*W*ILLS

of

RICHMOND COUNTY, VIRGINIA

1699–1800

*W*ILLS

of

RICHMOND COUNTY, VIRGINIA

1699–1800

By
Robert K. Headley, Jr.

CLEARFIELD

Reprinted for
Clearfield Company, Inc. by
Genealogical Publishing Co., Inc.
Baltimore, Maryland
1993, 1995, 1998, 2002

To the memory of my mother,

Marjorie H. (Smoot) Headley

(1911-1982)

INTRODUCTION

The will abstracts and inventories in this collection are
taken from eight will books of Richmond County:

> Wills and Inventories, 1699-1709
> Wills and Inventories, 1709-1717
> Will Book 4, 1717-1725
> Will Book 5, 1725-1753
> Will Book 6, 1753-1767
> Will Book 7, 1767-1787
> Will Book 8, 1787-1794
> Will Book 9, 1794-(1800)

Will Book 1, presumably dating from 1692--the year Richmond County
was formed out of part of Old Rappahannock County--to 1699 is not
extant. It is possible that there never was a Will Book 1. According to an entry on pp. 38-39 of Deed Book 17 (1793-1802),
dated 24 May 1794, the Justices of Richmond County met at the
Clerk's Office and examined the state thereof, and they reported:
"The following books from age and use are much out of repair as
follows, viz. No. 10 to be furnished with an index; wills, etc.
from 1692 to 1699 want transcribing and also from 1699 to 1709 .
. . ." Even more troubling is another part of the same entry:
". . . the clerk offered to our view sundry old wills, deeds, etc.
which appear to have been offered to court but have not yet been
recorded, on which we make no other report." In order, partially,
to make up for this lacuna, genealogical data on probates during
the period 1692-1699 has been extracted from Order Book 1 (1692-
1694) and Order Book 2 (1694-1699). These extracts have been
collated with those published in 1925 by E. C. Delano.

I have tried to abstract all of the information of value to
genealogists from these records. In some cases this involved
considerable data, in others, very little. I regret that many
testators did not even name their spouses or all of their children.
I have used my own discretion in some of these abstracts, and,
when I found a particular document interesting either as social
commentary or simply on its own merit, I have provided a fuller
abstract. Where possible, in order to provide additional data,
I have supplied notes extracted from several other works on
Virginia genealogy or from other records of Richmond County.
These will be found in the "List of Sources and Abbreviations."
Two are worthy of further note here because of their excellence
and because of the great use made of them herein. These two works
are: Marriages of Richmond County and North Farnham Parish
Register, both by George H. S. King. The reader is directed to
their pages for further information on the families of Richmond
County.

The entries, which consist mainly of wills and inventories,
are arranged chronologically by will book. Each will abstract
contains the name of the testator or testatrix, often the parish
or residence, the date the will was written, the date it was
proved, the names of the legatees, the names of the executor(s),

and the names of the witnesses. All surnames have been printed
in capitals. Unless otherwise noted, the legatees have the same
family name as the testator. Most of the nuncupative wills have
been given in full. For inventories, the name of the person whose
estate is inventoried and the date the inventory was recorded are
given. In some cases, when no other date was provided, the date
of the court order for the inventory is given. The various abbreviations used in the abstracts are explained in the "List of
Sources and Abbreviations." In certain cases additional notes
from other sources are provided. These notes are in square brackets following the will or inventory.

The handwriting of the vast majority of these instruments was
exceptionally clear, although, inevitably, some words were difficult
to read. In those cases where I could make a reasonable guess, I
did so, and placed square brackets around the tentative word. In
other places, where I filled in obvious gaps or omissions, I also
used square brackets. As far as spelling and grammar are concern-
ed, I have tried to normalize the spellings of all common names,
but I have retained the original spellings of the more unusual
names and the original wording of most of the longer textual abstracts.

A word concerning the index may be helpful here. There are
two indexes: an "Index of Place Names" and an "Index of Personal
Names." Each name has been indexed, but only once per page. As
much as possible, the individuals belonging to the same family
were grouped under the most common, modern spelling of their sur-
name, no matter how the name is spelled in the abstract. Thus,
under DOBYNS will be found individuals whose names were spelled
DOBINS, DOBBINS, or DOBYNS in the abstracts. Cross-references
are provided to the most common spellings.

Errors of omission and commission will inevitably be found
in this work despite my best efforts to avoid them. I will be
grateful to those who point them out to me.

I would like to thank the Interlibrary Loan Services of the
Virginia State Library and the Prince George's County (Maryland)
Library for providing me with the microfilm copies of the Richmond
County records from which I did the bulk of the abstracting; the
personnel at the Richmond County Courthouse in Warsaw; my friend
Robert Barnes for his valuable advice and friendship during all
stages of this work; my family--Anne, Sarah, and Amy--for helping
me and putting up with me during the long preparation of this
book; my mother and father for giving me the family pride that has
spurred my genealogical researches; and Dr. Michael Tepper of the
Genealogical Publishing Company for his patience and support.

Robert K. Headley, Jr.

University Park, Maryland

CONTENTS

LIST OF SOURCES AND ABBREVIATIONS

AB	account book
ac.	acres
adm.	administrator, administratrix
admin.	administration
b.	born
bef.	before
b-i-l	brother-in-law
bro.	brother
ca.	circa
chil.	child(ren)
cod.	codicil
Col.	colonel
cr.	creek
d.	died
dau.	daughter
daus.	daughters
DB	deed book
dec'd	deceased
dep.	deposition
d-i-l	daughter-in-law
div.	divided
eld.	eldest
eq. div.	equally divided
est.	estate
ex.	executor, executors, executrix
f.	folio (WB 2 is numbered in folios rather than pages; each folio has a recto (r.)--the right-hand page-- and a verso (v.)--the left-hand page.)
Farn. Par.	Farnham Parish (see: NFP)
f.inv.	further inventory
f-i-l	father-in-law
fol.	following
fr.	friend(s)
grchil.	grandchild(ren)
grdau.	granddaughter
grson.	grandson
Han. Par.	Hanover Parish--formed from the portion of St. Mary's Parish north of the Rappahannock River in 1714. Hanover Parish and the upper part of Sittenburne Parish became part of King George Co. in 1721.
husb.	husband
illeg.	illegible
inv.	inventory
Lanc.	Lancaster Co., Virginia
Lun. Par.	Lunenburg Parish--formed in 1732 from Sittenburne and part of North Farnham Parishes; it includes all of Richmond Co. north and west of Totuskey Cr. - Bramham's Mill Creek.
mar.	married
MR	Miscellaneous Records, 1704-1724, Richmond Co. (Abstracted by Beverley Fleet in _Virginia Colonial Abstracts_, Vol. XVII, 1943.)

MRC	Marriages of Richmond County Virginia 1668-1853, by George H. S. King, Fredericksburg, 1964.
nd.	no date
nfi.	not further identified
NFP	North Farnham Parish--that portion of Farnham Parish north of the Rappahannock River; formed in 1683; roughly the southeastern half of Richmond Co.
NFPR	The Registers of North Farnham Parish 1663-1814 and Lunenburg Parish 1783-1800, Richmond County, Virginia, by George H. S. King, Fredericksburg, 1966.
no ex.	no executor(s) named
nunc.	nuncupative (will)
OB	order book
ord.	[pursuant to a court] order of . . . .
p.	page
plant.	plantation
pres.	presented
prob.	probate
prov.	proved
r.	recto (see: f.)
Rapp.	Rappahannock Co.
RCV	Richmond County, Virginia. A Review Commemorating the Bicentennial, Elizabeth Lowell Ryland, ed., Warsaw, 1976.
rec.	recorded
rel.	relationship
ret.	returned to court
St. M. Par.	St. Mary's Parish--formed in 1677 out of the north-western portion of Sittenburne Parish. In 1714 its northern half in Richmond Co. became Hanover Parish.
sd.	said
sec.	security
s-i-l	son-in-law
sis.	sister
Sitt. Par.	Sittenburne Parish--formed in 1661 from the western portion of Farnham Parish. In 1704 the parish was divided and the portion north of the Rappahannock retained the name Sittenburne. In 1732 it was di-vided between Hanover Parish in King George Co. and the new parish of Lunenburg in Richmond Co.
v.	verso (see: v.)
wid.	widow
wits.	witnesses
WLC	Abstracts Lancaster County, Virginia, Wills 1653-1800, by Ida J. Lee, Richmond, 1959.
WRC	Wills of Rappahannock County, Virginia 1656-1692, by William M. Sweeny, Lynchburg, 1947.
WWC	Wills of Westmoreland County, Virginia, 1654-1800, by Augusta B. Fothergill, Richmond, 1925.

*W*ILLS

of

RICHMOND COUNTY, VIRGINIA

1699–1800

ORDER BOOK 1 (1692-1694)

p. 35 - Giles WEBBE; will presented by Mrs. Margaret WEBBE, ex;
         prov. by John TAVERNER and John PARKER, wits; prob. to
         ex; 3 Aug 1692.
p. 84 - Elizabeth LLOYD; will pres. by Mrs. Elizabeth CARTER, ex;
         prov. by John TAVERNER and Margaret LEGGINS (who was un-
         able to come to court because of imminent childbirth),
         wits; 1 Feb 1692/93. [Elizabeth LLOYD was the wife of
         John LLOYD and dau. of Col. John CARTER. OB 1, p. 168]
p. 85 - Elias YATES; will pres. by Mary YATES, ex; prov. by Mr.
         Thomas LLOYD and William SMITH; prob. to ex; 1 Feb 1692/93.
         [Elias YATES mar. Mary HUDSON by 1679. MRC, p. 238. Their
         dau., Priscilla, was b. in 1681. NFPR, p. 207.]
       - Francis DOUGHTY; will pres. by William BERRY, ex; prov. by
         Sem COX and Benj. HENSLE; prob. to ex; 1 Feb 1692/93.
p. 87 - Robert BAYLIS, Sr; will pres, by Thomas and John BAYLIS, ex;
         prov. by Samuel SANFORD and John TAVERNER, wits; prob. to
         his sons, the ex; and William BAYLIS, a grson. 5 Apr 1693.
         [Robert BAYLIS, Sr. desired his grson., William BAYLIS (son
         of Jane BAYLIS), and his grdau., Amadine BAYLIS (dau. of
         Thomas BAYLIS), to have two featherbeds, acc. to depositions
         by Jane BAKER and James SAMFORD. MR, p. 8a]
p. 88 - Roger RICHARDSON; will pres. by the wid., Elizabeth, ex;
         prov. by Nebu. JONES, Mary HEWS, and Elizabeth PACKFORD;
         prob. to ex; 5 Apr 1693.
p.122 - Henry THACKER; will pres. by Matilda THACKER, ex; prov. by
         Joshua DAVIS, wit; prob. to ex; 2 Aug 1693. [Matilda
         THACKER probably mar. (2) John WILLIS, 1693. DB 1, p. 84]
p.139 - John PITMAN; will pres. by the relict Rebecca PITMAN, ex;
         prov. by Joseph HENNINGS (who wrote the will) and Henry
         ARKHILL, wits; prob. to ex. 4 Oct 1693.
p.145 - John RICE; will pres. by Capt. Samuel TRAVERS, one of the ex;
         prov. by John POND, Walter PAVEY, William WITT, and Cornelius
         KINSELLOE, wits; prob. to Col. John STONE and Capt. Samuel
         TRAVERS, ex; 6 Dec 1693. [John RICE mar. Rebecca TRAVERS.
         MRC, p.169]
p.155 - David PURSELL; will pres. by Belinda PURSELL, ex; prov. by
         Daniel JACKSON, Thomas NEWMAN, and Evan THOMAS, wits; prob.
         to ex; 3 Jan 1693/94. [David PURSELL mar. Belinda, probably
         a dau. of Joshua LAWSON. MRC, p. 164. They had the fol.
         chil: Henry (1682), John (1683), David (1686), William
         (1688), Tobias (1691). NFPR, p. 153]
p.165 - John MORRIS; will pres. by Elizabeth MORRIS, ex; prov. by
         Isaac WRIGHT and John HARTFORD; prob. to ex; 7 Mar 1693/94.
p.169 - Matthew BOWEN; will prov. by Allen MOUNTJOY, Rebecca HUNSEMAN,
         and David COLEBURNE, wits; prob. to ex; 7 Mar 1693/94.
       - Bridget EALE; will prov. by Thomas DEADMAN and William CLEATON,
         wits; prob. to George and William EALE, ex; 7 Mar 1693/94.
       - William HASLE; will pres. by Anne HASLE, ex; prov. by William
         SISSON and Thomas WALKER, wits; prob. to ex; 7 Mar 1693/94.
p.186 - James SCOTT; adm. of his est. to Mary SCOTT his wid. on 4
         Apr 1694; rec. 6 Jun 1694.
       - Richard WINTER; will pres. by Capt. Alexander SWAN, surviving
         ex; prov. by Henry HOW and Lawrence PRESCOTT, wits; 6 Jun
         1694. [Richard WINTER mar.Abigail _(?)_. DB 1, p. 44]

ORDER BOOK 2 (1694-1699)

p. 12 - Luke BILLINGTON; ordered that the est. of Luke BILLINGTON,
         Jr., dec'd, be separated and set apart out of and from the
         est. of Dennis McCARTY, dec'd. 6 Sep 1694.
p. 16 - Isaac WEBB; will pres. by John WEBB, ex; prov. by Samuel
         PEACHEY and John SUGGETT. 5 Dec 1694. [An Isaac WEBB mar.
         Mary BEDWELL, 6 Apr 1678. NFPR, p. 195]

p. 18 - Dennis McCARTY; the est. of Dennis McCARTY, dec'd, not already inventoried, to be appraised; 5 Dec 1694. [Dennis
McCARTY mar. Elizabeth BILLINGTON. MRC, p. 123; He nominated
two of his children, Daniel and Katherine, both minors, his
joint executors. OB 1, p. 174]

p. 27 - Daniel BOURNE; order of administration granted to Anne BOURNE
upon the est. of her deceased husband Daniel; 6 Feb 1694/95.
- Evan WILLIAMS; will pres. by ex; prov. by George LODGE and
Stephen FENELL; prob. to ex; 6 Feb 1694/95.

p. 47 - Est. of Martha STOPFORD, dec'd, to be appraised; 1 May 1695.

p. 55 - Henry BURDETT; will pres. by Thomas NEWMAN, ex; prov. by
Elizabeth BURGESS, Mary MORRELL, and Thomas ROSE, wits; prob.
to ex; 5 Jun 1695.
- Anthony SAVAGE; will pres. by Francis THORNTON, ex; prov, by
Thomas PARKER; prob. to ex; 5 Jun 1695.

p. 56 - Joseph DAVIS; will pres. by Catherine DAVIS, ex; prov. by
Edward JONES and Thomas GLADMAN; 5 Jun 1695. [Joseph, the
son of Joseph and Catherine DAVIS, b. 9 Jan 1693. NFPR, p.41]
- Thomas REYLY; will pres. by Elizabeth REYLY, ex; prov. by
John BAPTIST and Richard WOOD; prob. to ex; 5 Jun 1695.
- William STARKE; will pres. by Frances STARKE, wid. and ex;
prov. by Thomas PARKER, Thomas PHILPIN, and Richard GRUBBS,
wits; prob. to ex; 5 Jun 1695.

p. 64 - John BAPTIST; will pres. by Anne BAPTIST, ex; prov. by
Thomas NEWMAN and Elizabeth BURGESS; prob. to ex; 7 Aug 1695.

p. 85 - Edward PRICE; will pres. by Anne PRICE, wid. and ex; prov.
by Andrew BOURNE and John BOURNE, wits; prob. to ex; 2 Oct
1695.

p.121 - Charles MINTHORN; admin. of his est. to his wid. Mary MINT-
HORN; 4 Mar 1695/96.
- William CLAPHAM; will pres. to court; prov. by John DEANE,
William COTTERELL, John SPENCER; prob. granted; 4 Mar 1695/96.

p.125 - John BROWN; admin. of his est. with the will annexed to Mrs.
Johanna BROWN, wid. and relict; 1 Apr 1696.

p.164 - Maxmilian ROBINSON; will pres. by Henindge ROBINSON, one of
the ex; will was prov. in the ecclesiastical court of the
Diocese of London; prob. to Henindge ROBINSON; 7 Oct 1696.

p.165 - Henry BERRY [Jr.]; will pres. by Sarah BERRY, ex; prov. by
Alexander SPENCE and James WOFENDALL; prob. to ex; 7 Oct
1696. [Henry BERRY, Jr. mar Sarah HARPER; she mar. (2) John
SPILLER. MRC, p.17; Henry BERRY, Jr. had land surveyed in
Stafford Co. in 1671; the deed mentioned his brother Richard
and William BERRY (no rel. stated). DB 2, p.31]

p.167 - John DALE; admin. of his est. to Mary DALE his wid.; 7 Oct
1696.

p.197 - Leonard ROBINSON; will pres. by Joseph DIKE, ex; prov. by
Thomas LEWIS and John WAKEMAN; prob. to ex; 2 Dec 1696.
- Isaac WRIGHT; admin. of his est. to John TAVERNER; Samuel
PEACHEY and Samuel BAYLEY, sec; 2 Dec 1696.

p.231 - Peter BURGESS; admin. of his est. to his wid. Elizabeth
BURGESS; 2 Jun 1697.

p.233 - William CLAPHAM; admin. with the will annexed granted to
Thomas RICHARDSON and Mary his wife, the relict of William
CLAPHAM; 2 Jun 1697.

p.247 - Henry LEWCAS; will pres. in court; prov. by John BATTIN and
Elias ROBINSON; 4 Aug 1697.

p.274 - John OAKLEY; will pres. by Thomas GLASCOCK; prov. by Richard
WHITE and Dr. Henry CLARKE, wits; 2 Mar 1697/98. [This is
probably the John OCKLY, aged 40 years or thereabouts, who
witnessed the will of Roger WATERS and was a legatee there-
to in 1685. WRC, pp. 115, 116]
- John WEBB; will pres. by Giles WEBB, ex; prov. by Samuel
SAMFORD and Thomas WHITE; cod. prov. by John BAKER; prob.
to ex; 2 Mar 1697/98. [A John WEBB mar. Mary SAMFORD, 14
Jul 1673; they had 3 chil: James (1673), Giles (1677),
Isaac (1681). NFPR, p. 195.]

3

p.275 - Francis ELMORE; will pres. by Thomas NEWTOWNE, ex, who relinquishes executorship; prov. by John HINDS and Richard
KNOWLES; admin. to John TARPLEY for and on behalf of the
orphans; 2 Mar 1697/98. [Francis ELMORE mar. (1) Anne ALLEN,
2 Dec 1677; they had the foll. chil: John (1685), Daniel
(1689). He probably mar. (2) Catherine _(?)_ and they had
a dau., Elizabeth (1693). NFPR, p. 59]
      - William DAVIS; will pres. by Nathaniel THRIFT, ex; prov. by
Elias HUGHS and Thomas LEWIS; prob. to ex; 2 Mar 1697/98.
[William DAVIS mar. Elizabeth THRIFT, 23 Apr 1677; they had
the foll. chil: William (1677/78), Jane (1680), Robert (1682),
Richard (1687). NFPR, p. 41, MRC, p. 51]
      - Ralph WHITING; will pres. by ex; prov. by John SILVESTER and
John HARDEY; prob. to ex; 2 Mar 1697/98. [John SIZE and
Thomasin WHITING were the ex. of Ralph WHITING. MR, p. 5]
p.276 - William DOWGAN; admin. of his est. to Hugh FRENCH; 2 Mar
1697/98.
      - Thomas SWINBURNE; will pres. by Martha, one of his children;
prov. by Paul MICOU and Stephen MANNERING; prob. to Martha
as surviving ex; 2 Mar 1697/98. [Thomas SWINBURNE mar.
Catherine PANNELL, wid. of Thomas PANNELL, ca 1678. MRC, p 200]
p.277 - John ALEXANDER; will pres. by ex; prov. by William MILLER;
prob. to ex; 2 Mar 1697/98.
p.294 - Samuel DAVIS; admin. of his est. to Grace BRYANT of Essex
Co., wid. (she being nearest of kin); William YATES, sec;
1 Jun 1698.
p.295 - Matthew [] BURROWS: admin. of his est. with the will annexed
to Patience BURROWS, his wid; 1 Jun 1698.
      - John PEIRCE, Gent; will pres. by Col. William PEIRCE, ex;
prov. by George GIBBS and Ralph BERKLEY; 1 Jun 1698. [John
PEIRCE mar. Hester (WALKER) TOMLIN bef. 1691. His will was
pres. by his father, Col. Wm. PEIRCE of West. Co. MRC, pp.
156-157.]
      - William SLOUGHTER; admin. of his est. to Mrs. Phebe SLOUGHTER;
Samuel PEACHEY and Thomas GLASCOCK, sec; 1 Jun 1698.
p.296 - Decemia DALTON; admin. of his est. to Samuel SAMFORD; 1 Jun
1698. [Decemia DALTON, cooper, mar. Joan _(?)_ ; they had
Decemia (1693). NFPR, p.39; DB 2, p.168]
      - William WHEELER; will pres. by Nathaniel POPE, wit; 1 Jun
1698.
p.297 - Edward LEWIS; admin. of his est. to Martha HAMMOND and Mary,
his wife, (as nearest of Kin); 1 Jun 1698. [Edward and Mary
LEWIS had the foll. chil: Elizabeth (1674), Joanna (1676),
Jane (1693), Lewis (1695). NFPR, pp. 115-116]
p.298 - John ALLIN; will pres. by Cornelius McCARTY, wit; 1 Jun 1698.
[A John ALLEN mar. Catherine MAJOR, 15 Nov 1678. NFPR, p.3]
      - Richard DUDLEY; will pres. by Richard JESPER, Sr. and Thomas
JESPER, ex; prov. by George MADOX and Henry HEYES, wits; 1
Jun 1698. [Alexander DUDLEY, the son of a Richard DUDLEY,
was a legatee of John STEPHENS of Rapp. Co. in 1661. WRC,
p. 66.]
      - John CARRELL; will prov. by John HARDY and Edward RUSSELL;
prob. to John SIZE, ex; 1 Jun 1698.
p.299 - Phillip COUZENS; will pres. by James TRENT, ex; prov. by
Francis STONE and Richard HAYDEN; 1 Jun 1698.
      - John JENNINGS; admin. of his est. to Anne JENNINGS, wid. and
relict; George PAYNE and Neb. JONES, sec; 1 Jun 1698.
      - Capt. Alexander NEWMAN; will pres. by Mrs. Elizabeth NEWMAN,
ex; prov. by William WOODBRIDGE and George WOODBRIDGE; prob.
to ex; 1 Jun 1698.
      - Richard SHIPPIE; will pres. by James SHIPPIE, ex; prov. by
Luke [?], William SIMMES, and George BARNETT; 1 Jun 1698.
p.300 - John KERBY; admin. of his est. to Elizabeth KERBY, wid;
George GIBBS and Thomas TAYLER, sec; 1 Jun 1698.

- Kitt (a Christian Indian); will pres. in court; prov. by
William HUTSON and Thomas DAVIS; prob. to John JONES, ex;
1 Jun 1698.
- William JEFFERYES; admin. of his est. to Thomas TAYLER;
1 Jun 1698.
- David ROSER; admin. of his est. to Margaret ROSER, wid;
Francis STONE and Francis TRIPLETT, sec; 1 Jun 1698. [David
ROSSIER mar. (1) Sarah SHERWOOD by 1688 and (2) Margaret
(?) . MRC, p. 173]

p.306 - Francis TAYLOR; will pres. by Charles SNEAD, ex; prov. by
John BERNARD; 1 Jun 1698. [Francis TAYLOR mar. Elizabeth
SNEAD by 1693. MRC, p.205]

p.311 - John LANDMAN; will pres. by ex; prov. by Abigall SISSON;
6 Jul 1698. [John LANDMAN was a son of William LANDMAN. DB
2, p.95]
- Robert SISSON; will pres. by Ralph BERKLEY, William LAWSON,
and Thomas LEWIS; 6 Jul 1698. [Robert and Abigail SISSON
had two chil: Mary (1692) and George (1695). NFPR, p.168]
- John TAVENER; will pres. by his dau. Sarah and his son James
TAVENER, ex; and Samuel PEACHEY and John BAKER; 6 Jul 1698.
[John and Elizabeth TAVERNER had at least five chil.; the
births of four of them are: Sarah (1679), Elizabeth (1681),
John (1682/83), Richard (1685). NFPR, pp. 181-182]
- Thomas TRIPLETT; will pres. by Margaret, ex; prov. by Peter
RAWLLS; 6 Jul 1698.

p.312 - Henry LEWIS; will pres. by Mary, his relict and ex; prov.
by William SMITH; 6 Jul 1698.
- William WHE[E]LER; will pres. by Lewis MARKHAM, ex; prov.
by Nathaniel POPE and Walther ANDERSON; 6 Jul 1698.

p.326 - William POWELL; admin. of his est. to Joseph DIKE; 6 Jul 1698.

p.330 - James KEY; admin. of his est. to Mrs. Mary KEY, wid; 6 Jul
1698.

p.331 - Edwin CONWAY; will pres. by Elizabeth, his wife, ex; prov.
by Alexander SPENCE and John SIZE; 6 Jul 1698. [Edwin CONWAY
mar. (1) Sarah WALKER and (2) Elizabeth THORNTON, 21 May
1695. MRC, pp. 43-44]
- William JETT; will pres. by Elizabeth, his wife, ex; prov.
by William UNDERWOOD and George GREEN; 6 Jul 1698. [William
JETT, the son of Peter JETT, mar. Elizabeth (HOSKINS) WOOD
by 1681. MRC, pp. 106-107]
- Richard WHARTON; will pres. by Neb. JONES and James SCOTT,
ex; prov. by John TILLETT and Thomas SMYTH; 6 Jul 1698.

p.332 - Peter BUTLER; admin. of his est. to Rebecca BUTLER; 6 Jul
1698.

p.335 - Richard TOMPKINS; will pres. by Rowland THORNTON, ex; prov.
by Nathaniel HALL; 8 Sep 1698. [Elizabeth PALMER was the
dau-in-law of Richard TOMPKINS. DB 1, p.71]
- John ROSE; admin. of his est. to his wid. Sarah ROSE; 8 Sep
1698.

p.338 - Thomas HARVEY; nunc. will pres. by Alexander SPENCE and
George GREEN, ex; prov. by John HAUKSFORD and John BENNETT;
8 Sep 1698.

p.343 - William TAYLOR; admin. of his est. to Margaret TAYLOR, his
wife; 8 Sep 1698.

p.344 - John PARTRIDGE; will pres. by Frances PARTRIDGE, ex; prov.
by John PECK and Mary WOOLLARD; 8 Sep 1698. [John PARTRIDGE
mar. Frances CRESWELL, 6 Apr 1678. NFPR, p.144]

p.345 - Angell JACOBUS; will prov. and rec. in this county; 8 Sep
1698. [Angell JACOBUS mar. (1) Elizabeth CLARK by 1688 and
(2) Anne VALLOTT, 12 Jul 1694. MRC, p.102]

p.348 - Henry TILLERY; will pres. by Mary TILLERY, ex; prov. by
John PECK; 3 Nov 1698. [Henry TILLERY mar. Mary WASCOLE,
7 Nov 1675; they had two chil: Henry (1679) and Mary (1685).
NFPR, p.187]

p.362 - John LEWIS; admin. of his est. to William COLSTON as greatest creditor; 1 Feb 1698.
p.369 - Dr. William BRUCE; admin. of his est. to Mrs. Elizabeth
NEWMAN as greatest creditor; 1 Mar 1698/99.
p.370 - John MORGAN; admin. of his est. to William COLSTON as greatest creditor; 1 Mar 1698/99.
p.405 - Richard METCALFE; admin. of his est. to Mrs. Anne METCALFE,
his wife; 3 Nov. 1698. [Richard METCALFE mar. (1) Elizabeth
FAUNTLEROY and (2) Anne STONE. MRC, p.131.]
     - Col. John STONE; will pres. by Mrs. Anne METCALFE; prov. by
Elias WILSON and Thomas LAWSON; 3 Nov 1698. [Col. John STONE
mar. Sarah ((?)) FLEET WALKER ca. 1670. MRC, p. 195.]
p.409 - William BROWN; will pres. and prov. by Alexander SPENCE and
John CRASK; prob. to Frances BROWN, ex; 3 Nov 1698. [William
BROWN mar. Frances the eld. dau. of William MOSS; he was
the son of William BROWN and had bros. John and Maxfield.
DB 2, pp. 1,2,37]
p.430 - Mary ANDERSON; admin. of her est. to Charles BARBER; 2 Aug
1699.
p.432 - John WOOLLARD; admin. of his est. to Rawleigh TRAVERS; 2
Aug 1699. [John and Mary WOOLLARD had at least five chil:
Mary (1682), John (1685), Rebeccah (1687), Richard (1691),
Elling (1696). NFPR, p. 205.]
p.490 - John BURNETT (minister of the Gospel); admin. of his est.
to Samuel PEACHEY; 1 Nov 1699.

WILLS AND INVENTORIES, 1699-1709

f1r - Anthony CARNABY, Farnham Par., will; prov. [11 Oct 1699]
[page mutilated]

f1v - Thomas BAYLIS, will; 25 Apr 1697, [27 Dec 1699]
land lying in the woods to be eq. div. among eight
chil: Robert, [Anne], Francis, [Catherine], [Mary],
[...]; land purch. from Alexander FLEMING, [...] ALGAR,
and Edward TAYLOR to son Thomas, if he has no heirs,
to son Robert; ex: wife; wits: Phillip HEMMINGS, Geo.
BLUFORD, Samuel SAMFORD.
[Thomas BAYLIS was the son of Robert BAYLIS, Sr. (d.
1692); he mar. (1) Catherine SAMFORD and (2) Sarah
(EDGCOMB) SUGGETT. MRC, p.12.]

f2v - Thomas LLOYD, inv; rec. 27 Oct 1699.

f7v - Thomas BAYLIS, inv. by Sarah BAYLIS; [nd]

f8v - Anthony CARNABY, inv; Oct 1699.

f9r - John PARKER, will; 13 Dec 1699, 3[0] Jan 1699/1700
Elias WILSON, Sr.; Terence WEBBE to be freed;
mentions a shallop with all the sails, rigging, and
other gear; [top of next f. mutilated] John BURKETT,
John JONES (son of Nebuchednezzer JONES); Richard
[HANEY]; Rawleigh TRAVERS and Thomas BEALE a gold ring
each; ex: Mr. William COLSTON; wits: Thomas DICKENSON,
Thomas NEWMAN.

f10r - Benjamin HENSLE, will; 28 Jan 1699, [8] Mar 1699/1700
wife Beatrice; son Benjamin the land I have by patent,
50 ac; sum of money to Elizabeth [TOBY] at the [BLUEBELL]
near St. Thomas Hospital in [Southwark]; no ex; wits:
Joseph WRIGHT, [Sem] COX.

- Elias WILSON, Sitt.Par., will; 2 Mar 1697/98, 6 Mar 1699/
  1700
    sons Henry all my part and share of 350 ac. bought of
    Thomas NORTON by me, John CARTON, and John [HUGHES],
    James 254 ac., Elias; dau. Elizabeth the wife of Edward
    [MOSELEY]; dau. Martha; grchil. Edward MORRIS, Charles
    [SNEAD],Jr., and Elias [SNEAD] sons to my dec'd dau.
    [Sheba]; ex: wife Susannah and son Elias; wits: Thomas
    LONG, Thomas BRADLEY. [A cod. nominates Capt. George
    TAYLOR, William COLSTON, and Edwin CONWAY as overseers.]

f11v - John FORD, will; [?], 6 Mar 1699/1700
    wife Patience; son John one shilling; ex: wife; wits:
    Henry CHAPPELL, Edward NEWTON,Sr., [Shelah] NEWTON.

- Stephen MANNERING,Sitt. Par., will; 6 Oct 1699, 6 Mar 1699/
  1700
    wife Joan; grson. John JONES; godson Stephen [FRAINUM];
    no ex; wits: Rowland THORNTON, Nabu. JONES. [A cod.
    appoints Dr. Paul MICOU, Rowland THORNTON, and Nabu.
    JONES to be overseers.]

f12r - William [PICKFORD], inv; 29 Apr 1700

- William WITT, inv; 29 Apr 1700

f13v - Edward WADHAM, inv; [15 May 1700]

f14r - Arthur SPICER, Sitt. Par., will; 18 Sep 1699, 3 Apr 1700
    all est. in England and elsewhere to son John; if he
    dies in his minority, everything to Lidia SPICER the
    eld. dau. of bro. John SPICER late of London dec'd;
    youngest sis. Elizabeth SPICER; [?] COLSTON, Capt.
    John BATTAIL, Mr. [?], and Mr. John LLOYD to be
    guardians to son during his minority; guardians to pay
    Frances ROBINSON dau. of Capt. Samuel BLOOMFIELD what
    is due her; son to be sent to England for his better
    education, that of the charter house I take to be the
    best; requests Col. CARTER of Lanc. Co. to accept the
    trouble of supervision; wits: John BURRETT, Mary HARDIDGE.
    [Arthur SPICER mar. by 27 Sep 1693 Elizabeth (JONES)
    BLOOMFIELD dau. of Thomas JONES. MRC, p. 193.]

f15r - Thomas PARKER, inv; 22 Aug.1700

f15v - William SMITH, will; 9 Feb 1699, 2 Oct 1700
    Abraham GOAD; John, William, and Hannah chil. of
    Abraham and Catherine GOAD; ex: wife Eve; wits: John
    PHILLIPS, Rich. SANDFOE, [Mary] DOSON.

f16r - John HUGH[ES], inv; 23 Aug 1700

f17v - Alvin MOUNTJOY, will; 28 Sep 1700, 1 Jan 1700/01
    son Thomas; if he has no heirs est. to daus. Sibella
    and Mary; wife Mary (now with child); ex. wife; wits:
    John KELLY, Amy KELLY. [Alvin MOUNTJOY mar., ca. 1690,
    Mary LANE dau. of William LANE. MRC, p. 140.]

- Henry CLARK, will; 29 Aug 1700, 1 Jan 1700/01
    eld. son Henry my plant. of 150 ac; dau. Elizabeth; son
    William all my land on the west side of my plant; son
    Alexander the upper part of my land on the north side
    of my plant; [mentions but does not name six youngest
    chil.]; fr. Charles BARBER; ex: wife; wits: Ralph
    ABINGTON, Robert HUGHES.

f18r - Leroy GEORGE, will; 16 Sep 1700, 1 Jan 1700/01
            kinsman Thomas WHITE; fr. Nicholas SMYTH; little bro.
            Edward READ; mother; Charles BARBER; ex: John WHITE
            and wife Margaret [GEORGE]; wits: Edward READ, Eliza
            READ.

f18v - William REYNOLDS, will; 22 Oct 1700, 1 Jan 1700/01
            sons Cornelius, John, and William; dau. Elizabeth; sons
            to be of age at 16; ex: bro. John REYNOLDS; wits: Wm.
            MARSHALL, Catherine JACKSON, Cornelius LAFFIN, Anne
            MARSHALL.

f19r - Rebecca THOMAS, will; 28 Dec 1700, 5 Mar 1700/01
            three godchil. [not named]; Bridget MACKLATHLIN; Corbin
            GRIFFIN; Thomas GRIFFIN; [William GRIFFIN, Jr.];
            Winifred GRIFFIN, Sr.; Winifred GRIFFIN, Jr.; ex:
            Winifred GRIFFIN, Jr.; wits: Thomas GRIFFIN, Elizabeth
            WRIGHT, Walter WRIGHT.

f19v - Humphry MEALEY, will; 14 Dec 1700, 5 Mar 1700/01
            Alexander [HUISON] part of my land during his life;
            ex: wife; wits: William WATSON, John DACOCKS.

      - Dr. Edward TALBOTT, inv; [nd]

f20v - William REYNOLDS, inv; 22 Apr 1700/01

f21v - Martin FISHER, Sr., Sitt.Par., will; 11 Jan 1699, 7 May 1701
            d-i-l Sarah 100 ac; all [other] lands to be eq. div.
            between son Martin and dau. Elizabeth [KITCHIN]; ex:
            son Martin and dau. Elizabeth; wits: William HUDSON,
            Richard HAYDEN, [Thomas PACEY].

f22r - John HARDY, St.M.Par., cooper, will; 12 Dec 1700, 7 May 1701
            [John] PHILPIN; Richard WEST; ex: John BOWLIN; wits:
            William JACKSON, Richard WEST, Joseph COTTON.

      - William BROCKENBROUGH, inv. pres. by Mary BROCKENBROUGH,
            the adm.; 28 May 1701.

f23v - William LAWFORD, inv. pres. by Isabell LAWFORD; [nd].

      - John WAKEMAN, inv; [nd].

f24r - William BAYLYS, inv; [nd].

f25r - Capt. Alvin MOUNTJOY, inv. pres. by Mary MOUNTJOY; 28
            May 1701.

f26r - Thomas NEWMAN, Sr., inv; [nd].

f26v - William HAMMACK, will; 11 Jul 1701, 2 Jul 1701
            200 ac. whereon I now live to my youngest son William;
            if he should die without issue, to go to dau. Elizabeth.
            eld. son William [sic] one shilling; son William to be
            of age at 18; dau. to be of age at 16; ex: son Richard;
            wits: Rebeccah KERTLEY, John HARTLEY, John BOHANNAH.

f27r - John INGO, Sr., NFP, will; 3 Jun 1701, 2 Jul 1701
            est. to son John; plant. and land I now live on to
            youngest son James; dau. Elizabeth ASCOUGH; Mary
            SALISBURY, when she shall be free; ex: wife Mary; wits:
            Anne ASCOUGH, Edward READ, Edward JEFFORY.

f28r - Walter PAVEY , inv; 21 Jul 1701.

f28v - Rowland THORNTON, inv; 21 Jul 1701.

f29r - William PEACHEY, inv; 21 Jul 1701.

f30r - James KEY, inv; taken [29] Oct 1698, rec. 21 Jul 1701.

f30v - Alvin MOUNTJOY, f.inv. pres. by his widow Mary MOUNTJOY;
          Sep 1701.

       - William COLSTON, clerk, will; 27 Oct 1701, 3 Dec 1701
          to be interred by the body of wife Anne; dau. Susannah
          150 ʟ to be paid out of money now in the hands of Capt.
          John PURVIS, merchant, in London; son William; son
          Charles 640 ac. bought of Capt. Thomas BEALE and Joseph
          RUSSELL; Thomas READ, that now lives with me, to have
          his maintenance out of my est. until 18 provided he
          continue with my two sons; Rawleigh TRAVERS; s-i-l
          Thomas BEALE; Rawleigh TRAVERS and Thomas BEALE to be
          ex. during the minority of sons William and Charles;
          wits: Daniel HORNBY, Thomas BARLOW, Ellen FOSTER.
          [William COLSTON, first clerk of the Rich. Co. court,
          mar. by 1681, Anne (GOOCH) BEALE, wid. of Capt. Thomas
          BEALE. MRC, p.42.]

f31v - Henry CHAPPELE, will; 10 Jun 1701, 3 Dec 1701
          Eliza HAMBLETON that now liveth with me the plant. and
          land; if she has no heirs, land to go to Anne HOPKINS
          dau. of George and Anne HOPKINS; ex: Eliza HAMBLETON;
          wits: Geo. HOPKINS, Anne HOPKINS, Patrick TIFFE.

f32r - Thomas ASCOUGH, Farn. Par, will; 21 Aug 1701, 3 Dec 1701
          mother Anne ASCOUGH; wife Elizabeth; son Christopher;
          no ex; wits: Luke MORGAN, John DOYLE. [Thomas ASCOUGH
          mar. Elizabeth INGO, dau. of John INGO, Sr.; she mar.
          (2) Leonard DOZIER. MRC, p.5.]

f32v - John PHILLIPS, will; 17 Jul 1701, 3 Dec 1701
          sons John plant. where I now live; Bryan land in Lanc.
          Co., Thomas, Tobias; daus. Mary, Anne, Elizabeth COLLIN;
          If sons die without lawful male issue, the plant. where
          I now live to go to the use of the Par. of North Farn.
          for a glebe and the plant. in Lanc. Co. to go to White
          Chapel Par. for a glebe; wife Mary; if wife doth come
          to poverty, ex. to allow her an honest maintenance so
          long as she doth remain Mary PHILLIPS; ex: sons John
          and Bryan; wits: John STOTT, James HARLEY, James HILL.
          [The birth records of the chil. of John PHILLIPS in the
          NFPR give his wife's name as Elizabeth. NFPR, p.147.]

f33v - Hugh FRENCH, St. M. Par, will; 20 Jan 1699/1700, 3 Dec 1701
          200 ac. in Maryland to be sold and money paid to son
          Hugh; dau. Mary 200 ac. bought of David [DARNELL]; sons
          Daniel and Mason; dau. Margaret 130 ac; ex: wife
          Margaret; wits: John BATTAILE, Wm. MARSHALL, Simon
          MILLER, John MILLER.

f34v - John EVANS, will; 3 Aug 1700, 3 Dec 1701
          all est. to John JONES on Totuskey Cr; no ex; wits:
          John JOHNSON, Thomas LEWIS, Benjamin LEWIS.

f35r - Thomas RADLEY, will; 3 Mar 1701, 3 Dec 1701
          son Thomas; daus. Patience, Isabella; ex: wife Isabella;
          wits: Dominick DAWSON, Rice WILLIAMS.

f35v - Arthur SPICER, Gent., inv. upon the several plant. of the
said SPICER in the county; 3 Dec 1701.

f37r - Rice WILLIAMS, will; 4 Aug 1701, 5 Feb 1701/02
wife Mary to receive rent from the land where Randal
DOUGLAS liveth; tract of land to dau. Elizabeth SETTLE;
grchil. Francis SETTLE; son Thomas; ex: son Thomas;
wits: Elizabeth JONES, John [FAVER].

f37v - Arthur SPICER, f.inv; 9 Mar 1701/02.

f41v - Francis TRIPLITT, will; 24 Nov 1700, 4 Mar 1701/02
wife Abigail 200 ac. which is to go to son Francis at
her death and if he has no heirs, to son William; wife
also to receive tract of land which is part of 1050 ac.
I took up lying between the lines of Capt. BALL, James
SCOTT, John NICHOLLS, and Samuel BOWEN, this land is
also to pass to son Francis; son William all land on the
south side of Tha[t]cher's Creek Branch; grson. Francis
TRIPLITT, son of my eld. son Thomas, a tract of land
near the land of George HAILE; if grson. Francis should
die without heirs, land to go to grson. Thomas TRIPLITT;
Francis JETT son of John and Elizabeth JETT; ex: wife
and son William; wits: John DEANE, Giles MATTHEWS,
Susan CAMMACK.

f42v - Rawleigh TRAVERS, Farn. Par., 20 Feb 1701, 4 Mar 1701/02
cousins Elizabeth, Winifred, and Rebecca TRAVERS; god-
son Rawleigh BROOKS 120 ac. out of the land I bought of
Zachariah NICHOLS; wife Sarah 400 ac. called "Exeter
Lodge", if she remarry, then to have only 300 ac; Capt.
Thomas BEALE; Mr. John TAVERNER; Mrs. PEACHEY; Mrs.
SLAUGHTER; Mrs. Sarah BAYLIS; Dr. Robert CLARKE, Edward
JONES; Samuel PEACHEY; sis. BEALE; no ex; wits: Samuel
PEACHEY, Robert CLARKE, Edward JONES.

f44r - John HENDERSON, inv; 10 Mar 1701/02.

f44v - Francis SETTLE, inv; 10 Mar 1701/02.

f45r - William GRIFFIN, inv. at his house, pres. by Mary BARKER,
relict and adm; 4 Apr 1702.

f45v - Col. Leroy GRIFFIN, inv. account at the house of Mrs.
Winifred GRIFFIN; 4 Apr 1702.

f46v - John PHILLIPS, inv; 4 Apr 1702.

f48r - Elizabeth ASCOUGH, NFP, wid., deed of gift to her dau. Anne
ASCOUGH to be delivered the day of her marriage or after;
19 Mar 1701/02, rec. [4] Apr 1702.

f48v - John BAKER, inv. pres. by Mrs. Jane BAKER, adm; [mentions
some property in West. Co.]; 26 May 1702.

f49v - William COLSTON, inv. pres. by Capt. Rawleigh TRAVERS and
Capt. BEALE, ex; 3 Jul 1702.

f53r - David DARNELL, inv; 9 Nov 1702.

f53v - Elizabeth GRADY, will; 10 Mar 1693/94, 4 Nov 1702
Mary SMOOT dau. of William SMOOT all land; ex: William
SMOOT; wits: Thomas DURHAM, Richard DRAPER, John RANKIN.

10

- William STROTHER, Sr., will; [30] Dec 1700, 4 [Nov] 1702
  eld. son William land whereon I now live; sons James,
  Robert, Benjamin, Joseph; grson. Will STROTHER; wife
  Dorothy; no ex; wits: James PHILLIPS, Edward LANGEDELL,
  William SMITH.

f55r - Hugh FRENCH, inv; [10 Nov 1702].

f56v - William HAMMOCK, account of est. by Richard HAMMOCK, ex; [nd].

- Henry SUTTLE, Farn. Par., will; 9 Sep 1701, 2 Dec 1702.
  John HOW; son Henry (under 14); child wife is now big
  with; ex: wife Mary; wits: Elizabeth SUTTLE, Jn. DOYLE.

f57v - Thomas ALGER, inv. pres. by Alexander FLEMMAN; 8 Feb 1702.

f58r - Capt. Rawleigh TRAVERS, inv. pres. by Capt. Thomas BEALE and
  Mr. John TAVERNER, ex; 9 Feb 1702/03.

f59v - John HENDERSON, account of est; [nd.]

- Richard JESPER, will; 11 Jun 1698, 3 Mar 1702/03
  son Thomas; son Richard Jr. the land I bought of Richard
  DUDLEY; dau. Sarah (under 16); grchil. William and Mary
  DUDLEY; ex: son Thomas and John THOMAS; wits: William
  LEE, Mary LEE, Henry HAYES.

f60v - Richard WHITE, Sitt. Par., will; 5 Feb 1702/03, 2 Jun 1703
  godson Bryan SISSON son of William SISSON in Farn. Par;
  godson Richard JONES son to Edward JONES in Nomini Par;
  wife Katherine; ex: wife; wits: William TALBERT, John
  DOYLE.

f61r - Sarah BAYLIS, NFP, will; 8 Mar 1699/1700, 2 Jun 1703
  sons John, Edgecomb, Thomas, and James SUGGITT; ex:
  son James; wits: John SHERDON, Joan TALBOT, John HUGHS.
  [Sarah EDGECOMB mar. (1) John SUGGITT and (2) Thomas
  BAYLIS. WRC, p. 145; MRC, pp. 12, 199.]

- John SIGES, will; 21 Aug 1702, 2 Jun 1703
  Sem WALTON; John and Thomas WALTON; wife and children
  [not named]; ex: wife; wits: John SKEY, Samuel WALTON,
  John WALTON, Mary [DOYLE].

f61v - Owen DERMOTT, inv. at the house of Michael CONNELE, pres.
  by Michael CONNELE; 7 [Jun] 1703.

f62v - William DAVIS, inv. pres. by Job HAMMOND; 7 Jun 1703.

- John [SIGES], inv; 8 Jul 1703.

f63v - Edward JONES, inv; 8 Jul 1703.

- Thomas WALKER, aged about 59 years; will; [31 Jan 1702],
  8 Jul 1703
  son Thomas the plant. where I now live; son William;
  Elizabeth WILLIAMS, Shaddrick WILLIAMS; Anne MUDY; daus.
  Sarah, Mary, Rachel, and Alice; wife Anne; ex: wife;
  wits: Lewis RICHARDS, George RICHARDS, James GRAHAM.

f64v - Pythagoras POWELL, will; 29 Oct 170[2], 7 Jul 1703
  whole est. to wife Sarah; Charles SNEAD to assist wife;
  no ex; wits: Alexander RIGGES, Mary SPOE.

f65r - Dennis MONY, inv; 14 Sep 1703.

- Joan L[L]OYD, will; 8 Jan 1703, 2 Feb 1703/04
dau. Susannah the wife of William PHILLIPS; son
Shaddrack WILLIAMS; dau. Anne the wife of James DEBORD;
dau. Ruth the wife of John CANTERBURY; grdau. Elizabeth
THORNHILL; d-i-l. Elizabeth WILLIAMS; s-i-l. George
THOMPSON to receive a boy named Thomas [BATTS] until
the boy is [20]; grdau. Susan PHILLIPS; grson. John
M'DANIEL; s-i-l. William PHILLIPS; s-i-l. John CANTER-
BURY; ex: s-i-l. George THOMPSON; wits: Robert THOMAS,
Deborah THOMAS, William YATES.

f65v - Zachary HEFFORD, will; 30 Sep 1703, 2 Feb 1703/04
dau. Mary the wife of William TAYLOR; sons John (age
14) and Zachary (age 4); ex: fr. John POUND Sr; wits:
John POUND Jr., Edmund NEALE, John CHARTARIS.

f66r - Zachary HEFFORD, inv; [7] Mar 1703/04.

f66v - Thad[deus] LYNSEY; inv. at the house of Alexander FLEMING;
[4 Mar] 1703/04.

      - Stephen LYNCH, inv; 4 Mar 1703/04.

f67v - Edward JONES, inv; [nd.]

      - Henry WILLIAMS, NFP, will; 25 Jan 1703/04, 1 Mar 1703/04
wife Lettice; dau. Mary the wife of Phillip HARRIS;
grdau. Sarah the dau. of Phillip HARRIS; son John all
land; son Thomas; daus. Sarah and Jane; ex: son John;
wits: Andrew DEW, Henry JENNINGS.

f69r - James GILBERT, NFP, will; 31 Jan 1701/02, 7 [Jun] 1704
wife; ex: fr. John MILLS Jr; wits: Edward WELCH, Jane
WILLIAMS, Thomas WHITE.

f69v - Thomas DUSEN, Farn. Par., Rapp. Co., will; 6 Aug 1691, 7
[Jun] 1704
entire est. to wife Susannah; ex: wife; wits: William
SMITH, James RANKIN, Charles DODSON. [Thomas DEWSIN,
aged 29 years or thereabouts, witnessed the will of
Geo. NICHOLLS in Rapp. Co. prior to 2 May 1677. WRC,p.50.]

f70r - Adam WOFFENDALE, will; 25 Apr 1703, 7 [Jun] 1704
if I die before I lay out 350 ac., sons HARRISON and
STROTHER to lay it out and each to receive 150 ac; daus.
Sarah and Mary; son Francis tract of land; ex: wife;
if my son Francis will not be ruled by his mother...he
should live with my son HARRISON and his mother to have
the benefit of his labor until he comes to age 21; wits:
John GRIMESLEY, Thomas ARNOLD, Andrew HARRISON. [The
wife of Adam WOFFENDALL was Honoria. DB 2, p. 61.]

f70v - Thomas SOUTHERN, will; 17 Apr 1704, 2 Aug 1704
son Thomas the dwelling plant; wife Eleanor; three daus.
[not named]; d-i-l. Mary SOUTHING; sons William and
James; ex: wife; wits: Christopher PETTY, [Bartholomew
Thomas Richard] DODSON, Charles DODSON. [The births of
the fol. chil. of Thomas and Eleanor SOUTHERN are rec-
in the NFPR, p. 173: Susannah (1691), Winifred (1693),
and Thomas (1695).]

f71r - [Mottrom] WRIGHT, inv. including that part of the est. which
is in the hands or custody of Mr. Joseph BELFIELD; 8
Aug 1704.

f71v - Nicholas LEWIS, inv. at the house of Charles SPOE; 4 [?]
        1704.

f72r - James SAMFORD, NFP, will; 27 Sep 1703, 2 Nov 1704
        plant. and 200 ac. to grson. Thomas SAMFORD; if he has
        no heirs, to grson. James SAMFORD; son Samuel shall live
        on the before bequeathed plant. of Thomas SAMFORD for
        and during his natural life; Elizabeth the wife of son
        Samuel; grsons William, Giles, and John SAMFORD; Samford
        JONES; Edward JONES; ex: son Samuel; wits: Giles WEBB,
        Richard TAYLOR, Edward JONES. [James SAMFORD may be the
        same James SAMFORD, aged 55 years or thereabouts, who
        witnessed the will of Roger BAGWELL in Rapp. Co., 26
        Mar 1679. WRC, pp. 86-87.]

f73v - William GLEW, inv. pres. by William GLEW, Jr., adm. and
        Constance the wife of Arthur [MAGAYAR]; 13 Jan 1704/05.

f74r - Francis TRIPLETT, inv. pres. by Mary TRIPLETT; 13 Jan 1704/05.

f75v - David GWYN, laying out and separating from the est. of
        David GWYN a [?] jointure bearing the date 28 Feb
        1680 made by William FAUNTLEROY and Catherine his wife
        to Richard LEE and Leroy GRIFFIN and their heirs; 15
        Mar 1704/05.

f76v - Avery NAYLOR, will; 24 Jan 1704/05, 7 Mar 1704/05
        wife Patience; godson Avery DYE son of Arthur DYE; for-
        gives and acquits Thomas NEWMAN of all debts; ex: wife;
        wits: [?] [PINKETT], James [MURPHY], Stephen
        [HUCHISSON].

f77r - Darby INGLISHBY, inv; 15 Mar 1704/05.

f77v - John SUGGITT, NFP, will; 16 Jan 1703, 7 Mar 1704/05
        [partially mutilated] dau. Elizabeth SUGGITT; bros.
        James, Edgecomb, Thomas; Thomas AYRES; William AYRES;
        b-i-l. William SMITH; Robert CLARK; in case dau.
        Elizabeth should die before marriage or age 21, her
        legacy to be eq. div. between wife and Thomas SUGGITT;
        ex: wife and bro. Thomas SUGGITT; wits: Robert CLARK,
        James MURPHY.

f78r - David GWYNN, will; 22 Feb 1702/03, 8 Mar 1704/05
        land in Essex Co. which I bought of Mrs. Margaret BLAGG
        and Mr. Richard WATTS to be given to two daus. Elizabeth
        and Sarah; if they have no heirs, then to dau. Catherine;
        if she has no heirs, to male issue of sis. Elizabeth
        GWYNN wife of Benjamin GWYNN in Bristol; if they have
        no male heirs, to bro. Edward GWYNN, clerk, in Wales;
        and if he has no heirs, then to the female heirs of
        Elizabeth the wife of Benjamin GWYNN; wife Katherine;
        sis. Mary all real est. in Wales in and about Harford
        West; sons-in-law William, Moore, and Griffin FAUNTLEROY;
        ex: wife; wits: Will. TAYLO[E], James SHERLOCK, Thomas
        BEALE.

f79r - William HANKS, inv; 10 May 1705.

f80v - Patrick LANGHEE , inv. [8] Jun 1705.

f81r - Maj. David GWYNN, inv; 8 Jun 1705.

f84r - Daniel HORNBY, NFP, will; 24 Aug 1705, 5 Sep 1705

13

son Daniel (under 16); dau. [not named]; dau. Frances
(under 16) to have liberty to live with whom she pleases;
Thomas BARLOW; ex: son, fr. John TAVERNER and Thomas
SUGGITT to be guardians; wits: Thomas BARLOW, Henry
JENNINGS.

f85r - Thomas BRADLEY, will; 9 Jul 1705, 5 Sep 1705
Elizabeth SMITH; wife Elizabeth; ex: wife; wits: John
GYLBERT, John KELLY, William SHAW.

- Charles TEBOE, St. M. Par., will; 3 Feb 1704/05, 3 Oct 1705
wife Frances; daus. Joan, Sarah, Anne, Frances, Martha,
eld. son Charles; youngest son John; no ex; wits: Wm.
MARSHALL, Lewis JONES, Richard TANKERSLEY.

f85v - Thomas TILLERY, will; 19 Jun 1705, 3 Oct 1705
son Job (under 20); bro. Job; if bro. Job should die,
son Job should go to Martin HAMMOND until he is of age;
wife Sarah; ex: wife; wits: Thomas JENKINS, James
COWARD.

f86r - Eve SMITH, NFP, will; 24 Apr 1704, 4 Oct 1705
grsons William GOAD and John GOAD; dau. Catherine to
have her father, John WILLIAMS', chest; grdau. Hannah
GOAD; ex: son Abraham GOAD; wits: William DODSON,
Charles DODSON Sr., Anne DODSON.

f87r - Richard GREENE, inv; [20] Nov 1705.

f88r - [mutilated] [?] HANKS, inv. at the house of William HANKS;
1 Feb 1705/06.

f89r - Daniel HORNBY , inv; 1 Feb 1705/06.

f89v - George TOMLIN, will; 15 Dec 1705, 6 Feb 1705/06
son George plant. I now live on with 140 ac. that I had
of my uncle TAYLOR, if son has no heirs, land to go to
dau. Anne; ex: wife Hannah; wits: James INGO, Sarah
LILLY, Henry STREET.

f90r - John MACKMELION [=McMILLION], will; 14 Oct 1701, 6 Feb 1705/
1706
dau. Charity; youngest dau. Catherine; John NEWMAN;
George NEWMAN; William COLEMAN; Maxfield BROWN; wife
Frances; ex: wife; wits: John FENNELL, Henry STREET.

f90v - [Alexander PETTENDRICKS], late of Liverpool, nuncupative
will at the house of Col. William TAYLOE; ex: fr. John
CHARTRES; rec. 5 Feb 1705.

- Eve SMITH, inv. at the house of Abraham GOAD, [5]
Feb 1705/1706.

f91r - Robert CLARK, Farn. Par., will; 12 Dec 1705, 6 Feb 1705/06
sons Robert, John, George, Thomas; dau. Catherine;
Capt. Charles BARBER; William SIMMS; ex: wife and son
Robert; wits: Charles BARBER, William SIMMS, Amy SIMMS.

f92r - William CLAYTON, will; 27 Dec 1705, 6 Mar 1705/06
two youngest sons Alexander and [Stephen] the plant.
and land I now live on; daus. Mary, Elizabeth, Hannah
(all under 16); son William (under 17); son Alexander
to receive spoon moulds; ex: wife; wits: John SEAMAN,
William LINTON, William LANDMAN.

f93r - John OLDHAM, inv. at the house of John OLDHAM; 14 Mar 170[5]/
        1706.

f94r - William WATTSON, inv; 14 Mar 1705/06.

f94v - William HANKS, f. inv. by his son, William HANKS, the adm.;
        14 Mar 1705/06.

      - [partially mutilated] Christopher JONES, will; 18 Oct 1705,
        6 Mar 1705/06
              [Margaret] DUDLEY dau. to Elizabeth DUDLEY; wife Elizabeth;
              no ex; wits: Nicholas SMITH, Elizabeth ELAM.

f95r - Charles DODSON, will; 11 Jan 1702/03, 6 Feb 1705
              son Charles the plant. formerly called [Col. Travers']
              Quarter with 150 ac; son Thomas the plant. formerly
              called The Rich Neck with 150 ac; son Bartholomew Richard
              the plant. known by the name of [Oak] Neck of 150 ac;
              son William the plant. in Hickory Neck of 150 ac; sons
              John and Lambert tracts of land; wife Anne; daus. Anne
              and Elizabeth; ex: wife; no wits; prov. by Christopher
              PETTY, 6 Feb 1705/06 and John BECKWITH, 6 Mar 1705/06.

f96r - James SPENDERGASS, inv; 14 Mar 1705/06.

f97v - Richard THODY, inv., pres. by Jane, his wid. at the house
              of Mrs. Katherine GWYNN; 14 Mar 1705/06.

f98r - Rawleigh TRAVERS, inv; 25 Apr 1706.

f100r - John FEBRUARY, inv; 25 Jul 1706.

      - George TAYLOR, Sitt. Par., will; 24 Jun 1706, 7 Aug 1706
              wife Susannah plant. where I now live on the west side
              of [?]; dau. Martha GAINES to have an English servant-
              man, John [HINTER] and a tract of land; George GAINES
              youngest son of Martha; Daniel eld. son of Bernard and
              Martha GAINES; Henry WILSON; Thomas DICKENSON who wrote
              this will; ex: wife; wits: Robert GORDEN, Elizabeth
              BRADLEY, Anna POST, Edward JEFFREY, Thomas DICKENSON.

f101r - John WILLIAMS, St. M. Par., will; 27 [Jan] 1704/05, [7 Aug
        1706]
              entire est. to Stephen FEWELL and his children; no ex;
              wits: Richard PEARLE, John OWEN, Richard ROSSER.

      - John OLDHAM, inv; [nd.].

f102r - Henry AUSTIN, will; 8 Feb 1687, 2 Oct 1706
              entire est. to wife Anne; ex: wife; wits: Thomas GUNSTON,
              Francis JORDAN, Walter WILLETT.

      - Charles DODSON, inv; 17 Oct 1706.

f103r - John KENYON, will; 29 Aug 1706, 2 Oct 1706
              son Abraham plant. that Thomas DECUS lives on containing
              550 ac; dau. Anne that plant. that John JONES Jr. lives
              on; dau. Sarah the plant. that John BARTHOLOMEW lives
              on containing 100 ac; son John remainder of land; ex:
              fr. Daniel MERRITT; wits: William THORNTON, [George]
              DAVIS, Sarah DAVIS. [John KENYON was the son of Abraham
              KENYON of Rapp. Co. DB 2, pp. 8, 11.]

f103v - Margaret CUNSTABLE, will; 25 Jun 1705, 6 Nov 1706
        nephew John TUNE all land and plant. on the west side
        of North Farnham Creek; if he has no lawful heirs, land
        to go to Mark TUNE son of Mark and Elizabeth TUNE;
        William son of Mark and Elizabeth TUNE; ex: Mark TUNE
        Sr.; wits: Robert NETHERCUTT, Austin BROCKENBROUGH.

f104v - [John KENYON], inv; 15 Nov 1706.

f105r - Elizabeth REED, inv; 14 Dec 1706.

f105v - [Tobacco paid for the use of John OLDHAM, dec'd]; signed
        by Anne OLDHAM, 5 Feb 1706/07.

      - Elias WILSON, will; 23 Dec 1706, 5 Feb 1706/07
        son Elias plant. of 400 ac. when he comes of age; wife
        Mary; bros. Henry and James; ex: wife; wits: Henry
        SEGER , Anne POST , John KELLY.

f106r - Daniel JACKSON, NFP; will; 13 Nov 1706, 5 Feb 1706/07
        son David the plant. whereon he now lives which is one
        half of the plant. where I now live; if he die without
        heirs, then plant. to go to son Nathaniel, and if he
        die without heirs, plant. to go to son Daniel; sons
        Nathaniel and Daniel also received other land; daus.
        Mary SETTLE, Sarah GOWER, and Anne HUTT; ex: son Daniel;
        wits: Joshua LAWSON, Stephen WELLS, Thomas DICKENSON.

f107r - Henry Parker TAYLOR, NFP, will; 24 Jan 1706/07, 5 Feb 1706/07
        Thomas WARD; Austin BROCKENBROUGH; father Henry PARKER;
        servant John SIMCOCK to be ex. in Virginia; wits: John
        CHARTERIS, Thomas WARD, Mary JONES.

f107v - John WALKER, of Rapp. Co., will; 22 Feb 1665, 3 Feb 1668,
        [rerecorded 14 Feb 1706/07]
        dau. Anne (mentions previous legacy to her from Francis
        BAYLIE); daus. Frances, Jane, Elizabeth; all land in
        Gloucester Co. to be eq. div. among four daus. Anne,
        Frances, Jane, and Elizabeth; daus. Sarah and Hester
        to receive all land in Rapp. Co. consisting of 1000 ac.
        (all daus. are under 16); wife Sarah 400 ac. in Rapp.
        Co.; ex: wife; wits: Richard FOX, Abraham WARREN;
        Cod. dated 6 Jul 1668 mentions that dau. Anne had, by
        that time, mar. John PAYNE. Prov. by the depositions
        of Richard FOX, aged 39 years or thereabouts, and Joseph
        CHISSEL, aged 27 years or thereabouts.

f109r - Luke WILLIAMS, NFP, will; 17 Apr 1706, 5 Mar 1706
        son John the plant. where I now live; fr. Martin SHERMAN
        the plant. he now lives on for his lifetime; son Henry
        the plant. where Judith·FOX lives; wife Mary the plant.
        where [?] now lives; nephews William FRESTOE, and
        Richard and Thomas SMITH; fr. Henry JENNINGS; John
        WILLIAMS and John HARRIS to have care of son John;
        Phillip HARRIS and Hugh HARRIS to have care of son
        Henry; ex: wife; wits: Richard HINDS, John MILLER,
        Henry JENNINGS.

f110r - Thomas WOODYATES of Bristol in the Kingdom of Great Britain,
        will; 20 Jan 1706/07, 5 Mar 1707
        friends Job HAMMOND Jr, William HAMMOND, John HAMMOND,
        Jane THORNE, Anne HAMMOND, Elizabeth HAMMOND; ex: Job
        HAMMOND Sr; wits: Martin HAMON, Martin HAMON Jr, John
        BURK.

- Susannah TAYLOR, inv; 15 Apr 1707.

f111v - Thomas WOODYATES, inv; 16 Apr 1707.

f112v - James TRENT, will; 5 Jan 1706, [1] Oct 1707
        daus. Elizabeth and Anne all the land I now possess;
        daus. Mary and Alice; wife Alice; ex: wife and John
        DEANE; wits: Giles MATTHEWS, John CURTIS, Elizabeth
        DEANE.

f113r - Henry CLEARKE, inv; 26 Dec 1707.

f113v - William STONE, statement of the mother Sarah STONE; 31 [Jan]
        [1707].

f114v - William STONE, Farn. Par., will; 7 Nov 1704, 31 Jan 1707/08
        sons Phillip, Joshua; s-i-l Robert SCOLFIELD; grsons.
        Gregory and John GLASCOCK; wife Sarah; daus. Elizabeth,
        Mary FANN; ex: wife; no wits.

f115r - John HAMMOCK, planter, will; [nd.], 15 Feb 1707/08
        son William; ex: son William; wits: Thomas BRYANT,
        Edward TALBERD, David BENEHAN.

f115v - James SPENDERGRASS, inv. at the house of Robert PORT, 15
        Feb 1707/08.

f116r - John HAMMOCK, inv. at the house of Thomas BRYANT; [nd.].

f116v - Mr. Gerrard [NEWTON], inv; 26 Apr 170[6].

f117r - George WOODBRIDGE, inv; 26 Apr 170[6].

f118r - John RICHARDSON, inv; 26 Apr 1706.

f118v - Peter EVANS, Sitt. Par., will; 13 Jun 1706, 3 Jul 1706
        sons Richard, Peter, and John; dau. Sarah; wife
        Elizabeth the plant. of 100 ac. where I live; after her
        death, to go to son Peter upon condition that he person-
        ally appear in the Colony of Virginia, otherwise to go
        to son John; daus. Elizabeth and Anne; ex: wife; wits:
        Matthew BURROWS, James DOWLING, Thomas DICKENSON.

f119v - Capt. John CLARK, inv. at the house of Mrs. Elizabeth
        CLARK; [?] Jul 1706.

f120r - George LODGE, St. M. Par., will; 1 Dec 1707, 7 Apr 1708
        son [Abslent] SPISER; no ex; wits: Anne FRANCE[S],
        Thomas ROBINSON.

f120v - Richard WHITE, will; 31 Oct 1706, 7 Jul 1708
        sons John, Thomas, William; daus. Hesther MILLS,
        Susannah ADCOCK; wife Sarah; all land to be eq. div.
        between sons Thomas and William; ex: son Thomas;
        wits: George MURDOCK, John WILLCOCK[S], John CALLEHAN.

f121r - Matthew BROOK, inv; [nd.].

f121v - John [SPRAGG], inv; 13 Sep 1708.

      - Owen McARTE, inv. at the house of Nathaniel HALL; [nd.].

f122v - [blank]

f123r - Thomas DEW, will; 23 Dec 1708, 2 Feb 1708/09
wife Jean; s-i-l William BAKER; d-i-l Elizabeth BAKER;
daus. Anne, Mary, and Elizabeth; son Thomas my Indian
woman, Gunn[o]r; son is to keep his sisters as long as
they stay with him; ex: son Thomas; wits: Peter KIPPAX,
George HABRON, Andrew DEW. [Thomas DEW was the son of
Andrew and Anne DEW; he married (1) Elizabeth BARBER
and (2) Jean BAKER. MRC, pp. 200,201.]

f123v - John GAYTHINGS, Farn. Par., will; 29 Nov 1708, 2 Feb 1708/09
sons Phillip (eldest), John, and Cobham (youngest);
wife Anne; dau. Winifred; ex: wife and son Phillip;
wits: Edward JONES, John BUXSTONE.
Cod.; 29 Nov 1708; Since I have further considered that
my oldest son Phillip may have peach drink and apple
drink to distill and make brandy and that I have made
no provision in my...will for his distilling the same,
now my will is further that my son Phillip shall and may
have free liberty of my still at such convenient time
as it may be spared on the plant. whereon I now live
to make use of it to his own benefit provided he brings
no other than what is or shall be of his own growth.
wit: William ALLGOOD.

f125r - John PRICE, will; 11 Sep 1707, 2 Feb 1708/09
land to cousin Edward PRICE; bro. Edward PRICE; cousin
John PRICE son of bro. Edward; no ex; wits: James [JONES],
Walter FRANCIS.

- Francis SETTLE, Farn. Par., will; 11 Jul 1707-12 Aug 1707,
2 Feb 1708/09
son John; son Thomas the plant. where he lives containing 200 ac. which I purchased of Richard RICE; grsons.
Francis SETTLE (son of Francis SETTLE) a tract of land
where Stephen WELLS now lives, Henry SETTLE (son of
Henry SETTLE dec'd) the plant. where I now live, Francis
SETTLE (son of Henry SETTLE dec'd); wife Mary; ex: wife,
son Thomas, and s-i-l Thomas WILLIAMS; wits: Thomas
SWINDLEY, Alexander [YOUNG], Thomas DICKENSON. [Francis
SETTLE Sr. mar. (2) Mary WILLIAMS, wid. of Rice WILLIAMS,
in 1702. MRC, p. 184.]

f126v - John CRASK, inv. at the house of James LOCKHART; 15 Mar 1708/
1709.

f127r - [Richard] SHIPPIE, inv; [15 Mar 1708/09.]

f128v - John SHORDON, will; [nd.], 1 Jun 1709
godson John DUNN (son of Patrick DUNN) 2 years schooling;
Daniel CAVENNER ; Ellen [EROCHE] and her son John; ex:
Ellen [EROCHE]; prov. by Samuel BACHEY and Richard
COOPER.

f129r - Thomas LEWIS, NFP, will; 20 May 1709, [1] Jun 1709
all land to son Thomas; if he has no heirs, to dau.
Deborah POUND; s-i-l John POUND Jr; ex: son Thomas and
dau. Deborah POUND; wits: Tobias PURCELL, Thomas
DICKENSON.

f130r - [A second recording of the will of Thomas LEWIS.]

f131r - Abraham MARSHALL, blacksmith, will; 3 Nov 1708, 6 Jul 1709
wife Thomasin use of plant. and lands in NFP, after her
death, to dau. Mary CAM[P]BELL, if she has no heirs,

18

to brother John MARSHALL of Bradfield in Berkshire in
the Kingdom of England, and if he has no heirs, to go
to John DURHAM (son of Thomas DURHAM) of NFP; s-i-l
Alexander CAM[P]BELL; ex: wife; wits: Thomas MORGAN,
Alexander THOMPSON, [Mil.] WALTERS. [The birth of Mary
MARSHALL, to Abraham and Thomasin, was recorded on 7
Jan 1699, yet apparently she had mar. Alexander
CAM[P]BELL by Nov 1708. NFPR, p. 126; MRC, p.32.]

f131v - James SHERLOCK, inv. of his movable est; 3 Aug 1709.

- Ralph MARE and Thomas WARD, late of this county, inventories;
4 Aug 1709.

f132v - Edward MONTAGUE, inv; 7 Sep 1709.

WILLS AND INVENTORIES, 1709-1717

p. 1 - John WILSON, will; 30 Jul 1707, 2 Nov 1709
bros. Henry and James; Maj. Edward MOSELEY; wife Frances;
wife to give two years of schooling to Thomas NEWMAN;
ex: wife; no wits; prov. by John KELLY and Elizabeth
BRADLEY.

p. 2 - Richard [FAULKNER], inv; 1 Feb 1709/10.

- Shadrack WILLIAMS, inv; 1 Feb 1709/10, Elizabeth WILLIAMS
adm.

p. 4 - Richard LEVACON, inv; 1 Mar 1709/10, George HOPKINS adm.

p. 5 - Bryan THORNHILL, nuncupative will; [25 Jan 1709/10, 1 Mar
1709/10
Be it remembered that on the 25th day of January last
past, Bryan THORNHILL, since deceased, was at the time
aforesaid, being then sick but in perfect sense and
memory, heard to say and declare in the presence and
hearing of us the subscribers that it was his will...
that he had then two horses and one mare and that he
was in hopes that by the produce of the mare his children might have, each of them, one and what else he had
he gave to his wife; witness our hands, John CANTERBURY,
Susannah PHILLIPS. Pres. by the relict, Elizabeth
THORNHILL, 1 Mar 1709/10.

- Giles MATHEWS, will; 13 Feb 1709/10, 5 Apr 1710
eld. daus. Mary and Ellinor 200 ac. to be eq. div.;
youngest dau. Jane; fr. John HIGDON; ex: John HIGDON
and dau. Mary; wits: Nath. POPE, Alex. SIM, Phillip
HARRALL.

p. 7 - Samuel BAYLY, NFP, will; 8 Feb 1709/10, 5 Apr 1710
dau. Joyce BARBER wife of Capt. William BARBER; wife
Anne; son Samuel; reading books to be eq. div. between
son Samuel and s-i-l William BARBER; ex: wife, son, and
s-i-l William BARBER; requests fr. Col. William TAYLOE
and Mr. Daniel McCARTY to see that will is performed;
wits: Charles BARBER, Thomas LEWIS.

p. 8 - Richard COLEMAN, NFP, will; 16 Mar 1709/10, 5 Apr 1710
Elizabeth TUNE wife of Mark TUNE; Barbary TOMSON wife
of James TOMSON; Timothy McDANIEL; John TAVERNER; James
WELCH; Samuel ANGEL; Judith HALL; Alexander FLEMING Jr;

John STEWARD; Charles STEWARD; James WELCH; the little
girl, Winifred, which was bound to me to go again to
her mother; Edward [PARTLEY]; Mary POWELL; James
STEWARD; ex: John TAVERNER and Mark TUNE; no wits.

p. 10 - Joshua DAVIS, will; 1 Mar 1708, 5 Apr 1710
land to be eq. div. between two sons Joshua and Samuel;
dau. Hester; Elizabeth CRAFORD; Mary QUIGS; ex: wife
Catherine, dau. Hester, sons Josuaway and Samuel; wits:
John GRIMSLEY, Thomas JONES.

p. 11 - Samuel BAILEY, inv; 8 Jun 1710.

p. 12 - Eleanor EACKES, inv. as she was ex. to John SHERDON, dec'd;
5 Jul 1710.

p. 13 - Manus McLAUGHLIN, Farn. Par., will; 23 Dec 1709, 5 Jul 1710
wife; daughters Bridget (eld.), Elizabeth, Anne, Sarah,
Priscilla (youngest); ex: wife; wits: Thomas GRIFFIN,
John HENLEY, Richard WAUGHAN. [Manus McLAUGHLIN mar.,
by 3 Jan 1694, Elizabeth WOODBRIDGE. MRC, p. 126.]

p. 14 - Joshua DAVIS, inv; 5 Jul 1710.

p. 16 - William PEMBERTON, inv; 5 Jul 1710.

p. 17 - Giles MATHEWS, inv; 5 Jul 1710.

p. 18 - John [JETT], Sitt. Par., will; 11 May 1710, 6 Sep 1710
son Francis 100 ac. I bought of Joseph SHIP; dau.
Abigail; son John the plant. and land whereon I now
live; son William; ex: Elizabeth and son Francis; wits:
Francis EAMES Sr., John [RAEW], John SKEY.

p. 20 - Manus McLAUGHLIN, inv. pres. by Elizabeth McLAUGHLIN his
ex; 6 Sep 1710.

p. 23 - William NELSON, planter, Farn. Par., will; 5 Mar 1710; 6
Sep 1710
fr. Dominick BENNEHAM; wife Frances; son James; asks
that Rawleigh DOWNMAN be guardian to son James; ex:
Rawleigh DOWNMAN; wits: Abraham PROCTOR, William FOSTER,
Thomas LEE.

   - [Henry WILTON], inv; 4 Oct 1710.

   - William HEAD, inv. pres. by Mary HEAD, ex; 4 Oct 1710.

p. 25 - Thomas MASON, inv; 4 Oct 1710.

p. 27 - Thomas TIPPITT, St. M. Par., will; 15 Feb 1699/1700, 6 Dec
1710
land to be eq. div. between wife Katherine and son
William; no ex; wits: Neal McCORMACK, John TAYLOR.

p. 28 - Sem COXE, will; 18 Oct 1710, 6 Dec 1710
to be buried in my own burying place by my late dear
dau., dec'd, at Robert PECK's plant; mentions John
COLLYER merchant in Bristol; water grist mill called
Head's Mill to Joseph DOWNING (son of George DOWNING
by Anne his wife); asks Anne the wife of George DOWNING
to look after Elizabeth COLLYNS, an orphan, until she
comes of age or marries; Sem RICHARDSON (son of James
RICHARDSON) to stay with my ex. or return to his father

which he pleaseth; Margaret BERRY (dau. of William
BERRY);[Robert TALIAFERRO and Margaret his now wife];
in case the sd. Joseph DOWNING should die without issue
...after the decease of his mother, then I give and
bequeath all and singular my lands, tenements, and
messuages to the use and behoof of the north side of
the par. of St. Mary's in the county of Richmond to buy
ornaments and other decent utensils for the two churches
therein; fr. Edward TURBERVILLE; ex: Benjamin DEVERILL
and George DOWNING; wits: Thomas EVANS, George ALSUP,
E. TURBERVILLE.

p. 30 - Edward NEWTON, will; 23 [?] 1710, 6 Dec 1710
leaves son Henry to James INGO for 3 years and also
an orphan boy called Edward CLARK belonging to him;
dau. Anne; son William; ex: James INGO; wits: Arthur
DYE, Robert HOPKINS, James NELSON.

p. 31 - James INNIS, will; 25 Dec 1709, 6 Dec 1710
wife; daus. Sarah, Elizabeth, and Hannah; son Enoch
the plant. where I now dwell; son James (under 18);
servant Hugh [MATEER] to be free two years before his
full time; ex: dau. Sarah; wits: John HUST, Jean HUST,
John BARTHOLOMEW Jr.; Cod. If either son dies before
he comes of age and leaves no children, land to go to
the survivor; if both die, land to go to dau. Sarah.

p. 33 - Bryan THORNHILL, inv; 6 Dec 1710.

- Elizabeth LOCKHART, wife of James LOCKHART, will; 26 Mar
1709/10, 6 Dec 1710
daus. Martha and Eleanor CRASKE; no ex; wits: Elizabeth
BROWN, James INGO. [Elizabeth MOSS mar. (1) Capt. John
CRASKE and (2) James LOCKHART ca. 1708. MRC, p. 120]

p. 34 - Henry JEN[N]INGS, inv. pres. by Eleanor JEN[N]INGS, adm;
6 Dec 1710.

p. 35 - Sem COX, inv; 3 Jan 1710/11.

p. 37 - John MILLS, Farn. Par., will; 30 Dec 1709, 7 Feb 1710/11
son John land where I now live; daus. Hannah, Hester,
Elizabeth GREEN; other sons Richard 50 ac., Thomas 50
ac., George (under 21), James (under 21); wife Hester;
ex: wife; wits: Winfred SOUTHERN, John RANKIN, Thomas
WHITE. [The birth of Elizabeth to John and Esther MILLS
is rec. in the NFPR in 1682, p. 129.]

p. 38 - Samuel COLE, will; 24 Sep 1710, 7 Feb 1710/11
Richard BRAMHAM Sr.; Richard BRAMHAM Jr.; George HEALE;
ex: fr. George HEALE; wits: William WEST, Arthur BIRD.

p. 39 - James MATHEWS, St. M. Par., will; 2 Feb 1707, 7 Mar 1710/11
wife Jennett; son Andrew; dau. Margaret the wife of
Richard TANKERSLEY; ex: wife; wits: John SOMMERVILLE,
John [GREEN], Edward TURBERVILLE.

p. 40 - Maurice CLARK, will; 28 Feb 1710/11, 7 Mar 1710/11
Peter WATERSON the plant. whereon I now live with 100
ac. of land next the river; servant man Dennis LINSY a
tract of land; John HOAGIN 75 ac. in Stafford Co.;
Thomas CONAWAY; Thomas WALTER; ex: Peter WATERSON; wits:
Thomas CONAWAY, John SMYTH, Edward LANGSDELL, Thomas
WALTER.

p. 41 - Col. William TAYLOE, inv; 7 Mar 1710/11.

p. 44 - Mary WAKEMAN, inv; 7 Mar 1710/11.

p. 45 - David SMITH, inv. pres. by Anne SMITH, adm; 20 Mar 1710/11.

p. 46 - David SMITH, f. inv; 2 May 1711.

p. 47 - George PAYNE Sr., will; 3 Feb 1710/11, 2 May 1711
        sons George and John tract of land to be eq. div; son
        Thomas; father Thomas [PACEY]; ex: bros. George and
        Daniel WHITE; wits: Henry AXTON, Jane [MURROW], [Margit
        CUSHEE]. [George PAYNE Sr. mar. Jane WHITE dau. of
        Thomas and Jane WHITE of West. Co. MRC, p.154.]

p. 48 - Henry CLARK, f. inv. ret. by Bartholomew Richard DODSON,
        adm; 2 May 1711.

     - [Sem] COXE, f. inv; 2 May 1711.

p. 49 - David MAGUYER, inv; 3 May 1711.

p. 50 - George PAYNE [Sr.], inv; 6 Jun 1711.

p. 52 - Edward NEWTON, inv; 6 Jun 1711.

p. 53 - [Mary] WAKEMAN, f. inv; 6 Jun 1711.

p. 54 - Peter ELLIS, will; [26 Feb 1706], 4 Jul 1711
        grson James ELLIS (son of Peter ELLIS Jr., dec'd) the
        plant. where his father died and was buried containing
        181 ac. lying on the s.w. side of the main swamp of
        Totuskey Creek; if he has no heirs, land to go to his
        sis. Catherine ELLIS; if she has no heirs, to dau. Anne
        ELLIS; and, if she has no heirs, to John POWELL; ex:
        wife Jane; wits: David SMITH, Edward JONES. [Peter,
        the son of Peter and Ellenor ELLIS, was b. 21 Apr 1670
        and Anne, the dau. of Peter and Jane ELLIS, was b. 2
        Jan 1696. NFPR, p. 58.]

p. 55 - Gerrard NEWTON, inv. of an est. set apart for the orphans;
        4 Jul 1711. [Gerrard NEWTON mar. Rebecca _(?)_ ; they had
        three chil., John, Rose, and Elizabeth. MRC, p. 146.]

p. 56 - William HEAD, inv; 17 Aug 1711.

p. 57 - Thomas SMITH, inv; 17 Aug 1711.

p. 58 - Interrogation put by John TARPLEY to Capt. William WOOD-
        BRIDGE, Mr. William FITZHERBERT, Mr. Dominick BENNEHAM,
        Madam Winifred GRIFFIN, and George GLASCOCK; 30 Jul 1711.
        [The witnesses responded to questions regarding who
        would receive the land of Capt. Alexander NEWMAN if he
        died without heirs. They agreed that Capt. NEWMAN had
        stated that it should go to Thomas NEWMAN, the son of
        Thomas NEWMAN "that lived above Rappahannock Creek"
        and who mar. the dau. of Elias WILSON dec'd. For
        further details see MRC, p. 146.]

p. 60 - Alexander FLEMMON [=FLEMING], will; 11 Nov 1710, [?]
        sons John the plant. where I now live, Alexander 50 ac.
        of land, William, Charles; dau. Margaret; Samuel KENNEDY;
        Elizabeth KENNEDY; Anne KENNEDY; wife Sarah; no ex;
        wits: Jane FOUSHEE, William SMITH, Will. BARBER.
        [Alexander FLEMING mar. Sarah KENNEDY, the dau. of John

22

KENNEDY, by 23 Mar 1690. MRC, p. 70.]

p. 62 - Alexander FLEMMING, inv; 10 Mar 1711/12.

p. 63 - James INNIS, inv. pres. by Mr. Thomas HOOPER and Sarah, his
wife; 10 Mar 1711/12.

p. 65 - Henry TODD, James STARK acknowledges that he received full
satisfaction of his share of Henry TODD's est. from
Jane TODD; 6 Mar 1711/12.

- John TAVERNER, NFP, will; 4 May 1711, 5 Mar 1711/12
nephews Thomas BEALE Jr, John BEALE, William BEALE, and
Isaac ALLERTON; niece Elizabeth BEALE; all land to wife
Rebecca; ex: wife; wits: Joseph BELFIELD, Charles
COLSTON, Thomas READ; [W.] ALLERTON. [John TAVERNER
mar. Rebecca TRAVERS dau. of Capt. Samuel and Frances
(ALLERTON) TRAVERS. MRC, p. 42.]

p. 67 - Winifred GRIFFIN, NFP, will; 10 Sep 1709, 5 Mar 1711/12
grdaus. Winifred PRESLEY (dau. of Col. Peter PRESLEY),
Winifred GRIFFIN, and Alice Corbin GRIFFIN; son Thomas;
s-i-l Col. Peter PRESLEY; ex: son Thomas; wits: John
TARPLEY, E. KIPPAX, William HANKS.
Cod., 5 Jan 1711/12, mentions daughter-in-law Elizabeth
GRIFFIN; wits: John TARPLEY, Mary NICKOLS. [Winifred
GRIFFIN was the wife of Leroy GRIFFIN; the births of
three of their chil. are rec. in the NFPR: Corbin
(1679), Winifred (1682), and Thomas (1684). NFPR, p.73.]

p. 69 - Giles MATHEWS, supplementary inv; 15 Mar 1711/12.

- Theodore [DUROSOU], Sitt. Par., will; 8 Feb 1711/12, 5 Mar
1711/12
Charles [SPOE] Jr.; goddau. Elizabeth FOUSHEE a parcel
of land containing 50 ac. near [Perpetoc] Creek; no ex;
wits: Matthew DAVIS, Alexander RIGG.

p. 70 - Mary WAKEMAN, supplementary inv; 13 Mar 1711/12.

- Theophilus KING, Farn. Par., will; 7 Aug [1711], 5 Mar 1711/
1712
Philip GAYTHINGS all my lands and living except my share
of corn for Dominick NUGENT; Matthew NOXEN; no ex; wits:
Philip HARRIS, Matthew NOXEN, Dominick NUGENT.

p. 71 - William FENTON, inv; 2 Apr 1712.

p. 73 - Elizabeth KING, relinquishment; 26 Mar 1711/12, 2 Apr 1712
Elizabeth KING, the wid. of Theophilus KING who died
intestate, relinquishes her right of adm. to Philip
GAYTHINGS; wits: Charles BARBER, Edward JONES.

- Ralph RUTTUR, will; [31] Dec 1711, 2 Apr 1712
fr. William DANIELE of St. Anne's Par., carpenter, land
in Essex Co. which I bought of Richard DAVISON containing
100 ac.; servant and shipmate John GEORGE; no ex; wits:
Joneth. GIBSON, Robert PAYNE, Susan MILLER.

p. 75 - Edward MOZINGO, will; 30 Jul 1711, 7 May 1712
sons Edward and John; wife Margaret; ex: wife and sons;
wits: Leonard DOZIER, John DOZIER, Edward BARROW.

p. 76 - John TAVERNER, inv. pres. by Rebecca TAVERNER, ex; 7 May 1712.

p. 78 - John OWENS, inv; 7 May 1712.

p. 79 - Ralph [RUTTER], inv; 7 May 1712.

p. 80 - Thomas TAYLOR, will; 29 Mar 1711/12, 4 Jun 1712
        sons Thomas, Benjamin, and John to be left at age and
        set at liberty at 16; eld. son Thomas 50 ac. binding
        on Lawrence TALIAFERRO; son Benjamin 50 ac. binding on
        John JONES; youngest son John 50 ac. between the lands
        of his brothers; no ex; wits: Job SHAPLES, Thomas
        SISSON.

     - William DOWNMAN, NFP, will; 23 May 1711, 4 Jun 1712
        son Rawleigh tract of land bought of Edward KING called
        "Mt. Sion" and 250 ac. bought of Charles CALE; son
        Robert 300 ac. near the branches of Totuskey; son
        Travers all the land I bought of Arthur [ATTEY] in the
        forest of Moraticon; son William what moneys son GLASCOCK
        owes me for the millstones and what belongs to them;
        daus. Million, Elizabeth, Priscilla; ex: wife; wits:
        Abraham GOAD, William ACKERS, William GOAD. [The births
        of the fol. chil. of William and Million DOWNMAN are
        rec. in the NFPR: Rawleigh (1680), Wilmoth (1681),
        Million (1683), William (1685), Robert (1686), Elizabeth
        (1688), Travers (1696), and a second son Travers (1700).
        p. 51.]

p. 82 - James WILSON, will; 20 Jul 1709, 4 Jun 1712
        son James land on which I now live; wife; three chil.;
        ex: wife; wits: Thomas SCARLOCK, Mary JONES, Thomas
        ROUT. [The births of three chil. to James and Mary
        WILSON were rec. in the NFPR: James (1703), Anne
        (1707), and John (1710). p. 203.]

p. 83 - Mrs. Elizabeth FOSSAKER, inv. pres. by the ex. Mrs. Eleanor
        SHIPPIE; 4 Jun 1712. [Elizabeth FOSSAKER was the wid.
        of John FOSSAKER and eld. dau. of George MOTT. MRC, p.
        71.]

     - Samuel PEACHEY, NFP, will; 2[9] Jan 1711/12, 4 Jun 1712
        nephews and nieces the sons and daus. of Nathaniel and
        Sarah PEACHEY, the sons and daus. of Will. and Anne
        [DEBAMORE], and the sons and daus. of John and Jane
        WILDMAN; wife; grson. Samuel PEACHEY; Catherine DOBYNS;
        James BIDDLECOMB; Robin HOOD Sr; William and Charles
        DOBYNS; Thomas THORNE; the eld. son of James BIDDLECOMB;
        Elizabeth LYNCH (the dau. of Stephen and Elizabeth
        LYNCH); goddau. the eld. dau. of James and Mary TARPLEY;
        Thomas BOWLES; sis. Jane WILDMAN; I give and devise 40
        shillings sterling for three years successively after
        my decease to be disposed of by my ex. in trust in manner
        following, that is to say that they shall send for some
        necessary clothing out of Great Britain and bestow the
        same upon some poor people of the parish that are not
        provided for by the parish; fr. Col. Willoughby ALLERTON,
        Capt. Daniel McCARTY, Mr. Daniel DOBYNS, and Capt. Thomas
        BEALE; grson Samuel PEACHEY the plant. I now live on and
        the next plant; ex: grson Samuel PEACHEY, Col. Willoughby
        ALLERTON, Capt. Daniel McCARTY, Daniel DOBYNS, and Capt.
        Thomas BEALE to be trustees, grson to be of age at 18;
        wits: Thomas THORNE, Thomas BOWLES, Edward JONES. [For
        further information on Samuel PEACHEY, see MR 1699-1724,
        p. 19.]

p. 87 - Edward MOZINGO, inv; 4 Jun 1712.

p. 88 - William BURGES, St. M. Par, nuncupative will
Published and declared the same before us on Thursday
23 Apr 1712 as follows: son Edward; daus. Elizabeth,
Sarah, and Mary; son Edward to go with Jeremiah BRONAUGH
until 21; wits: Richard COPELY, Rebecca COPELY; prov.
4 Jun 1712.

p. 89 - James WILSON, inv; 2 Jul 1712.

- Edmund OVERTON, inv; 2 Jul 1712.

p. 91 - Theophilus KING, inv; 2 Jul 1712.

p. 92 - John DEANE, Sitt. Par., will; 15 Feb 1711/12, 2 Jul 1712
son Charles all the land whereon I now live with 100
ac. known as "Ireland" in Sitt. Par; land at Port
Tobacco in Essex Co. to sons John and William; ex:
sons Charles and John; wits: Henry AXTON, Thomas
WATERS, Jane [BRANCH]. [John DEANE mar. (1) Jane
WALKER by 1683 and (2) Elizabeth THATCHER. MRC, p. 53.]

p. 94 - John DEANE, inv; 6 Jul 1712.

p. 97 - [Francis] JETT, inv; 6 Aug 1712.

p. 98 - William DOWNMAN, inv; 7 Aug 1712.

p.102 - Theodore [DUROSOU], inv; 7 Aug 1712.

p.103 - John BATTEN, NFP, will; 3 May 1712, 3 Sep 1712
land to grdau. Phyllis LUCAS; land upon the riverside
joining upon my s-i-l Francis LUCAS to dau. Elizabeth
DOBYNS; ex: wife, dau. Elizabeth DOBYNS, and grdau.
Phyllis LUCAS; wits: Richard [DOWDY], John MILLER,
Thomas THORN. [John BATTEN mar. Elizabeth (?) ; she
mar. (2) John WILLIAMS, and (3) William STOKES. MRC,
pp. 11-12.]

p.105 - William BURGES, inv; [3] Sep 1712.

p.106 - Mary PHILLIPS, wid; will; 21 Oct 1702, 3 Sep 1712
son Richard FORRISTER 231 ac. of land; dau. Frances
BRADSHER; eld. s-i-l Nicholas GEORGE; ex: son Richard
FORRISTER; wits: John HARPER, Robert ROUNDS, William
DOWNMAN.

- Jeremiah HOOK, inv; 4 Sep 1712.

p.107 - Matthew LYNCH, inv; 1 Oct 1712.

p.108 - John WILLIMOTT of the Par. of St. Dunstan[s], Stepney, in
the Co. of Middlesex, mariner, now in the river of Gambia,
will; 6 Jul 1712, 5 Nov 1712
I bequeath to my father and mother WILLIMOTT and ordain
my only and sole ex. 22 ounces and half of gold and
the profit of nine [slaves] when sold at [Virginia or
Jamaica] and my wages and servants that shall be due to
me on board the ship Mary and Elizabeth and [?] mark
'EW' that's now on board, they paying all my just and
due debts and what money shall be found remaining, I
give and bequeath unto my loving wife Radygon WILLIMOTT
and I likewise give and bequeath unto my sd. wife...
all my plate goods and chattels and etc. to be at her

disposing after my decease as she shall think fit;
whereas I deliver the key of my chest where my gold is
lock in and all papers and accounts into the hands of
William COURTNY, Nathaniel DAVIS, and Francis WOOD, and
William [NOULTON] which are to see that nothing of my
things be made away with or [embezzled], but to be delivered to my ex., adm., or assigns as above mentioned,
willed and bequeathed, ratifying and confirming this
and no other to be my last will and testament, in witness
whereof, I have hereunto set my hand and seal the day
and year above written; wits: Will COURTNEY, Nathaniel
DAVIS, Francis WOOD, William NOULTON.
And, whereas I stood obligated in England to find Nathaniel DAVIS, my 2d mate, one slave, and James DENISON,
[my doctor], one slave, and have brought each of them
a slave which is now on board and though the two slaves
should die is now on board, they can't claim no [debts]
dues and demands whatever on me.
                              /s/ John WILLIMOTT

p.110 - Cyprian PROU, will; 16 Oct 1712, 5 Nov 1712
        daus. Mary, Elizabeth, Margaret, Susan, and Frances;
        s-i-l William [PAYNE]; Isaac FEBRUARY; ex: daus. Mary,
        Susan, and Frances; wits: Thomas PANNELL, Thomas SHIP,
        Joseph BERRY.

p.111 - James COLEMAN, inv; 3 Dec 1712.

p.112 - John BATTEN, inv; 4 Feb 1712/13.

p.115 - Edward KIPPAX, inv; 4 Mar 1712/13.

p.117 - John GLENDENING, inv; 4 Mar 1712/13.

p.118 - Mrs. Winifred GRIFFIN, inv. pres. by Thomas GRIFFIN, ex;
        4 Mar 1712/13.

p.120 - William JORDAN, inv; 1 Apr 1713.

p.121 - William MARCH, inv; 1 Apr 1713.

p.122 - Francis STONE, will; 19 Jan 1712/13, 6 May 1713
        all lands to be eq. div. between sons Francis and
        David; ex: wife; wits: John GILBERT, Anthony PATON,
        Isaac TRUCK.

      - Anne A[U]STIN, wid., NFP, will; 19 Jan 1711/12, 6 May 1713
        tract of land where I now dwell, formerly purchased by
        my late husband, Henry ASTIN, of Mr. William FAUNTLEROY,
        to my nephew Austin BROCKENBROUGH; nephew Austin also
        to receive a tract of land in Rich. Co. near the wid.
        GREEN; nephew William BROCKENBROUGH 240 ac. near
        Totuskey Mill; nephew Newman BROCKENBROUGH; niece
        Elizabeth DICKENSON (wife of Thomas DICKENSON); Mary
        the dau. of Jane and Owen JONES; 4000 lbs of tobacco
        to the poor of NFP; ex: nephew Austin BROCKENBROUGH;
        wits: Samuel GODWIN, George WHARTON, Arthur BIRD,
        William DAVIS.

p.124 - Hugh HARRIS, Farn. Par., will; 7 Nov 1712, 6 May 1713
        sons John and Hugh the lands that belonged to my deed
        of sale bought of Col. Samuel GRIFFIN except what I
        have already by deed given to my son Philip; William
        MILLER; grdau. Mary HARRIS; grdau. Anne HARRIS (dau.
        to Philip HARRIS; John WILLIAMS (son to Luke WILLIAMS);

William and Samuel OLDHAM (sons to John OLDHAM); Anne
WILLIAMS (dau. to John WILLIAMS); wife; John DAVIS an
orphan bound to me; ex: wife and son Hugh; wits: John
DAVIS, John MORGAN, Edward JONES.

p.126 - Thomas TAYLOR, will; 4 Jun 1712, 7 May 1713
        sons Thomas, Benjamin, and John; no ex; wits: Thomas
        [STOONE], Job STAPPLES.

      - Zachariah NICHOLLS, inv; 7 May 1713.

p.127 - Thomas TAYLOR, inv; 7 May 1713.

p.128 - Hugh HARRIS, inv; 3 Jun 1713.

p.130 - Mrs. Anne AUSTIN, inv; 3 Jun 1713.

p.134 - William TALBOT, inv; 3 Jun 1713.

p.136 - Francis STO[RNE], inv. [pres. by] ex. Mary STORNE; 3 Jun 1713.

p.138 - Cyprian PROU, inv; 5 Aug 1713.

p.141 - James TARPLEY, Farn. Par., will; 12 Dec 1711, 5 Aug 1713
        sons Thomas and Charles 260 ac. on Farnham Creek, James
        the land whereon I now live, and William; daus. Mary,
        Elizabeth, and Lucy; ex: wife, brother John, William
        BARBER, and Charles BARBER; wits: Stephen [GUPTON],
        William CLARK, William [GUPTON]. [The births of the
        fol. chil. to James and Mary TARPLEY are rec. in the
        NFPR: John (1690), Mary (1691), James (1692), William
        (1695), Thomas (1697), and Elizabeth (1701). NFPR, p.180.]

p.142 - Capt. Henry BRERETON, inv; 5 Aug 1713. [Sarah, the wid. of
        Capt. Henry BRERETON, mar. (2) William WOODBRIDGE in
        Jul 1713. MRC, p.235.]

p.144 - Thomas SUGGITT, inv. pres. by Mrs. Rebecca SUGGITT, adm;
        6 Aug 1713.

p.146 - James TARPLEY, inv. pres. by Mrs. Mary TARPLEY, wid. and
        relict; 2 Sep 1713.

p.148 - William GOODRIDGE, NFP, will; 12 May 1713, 2 Sep 1713
        wife Tomasin; son William all land in Lanc. Co. which
        I bought of Richard ALDERSON and John [BUXTON]; other
        chil. Moses and Elizabeth; desires Mr. Rawleigh CHINN
        to have the care of the three chil. until age 21; ex:
        fr. Rawleigh CHINN; wits: none given, but prov. by the
        oaths of Dorothy and Thomas DURHAM.

p.150 - Mrs. Patience HARRIS, her part of her dec'd husband's
        est.; 2 Sep 1713.

      - Mr. Hugh HARRIS, his part of his dec'd father's est; 2
        Sep 1713.

p.151 - [William] PEACHEY, will; May 1713, 2 Sep 1713
        grdaus. Mary and Elizabeth TARPLEY; dau. Mary TARPLEY;
        chil. of James BIDDLECOMB; chil. of dau. Elizabeth JONES;
        ex: none named; pres. by Mrs. Mary TARPLEY and prov. by
        the oath of John TARPLEY Gent.

p.152 - Philip BROWNE, inv; 2 Sep 1713.

p.153 --Jeremiah HOOK, supplementary inv; 2 Sep 1713.

- John MEADE, will; [4] May 1711, 7 Oct 1713
  wife Susannah; chil. [unnamed]; ex: wife; wits: William
  PHILLIPS, John NEWMAN.

- William SOUTHERNE, inv; Winifred SOUTHERN ex; 7 Oct 1713.

p.155 - William GOODRIDGE (or GUTTRIDGE), inv. by Rawleigh CHINN,
  adm; 4 Nov 1713.

p.156 - William YEATS, inv; 4 Nov 1713.

p.157 - John MEADE, inv; 4 Nov 1713.

p.158 - George ERWIN, will; 23 Oct 1713, 4 Nov 1713
  On 23 Oct. the sd. George ERWIN called us the subscribers
  and declared these following words, that he gave to his
  goddau., Millicent VEALE...to be delivered to Morris
  VEALE father to the sd. Millicent...[also mentioned
  ERWIN's wife Sarah]; wits: John JENNINGS, Mary JENNINGS.

p.159 - Joseph BARKER, will; 9 Jun 1713, 4 Nov 1713
  wife one half of est; son Edmond one half of est; ex:
  son Edmond; wits: John CHAMPE, John HILL, Eliz. HILL.

p.160 - Joseph BARKER, inv; [nd.]

p.161 - George ERWIN, inv; 2 Dec 1713.

p.163 - Anne GLASCOCK, will; 6 Feb 1713, 7 Apr 1714
  grson. John TARPLEY tract of land between the land of
  Henry CLARK and his father, Capt. John TARPLEY; grson.
  Anthony SYDNOR 150 ac., if he has no heirs, to grdau.
  Anne BARBER; son George GLASCOCK; daus. Anne TARPLEY,
  Frances BARBER, Joan LAWSON, and Mary HIPKINS; grson.
  George GLASCOCK; ex: s-i-l Charles BARBER and Rowland
  LAWSON; wits: Joseph BRAGG, William DOWNMAN, Thomas
  GLASCOCK.

p.165 - Thomas BROOME, Farn. Par; will; 26 Dec 1713, 3 Mar 1713/14
  all books to William DARE of St. Mary's White Chapel;
  rest of est. to Mrs. Elizabeth DENTON, Sarah Broome
  DENTON, Thomas Broome DENTON, and Joseph Broome DENTON;
  ex: Elizabeth DENTON; wits: Catherine [SOFFEL], Edward
  GEFFEREY.

- Anne GLASCOCK, inv. by Thomas GLASCOCK ex; 7 Apr 1714.

p.168 - George GLASCOCK, will; 20 Jan 1713/14, 7 Apr 1714
  sons William and George the plant. where I now live and
  the plant. I bought of the INGO's, to them and their male
  heirs; if neither has heirs, land to go to two younger
  sons, Thomas and John; fr. [Mr.] GRIFFIN; fr. Capt.
  George ESKRIDGE a silver-hilted sword; wife Million; ex:
  wife; desires Thomas GRIFFIN, Capt. George ESKRIDGE, Mr.
  Thomas GLASCOCK, and Mr. Robert DOWNMAN to assist wife;
  wits: Robert DOWNMAN, John HIPKINS, Samuel BAKER.

p.169 - William SMITH, inv; 7 Apr 1714.

p.170 - Col. Samuel PEACHEY, inv; 7 Apr 1714 [includes the following
  servants: Thomas ROBERTS, Mary PEACOCK, Isaac EACHE, and
  John SHURDEN.]

28

p.172 - Inv. of third part of the est. of Col. Samuel PEACHEY
        delivered to Mrs. Mary PEACHEY wid. and relict.

p.173 - John WOOLLY, inv; 5 May 1714.

p.174 - Andrew DEW, will; 16 Oct 1711, 5 May 1714
        son Andrew DEW alias RICE 300 ac. in Sitt. Par; son
        Samuel DEW 200 ac. in Sitt. Par. purchased of my bro.
        Thomas DEW; son Andrew DEW the plant. where I now live;
        ex: wife Flora; bro. Mark TUNE and Austin BROCKENBROUGH
        to assist wife and chil.; wits: John WILLIAMS, Thomas
        DEW, John DALTON. [The births of the fol. chil. to
        Andrew and Flora DEW are rec. in the NFPR: Ishmael
        (1700), Andrew (1702), Samuel (1705), Thomas and
        William (twins, 1711). NFPR, p. 44.]

      - BROOME's inv; 5 May 1714.

p.178 - Division of est. of William SMITH, dec'd; 5 May 1714
        [mentions sons Thomas, James, and William, and William
        CARTER.]

      - Henry EAST, inv. pres. by Capt. William BARBER, adm; 6 May
        1714.

p.179 - Patience [CLEVES], will; 27 Feb 1713/14, 2 Jun 1714
        Avery DYE; grson. John FORD; Henry BRUCE Sr. to have
        custody of John FORD; ex: Henry BRUCE; wits: William
        BRUCE, [?], [?].

p.180 - Andrew DEW, inv; 2 Jun 1714.

p.182 - Cormac [KAVEY], inv. pres. by Mary [KAVEY]; [2] Jun 1714.

p.184 - Further inv. of GLASCOCK; 2 Jun 1714.

      - George GLASCOCK, inv; 2 Jun 1714.

p.187 - William [ACKER], inv; 2 Jun 1714.

p.189 - Jane PRESCOTT, inv. by Charles BOWLES adm; 7 Jul 1714

p.190 - Edward JEFFEREY, NFP, will; 18 Apr 1714, 7 Jul 1714
        Wilson CHARLTON; father Thomas CHARLTON; daus. Prudence
        PALMER, Elizabeth MISKELL, Esther CHARLTON, and Margaret
        [?]; grdau. Elizabeth JEFFEREY; grson. William MISKELL;
        son John; wife Elizabeth; ex: wife; wits: Thomas
        BRYANT Jr; Samuel BAKER.

      - Patience CLEVES, inv; 7 Jul 1714.

      - John FORD, inv; 7 Jul 1714.

p.192 - James BURN, inv; 7 Jul 1714.

p.193 - Edward JEFFEREY, inv; 4 Aug 1714.

p.195 - Thomas ISAACK, inv; 4 Aug 1714.

p.197 - John PHILLIPS, inv; 4 Aug 1714.

p.198 - John WOOLEY, f. inv; 4 Aug 1714.

      - Charles COLLINS, inv; 4 Aug 1714.

- Philip BROWN, f.inv; 5 Aug 1714.

p.199 - John NEWBOURGH, will; [17] Aug 1714, 1 Sep 1714
whole est. to Joseph AMMON; ex: Joseph AMMON; wits:
John TIPPETT, Sarah TIPPETT, J. [SKEY].

- William McDANIEL, inv. at the house of Anne McDANIEL the
adm; 1 Sep 1714.

p.200 - Edward PARTLETT, inv; 1 Sep 1714.

p.201 - John NEWBOURGH, inv; 6 Oct 1714.

p.202 - John WHITE, inv; 6 Oct 1714.

p.204 - William POWELL, inv; 2 Feb 1714/15.

p.205 - John WILLIAMS, inv; 4 May 1715.

- Thomas DICKENSON, inv; 4 May 1715.

p.208 - DICKENSON's f.inv; 4 May 1715.

- John KELLY, will; 7 Oct 1714, 4 May 1715
son John the plant. where I now live; if he has no heirs,
to go to son Matthew; if he has no heirs, to youngest
son Alexander; if he has no heirs, to daus. Elizabeth
and Mary; sons Matthew and Alexander 100 ac; eld. dau.
Elizabeth 50 ac. lying in the Great Fork of Rappahannock
Creek; wife Amy; ex: wife; bro. Matthew KELLY and
William CARTER with James WILSON to be trustees; wits:
Matthew KELLY, Thomas MOUNTJOY, Henry WILSON, John
MORTON Jr.
Cod. In consideration of my three sons, John, Matthew,
and Alexander staying til they come to age, it is my
will that they shall have each of them one year's
schooling and my dau. Mary likewise to have one year's
schooling.

p.210 - Thomas DURHAM, NFP, will; 4 Aug 1711, 1 Jun 1715
wife Dorothy the plant; after her death, to son Thomas
and Mary his wife; son John; dau. Mary DODSON; grson.
Thomas DODSON; ex: wife; no wits. [The births of the
fol. chil. to Thomas and Dorothy DURHAM are rec. in the
NFPR: Mary (1686), Thomas (1690), John (1698). NFPR,
p.56. Dorothy DURHAM was probably related to William
SMOOT Sr; she mar. (2) Jeremiah GREENHAM, Feb 1714/15.
MRC, p.81.]

p.212 - Thomas DURHAM, inv; 6 Jul 1715.

p.214 - John WILLIS, Han. Par; will; 7 Jun 1715, 6 Jul 1715
s-i-l Thomas JAMES and Mary his now wife the plant.
where they now live; David JAMES (son of Thomas); Mary
COLLINS (under 16) which now liveth with me the tract
of land on which William PULLIN now liveth; if she die
without heirs, land to go to son Charles WILLIS; son
Charles the plant. and land I now live on; John WILLIS
(son of Charles); mentions late wife Matilda; dau.
Susannah; Mary GARDNER; Isaac ARNOLD and William WILLIS
to be guardians to Mary COLLINS; ex: son John and Isaac
ARNOLD; wits: Thomas PARKER, Augustine BLAKE, Eleanor
[NASH]. [John WILLIS Sr. mar. (2) Matilda THACKER in
1693. MRC, p.232.]

p.217 - John KELLY, inv; 6 Jul 1715.

p.219 - Thomas WHITE, Han. Par, will; 27 Apr 1715, 7 Sep 1715
Richard PEARLE; wife Frances whole est; ex: wife;
wits: Richard PEARLE, Thomas MACDANIEL, Thomas PORCH.

- John WILLIS Sr, inv; 7 Sep 1715.

p.222 - Francis TERRETT, inv; 7 Sep 1715.

p.223 - John KELLY, f.inv; 7 Sep 1715.

p.224 - John HUGHS, inv; 5 Oct 1715.

- Edward JONES, Farn. Par, will; [nd.], 5 Oct 1715
sons Samford, John all the lands I lately entered and
patented, that is, what lay between the line of John
WILLIAMS and the line of Miles [HUGALL] to the land
of Mr. SAMFORD; also the surplus land between the land
of John WILLIAMS and the line of Mr. Samuel SAMFORD as
by a survey made by Capt. Charles BARBOUR, Edward, and
Charles; sons Edward and Charles to have all the land
that I possess by the church which I bought of Mr.
Richard KING; dau. Alicia PAYNE; ex: sons Edward and
Charles; wits: Rawleigh BROOKS, Reuben CALVERT.
Cod. 3 Sep 1715, wool to be div. between John, Edward,
and Charles JONES; Susan KING to have jacket and coat
out of it; wit: Thomas NASH. [Edward JONES mar. Alicia
LUNN (wid. of William LUNN and dau. of James SAMFORD),
27 Aug 1679. The births of their fol. chil. are on
record: John (1680), Mercy (1682), Samford (1684),
Charles (1697). NFPR, p.106.]

p.227 - Alexander [MASH], Sitt. Par, will; 22 Oct 1715, 2 Nov 1715
fr. John GILBERT all est; ex: John GILBERT; wits:
Andrew BAKER, Foukes JONES.

p.228 - John SIMMONDS, NFP, will; 27 Aug 1715, 5 Oct 1715
Patience BRYAN; Abraham DEAL; Isaac (the son of
Abraham PROCTER); Thomas DALE a set of cooper's tools;
Daniel BEACHAM; Rawleigh DOWNMAN tract of land; re-
maining land to be div. between Abraham [DALE] and
Thomas YOUNG together with the plant. I now live on,
after the death of my wife Elizabeth; Will DODSON;
Thomas GLASCOCK; Capt. TARPLEY; Will JOBSON; ex:
Rawleigh DOWNMAN and Thomas GLASCOCK; wits: Thomas
DURHAM, Thomas READ, Gilbert LOWDING.

p.229 - Edward JONES, inv; 2 Nov 1715.

p.231 - Alexander [MASH], inv; 4 Jan 1715/16.

p.232 - Quintilian SHERMAN, inv; 4 Jan 1714 (sic).

p.233 - John SIMMONDS, inv; 1 Feb 1715/16.

p.234 - Margaret CAMMACK,being very ancient and weak in body, will;
24 Mar 1709, 7 Mar 1715/16
est. to be div. into three eq. parts, one to dau.
Margaret MICOU, one to dau. Susan FOSTER, and one to
be div. between dau. Mary [STORNE] and sons William and
David; other sons Sylvester THATCHER and John CAMMACK;
other daus. Mary RICHARDSON and Elizabeth DEANE; ex:
Paul MICOU and John FOSTER; wits: Isaac TRUCK, John
PLAILE.

p.235 - John [HOAKINS], Han. Par., will; 16 Jan 1715/16, 7 Mar
1715/16
now wife Elizabeth, being at this time very sick and
weak; if she dies, freeman John SUTTLE Jr, which now
liveth with me, to remain and live on the plant. whereon my family now liveth; sons William, John, Benjamin,
and James; daus. Sarah and Elizabeth; Richard and James
BUTLER to care for six children, but, in case Henry
WOOD doth think fit to take son William, I desire he
may have him, providing the said Henry will learn him
the trade and calling of a plasterer; Richard BUTLER
to take son John and daus. Sarah and Elizabeth; James
BUTLER to take sons Benjamin and James until age 20.
ex: fr. Isaac ARNOLD; wits: Isaac ARNOLD, Rebecca BUTLER,
John SUTTLE.

p.237 - Richard TALIAFERRO, inv. pres. by Thomas TURNER adm; 7 Mar
1715/16. [Richard TALIAFERRO mar. Sarah [?], dau. of
Martha WINFIELD. They had the fol. chil: Martha,
Richard, Catherine, and Sarah. MRC, p.203.]

p.238 - George BRUCE, NFP, being very aged, will; 24 Aug 1713,
9 Mar 1715/16
sons George, Charles, William, [Hensfield], and John
the plant. whereon I now live; dau. Jane (the wife of
Joseph RUSSELL); ex: son John; wits: Samuel BAILEY,
Elizabeth BAILEY, Marmaduke BECKWITH, Thomas DICKENSON.

p.239 - John MASON, Sitt. Par., will; 18 Dec 1704, 4 Apr 1716
whole est. to wife Mary; ex: wife; wits: Nabu. JONES,
Charles KILL.

p.240 - James STOREY, inv; 4 Apr 1716.

p.241 - Richard PEARL Jr, inv; 4 Apr 1716.

p.242 - Bernard IRISH, inv. pres. by Ruth IRISH adm; 4 Apr 1716.

p.243 - Robert PORT, inv; 4 Apr 1716. [Robert PORT mar. Hannah
[?] HARBIN, TAYLOR, HUGHES by 1701. MRC, p.160.]

p.244 - Lawrence BARKER, inv; 4 Apr 1716. [Lawrence BARKER mar. Mary
SKELDERMAN by 1714; they had two chil: Lawrence and
Elias. MRC, p.10.]

p.245 - John [SINKLER], inv. pres. by the adm. Dennis CONNELLY;
4 Apr 1716.

p.246 - James STROTHER, will; 5 Jan 1710, 4 Apr 1716
bro. Joseph; ex: bro. Joseph; wits: William WEBSTER,
Doraty STROTHER.

p.247 - William LAMBERT, will; 9 Jan 1715, 4 Apr 1716
sons William the plant. whereon I now live, John 141
ac. of land bought of Samuel STANFORD and his son
William, and Hugh; daus. Elizabeth 50 ac. of land
bought of John POUND on the west side of Totuskey Creek,
Anne, [Ellinor], and Mary; sons William and John and
dau. Elizabeth to live with son Hugh and serve him
until they arrive to age 17; ex: son Hugh; wits: John
HARTLEY, Robert GAILLE, Sarah HUTCHINS.

p.248 - Augustine BLAKE, inv. at the house of William PITTMAN; 5
Apr 1716.

32

p.249 - George BRUCE, inv. pres. by John BRUCE; 5 Apr 1716.

p.250 - Charles DODSON, Far. Par., will; 8 Jul 1715, 2 May 1716
          son Charles all land between spring branch and the
          branch that parts my land from the land of Thomas
          DODSON; son Fortunatus all land below my spring branch;
          wife Anne; ex: wife; wits: Bartholomew R. DODSON,
          George PETTY.

      - John MASON, inv. by Mary MASON; 2 May 1716.

p.251 - John ROBINSON, inv; 2 May 1716.

p.252 - Madam Mary PEACHEY, inv; 2 May 1716.

p.254 - James STROTHER, inv; [2] May 1716.

p.256 - Margaret CAMMACK, inv; 2 May 1716.

p.259 - George PHILLIPS, will; 20 Apr 1716, 2 May 1716
          all land to sons George and James; wife Martha; daus.
          Margaret, Martha, and Mary; ex: fr. Joseph STROTHER
          and Thomas PANNELL; wits: Benjamin PORTER, Thomas NORMAN,
          Robert BUTLER. [George PHILLIPS mar. Martha SWINBURNE
          in 1698. MRC, p.158.]

      - William FITZHERBERT, inv. at the house of Capt. William
          WOODBRIDGE; 2 May 1716.

p.260 - John WILLIS, f. inv; 2 May 1716.

p.261 - John JONES, inv; 2 May 1716.

p.262 - William LAMBERT, inv; 2 May 1716.

p.264 - James SHAW, inv. at the house of Elizabeth SHAW; 2 May 1716.

p.265 - James BUTLER, Washington Par, West. Co, will; 26 Jan 1715,
          2 May 1716
            bro. Richard BUTLER; land and plant. to wife Sarah;
            daus. Elizabeth 50 ac. and Sarah 50 ac; ex: wife; wits:
            George URIELL, Robert BRYAN, William BRIDGES.

      - Thomas PRENTIS, inv; 2 May 1716.

p.266 - James BIDDLECOMB, inv; 3 May 1716.

      - James BUTLER, inv; 6 Jun 1716.

p.267 - George PHILLIPS, inv; 6 Jun 1716.

p.268 - Charles DODSON, inv. pres. by the adm. Anne DODSON; 6 Jun
          1716.

p.269 - BRUCE's f. inv. by John BRUCE; 6 Jun 1716.

p.270 - William SMOOT, NFP, will; 24 Feb 1715, 4 Jun 1716
          grchil. Margaret, Joseph, and Sarah DURHAM; son-in-law
          Thomas DURHAM; wife Jane use of plant. and lands, after
          her death, to go to three grchil; ex: wife; wits: John
          DURHAM, Abraham DALE, Brian MUCKLEROY. [Mary, the dau.
          of William and Jane SMOOT, mar. Thomas DURHAM ca. 1710.
          MRC, p.250.]

p.271 - John HO[A]KINS, inv; 4 Jul 1716.

p.272 - Robert DOWNMAN, Farn. Par., will; 7 Mar 1715, 4 Jul 1716
all land to bros. William and Travers; godson John
GLASCOCK; sisters Million GLASCOCK, Elizabeth DOWNMAN,
and Priscilla DOWNMAN; brother Rawleigh; ex: bros.
Rawleigh and William; wits: Thomas DALE, Anne TARPLEY,
Mary NICKOLS.

p.273 - Peter TAFF, inv. at the house of Elizabeth TAFF; 4 Jul 1716.
[Peter TAFF mar. Elizabeth (WOODBRIDGE) McLAUGHLIN;
they had two sons, Thomas and John. MRC, p.202.]

p.274 - Thomas KENDALL Jr., inv; 1 Aug 1716.

p.276 - James PHILLIPS, inv; 1 Aug 1716.

p.277 - Francis STONE; inv; 1 Aug 1716.

p.278 - William PANNELL, will; 13 Dec 1715, 1 Aug 1716
son William all land and marsh lying on the south side
of the main road of Rich. Co; son David all land on the
north side of the main road now in the hands of William
PILLKINGTON by virtue of a lease; son George all land
due to me by virtue of a will made by one William
SERGEANT formerly, dec'd; daus. Elizabeth, Frances,
Catherine, and Mary; also mentions a tract of 220 ac.
purchased of Andrew HARRISON and Edward CARRILL part
in Rich. Co., part in West. Co., and part in Stafford
Co.; wife; ex: wife, asks fr. Capt. Nicholas SMITH to
aid wife; wits: Jasper COFTON, John JONES, William
DEEKINS, Thomas HUMPHREYS. [William PANNELL mar. Frances
STERNE by Jun 1698. MRC, p.154.]

p.279 - William SIMMS, Sitt. Par., will; 28 Apr 1716, 1 Aug 1716
son Thomas all lands in Rich. Co., if he has no heirs,
said lands to go to the churchwardens of Sitt. Par.
"for the time being"; ex: Capt. Nicholas SMITH and
George WHITE, both of Sitt. Par.; asks WHITE to care
for son Thomas until age 20; wits: John [BAGGE], [Will
...], Edward HINKLY.

p.281 - Frances LAMPTON, will; 24 Apr 1716, 1 Aug 1716
cousin John MARTIN Jr. the tract of land where Richard
CRAFORD is now living; cousin Francis MARTIN (bro. to
John) the tract of land where James CLARK is now
living; son and d-i-l William and Anne LAMPTON; no ex;
wits: Mary MARTIN, Thomas [MacDUNIL], Elizabeth SPEARS.
[Frances LAMPTON was the 2d wife of William LAMPTON whom
she mar. in Nov 1715; at that time she was the wid. of
Thomas WHITE. MRC, p.114.]

     - Charles DODSON, f.inv; 5 Sep 1716.

     - Dominick BENNEHAM, Farn. Par., will; 16 Apr 1716, 5 Sep 1716
sons Alexander and Dudley; grsons. Dominick NUGENT and
Isaac PROCTER; wife; daus. [unnamed]; ex: wife and son
Alexander; wits: Tobias PHILLIPS, Samuel STEELE, William
DOWNMAN. [Dominick and Elizabeth BENNEHAM had five
chil. according to the NFPR, p. 14: Elizabeth (1692),
Alexander (1695), Frances (1697), Mary (1700), Dudley
(1713); Dominick died 27 Apr 1716.]

p.282 - Alexander SPENCE, inv; 5 Sep 1716.

     - William PANNELL, 5 Sep 1716.

p.284 - Thomas GOFF, inv; 5 Sep 1716.

    - Robert DOWNMAN, inv; 5 Sep 1716.

p.286 - William SMOOT, inv; 5 Sep 1716.

p.287 - William SIMS, inv; 5 Sep 1716.

p.289 - Dominick BENNEHAM, inv; 3 Oct 1716.

p.290 - Benjamin DEVERALL, will; 22 Oct 1716, 5 Dec 1716
bro. Joseph (of England) and bro's two chil. John and
Susannah; cousin William MORGAN; Mary TAYLOR (wife of
Humphrey TAYLOR); wife Rachel; dau. [unnamed]; chil. of
sis. Hannah MORGAN; ex: wife, dau., bro. Joseph, fr.
William BRONAUGH and Samuel MATHEWS; wits: Benjamin
STROTHER, William MORGAN, John DAVIS. [Rachel DEVERALL
wid. of Benjamin and Jeremiah DEVERALL, surgeon, both
of Bristol, England, appointed Charles BURGES of Va.
their attorney, 25 Jul 1717, 20 Feb 1719/20. MR, pp.
95a, 112a.]

p.291 - Roger RICHARDSON, Sitt. Par., will; 20 Nov 1716, 5 Dec 1716
bros. Thomas and William; sis. Mary; Elizabeth RICHARD-
SON; Sarah PHILLIPS, Mary JONES; Thomas HUGHS; ex. bro.
Thomas; wits: Henry AXTON, Joseph BURGES, Thomas
MORGAN.

p.292 - Thomas KINGCART, inv; 2 Jan 1716/17.

    - Benjamin DEVERALL, inv. pres. by Capt. Samuel MATHEWS, adm;
6 Feb 1716.

p.297 - Alexander DONIPHAN, will; 20 Sep 1716, 6 Feb 1716/17
son Alexander 250 ac. in the fork of Rappahannock
bought of George JONES dec'd; Stephen BOWEING the other
250 ac. of land joining the aforesaid tract; son Mott
180 ac. out of a tract bought of Joshua DAVIS being
330 ac. lying back of my river land; if he has no heirs,
to go to grson. Giles TRAVERS; son Robert; dau.
Margaret 70 ac. bought of Joshua DAVIS; dau. Elizabeth
remainder of 80 ac. and her mother's wedding ring; wife
Susannah, having kept her est. apart, and taken it to
herself and desiring nothing of mine...; dau. Anne;
ex. to give Mrs. Mary BELFIELD a ring of 12 shillings
price; ex: son Robert; wits: Peter LOWD, Elias POWELL,
Robert FASSAKER. [Alexander DONIPHAN mar. his 2d wife,
Margaret MOTT, by Nov 1691; she d. prior to Mar 1709.
MRC, p.57.]

p.298 - Mark RYMER Jr., will; 23 Nov 1716, 6 Feb 1716/17
wife Margaret; dau. Catherine; ex: fr. William THORNTON
and wife; wits: Thomas BENSON, Thomas HAZZARD. [Mark
RYMER Jr. mar. Margaret PROU in Feb 1712/13. After his
death, Margaret became the concubine of the Rev. Mr.
John PRINCE. MRC, p.176.]

p.299 - James SAMMON, inv; 6 Feb 1716/17.

p.300 - John COMBES, Han. Par., will; 11 Dec 1716, 7 Feb 1716/17
youngest son Mason 200 ac. on the branches of [Punan's]
End in the co. of Essex being part of a dividend of
land formerly belonging to Warwick CAMMOCK; dau. Elizabeth KENDALL; wife Hannah and six chil; son Archdell;

daus. Judith, Mary, Sarah, and Aime; if son Archdell
should be so unkind as by force to cause his mother
...to leave as dispossessed the house and habitation
I now live in...my sd. wife to take as her proper goods
all his part of my personal est. before given to the
sd. Archdell excepting 1 shilling; wife to have care
and custody of dau. Aime and son Mason until 18 or
married; ex: wife and John ANDERSON; wits: Isaac ARNOLD,
Charles WILLIS, Mary JAMES.

p.301 - John COMBES, inv; 3 Apr 1717.

p.302 - Mark RYMER Jr., inv. pres. by Margaret RYMER wid.; 3 Apr
1717.

p.303 - Thomas PORCH, inv; 3 Apr 1717.

p.304 - Robert PAINE, Han. Par., will; 16 Mar 1717, 3 Apr 1717
I bequeath unto the poor people of Sepulchre's Par.
in London money I have in the hands of William DAWKINS,
merchant, in London; wife's bro., Mr. Henry WILLIAMSON,
in London; sisters Elizabeth and Jane; goddau. Barbary
(dau. of William CARTER); Eleanor and Will CARTER; goddau. Barbary (dau. of Samuel KERCHAVELL); Owin JONES;
Mrs. Elizabeth GIPSON; godson Robert STROTHER; David
JONES (son of Lewis JONES); Robert TAYLOR; goddau.
Mary TUTT; Halbert RAPHELL; I give for the use of the
church in Han. Par. one [chusion] and pulpit cloth...
and a poor plate to receive the communion in, the 10
Commandments, and the Lord's Prayer to set in the
church; fr. Francis SLAUGHTER Sr. and Samuel WHARTON;
ex: Francis SLAUGHTER Sr. and Samuel WHARTON; wits:
Simon MILLER, William [SIES], Lewis JONES.

p.306 - William WILLIS, inv; 3 Apr 1717.

p.307 - Richard COPPLY, Han.Par., will; 19 Aug 1716, 3 Apr 1717
all est. to wife Rebecca; no ex; wits: John GLENDENNING,
Samuel KERCHAVELL, Joseph ARMSTRONG.

p.308 - Thomas WOOD, NFP, will; 2 Nov 1716, 3 Apr 1717
son Thomas the old plant. where my father lived; son
Samuel the plant. where I now live; sons William and
John; dau. Mary; John HAMON; desires son Thomas and
dau. Mary to stay with Richard HINDS until 18; sons
Samuel, William, and John to stay with Capt. William
BARBER until 18; ex: Capt. William BARBER and Richard
HINDS; wits: Samuel BAKER, Edward MORRIS, John HAMON.

p.309 - Samford JONES, will; 1 Nov 1716, 3 Apr 1717
bro. Edward the order of court which I had against him
as being my father's ex. with cost; bro. John all the
land lying between the old line of James SAMFORD and
the line of John WILLIAMS; cousin Anne PAINE; ex. bro.
Charles; wits: Luke HANKS, William DUDLEY, John HAMMOND.
[Samford JONES d. 27 Sep 1716. NFPR, p.106.]

    - William GOFFE, f. inv; 3 Apr 1717.

p.311 - Richard BENGEY, Cople Par., West. Co., will; 30 [Jan] 1716/
1717, 3 Apr 1717
grchil. Charles and Joseph RUSSELL 100 ac. in Rich. Co.
whereon Charles RUSSELL lived; grdau. Jane [BENGEY] 60
ac. between the new ground and the head of Fox Grape
Swamp; son John remaining land; grdau. Anne BENGEY;

grdau. Eleanor CROUCHER; John CROUCHER in consideration of his trouble in burying me; ex: son John; wits: Richard WYATT, Gabriel [ELLCORSEN].

p.312 - Alexander DONIPHAN, Gent., inv. pres. by Robert DONIPHAN; 3 Apr 1717.

p.315 - Robert GREGORY, inv; 3 Apr 1717.

- [Roger] RICHARDSON, inv.,Thomas RICHARDSON ex; 3 Apr 1717.

p.316 - Jane DEW, NFP, will; 25 Jan 1716/17, 3 Apr 1717
        dau. Elizabeth BAILEY (wife of Samuel BAILEY); son William BAKER all lands; Sarah BAILEY (cousin to William BAILEY); ex: son William BAKER; wits: Anne BLUFORD, Sarah JEFFRIES, Samuel BAKER.

p.317 - James ELKINS, inv; 1 May 1717.

p.318 - Thomas WOOD, inv; 1 May 1717.

p.319 - Luke WILLIAMS, inv. at the house of Mary BAKER, formerly Mary WILLIAMS, his ex; 1 May 1717.

p.320 - Samford JONES, inv; 1 May 1717.

p.321 - Robert PAYNE, inv. pres. by Capt. Francis SLAUGHTER and Samuel WHARTON; 1 May 1717.

p.323 - Richard BENGEY, inv; 1 May 1717.

- Sarah STONE, wid. and relict of William STONE of Rich. Co., will; 2 Jul 1711, 1 May 1717
        dau. Elizabeth DAWSON (now wife of William DAWSON) a tract of land near the lands of George GLASCOCK and James TUNE [containing] 40 ac. which sd. land was bought of my son Philip STONE by the sd. William DAWSON; ex: son William STONE; wits: Joseph STONE, Thomas DRAPER, Leonard HART.

p.324 - Henry HAWES, will; 22 Mar 1711/12, 1 May 1717
        all est. to wife Anne; son Henry (under 21); fr. Thomas JAMES to care for son's est. if wife dies; ex: wife; wits: William JENKINS, Mary COLE, John KELLY. [Henry HAWES mar. Anne SKELDERMAN. MRC, p. 90.]

p.325 - Austin BROCKENBROUGH, will; 20 Feb 1716/17, 1 May 1717
        bro. William tract of land in Rich. Co. which I had in exchange of other land with Capt. Charles BARBER; bro. Newman; wife Mary; son William rest of land including tract called Mulberry Island; mentions b-i-l Thomas DICKENSON dec'd; sis. Elizabeth DICKENSON and her son Metcalfe; ex: wife and bros. William and Newman; wits: John METCALFE, Elizabeth LONGWORTH, Samuel GOODWIN. [Austin BROCKENBROUGH mar. Mary METCALFE in Aug 1714; she mar. (2) John SPICER. MRC, p.24.]

p.327 - DEW's inv; 1 May 1717.

p.329 - John CAMMACK, inv; 2 May 1717.

p.330 - Richard COPLEY, inv; 5 Jun 1717.

p.332 - Sarah STONE, inv. pres. by William STONE ex; 5 Jun 1717.

37

p.333 - Thomas SMITH, Farn. Par., will; 20 Jan 1716/17, 5 Jun 1717
           everything to wife Margaret; dau. [Jesse] to receive
           land after her mother's death; ex: wife; wits: William
           SMITH, Samuel POUND, Robert SMITH.
           Cod. After wife's decease, chil. [Jesse] and Elizabeth
           to have their part of the est.

       - Stephen GUPTON, will; 8 Oct 1716, 5 Jun 1717
           son Stephen my now dwelling plant; dau. Joyce my plant.
           where Matthew NOXAM dwells; bro. William; son to be
           brought up at the discretion of his uncle, Thomas
           HARFORD, after wife's death; dau. Joyce may be brought
           up at the discretion of Thomas NASH and to learn to
           read; ex: Thomas NASH, Thomas HARFORD, Henry HARFORD.

p.334 - Henry HAWS, inv; 5 Jun 1717.

p.335 - Austin BROCKENBROUGH, inv; 5 Jun 1717.

p.339 - Edward BRUMLOE, inv; 3 Jul 1717.

p.340 - Stephen GUPTON, inv; 3 Jul 1717.

p.342 - Thomas SMITH, inv; 3 Jul 1717.

p.343 - William COLLINS, inv; 3 Jul 1717.

p.344 - William UNDERWOOD, Sitt. Par., will; 19 Jul 1717, 7 Aug 1717
           son John the reversion and reversions of one water mill
           now in the hands of Richard TUTT and 300 ac. of land;
           son William all land and plant. within the isthmus or
           neck of land where I now live; dau. Mary TUTT 200 ac.
           beginning at the Rich Fork Point; dau. Sarah GILBERT;
           200 ac. beginning at the Beaver Dam; grsons. John and
           William THATCHER 200 ac. of land; dau. Elizabeth
           THATCHER; ex: sons John and William; wits: William
           PULLEN, Catherine PULLEN, Margaret BURKE.

p.345 - John BARRETT, inv; 7 Aug 1717.

p.346 - William UNDERWOOD, inv; 4 Sep 1717.

p.348 - George HELLAND, Sitt. Par., will; 26 Aug 1717, 4 Sep 1717
           eld. son Jehosephat all worldly est; desires son to be
           sent to uncle Jehosephat HELLAND living in Lewis' Town
           or, in case of his death, to Cornelius EDMONDS; ex:
           Cornelius EDMONDS; wits: Joseph CHAPMAN, Charles DEANE.

p.349 - George GAYDON, inv; 4 Sep 1717.

p.350 - ERWIN's f.inv. by the [wid.], Sarah KEMP; 2 Oct 1717.

       - Anne DEW, inv; 2 Oct 1717.

p.351 - Robert PAINE, f.inv; 2 Oct 1717.

p.352 - John CANTERBURY, inv; 2 Oct 1717.

p.353 - John MANEAR, will; 10 Sep 1716, 6 Nov 1717
           50 ac. to be eq. div. between wife and sons William and
           Usher; dau. Catherine; wife's eld. dau. Anne; no ex;
           wits: William STONE, Joshua STONE, Richard BROWN. [Usher,
           the son of John and Anne MANEAR, was b. 31 Aug 1715.
           NFPR, p.125.]

38

- John HIPKINS, will; 18 Mar 1716/17, 6 Nov 1717
  [Mary] NICKELS; son Samuel; if son dies before 21 or
  without issue, all est. to be eq. div. between John
  TARPLEY Jr. and Mrs. Anne TARPLEY (the wife of John
  TARPLEY Sr.); son to remain with John TARPLEY until
  18; ex: John TARPLEY Sr; wits: John TARPLEY, John
  BROWN, Thomas TARPLEY. [John HIPKINS mar. Mary GLASCOCK
  in Feb 1712/13. MRC, p.95.]

WILL BOOK 4, 1717-1725

p. 1 - William SMITH, inv; 4 Dec 1717.

p. 3 - John HIPKINS, inv; 4 Dec 1717.

      - William JOBSON, inv; 4 Dec 1717. [A William JOBSON mar.
        Bridget McLAUGHLIN by 1715. MRC, p.107.]

p. 4 - James BUTLER, f.inv; 4 Dec 1717.

p. 5 - Andrew MATHEWS, inv; 4 Dec 1717.

p. 6 - Joshua LAWSON, will; 11 Jan 1715/16, 4 Dec 1717
        Anne LLOYD, wid., 200 ac. and plant. (she had served
        him for 22 years); son William half of personal est.,
        household goods, and stock; no ex; wits: David JACKSON,
        Daniel JACKSON, Austin JONES.

p. 7 - William STEWART, inv; 4 Dec 1717.

p. 9 - John MUNEER, inv. by Anne MUNEER, adm.; 5 Feb 1717/18.

p.10 - William SMITH, f.inv; 5 Feb 1717/18.

p.11 - John POUND, will; 26 Jan 1716/17, 5 Feb 1717/18
        eld. son John one shilling; son Thomas the forest plant.
        and six head of cattle; if Thomas die without heirs, to
        go to [son] John's eldest son; son Samuel; dau.
        Margaret SMITH; wits: Sarah POUND, Zachariah HEFFORD,
        John NEWMAN. [John POUND mar. Deborah LEWIS, ca. 1709.
        MRC, p.160; NFPR, p.149.]

      - William LEE, inv; 5 Feb 1717/18.

p.13 - Patrick CARNEY, will; 15 Jan 1717/18, 6 Feb 1717/18
        godson Thomas BRYON; David DAILEY; Mary YEATS; wits:
        Elias YEATS, [John] DAILEY.

      - George HELLAND, inv; 6 Feb 1717/18.

p.14 - Patrick CARNEY, inv; 6 Feb 1717/18.

p.15 - John POUND, inv; 5 Mar 1717/18.

p.17 - Fookes JONES, Sitt. Par., will; 2 Feb 1717/18, 5 Mar 1717/18
        all est to s-i-l Samuel NICOLLS; wits: John GILBERT,
        Andrew BAKER.

      - Joshua LAWSON, inv; 5 Mar 1717/18.

p.18 - William BRONOUGH, will; 3 Sep 1717, 2 Apr 1718
        wife Anne; eld. son David the plant. that belonged to
        my bro. David BRONOUGH containing 150 ac; son Jeremiah
        135 ac. binding upon the land of George BRONOUGH;

bro. Jeremiah BRONOUGH; ex: wife; wits: Joseph CROUCH,
William PROCTOR, Henry MACKI[E].

- Job HAMON, will; 22 Mar 1717/18, 2 Apr 1718
    sons William, John, and Job [their legacy included
    some Indian slaves]; dau. Joyce; Hannah HAMON (dau.
    of son William); Philemon BIRD; ex: sons William and
    John; wits: Richard WOOLLARD, John WOOLLARD, Anne
    BLEWFORD.

p.20 - Catherine WATTERS, relict of Petter WATTERS, will; 2 Jan
    1717/18, 2 Apr 1718
        eld. dau. Margaret; dau. Bersheba; servant William
        WHITE; ex: John AMBROS; wits: John SMITH, John HULL.

p.21 - John SMITH, Sitt. Par., will; 10 Mar 1717/18, 2 Apr 1718
        wife Christian; dau. Anne; wife's dau. Mary; goddau.
        Abigail JONES; Winifred JONES; Alice the dau. of
        William KING; ex: wife; wits: Edward HINKLEY, John
        HILL, John WELLS.

p.22 - Peter EVANS, inv; 2 Apr 1718.

- Fookes JONES, inv; 2 Apr 1718.

p.23 - William SMITH, inv; 4 Jun 1718.

p.24 - Rebecca ROBINSON, inv; 4 Jun 1718.

- Job HAMON, inv; 4 Jun 1718.

p.26 - Silvester THATCHER, will; 18 Jul 1717, 4 Jun 1718
        wife Elizabeth; sons John, William, Samuel, Silvester,
        and Thomas; son Silvester to receive all the plant.
        where John GILBERT lives, if he die without heirs, to
        be div. between sons John and William; sons Samuel and
        Thomas to receive the plant. whereon I now live, if
        they die without heirs, then to sons John and William;
        daus. Margaret and Elizabeth; ex: wife; wits: John
        PITTMAN, George MICHEL, Wilmouth MICHEL. [Silvester
        THATCHER mar. Elizabeth UNDERWOOD. MRC, pp. 207, 268.]

p.27 - James THORNE, inv; 4 Jun 1718.

- Catherine WATERSON, inv. by John AMBROS ex; 4 Jun 1718.

p.29 - James SCOTT, will; 1 May 1718, 4 Jun 1718
        eld. son James the plant. whereon I now live; youngest
        son Paul land in Essex Co; dau. Margaret to have the
        land known by the name of the Indian Ridge and the two
        plants. whereon Alexander [SINNER] and John TIPPETT
        lived if sons die without heirs; ex: wife Elisabeth,
        Paul MICOU, William MONTRON, and son James (when 18);
        wits: Luke DICKSON, Elizabeth ANDRES, Sarah DICKSON.
        [James SCOTT mar. Elizabeth MICOU, dau. of Dr. Paul
        MICOU of Essex Co. MRC, p.182.]

p.30 - Anne LLOYD, inv. at the house of Gabriel PACKET; 4 Jun 1718.

- Mark TUNE, NFP, will; 21 Sep 1717, 4 Jun 1718
    sons William, Mark, Thomas, James, Lewis, John; daus.
    Anne and Elizabeth; fr. James and Barbary TOMSON to
    take daus. until they come of age; son John to live
    on the plant. where I now live and keep his four [sic]
    brothers in Christian manner until they come to age

18; ex: son John; wits: John HARRIS, Hugh HARRIS, Thomas DEW.

p.31 - Charles KILL, inv; 4 Jun 1718.

p.32 - Henry SEAGAR, NFP, will; 27 Feb 1717, 4 Jun 1718
Christopher ASCOUGH and Anne ASCOUGH (son and dau. of Thomas ASCOUGH); Thomas Wright BELFIELD (son of Joseph BELFIELD); Henry and Mary SISSON (chil. of William SISSON); ex: Henry SISSON; wits: John DOZIER, Edward HINKLY, Marmaduke BECKWITH. [Henry SEAGAR mar. Mary HUDSON, wid. of Bryan HUDSON. MRC, p.183.]

p.33 - Luke THORNTON, inv; 4 Jun 1718.

p.34 - William ROGERS, verbal will; 19 Feb 1717, 4 Jun 1718
all est. to dau. Rebeckah; no.ex; wits: Charles SNEAD, Thomas TURNER, William HUNT.

p.35 - Hannaball NICHOLAS, inv; 2 Jul 1718.

      - John DOYLE, inv; 2 Jul 1718.

p.38 - William ROGERS, inv. at the house of Thomas TURNER; 2 Jul 1718.

p.39 - Thomas WILLIAMS, inv. by Catherine WILLIAMS; 2 Jul 1718.

p.40 - Michall CONN[E]LL, will; 13 Apr 1718, 2 Jul 1718
all land to sons Edward and Michall; dau. Sarah; requests remaining est. be eq. div. into four parts by James FOUSHEE, Giles WEBB, Francis LUCAS, and Robert BAYLIS and asks that est. not be appraised; ex: son Edward; wits: Patrick DORRAN, Henry WOODCOCK, Robert BAYLIS.

p.41 - William BRONOUGH, inv. by Anne BRONOUGH ex; 2 Jul 1718.

p.42 - Henry SEAGAR, inv. by Briant SISSON, ex; 6 Aug 1718.

p.44 - John POORE, Farn. Par., will; 1 Jul 1718, 6 Aug 1718
godson [Denisead] CARROLL and his sis. Frances [?]; Sarah [WISDELL] (dau. of Richard); John [BLU..ER]; ex: Richard [WISDELL]; wits: Gilbert METCALFE, William PHILLIPS Jr.

p.45 - Joseph DEEKE, will; 8 Oct 1716, 6 Aug 1718
wife Catherine; daus. Elizabeth, Catherine, and Mary; son Joseph land at Rappahannock; son John plant. on Totuskey Creek; ex: wife and dau. Elizabeth; wits: Daniel BENTLEY, Thomas JASPER, Will BARBER. [Joseph DEEKE mar. Catherine LEWIS bef. Mar 1704/05. MRC, p.53.]

p.46 - Mark TUNE, inv. by John TUNE; 6 Aug 1718.

p.48 - Edmund McLYNCH, will; 1 Apr 1718, 6 Aug 1718
wife [Joan] 30 ac. of land remaining from the land sold to William BROWN joining upon James HARRISON's line; upon wife's death to go to son Edmund McLYNCH (son of Joan McLYNCH); if son dies without heirs, then to go to Mary and Elizabeth JONES (daus. of the sd. Joan McLYNCH); ex: wife; wits: Dan. GAINES, Mary DOYLE, Thomas [WESTT].

      - William HAMOND, inv. at the house of Mary HAMOND, 6 Aug 1718.

p.49 - [Cormac] L. MACCENEY, inv; 6 Aug 1718.

p.50 - An account of the estate my father was possessed at his
      death. [in margin] CONNELL's inventory; [6 Aug 1718].

p.51 - Sarah TALIAFERRO, Han. Par., will; 4 Feb 1717, 6 Aug 1718
      son Richard money which is now in the hands of Maj.
      [Terrin] TROTT in Bermudas; daus. Catherine, Sarah,
      and Martha; Catherine (dau. of son Richard); remainder
      of est. to son Richard and his heirs whether in Virginia,
      the West Indies, or New England, or elsewhere; fr. Capt.
      Nicholas SMITH to care for est. and dau. Martha; ex:
      son Richard; wits: Francis SLAUGHTER, Henry LONG.
      [Sarah TALIAFERRO was the wid. of Col. Richard TALIA-
      FERRO. MRC, p. 203.]

p.52 - John DOYLE, will; 17 Feb 1717, 6 Aug 1718
      sons: John, James, and Daniel; daus. Ellinner, Elizabeth,
      and Catron; Capt. Charles BARBER and Capt. George
      [ESCREDY] to aid and assist wife; ex: wife Mary; wits:
      Patrick DOON, Francis LUCAS.

p.53 - Nicholas RODGERS, Sitt. Par., will; 7 Jun 1718, 6 Aug 1718
      wife Elizabeth; s-i-l John FORD; no ex; wits: Henry
      BRUCE, Mary BRUCE. [Nicholas RODGERS mar. Elizabeth
      FORD, wid. of John FORD Jr., in 1714. MRC, p.173.]

p.54 - Sylvester THATCHER, inv; 7 Aug 1718.

p.55 - Archibald JOHNSTONE, inv; 2 Sep 1718.

     - James SPENDERGRASS, inv; 3 Sep 1718.

p.56 - Joseph SMITH, inv. pres. by Gilbert METCALF; 3 Sep 1718.

     - Joseph DEEK, inv; 3 Sep 1718.

p.58 - William TAYLOE, inv; 3 Sep 1718.

p.59 - Thomas ROGERS, inv; 3 Sep 1718.

p.60 - Hannaball NICHOLAS, f. inv; 3 Sep 1718.

p.61 - John POORE, inv; pres by Richard [WISDELL]; 3 Sep 1718.

p.62 - James SCOTT, inv; 1 Oct 1718.

p.65 - Peter DARBY, inv; 1 Oct 1718.

p.66 - John ARMSTRONG, Han. Par., will; [nd.], 5 Nov 1718
      son Joseph "I have done what I am able for him and
      also for my daughter Phebe;" son John; dau. Elizabeth;
      four other chil. [not named]; ex: wife; wits: Richard
      PEARLE, John ARMSTRONG Jr.

p.67 - Simon GRIFFITH, inv; 5 Nov 1718.

     - Stanley GOWER, will; 17 Sep 1718, 5 Nov 1718
      s-i-l Edward SPENCER; Anne GOWER (dau. of John GOWER);
      Sarah PAVEY; William SIDEBOTOM, Henry BRAINE; bro. John
      GRIMES; brother's dau. Margaret GOWER; ex: John GOWER;
      wits: David WILLIAMS, Mary WILLIAMS, Henry BRAINE.
      [Stanley GOWER of West. Co. mar. Winifred SPENCER, wid.
      of Edward SPENCER, Jun 1714. MRC, p.80.]

p.68 - Elizabeth GUPTON, inv; 5 Nov 1718.

p.69 - James TOONE, Farn. Par; will; 6 Dec 1718, 4 Feb 1718/19
        bro. Henry FANN (son of John and Mary FANN) a tract
        of land between the line of Mr. GRIFFIN and a branch
        known by the name of Christopher's Branch line;
        William DRAPER (son of Thomas DRAPER); Sarah DRAPER
        a tract of land; f-i-l John FANN to be ex; wits:
        William BROCKENBROUGH, William TARPLEY, Matthew
        [NOXAM].

p.70 - Charles NEAL, NFP, will; 27 Jan 1718/19, 5 Feb 1718/19
        son Charles; wife and three chil. [nfi.]; ex: wife;
        wits: Hugh HARRIS, John WILLIAMS.

      - Further inventory of my uncle William FITZHURBERT by
        William WOODBRIDGE adm; 5 Feb 1718/19.

p.71 - John ARMSTRONG, inv; 5 Feb 1718/19.

      - William TILLER, Sitt. Par. will; 20 Feb 1718/19, 4 Mar
        1718/19
        wife Mary all the land bought from Samuel NICHOLLS;
        son John; dau. Margaret, always provided she marrieth
        a man without land, if she marries a man with land
        then everything to son John; chil. Mary [SL.IP],
        Elizabeth THOMAS; no ex; wits: John GILBERT, Thomas
        EVANS, Thomas BUTLER.

p.72 - John HOXFORD, will; 31 Aug 1718, 5 Mar 1718/19
        wife Elizabeth 50 ac. in Han.Par; ex: wife; wits:
        Henry WOOD, Charles POWELL.

p.73 - John SCURLOCK, St. Mary's White Chapel Par., Lanc. Co.,
        will; 7 Dec 1718, 4 Mar 1718/19
        bro. Daniel SCURLOCK; cousin John SCURLOCK; Charles
        NORRIS; ex: bro. Daniel; wits: Thomas DURHAM, John
        DURHAM.

p.74 - James TOONE, inv. by John FANN; 4 Mar 1718/19.

p.75 - Charles NEAL, inv. by Anne NEAL ex; 4 Mar 1718/19

p.76 - Stanley GOWER, inv; 4 Mar 1718.

p.77 - Francis SLAUGHTER, Han. Par., will; 6 Nov 1718, 4 Mar
        1718/19
        daus. Martha, Mary, and Elizabeth; wife; s-i-l John
        TAYLOR to be ex; wits: Anne MARSHALL, John SUTTLE,
        Joseph SUTTLE. [Francis SLAUGHTER mar. (2) Anne HUDSON
        in Aug 1711. MRC, p.189.]

p.78 - Anne DODSON, will; 4 Apr 1718, 4 Mar 1718/19
        sons Charles, William, and James; dau. Mary; ex: son
        Charles; wit: Bartholomew Richard DODSON.

      - James HARTLEY, will; 31 Dec 1718, 4 Mar 1718/19
        money to be paid to my loving father Robert HARTLEY
        living in England in [Cobon] Parish, Lancashire and
        if my father Robert HARTLEY and my mother Jeanette
        should be dec'd before they receive the money, it is
        to be eq. div. among my three bros. Robert, John, and
        Lawrence HARTLEY; Mr. Robert KIPPAX; landlady Anne
        NASH; ex: Thomas NASH; wits: Peter KIPPAX, Daniel
        BENTLEY, William NICKOLLS.

p.79 - Teliff ALDERSON Jr., Farn. Par., will; 28 Dec 1718, 4 Mar 1718/19
    wife Rebecca; dau. Sarah; ex: wife; wits: William HAMMACK, John ALDERSON, Benedic HAMMACK. [Teliff ALDERSON mar. Rebecca HATTON. MRC, p.1.]

p.80 - Samuel MATHEWS, will; 16 Nov 1718, 4 Mar 1718/19
    eld. son John 600 ac. of land above the falls of the Rappahannock River in Rich. Co; son Baldwin the other 600 ac. part of the same tract bought of Mr. Joseph WAUGH of Stafford Co; two sons to be bound out as apprentices, eld. to a master of a ship to serve until he is 21, second to a good house carpenter to serve until he is 21; son Francis tract of land where I now live, but if my wife should now be with child, of a son, then my land to be eq. div. between them two; eld. dau. Elizabeth; dau. Mary 150 pounds sterling provided a bond be given up which brother Braxton extracted from me upon the day I was married to Catherine DUNSTALL when I was very much in drink and if either of them or both of them should die before the day of marriage or attain to the age of 21, that their money return to my est. and into the hands of my loving wife Margaret; very good fr. John BAYLER, Joseph STRAWTHER, and William [SKRINE] and my loving kinsman [Cole] DIGGS and Baldwin MATHEWS to advise wife; ex: wife; wits: Jeremiah BRONOUGH, John FERGUSON, Joshua FERGUSON. [Capt. Samuel MATHEWS mar. (1) _(?)_ PAULLIN, (2) Catherine DUNSTALL, 1706, and (3) Margaret _(?)_. MRC, pp.129-130.]

p.81 - Alexander CLAYTON, f.inv.; 4 Mar 1718/19.

  - Thomas CLARK, Farn. Par; will; 27 Dec 1718, 4 Mar 1718/19
    wife Elizabeth; mother Katherin G. CLARK; bro. Robert CLARK's chil.; will and desire is that my wife and my mother should live together; ex: wife; wits: Andrew MORGAN; Louis PUGH, Katherin CLARK.

  - Thomas PANNELL, will; 9 Oct 1718, 4 Mar 1718/19
    daus. Isabel and Elizabeth; sons William, Thomas; son Thomas to the care and management of Joseph STROTHER until age 18; I leave to Joseph STROTHER and his wife Margaret my dau. Catherine til she arrive to the age of 17; I leave to my loving wife Sarah my dau. Mary til she shall arrive to the age of 17, but, if wife dies, dau. is left to her own disposal; I give to the child my wife now goes with, if it be a son, all my land, and in case it be a dau. I give all my land to my son Thomas; ex: wife; wits: Benjamin GRUBS, Anthony SEALS, Joseph STROTHER.

p.83 - Samuel COATES, inv; 4 Mar 1718/19.

  - Samuel BAKER, inv; 6 Mar 1718/19.

p.84 - Teliff ALVERSON [or ALDERSON, in margin], inv; 1 Apr 1719.

p.85 - John SCURLOCK, inv; 1 Apr 1719.

p.86 - Ed[mund] McCLENCEY [or McLINCHE, in margin]inv; 1 Apr 1719.

p.87 - Thomas CLARK, inv; 1 Apr 1719.

p.88 - Anne DODSON, inv. by the ex. Charles DODSON; 1 Apr 1719.

- William TILLER, inv; [nd.]

p.90 - George HABRON, inv. by the adm. Samuel BAILEY; 1 Apr 1719.

- William COMBS, inv; 1 Apr 1719.

p.91 - John JONES, of [Sisell] Par., will; 15 Mar 1718/19, 1 Apr 1719
      sis. Anne DEANE and her husband Charles; Burkett EDMONDS; Cornelius EDMONDS; Thomas BROCK; ex: Thomas BROCK; wits: John THOMAS, George WHITE, Cor. EDMONDS.

- Thomas POUND, inv; 1 Apr 1719.

p.92 - John POUND, inv; 1 Apr 1719.

p.93 - Thomas PANNELL, inv. by the ex. Sarah MORGAN; 1 Apr 1719.

p.94 - George ALSUP, inv; 1 Apr 1719.

p.96 - Peter KIPPAX, rector of NFP, will; 16 Nov 1718, 1 Apr 1719
      land and negroes to be sold and money remitted to my loving bros. Richard and Edward KIPPAX of Marsden; the Rev. Ralph BUCKER; fr. Mr. Thomas GRIFFIN; Mr. Thomas BAILE; and Capt. Charles BARBER; Patrick DUNN and James HARTLEY; ex: Thomas GRIFFIN, Thomas BAILE, and Capt. Charles BARBER; wits: Giles WEBB, Patrick DUNN, John NAYLOR.
      [Cod. mentions: James SWINTON, Thomas JENNINGS, Thomas NASH, and John NAYLOR.]

p.97 - Thomas BRYAN Sr. of NFP, will; 26 Oct 1717, 2 Apr 1719
      all land to son Thomas; wife Eleanor; grson. George BRYAN alias [ASBUN] the son of my eld. son John; daus. Winifred McKAY and Margaret BRANNAN; no ex; wits: George MURDOCH, Alexander BENNEHAM, James HINDES.

- Eleanor BRYAN, relict and ex. of Thomas BRYAN, will; 8 Jan 1718, 2 Apr 1719
      est. to be eq. div. between son Thomas and dau. Mary; ex: dau. Mary; wits: Alexander BENNEHAM, James HINDS.

p.98 - Thomas BRYANT [BRYAN in margin], inv; 6 May 1719.

p.99 - Thomas CAVERNER, inv. by the adm. Stephen WELLS; 6 May 1719.

- John JONES, inv; 6 May 1719.

p.101 - John [HARFORD], inv. by Thomas JEFFRIES; 6 May 1719.

p.102 - Patrick CRUSE, inv; 6 May 1719.

p.103 - Joshua STONE, inv. by the adm. Mary STONE; 6 May 1719.

- TOONE's est., f. inv; 6 May 1719.

p.104 - Francis ARMSTEAD, will; 8 Apr 1719, 6 May 1719
      dau. Elizabeth (under 16) 85 ac. in Rich. Co; son John (under 18) rest of land; if son leaves no heirs, land is to go to Francis ARMSTEAD (the son of Rolfe ARMSTEAD); wife Sarah to be ex; wits: Thomas HARPER, William SMITH; William PICKRELL.

- HIPKINS f. inv; 6 May 1719.

p.105 - Daniel CAVERNER, inv; 6 May 1719.

- Peter KIPPAX, inv; 6 May 1719.

p.107 - Elizabeth HALL, verbal will; [nd.], 7 May 1719
This being a just and true account of the last will
and testament of Elizabeth HALL by word of mouth taken
within 24 hours after her departure out of this life
from the witnesses hereafter mentioned; Joseph WHING,
Aguthey WHING, and Elizabeth HINSON all testified that
Elizabeth HALL wanted Daniel WHITE to be her ex; and
that George HINSON should have her youngest dau.

p.108 - Elizabeth HALL, inv. by Daniel WHITE; 3 Jun 1719.

- William BENNETT, inv; 3 Jun 1719.

p.109 - Alexander BENNEHAM, inv; 3 Jun 1719.

p.110 - Thomas LEE, inv; 3 Jun 1719.

- Francis ARMSTEAD, inv; 3 Jun 1719.

p.112 - Francis SLAUGHTER, inv; 3 Jun 1719.

p.113 - Capt. Samuel MATHEWS, inv; 3 Jun 1719.

p.115 - William STONUM, inv; 1 Jul 1719.

p.116 - John LINKHORN, inv; 1 Jul 1719.

p.117 - William HODSKINS, will; 20 Dec 1718, 1 Jul 1719
everything to wife Mary and she is to be ex; wits:
Richard EVANS, Dorita CROUCHER, John NEWMAN.

- William SISSON, inv. at the house of Bryan SISSON; 1 Jul
1719.

p.119 - Peter EVANS, inv; 1 Jul 1719.

- Richard DAVIS, inv; 1 Jul 1719.

p.120 - Thomas FITZHUGH, of Stafford Co., will; 20 Dec 1717, 1 Jul
1719.
bros. Henry, George, and John; fr. Thomas GREEN; Mr.
BUTLER; wife Anne; dau. Mary; bro. Henry to have care
and tuition of dau. Mary until she marries or reaches
18; mentions debts to several persons in New England;
ex: bros. Henry, George, and John; wits: James GREEN,
Henry BUTLER. [Thomas FITZHUGH mar. Anne Fowke (MASON)
DARRELL, wid., ca. 1716. MRC, p.69.]

p.122 - John SANDERS, inv; 1 Jul 1719.

- John PECK, inv; 1 Jul 1719.

- William HOSKINS, inv. by Mary HOSKINS, ex.; 5 Aug 1719.

- Stanley GOWER, f. inv; 5 Aug 1719.

p.124 - James HARTLEY, inv; 5 Aug 1719.

p.125 - William LAMAS, inv.; 5 Aug 1719.

- Francis ARMSTEAD, f. inv; 5 Aug 1719.

- Elizabeth GUPTON, f. inv; 5 Aug 1719.

p.126 - Patrick DUNE, will; 21 Apr 1719, 5 Aug 1719
        wife; sons Robert and John; s-i-l Samuel WEATHERS;
        fr. Thomas NASH, Thomas NASH Jr; Giles WEBB; ex: wife;
        wits: Daniel BENTLEY, Thomas NASH, Edward JONES.

       - Thomas WHITTLE, NFP, will; 12 Jun 1719, 5 Aug 1719
         entire est. to wife Elizabeth and she to be ex; wits:
         William FORRESTER, John [BANFOLD], John CURRY.

p.127 - Thomas WHITTLE, inv; 2 Sep 1719.

p.130 - Patrick DUNN, inv. at the house of Anne DUNN; 2 Sep 1719.

p.131 - George GREEN, will; 9 Jun 1716, 2 Sep 1719
        wife Elizabeth; sons John, Thomas, George, Jozef,
        William, Samuel, Daniel, Isaac to have all land, and
        Robert; daus. Elizabeth and Grace; no ex; wits: Neall
        MCORMICK, William TIPPETT.

p.132 - Thomas RITCHASON [RICHARDSON], Sitt.Par., will; 3 Nov 1717,
        2 Sep 1719
        son Clapam all lands and he to be ex; wits: George
        WHITE, Thomas ADDOMES, Elizabeth WHITE. [Thomas
        RICHARDSON mar. Mary (THATCHER) CLAPMAN by 7 Oct 1696.
        MRC, p.171.]

       - Charles ELLS, inv. at the house of the adm. Elizabeth SHAW;
         7 Oct 1719.

p.133 - Thomas RITCHASON, inv; 4 Nov 1719.

p.135 - Peter ELMORE [Jr.], inv; 4 Nov 1719.

       - Thomas REED, Farn.Par., will; 24 Apr 1719, 2 Dec 1719
         son John; wife Catherine; ex: wife; wits: Abraham
         DALE, William FORRESTER.

       - Martin KEMP, will; delivered 9 Nov 1719; 2 Dec 1719
         Edward THOMLINSON now living at my house one half of
         est; the chil. of Morris NEAL: Millisent, Susannah, and
         Morris Jr; I give and bequeath to my two kinswomen
         living in Essex Co. one shilling apiece in bar of all
         further demand; no ex; wits: Elizabeth SPERRIN,
         Edward THOMLINSON.

p.137 - William COMBS, f. inv; 2 Dec 1719.

       - Thomas REED, inv; 3 Feb 1719/20.

p.138 - John BIRKET, will; 10 Dec 1719, 3 Feb 1719/20
        dau. Mary BROCK the plant. commonly called "The Quarter";
        dau. Margaret PRAT the plant. where I now live contain-
        ing 200 ac; dau. Elizabeth WHITE the plant. where
        George WHITE now lives containing 150 ac; dau. Anne
        EDMONDS the plant. where Cornelius EDMONDS now lives
        containing 150 ac; grson. John JONES; good fr. Col.
        William ROBINSON; ex: fr. Col. William ROBINSON and Mr.
        John GILBERT; wits: Luke DICKSON, Thomas HUGHS, James
        STREELY. [John BIRKET mar. Anne MILLS prior to 1676.
        MRC, p.18.]

p.139 - Martin KEMP, inv; 3 Feb 1719/20.

p.141 - Robert TAYLOR, inv; 2 Mar 1719/20.

p.142 - Richard DAVIS, f.inv; 2 Mar 1719/20.

      - David PURSELL, inv; 2 Mar 1719/20.

p.143 - John FANN, inv. by Mary FANN; 3 Mar 1719/20.

p.144 - Robert AYRES, inv. by the adm. Susannah AYRES; 3 Mar 1719/20.

p.145 - George GREEN, inv; 6 Apr 1720.

p.146 - John MANNING, inv; 6 Apr 1720.

      - Thomas FITZHUGH, inv; 6 Apr 1720. [mentions the following
            servants: Giles HICKS, Samuel RIDGWAY, (Jane) ENGLISH.]

p.148 - Robert HARRISON, will; 25 Jan 1719, 6 Apr 1720
            son William 50 ac. of land part of 150 ac. given me by
            Adam WOFFENDALL; son Robert half the tract I now live
            on when he reaches age 18; the other half to my wife
            Mary and after her death, to son George; son Aaron the
            other 100 ac. of the land given me by Adam WOFFENDALL
            when he reaches age 18; daus. Priscilla, Martha, and
            Mary; bro. Andrew HARRISON to be trustee and overlooker
            of my est; ex: wife and son Robert; wits: Aaron
            THORNLEY, Richard WILKINS. [Robert HARRISON mar. (1)
            Elizabeth WOFFENDALL and (2) Mary __(?)__. MRC, p.89.]

p.149 - Robert HARRISON, inv; 4 May 1720.

p.151 - Elizabeth SPENCE, inv; 4 May 1720.

      - Simon MILLER, Han. Par., will; 1 Dec 1719, 4 May 1720
            son Simon all land from the river to the Schoolhouse
            Swamp with the two plant. and all improvements; if
            he has no heirs, then land is to go to dau. Jane; dau.
            Eleanor all land on the backside of the Schoolhouse
            Swamp inclusive of the sd. swamp; son Simon shall be
            at age to choose his guardian when 16; ex: dau. Eleanor
            and William SMITH that boards at my house; wits:
            Jonathan GIBSON, William [SISE], Elizabeth GIBSON.

p.152 - John WHARTON, inv; 1 Jun 1720.

p.154 - Simon MILLER, inv. by William SMITH, ex; 1 Jun 1720.

p.155 - Charles HARVEY, will; 9 May 1720, 1 Jun 1720.
            Jane CARTER; Giles CARTER; John REED; William CARTER
            (the son of Giles); James [LEG]; Patrick GORMELEY;
            Jane CARTER's children; ex: fr. Jane CARTER; wits:
            William CARTER, Richard CLAXTON, Giles CARTER.

p.156 - Elizabeth BARRETT, inv; 1 Jun 1720.

p.157 - Margaret MARKHAM, inv; 1 Jun 1720.

      - John WILLIAMS, inv. by the adm. Joshua WILLIAMS; 6 Jul 1720.

p.158 - William CARTER, inv. at the house of Jane CARTER; 6 Jul 1720.

      - Charles HARVEY, inv. at the house of Jane CARTER; 6 Jul 1720.

p.159 - William JENKINS, inv; 7 Dec 1720.

48

p.160 - Richard HILL, will; 13 Nov 1720, 7 Dec 1720
        son John land and plant. whereon I now live after my
        wife, Elizabeth's, decease; daus. Mary JENNINGS and
        Elizabeth JEFFRYES; ex: wife; wits: Dan. GAINES, John
        JENNINGS, Dan. [KILLY].

p.161 - Robert GALLOP, will; prov. 7 Dec 1720
        Monday, May 23, 1720, on this day, Henry GALLOP age
        67, Richard ELKINS age 51, and William BROWN age 56,
        at the request of Eleanor GALLOP, wid. and relict of
        Robert GALLOP dec'd, came personally before me and
        made oath that on Friday last, the 20th instant, they
        heard Robert GALLOP declare as his last will that his
        two daus. by name Eleanor and [Tolis] should have all
        his land at Deep Run in this county to be eq. div.
        to them...and soon after on the same day departed
        this life and further saith not....

p.162 - James CUSHYON, will; 25 Apr 1720, 7 Dec 1720
        est. to be div. between wife Mary and Mary [RENES]
        her dau.; John BOWLING; ex: wife and John BOWLING;
        wits: Walter ANDERSON, William PANNELL.

p.163 - Thomas BRYANT, inv; 1 Feb 1720/21.

      - Anne LEWIS, inv; 1 Feb 1720/21.

p.164 - John DAYLE (or DAILEY), inv. by Thomas PHILLIPS and Mary
        his wife adm; 1 Feb 1720/21.

p.166 - William REED, of Han. Par., will; 11 Dec 1720, 1 Feb 1720/21
        eld. son Samuel; son Thomas; wife Abigail; s-i-l
        Samuel KENDELL; no ex; wits: Isaac ARNOLD, William PITMAN,
        William PULLEN.

      - Richard HILL, inv; 1 Feb 1720/21.

p.167 - Robert GALLOP, inv. by Eleanor GALLOP adm; 1 Feb 1720/21.

p.168 - James CUSHION, inv; 1 Feb 1720/21.

p.169 - Richard HINDS, will; 7 Jan 1718/19, 1 Mar 1720/21
        sons Thomas, Charles, and James all land; wife Mary;
        dau. Mary; ex: wife and son Thomas; wits: Thomas WOOD,
        Elizabeth STEEL, Gabriel [ALLOWAY].

p.170 - George HOPKINS, of Sitt. Par., will; 17 Aug 1719, 1 Mar
        1720/21
        wife Frances; daus. of wife Catherine DYE (wife of
        Avery DYE) and Charity BAYLY (wife of William BAYLY);
        ex: wife; wits: John NEWMAN, George NEWMAN, Elizabeth
        NEWMAN. [George HOPKINS mar. Frances WILSON wid. of
        John WILSON in Oct 1710. MRC, p.97.]

p.171 - William REED, inv; 1 Mar 1720/21.

p.173 - William SMITH, inv; 5 Apr 1720/21.

p.174 - George HOPKINS, inv; 5 Apr 1720/21.

p.175 - Francis SLAUGHTER, additional inv; 5 Apr 1720/21.

      - Simon MILLER, additional inv; 5 Apr 1720/21.

p.176 - James NELSON, Sitt. Par., will; 24 Feb 1720, 5 Apr 1720/21
        fr. William FAUNTLEROY all plant. and land whereon I
        now live in Sitt. Par. formerly belonging to Henry
        CHAPPELL; Elizabeth MOREEN (dau. of William MOREEN);
        no ex; wits: Samuel GODWIN, George NEWMAN, John ALLEN.

      - Richard HINDS, inv; 5 Apr 1720/21.

p.178 - William BARBER, Farn. Par., will; 10 Mar 1719, 7 Jun 1721
        daus. Mary LEWIS, Lucy BAKER; cousin Thomas BARBER;
        Samuel WOOD; Mary WOOD; daus. Joyce, Anne all land in
        Sitt. Par. to be eq. div. between them; wife to receive
        half of my mill; son Samuel when 18 to receive the
        other half of the mill and after his mother's death
        to have all of it; ex: wife and son Samuel; bro. Charles
        BARBER and cousin John TARPLEY to be trustees; wits:
        Samuel ALGAR, Thomas NASH Jr., Robert JOHNSON. [Capt.
        William BARBER mar. Joyce BAYLEY by Aug 1694. MRC, p.9.]

p.179 - Jefry REANOLDS, will; 13 Mar 1720/21, 7 Jun 1721
        son John piece of land bought of John SIMONDS; dau.
        Elizabeth; dau. Susannah all land that is on the north
        side of the Middle Swamp which I bought of John [MURTO]
        which land William HEADLEY now lives on; orphan boy
        John KILLEY to be free at 19 unless he has a year's
        schooling then to serve while he is one and twenty;
        and my will is that my son John shall be free as soon
        as, please God, I am deceased; ex: wife; wits: Joseph
        SEAMONS, Richard ALDERSON.

      - NELSON's inv; 7 Jun 1721.

p.180 - John GARTON, inv; 7 Jun 1721. [For further information on
        John GARTON, see MRC, p.154.]

p.181 - George HOPKINS, f.inv; 7 Jun 1721.

      - William SMITH, f.inv; 7 Jun 1721.

      - Henry WEBSTER, inv; 5 Jul 1721.

p.182 - Jefry REANOLDS, inv; 5 Jul 1721.

p.183 - Arthur McGWYER, inv. at the house of Mary McGWYER; 5 Jul 1721.

      - Richard WOOD, Farn. Par., will; 9 Jan 1717/18, 5 Jul 1721
        wife Mary all land; ex: wife; wits: John TABOT, Mary
        TABOT, Edward BARROW.

p.184 - John GLOW, will; 16 May 1721, 5 Jul 1721
        George TAYLOR (son of Simon TAYLOR) 100 ac.; sisters
        Mary and Elizabeth MACKGUYER remainder of land to be
        eq. div.; John TAYLOR (son of Simon TAYLOR) to be ex;
        wits: Thomas JESPER, Charles JONES, George HENDERSON.

      - Edmond DOBBINS, inv. by Mary DOBBINS adm.; 5 Jul 1721.

p.185 - William ROBINSON, inv; 5 Jul 1721.

p.186 - Capt. William BARBER, inv; 5 Jul 1721.

p.188 - Robert FRISTO, inv. by Anne FRISTO; 5 Jul 1721.

p.189 - Richard WOOD, inv; 2 Aug 1721.

p.190 - John PEIRCE, inv; 2 Aug 1721.

- Daniel BENTLEY, will; 19 Mar 17[20], 2 Aug 1721
    sons Daniel and James; son James to the care of son
    Daniel until 18; land to wife during her life; ex: wife;
    wits: William GUPTON, Marget SMITH, Thomas NASH.

p.191 - Thomas FRANKLIN, inv; 2 Aug 1721.

p.192 - Thomas EARTH, will; 23 May 1721, 2 Aug 1721
    wife; wife's three chil. Mary, John, and Edward SINGER;
    godson Thomas MORGAN; no ex; wits: John ALDERSON,
    William TAYLOR.

- John GLOW, inv; 2 Aug 1721.

p.193 - Robert NEATHERCOTE, inv; 6 Sep 1721. [A Robert NETHERCUTT,
    the son of John and Mary NETHERCUTT, was b. in 1686.
    NFPR, p.137.]

p.194 - Thomas EARTH, inv; 6 Sep 1721.

p.195 - Daniel BENTLEY, inv; 6 Sep 1721.

p.196 - DEEK's f. inv; 4 Oct 1721.

- Mary CARPENTER, Farn. Par., will; 22 Dec 1721, 3 Jan 1721/22
    Frances BARBER; Jean LAWSON; Elizabeth and Anne (daus.
    of Charles BARBER); Mary BARBER; Thomas and Charles
    (sons of Charles BARBER); Anne (dau. of Thomas GRIFFIN);
    Thomas GRIFFIN and his wife; bro. Thomas GLASCOCK; John
    and Thomas (sons of Thomas GLASCOCK); Capt. William
    WOODBRIDGE; Samuel HIPKINS; John TARPLEY Jr; John
    TARPLEY Sr; Winifred and Alice (daus. of Thomas GRIFFIN);
    Anne (wife of John TARPLEY); Million GLASCOCK; Elizabeth
    DOWNMAN; all land in Lanc. Co. to Anne the wife of Col.
    John TARPLEY; William GLASCOCK; Sarah (dau. to Thomas
    GLASCOCK); ex: John TARPLEY Sr. and John TARPLEY Jr.;
    wits: Alexander MATSON, John BROWN, [Hanner KELLIE]
    [Mary CARPENTER may have been the wife of Thomas
    CARPENTER whose will was rec. 10 Jul 1728 in Lanc. Co.
    WLC, p.35.]

p.198 - William COLSTON, will; 10 May 1721, 3 Jan 1721/22
    wife Mary; dau. Mary; other dau. unnamed; ex: wife and
    Mr. William DAINGERFIELD of Essex Co; wits: Reuben
    WELCH, Anne WEBB, Joseph BROWN. [William COLSTON mar.
    Mary MERIWETHER; they had two chil. Mary and Frances.
    MRC, p.42.]

p.199 - Mark THORNTON, inv. by Mary THORNTON relict and wid; 7 Mar
    1721/22.

- William REED, f. inv; 7 Mar 1721/22.

p.200 - Edward BARROW, will; [nd.], 7 Mar 1721/22
    son Edward all land and plant. whereon I now live also
    est. in England; wife Anne; dau. Anne 300 ac. at the
    deep run commonly called The Land at the Marsh in King
    Geo. Co.; dau. Margaret; fr. Capt. George ESKRIDGE and
    Maj. Nicholas SMITH; ex: wife and son Edward; wits:
    Robert JONES, Joseph BELFIELD, John MORTON. [Edward
    BARROW mar. Anne (STONE) METCALFE wid. of Richard
    METCALFE ca. 1700. MRC, p.11.]

p.201 - Edward BARROW, inv; 22 Mar 1721/22.

p.202 - Robert REANOLDS, inv; 4 Apr 1722.

p.203 - William COLSTON, inv. by Mary COLSTON ex; 4 Apr 1722.

p.206 - Thomas WELCH, Farn. Par., will; 10 May 1720, 4 Apr 1722
        wife Elizabeth; wife's son William all lands in Rich.
        Co.; dau. Margaret; no ex; wits: Thomas LAIN, John
        WOOD, Samuel STEEL.

p.207 - Frances CAVERNER, inv; 2 May 1722.

p.208 - Elisha JONES, inv; 2 May 1722.

p.209 - Thomas WELCH, inv; 2 May 1722.

      - John MORTON, Sitt. Par., will; 27 Jul 1721, 2 May 1722
        son Richard land which I bought of Lawrence BARKER;
        sons James and Thomas lands and plant. where I now
        live after the decease of wife Deborah; if they have
        no heirs, to Mary and Winifred MORTON; sons William
        and John; no ex; wits: J. DAVIS, Math. DAVIS.

p.210 - MORTON's inv. by Deborah MORTON; 6 Jun 1722.

p.211 - Edward BUCKLEY, inv; [nd.]

      - Mrs. Mary CARPENTER, inv; 1 Aug 1722.

p.212 - William GUPTON, inv. by Eleanor the adm; 5 Sep 1722.

p.213 - Henry BRUCE Jr., inv; 3 Oct 1722.

      - John BROWN, inv; 6 Feb 1722/23.

p.214 - Henry STREET, inv; 6 Feb 1722/23.

p.216 - Henry HEDLE [=HEADLEY], will; 25 Feb 1722/23, 3 Apr 1723
        wife Jean all land; sons John and Henry; no ex;
        wits: John HUGHLETT, Ellinor ALVORSON, William HILL.

      - George BLUFORD, inv. at the house of John HILL; 1 May 1723.

p.217 - Richard GIBBS, inv; 1 May 1723. [Richard and Anne GIBBS had
        a dau. Penelope b. 1 May 1722. NFPR, p. 68.]

p.218 - James FARRILL, inv; 1 May 1723.

      - Frances LUCAS, inv; 1 May 1723.

p.220 - Henry HEDLE, inv; 1 May 1723.

p.221 - John DAVIS, Sitt. Par., will; 28 Jan 1722/23, 1 May 1723
        dau. Catherine TAYLOR; sons Matthew, Walter, William,
        George, and Peter; wife Esther; ex: wife; wits: John
        [WELLS], William DOYLE, Susannah DAVIS.

      - Bartholomew BAKER, NFP, will; 31 Dec 1722, 5 Jun 1723
        plant. and land to wife Elizabeth, then to son William;
        if he has no heirs, then to Samuel BAKER, and if he has
        no heirs, to Bartholomew BAKER; all personal est. to
        wife during her life, then to her six chil: William,
        Samuel, Bartholomew, Constant, Patience, and Elizabeth
        BAKER and the child that my wife is now laboring with;

ex: wife; wits: Edward HINKLEY, John [CHAMPE], John MARKS.

p.222 - John DAVIS, inv; 4 May 1723.

p.223 - Bartholomew BAKER, inv; 3 Jul 1723.

p.225 - Elizabeth BRADLEY, Sitt. Par., will; 23 Sep 1723, 6 Nov 1723
grson. Barnaby WELLS; grson. John WELLS (son of my s-i-l
John WELLS) 100 ac. whereon I now live, if he has no
male heirs, land to be returned to my s-i-l John WELLS
and after his decease to go to my grson. Thomas POUND;
grson. George WELLS; s-i-l John WELLS all my handi-
crafts tools as coopers, carpenters, joiners, etc. and
the chest they are put into; dau. Margaret PURSELL;
Elizabeth SMITH; grchil. Thomas POUND, Elizabeth POUND,
and Catherine PURSELL; ex: s-i-l John WELLS and Tobias
PURSELL; wits: D. GAINES, James WILSON.

p.226 - William FORREST, inv; 4 Dec 1723.

p.227 - Stephen WELLS, inv. by Elizabeth WELLS adm.; 1 Jan 1723/24.

p.228 - Elizabeth BRADLEY, inv; 1 Jan 1723/24.

p.229 - John DAVIS, inv. at the house of John MORTON; 1 Jan 1723/24.

p.230 - Henry RAVNELL, will; 14 Apr 1723, 4 Mar 1723/24
godson William GRIFFIN; William GRIFFIN, my godson's
father and he to be ex; wits: Thomas CLATON, Richard
CLAXTON, Anne GRIFFIN.

p.231 - William SMITH, Farn. Par., will; [nd.], 4 Mar 1723/24
daus. Elizabeth CLARK, Mary WILLIAMS, Catherine SMITH;
wife Anne; son John the plant. whereon I now live; son
Robert; grsons. Francis LUCAS. Stephen LUCAS; son and
eld. dau. of son Robert; the land that belongs to me
by the riverside to wife and son John; ex: wife; son
Robert and Roger WILLIAMS to be overseers to look after
my son John if his mother shall decease before he is
of age or capable of managing it himself; wits: Joseph
SEAMANS, Tobias PURSELL.

- William SMITH, inv; 1 Apr 1724.

p.233 - William BROWNE, Sitt. Par., will; 14 Jan 1723/24, 6 May 1724
s-i-l Joseph AMBROSE all my land on the easternmost side
of Stony Hill Branch where Matthew [BEANE] formerly
lived; if he has no heirs, then to my two daus. [Mason]
and Eleanor; fr. Henry and James WILSON; no ex; wits:
D. GAINES, William BRUCE, Henry RAVENER.

p.234 - Matthew DAVIS, will; 26 Dec 1722, 3 Jun 1724
son Crighton land whereon I now live; if he has no heirs,
then to son Matthew, and if he leaves no heirs to loving
wife Frances; dau. Winifred; ex: fr. John MORTON; wits:
William PAYNE, William DAVIS.

p.236 - William BROWN, inv; 1 Jul 1724.

p.237 - Matthew DAVIS, inv. by Frances DAVIS adm; 1 Jul 1724.

p.239 - Daniel McCARTY, inv. at his Farnham and Mangorite Quarters
in Rich. Co.; 1 Jul 1724. [Daniel McCARTY mar. (1)
Elizabeth (POPE) PAYNE, 19 Oct 1698, and (2) Anne

(LEE) FITZHUGH by May 1719. His will was prov. in
West. Co. MRC, p.123; WWC, p.79.]

p.240 - Charles SNEAD, Sitt. Par., will; 4 Apr 1724, 5 Aug 1724
dau. Elizabeth KEITH; grdau. Sarah KEITH; son Charles
a parcel of land, if he has no heirs, then to son
James; wife Sarah; ex: wife and son Charles; wits:
Richard CLAXTON, William GRIFFIN, Edward LAMBURT.

p.242 - Charles SNEAD, inv; 7 Oct 1724.

     - Jeane TODD, inv; 7 Oct 1724.

p.243 - Daniel CHILD, inv; 4 Nov 1724.

p.244 - John GITHINGS, inv; 4 Nov 1724.

     - Francis YEATES, inv; 4 Nov 1724.

p.245 - McCARTY's f.inv; 4 Nov 1724.

p.246 - Edgcomb SUGGITT, inv. by Charles BARBER adm; 2 Dec 1724.

p.247 - Richard FOWLER, Farn. Par., will; 2 Jan 1717/18, 2 Dec 1724
wife Mary; daus. Mary, Elizabeth. and Martha; son
David the plant. my b-i-l Robert RENOLDS now lives on
and to have it in his possession at the age of 16; the
child my wife now goes with, if it be a boy, the plant.
I now live on; ex: wife; wits: Abraham DALE, Thomas
MILLS, William SMITH.

p.248 - William SMITH, f.inv; 2 Dec 1724.

     - Capt. Charles COLSTON, inv; 2 Dec 1724. [Capt. Charles
COLSTON mar. Rebecca (TRAVERS) TAVERNER in May 1713.
MRC, p.42.]

p.252 - Francis YEATES, f.inv; 27 Jan 1724/25.

p.253 - Richard FOWLER, inv; 3 Feb 1724/25.

p.254 - John COUS, NFP, will; 5 Jan 1724/25, 3 Feb 1724/25
William DOZIER (son of John and Sarah DOZIER) 300 lbs.
of tobacco toward his schooling; Mary WELCH (dau. of
Richard and Mary WELCH); John LEE; father George COUS
bro. Thomas COUS, and Sis. Elizabeth all living at
[Heierbe] near Cockermouth about 12 miles from White-
haven; ex: Col. John TAYLOE; wits: Thomas LEWIS, John
DOZIER, Samuel POUND.

p.255 - James INGO, will; 30 Dec 1722, 4 Feb 1724/25
s-i-l Richard BARNES; daus. Frances BARNES, Mary my
plant. and all the land; wife Frances; no ex; wits:
John GORAM, William CRASK, William DICKSON, Math. DAVIS.
[James INGO mar. Frances (MOSS) BROWN, wid. of William
BROWN, by Feb 1704. MRC, p.101.]

p.256 - Patrick NEALE, inv; 3 Mar 1724/25.

p.257 - John THOMAS, inv; 3 Mar 1724/25.

p.258 - James INGO, inv. at the house of James INGO and at the house
of William KILLBEE; 3 Mar 1724/25.

p.260 - William BROWN, f.inv; 3 Mar 1724/25.

54

- William GRIFFIN, Sitt. Par., will; 2 Mar 1724/25, 7 Apr
  1725
            sons John the plant. whereon I now live and all the
            land, William the plant. whereon Henry RAVNELL did
            live with all the land, if either of the above two sons
            die before they reach 24, land to go to son Charles,
            if both sons die...then son Joseph to have one of the
            plants.; wife Anne; wife of Richard CLAXTON; ex: wife
            and son John; wits: Christopher BUTLER, Richard CLAXTON,
            Thomas CLAYTON.

p.261 - Elizabeth WELLS, Farn.Par., will; 10 Feb 1724, 5 May 1725
            Richard LOSSON; Elizabeth WELLS; my son Thomas Williams
            WELLS I leave him to Richard LOSSON while the age of
            21 to have at his freedom one suit of apparel; Absolom
            WELLS; Sarah LOSSON; sons Francis SETTLE and Stephen
            WELLS; no ex; wits: Henry SETTLE, Daniel JACKSON, Henry
            SPURRIER. [Elizabeth WELLS was the dau. of Rice WILLIAMS
            and wid. of (1) Francis SETTLE Jr. and (2) Stephen
            WELLS. MRC, p.228.]

      - Elizabeth WELLS, inv; 5 May 1725.

p.262 - William GRIFFIN, inv; 5 May 1725.

p.263 - Henry RAVENELL, inv; 5 May 1725.

      - Mary HINDS, inv. by the adm. John WILLIAMS; 2 Jun 1725.

p.265 - Henry BURDITT, Sitt. Par., will; 29 Nov 1723, 2 Jun 1725
            plant. and land in Sitt. Par. to Thomas THORNTON and
            his wife Susannah and to John NEWMAN and his wife
            Elizabeth; plant. and land in NFP whereon John WALKER,
            Jane TODD, John MOLLONY, and Humphry THOMAS now live
            containing about 500 ac. to the sd. Humphry THOMAS and
            his wife Jane, after their decease, to their chil.
            William, John, David, and James THOMAS and William
            [LIMAS] and Sarah MOUNTJOY; fr. Capt. Thomas BEALE;
            my right of the land whereon Leonard HILL now lives in
            Essex Co. to my fr. George BROWN of West. Co.; Elizabeth
            BRUCE (dau. of Henry BRUCE); right and title of the
            piece of land as I am informed was bequeathed to me by
            Madam HULL to Edward HINKLEY of the county aforesaid;
            orphan boy that now lives with me named William [LIMAS]
            to remain with Thomas THORNTON and he to learn him to
            read and write; the orphan girl to remain with the sd.
            John NEWMAN and he to learn her to read and sew; ex:
            Thomas THORNTON and John NEWMAN; wits: Avery DYE, George
            NEWMAN, George FILKIN.

p.267 - Robert BAYLIS, Farn. Par., will; 30 Jan 1724/25, 7 Jul 1725
            Mr. Newman BROCKENBROUGH a small piece of land contain-
            ing 10 ac. lying to the west of the Mill Swamp; bro.
            Thomas all the land that I have any right to on the
            hills between the main swamp and the Gun Branch; Mr.
            Giles WEBB the plant. whereon I now live with 300 ac.
            thereunto belonging; daus. Elizabeth and Frances; son
            Thomas; cousin Giles WEBB and his son John Spann WEBB
            to be ex; wits: Joyce LEWIS, Ama[dine] HAMMON, James
            SAMFORD. [Robert BAYLIS mar. Ellin McCARTY in Nov 1711.
            MRC, p.12.]

p.268 - Henry BURDITT, inv; 7 Jul 1725.

WILL BOOK 5, 1725-1753

p. 1 - Robert BAYLIS, inv; 4 Aug 1725.

      - Thomas FRANKLIN, f.inv; 1 Sep 1725.

      - John COUSE, inv; 6 Oct 1725.

p. 2 - Thomas HINDS, inv; 1 Dec 1725.

p. 3 - John WEBB, inv. pres. by Barbary WEBB adm; 3 Nov 1725.

      - John BENGER, Farn. Par., will; 25 Oct 1725, 1 Dec 1725
            dau. Anne all land in Rich. Co., if she has no heirs,
            land to go to sis. Winifred; dau. Jane; b-i-l John
            CRUCHER and wife Anne to care for chil. until age 18;
            ex: b-i-l and wife Anne; wits: Lewis PUGH, Edward GILL.
            [John BENGER d. 31 Oct 1725. His first wife was evident-
            ly named Mary; she d. 6 May 1724. NFPR, p.14.]

p. 4 - John BENGER, inv; 5 Jan 1725/26.

      - John YEATS, inv; 2 Feb 1725/26.

p. 5 - Isabell SAMFORD, wife of Samuel SAMFORD, Farn. Par., will;
        29 Jul 1724, 2 Feb 1725/26
            all land in Middlesex Co. to be eq. div. between husband
            Samuel and Elizabeth SAMFORD (wife of Will SAMFORD);
            Anthony DODSON; sons John and Samuel; Keene (son of
            Will SAMFORD); dau. Elizabeth; ex: husband and son
            Samuel; wits: Newman BROCKENBROUGH, Thomas SAMFORD,
            Robert BAYLIS. [Isabell SAMFORD d. on 29 Nov 1725.
            NFPR, p.161. She was the wid. of Patrick LANGHEE and
            the second wife of Samuel SAMFORD. MRC, p.177.]

p. 6 - Eliza JESPER, wid. and relict of Richard JESPER, will; 21
        Jun 1717, 2 Mar 1725/26
            grdau. Elizabeth DODSON; sons William and Alexander
            CLARK; ex: sons William and Alexander; wits: John
            HUGHLETT, William DUDLEY, William MARSHALL.

      - Luke THORNTON, NFP, will; 29 Jan 1725, 2 Mar 1725/26
            son Thomas my land in West. Co. beyond Pantico; grsons.
            William, Mark, and [Rowland] THORNTON; dau. Anne
            MOUNTJOY; grdau. Sarah JONES; son Matthew; dau. Elizabeth
            NASH; ex: dau. Anne MOUNTJOY and grdau. Sarah JONES;
            wits: Marmaduke BECKWITH, William SISSON, Michael
            WINDER.

p. 7 - Elizabeth JESPER, inv; 6 Apr 1726.

p. 8 - Elizabeth HILL, inv; 6 Apr 1726.

p. 9 - Luke THORNTON, inv; 6 Apr 1726.

p.10 - Susannah PHILLIPS, NFP, will; 17 Jan 1725, 6 Apr 1726
            son David land and plant. I now live on; dau. Catharine;
            ex: son David; wits: John BRANHAM, Jane WILLKINSON,
            Robert TAYLOR.

p.11 - Susannah PHILLIPS, inv; 4 May 1726.

      - Francis WILLIAMS, inv; 1 Jun 1726.

      - Edward WILLIAMS, inv. at the house of Francis WILLIAMS;
        1 Jun 1726.

56

p.12 - George GAINS, Sitt. Par., will; 28 Apr 1726, 1 Jun 1726
        bro. Daniel and his wife may live on plant. they now
        live on until my son Bernard comes to age; wife Eleanor;
        dau. Margaret; ex: wife; wits: Elizabeth DOYLE, Patience
        BAKER, Alvin MOUNTJOY, John MORTON.

p.13 - George GAINS, inv; 6 Jul 1726.

     - John WALKER, inv; 6 Jul 1726.

p.14 - William DEBELL, inv; 6 Jul 1726.

     - Isabel SAMFORD, inv; 6 Jul 1726.

     - Joshua HIGHTOWER, will; 14 Apr 1726, 3 Aug 1726
        wife; sons Charnel and Thomas; four other chil.; ex:
        wife; wits: Charles DOBYNS, Henry WILLIAMS. [Thomas
        HIGHTOWER was b. to Joshua and Eleanor HIGHTOWER on
        20 Mar 1712. NFPR, p.93.]

p.15 - Thomas FRESHWATER, Farn. Par., will; 29 Mar 1726, 3 Aug 1726
        son George all land...bounded by the land I gave to my
        son Thomas, which land is all the upper part of my
        patent to the branch that divides this plant. and the
        land which I sold to Col. BARBER being that part of my
        patent which lies on the northwest side of the road and
        that below the line formerly made by a jury for Edward
        MOUNTAGUE dec'd; wife Mary; ex: wife; wits: Charles
        BARBER Jr, John McLAUGHLIN. [Thomas FRESHWATER mar. Mary
        HUDSON dau. of Bryan and Mary HUDSON by 3 Oct 1699. MRC,
        p. 74. The births of three of their chil. are rec. in
        the NFPR: Anne (1707), John (1712), and Mary (1717).
        NFPR, p.64.]

     - Bartholomew [SCALLAGHAM], inv. by Andrew HALEY adm; 3 Aug
        1726.

p.16 - Thomas FRESHWATER, inv; 7 Sep 1726.

     - Joshua HIGHTOWER, inv. at the house of Eleanor HIGHTOWER;
        7 Sep 1726.

p.17 - Patrick SHORT, Farn. Par., will; 14 Aug 1726, 7 Sep 1726
        daus. Eleanor and Anne; sons William and Patrick; wife
        Anne; mentions money owed by Thomas BRIDGEFORD and Lewis
        PUGH; ex: wife; wits: Lewis PUGH, Elizabeth WEBSTER.

p.18 - Peter ELMORE, Farn. Par., will; 5 Sep 1720, 5 Oct 1726
        wife Charity; grsons William ELMORE, Charles ELMORE,
        William ERRITT, George PETTERY, Josias ELMORE, Thomas
        ELMORE, John ELMORE, and Beck ELMORE; dau. Frances;
        ex: wife; wits: Bartholomew Richard DODSON, Thomas
        DODSON, William HUEITT.

     - Patrick SHORT, inv; 5 Oct 1726.

p.19 - George PETTY, will; 15 Aug 1726, 5 Oct 1726
        whole est. to bro. Christopher PETTY; ex: brother; wits:
        Charles BRUCE, John JENNINGS, William EVERETT.

p.20 - John GOWER, will; 8 Dec 1725, 5 Oct 1726
        son Travis; daus. Anne [THIFET], Winifred, and Elizabeth;
        wife Susannah; ex: wife and son; wits: William TOURNEY,
        Zacharias HEAFORD.

p.21 - John BOOTH, inv. pres. by Richard BOOTH adm; 5 Oct 1726.

- COLSTON's inv; 5 Oct 1726.

- George PETTY, inv; 2 Nov 1726.

p.22 - Peter ELMORE, inv; 2 Nov 1726.

p.23 - John GOWER, inv; 2 Nov 1726.

p.24 - Robert DUN, will; 25 Aug 1726, 2 Nov 1726
       land to wife Elizabeth and after her death to Harrabin
       MOORE; ex: wife; wits: Willoughby BRERETON, William
       MOORE, John NAYLOR.

p.25 - RIERDEN's inv; 2 Nov 1726.

- Anne STREET, inv; 2 Nov 1726.

- John SMITH, NFP, nunc. will; 22 Nov 1726, 7 Dec 1726
       SMITH stated that he gave all his est. to his wife
       Margaret, in the presence of the Rev. John GARZIA,
       minister, William THRIFT, Anne THRIFT, and Dr. Robert
       TAYLOR.

p.26 - William CLARKE, will; 21 Apr 1726, 7 Dec 1726
       wife Mary; son Henry (under 20) plant. where I formerly
       lived and that part of my land which my bro. Henry
       bought of George GLASCOCK containing about 30 or 40
       ac.; ex: wife; wits: Alexander CLARK, George HILL.
       [The births of the fol. chil. to William and Mary
       CLARKE are recorded in the NFPR: Henry (1713), Alice
       (1716); William CLARKE d. 23 Apr 1726. NFPR, pp.31,32.]

- Thomas SMITH, will; 20 Nov 1726, 7 Dec 1726
       son Peter; desires that Edmund NORTHERN and his wife
       Elizabeth may have his two sons Peter and Thomas to
       use them at their own discretion til they are 18; ex:
       Edmund NORTHERN; wits: Joseph RUSSELL Jr, John REYNOLDS.

- Charles BARBER, Farn. Par, will; 23 Nov 1726, 1 Feb 1726/27
       wife Frances; sons Thomas, Charles that part of my land
       where I now live containing 200 ac. more or less and
       also 750 ac. which is one half of my land in Stafford
       Co. said land there to be div. into two eq. parts and
       son Charles to have his choice; son William the rest of
       my land in general; daus. Mary, Anne, Elizabeth, and
       Frances; ex: wife, sons Thomas and Charles; wits:
       Archbald JOHNSTON, Samuel BARBER.
       [cod.] It is my will and pleasure that what land I gave
       my son Charles I give it to my son Thomas; [nd.]

p.27 - William WOODBRIDGE, NFP, will; 16 Nov 1726, 1 Feb 1726/27
       cousin George WOODBRIDGE the plant. I bought of Francis
       WILLIAMS 300 ac. to be made good out of that I bought
       of Thomas MOUNTJOY; dau. Elizabeth remaining 500 ac. of
       land I bought of Thomas MOUNTJOY and all slaves at
       Rappahannock Plant; executor to buy 200 ac. of good
       plantable land near the falls of our river and give it
       to William ROBERTSON the son of Anne ROBERTSON; son
       John; ex: son John; wits: Nath. NORTON, John [DEPLICH],
       Susannah HINDES. [Maj. William WOODBRIDGE mar. (1)
       Sarah KEENE and (2) Sarah BRERETON, 1713. MRC, pp.234,
       235. William ROBERTSON, the bastard son of Anne, was
       b. 18 Jan 1725. NFPR, p.158.]

p.28 - Rebecca COLSTON, NFP, will; 27 Dec 1726, 1 Feb 1726/27
tract of land and plant. in North. Co. called The
Lodge to son Charles, he lacking heirs, to son Travers,
and he lacking heirs, to dau. Susannah; son Travers
all land belonging to the Forest Quarter; daus. Elizabeth,
Winifred; sis. Winifred TRAVERS to have a suitable
maintenance out of my est. during her living single;
ex: fr. Daniel HORNBY; wits: John HAMMOND, William
RUSSELL.

p.29 - Francis GOWER, NFP, will; 14 Dec 1726, 1 Feb 1726/27
est. to be eq. div. between wife [Rachel] and children
including the child wife now goes with; dau. Anne; ex:
wife; wits: John BRAMHAM, John CAMPBELL. [Francis and
Rachel GOWER had two children, Anne and Francis. MRC,
p.254 and NFPR, p.72.]

- William CLARK, inv; 1 Feb 1726/27.

p.30 - Andrew DEW, NFP, will; 13 Nov 1726, 1 Feb 1726/27
bros. Thomas and William; ex: bro. Ishmael; wits: Hugh
HARRIS, Margaret MADDOCK, Thomas DEW.

- Benjamin TALBUTT, Sitt. Par., will; 24 Dec 1726, 1 Feb 1726/
1727
sons William, Benjamin, Daniel, and Samuel; bro. Samuel
TALBUTT; son William to receive a pair of pistols,
holsters, and a breastplate; [Pursley] NEALE; ex: wife
and fr. Wharton RAMSDELL; wits: Joseph BELFIELD, Thomas
GEARINGS.

p.31 - George THOMAS, NFP, will; 5 Jan 1726/27, 1 Feb 1726/27
James THOMAS Jr; John THOMAS; bro. James; Mrs. Elizabeth
MIDDLETON; sis. Catharine LANDMAN; ex: sis. Catharine;
wits: B.D. MIDDLETON, Benjamin MIDDLETON.

p.32 - Charles LEWIS, will; 17 Nov 1726, 1 Feb 1726/27
sons Edward and Charles; daus. Catharine and Betty;
mentions wife and five chil.; ex: fr. Samuel BARBER
and Thomas NASH Sr; wits: Patrick MILLER, John HAMMOND.
[The births of the foll. chil. to Charles and Mary
LEWIS are rec. in the NFPR: Joyce (1712), Kathrine
(1715), Edward (1718), Charles (1720), and Betty (1722).
NFPR, p.116.]

- Thomas SMITH, inv; 1 Feb 1726/27.

- Samuel TALBERT, NFP, will; 16 Dec 1726, 1 Feb 1726/27
bro. Benjamin; wife Elizabeth; ex: wife; wits: Robert
BUCKLEY, Thomas GEARING.

p.33 - George HINSON, Sitt. Par., will; 22 Nov 1726, 1 Feb 1726/27
son William 100 ac. in West. Co., if he has no heirs,
to dau. Frances; other chil. Mary and Martha; ex: bro.
William BAILEY; wits: Edward TOMLINSON, Richard CLIFTON.

- William MORGAN, will; 6 Dec 1726, 1 Feb 1726/27
sons Joshua, Will, John, Thomas, Robert; wife Elizabeth;
daus. Anne LAMBERT, Mary HARRIS, Anne MORGAN (sic),
Elizabeth, and Judith; ex: wife and Will STONE; wits:
Will HARTLEY, Richard BROWN, Philip HARRIS.

- James STARKS, Farn. Par., will; [nd.], 1 Feb 1726/27
son Henry and rest of chil. [nfi.]; wife Eleanor; ex:
wife; wits: Anne RAYNOLDS, John RAYNOLDS.

- John SMITH, inv; 1 Feb 1726/27.

p.35 - David WILLIAMS, will; 24 Dec 1726, 1 Feb 1726/27
        all land to sons Owen and David; daus. Joan, Anne, Mary
        Anne; child wife now goes with; wife Mary to be ex;
        wits: Benjamin RUST, John BRAMHAM, John CAMPBELL.

    - Mary WILLIAMS, will; [nd.], 1 Feb 1726/27
        mentions est. of her dec'd husb; sons Owen and David;
        daus. Mary Anne, Anne, Joan; est. to be in the hands
        of Benjamin RUST until chil. come of age; ex: Benjamin
        RUST; wits: John and Sarah CAMPBELL.

    - Henry STREET, verbal will; 3 Jan 1726/27, 1 Feb 1726/27
        desires est. to be eq, div. between Anne BECKUM and
        George TOMLIN; no ex; wits: William CRASK, Frances
        BARNES.

p.36 - Thomas STANFIELD, NFP, will; 12 Jan 1726/27, 1 Mar 1726/27
        "lawfully begotten" son Marmaduke (under 21) all land;
        dau. Betty (under 18); wife Mary; Henry MISKELL; William
        BROCKENBROUGH and Henry MISKELL to care for chil. and
        wife; ex: wife; wits: Thomas DEW, John WILLIAMS, Henry
        MISKELL. [Thomas STANFIELD mar. Mary DALTON ca. 1722.
        MRC, p.194. Betty STANFIELD was b. 1723 and Marmaduke
        was b. 1724/25. NFPR, p.174.]

    - Col. Charles BARBER, inv; 1 Mar 1726/27.

p.39 - Maj. John WOODBRIDGE, inv; 1 Mar 1726/27.

p.41 - David WILLIAMS, inv; 1 Mar 1726/27.

p.42 - Mary WILLIAMS, inv; 1 Mar 1726/27.

p.43 - Andrew DEW, inv. pres. by Ishmael DEW the ex; 1 Mar 1726/27.

p.44 - Mark TUNE, inv. pres. by John TUNE; 1 Mar 1726/27.

    - Charles LEWIS, inv; 1 Mar 1726/27.

p.45 - James STARK, inv; 1 Mar 1726/27.

    - George THOMAS, inv; 1 Mar 1726/27.

p.46 - Benjamin TALBUTT, inv; 1 Mar 1726/27.

p.47 - James HARRISON, inv; 1 Mar 1726/27.

p.48 - Samuel TALBUTT, inv; 1 Mar 1726/27.

p.49 - Henry STREET, inv; 1 Mar 1726/27.

p.50 - George HINSON, inv; 1 Mar 1726/27.

p.51 - William MORGIN, inv; 1 Mar 1726/27.

p.52 - Francis GOWER, inv; 1 Mar 1726/27.

p.53 - Deborah POUND, inv; 1 Mar 1726/27.

    - John SEAMAN, inv; 1 Mar 1726/27

p.54 - Elizabeth LUCAS, nunc. will; 19 Dec 1726, [1 Mar 1726/27]
        Elizabeth LUCAS of the county of Rich. and Parish of

North Farnham being sick and weak being asked whether
she was willing to make a will, she said, yes; and she
was asked again who she was willing to give what she
had to: she said Betty [BAROH] and we do believe she
was in her perfect sense. Given under our hands this
19th day of December 1726; Thomas BARBER, [Lillias]
CRAGHEAD, Hester [JAGARS].

- John SMITH, f.inv; 1 Mar 1726/27.

- Charles WILKINSON, inv; 5 Apr 1727.

p.55 - Edward HINKLEY, inv; 5 Apr 1727.

- William LANDMAN, inv; 5 Apr 1727.

p.56 - Giles SAMFORD, will; 19 Dec 1726, 5 Apr 1727
        sis. [Elizabeth] SAMFORD; bros. John, Samuel all of
        the est. given me by my grfath. James SAMFORD; godson
        Keen SAMFORD; ex: sis. Elizabeth; wits: Samuel SAMFORD,
        James WEBB, Anne BOUFORD. [Giles SAMFORD, the son of
        Samuel and Elizabeth (KEENE) SAMFORD, d. 15 Feb 1726/
        1727. NFPR, p.161, MRC, p.261.]

- Thomas STANFIELD, inv. pres. by the ex. Mary STANFIELD;
  5 Apr 1727.

p.57 - Matthew THORNTON, Sitt. Par., will; 30 Nov 1726, 5 Apr 1727
        sons Hopkins and Matthew my whole tract of land, the
        lower part to Hopkins and the upper part to younger son
        Matthew; wife Ellen; daus. Ellen, Rebecca CRASKE; no
        ex; wits: Avery DYE, John NEWMAN, James WILSON.
        [Matthew THORNTON mar. twice; by his first wife Elizabeth
        HOPKINS he had three chil., Hopkins, Matthew, Rebecca;
        and by his second wife Eleanor CRASKE he had two chil.,
        Craske and Ellen. MRC, p.211.]

p.58 - John DAVIS, inv. at the house of Anne DAVIS adm; 5 Apr 1727.

p.59 - Martin SHERMAN, will; 11 Mar 1726/27, 5 Apr 1727
        sons Martin and Benjamin; dau. Elizabeth WOODCOCK;
        wife Mary; Elizabeth and Mary Ann BAKER; nephew Gregory
        GAYDEN; ex: son Martin; wits: John HAMMOND, Henry
        WILLIAMS.

- Thomas TAYLOR, will; 15 Mar 1726/27, 5 Apr 1727
        wife Elizabeth; cousins Thomas TAYLOR, Mary TAYLOR,
        George TAYLOR, Peter EVANS, John POUND (son of Samuel
        POUND), and Catharine TAYLOR; wishes Thomas TAYLOR and
        John CROLEY to have two years schooling at the charge
        of my wife and George TAYLOR; ex: wife and cousin George
        TAYLOR; wits: Robert TOMLIN, William SISSON. [The est.
        of Thomas TAYLOR was div. between George TAYLOR and
        Elizabeth TAYLOR, 2 Aug 1727. AB1, p.11.]

p.60 - Winifred MONEY, NFP, nunc. will; 26 Feb [1726/27], 5 Apr
  1727
        On 26 Feb. last, Winifred MONEY called David MORGIN,
        Winifred MORGIN, and Catharine [BATTS] and desired
        them to bear witness that she gave all her est. to her
        dau. Catharine LANDMAN.

- Robert DUNN, inv; 3 May 1727.

p.61 - Anthony DOWDEN, inv. pres. by Sarah DOWDEN adm; 3 May 1727.

p.62 - John PETTY, inv; 3 May 1727.

- Patrick SHORT, f.inv; 3 May 1727.

p.63 - Thomas WOOD, Farn.Par., will; [10] Jan 1726/27, 3 May 1727
        wife Elizabeth; dau. Mary Anne all land; ex: wife;
        wits: Thomas SMITH, Thomas DEW, [John MILLNER].

- Martin SHERMAN, inv; 3 May 1727.

p.65 - Mrs. Rebecca COLSTON, inv; 3 May 1727.

p.67 - Thomas TAYLOR, inv. delivered by Elizabeth TAYLOR and George
        TAYLOR ex; 3 May 1727.

p.70 - Christopher PETTY, NFP, will; 1 Mar 1726/27, 3 May 1727
        whole est. to Thomas LEGG and sis. Prudence PETTY;
        bro. William PETTY; bro. Thomas LEGG; no ex; wits:
        William DAVENPORT, Edward REED.

- Winifred MONEY, inv; 3 May 1727.

p.71 - Matthew THORNTON, inv; 3 May 1727.

p.72 - Henry BRUCE, Sitt. Par., will; 9 Nov 1722, 7 Jun 1727
        four sons Andrew, John, Joseph, and Benjamin; two daus.
        Mary and Elizabeth; wife Mary; ex: wife; wits: Sarah
        YOUNG, James SHELTON, Robert WELSH.

p.73 - Thomas GRAY, inv; 7 Jun 1727.

- Thomas BRYANT, NFP, will; 10 Feb 1726/27, 7 Jun 1727
        land to son Robert; sons James, Fauntleroy, Peter;
        youngest son Charles; wife Elizabeth; no ex; wits:
        Thomas WHITE, Thomas GEFFERY, Henry MISKELL.

p.74 - Thomas WOOD, inv; 7 Jun 1727.

p.75 - William DOWNMAN, NFP, will; 31 Mar 1726/27, 8 Jun 1727
        sons Travers and William; dau. Priscilla HEALE; grsons.
        William and Rawleigh (sons of son Rawleigh); sister
        Elizabeth [WORMLEY]; daus. Elizabeth, [Million] GLASCOCK;
        ex: sons; proved by the oaths of William GLASCOCK,
        Tobias PHILLIPS, Caran BRANHAM.

p.76 - Henry BRUCE, inv; 5 Jul 1727.

p.77 - Inv. of tobacco belonging to Christopher PETTY [Jr], dec'd;
        5 Jul 1727.

p.78 - Thomas JAMES, will; 27 Apr 1727, 5 Jul 1727
        son Thomas all land on north side of a small run which
        lies below my house; dau. Jane rest of land; wife Grace;
        other chil. [Honour]; ex: wife; wits: Nicholas MINOR,
        Charles ROBINSON. [Thomas JAMES mar. the wid. Grace
        KIRKHAM in 1714. MRC, p.102.]

p.79 - Thomas BRYAN[T], inv; 5 Jul 1727.

p.80 - Patrick BRADLEY, inv; 5 Jul 1727.

p.81 - Winifred GOWER, NFP, will; 20 May 1727, 5 Jul 1727
        sis. Elizabeth GOWER; cousins Frances GOWER and Esther

THRIFT; Esther MERCHANT; sis. Anne THRIFT; ex: [Uncle]
Stanley GOWER and bro. William THRIFT; wits: Thomas
PAIN, Frances GOWER. [Winifred GOWER was the wid. of
Stanley GOWER. MRC, p.80.]

p.82 – Winifred GOWER, inv; 2 Aug 1727.

- William MORGAN, f.inv; 2 Aug 1727.

- [Thomas] JAMES, inv; 2 Aug 1727.

p.84 – Giles SAMFORD, inv. at the house of Elizabeth SAMFORD ex;
2 Aug 1727.

p.85 – William MORGAN, inv; 6 Sep 1727.

- Elizabeth WEBSTER, wid., Farn. Par., will; 12 Nov 1725,
6 Sep 1727
dau. Judith; sons Henry and George; ex: son Henry;
desires Henry WEBSTER to take diligent care of his
bro. and sis. George Leazur WEBSTER and Judith WEBSTER,
and sis. Joyce WEBSTER is to live with him if she likes
of it; wits: Lewis PUGH, Henry KILLBORN.

p.86 – Thomas CRIBBIN, inv; 6 Sep 1727.

- Elizabeth WEBSTER, inv; 5 Oct 1727.

p.87 – Thomas MILLS, inv; 1 Nov 1727.

- Mr. William DOWNMAN, inv; 3 Jan 1727/28.

p.89 – William MORGAN, f.inv; 3 Jan 1727/28.

- Samuel BAILEY, will; 25 Aug 1725, 3 Jan 1727/28
son William all land at Rappahannock, if he has no
heirs, to son John, and if he has no heirs, to dau.
Sarah; son Samuel all land where I now live; ex:
William BRUCE; wits: Charles BARBER, John FOUSHEE.

p.90 – John CANE, inv; 6 Mar 1727/28.

p.91 – Samuel BAILEY, inv. pres. by William BRUCE ex; 6 Mar 1727/28.

p.94 – James STARK, f.inv; 6 Mar 1727/28.

- George THOMAS, f.inv; 6 Mar 1727/28.

- John HILL, will; 24 Mar 1727/28, 3 Apr 1728
plant. and all land to wife, after her death to be eq.
div. between s-i-l Robert RUNNELS and d-i-l Rebecca
RUNNELS and she is to have the upper part where the
plant. now is; ex: wife; wits: Dominick NEWGENT, James
WILSON, John HIGHTOWER.

p.95 – Samuel BAILEY, f.inv; 3 Apr 1728.

- Richard BRAMHAM, NFP, will; 4 Apr 1728, 1 May 1728
son Richard; son John; wife; ex: wife; wits: Robert
TOMLIN, Edward GILL, Elizabeth GILL.

p.96 – Ishmael DEW, will; 4 Apr 1728, 1 May 1728
bros. Thomas and William tract of land in Sitt. Par;
Jane PALMER; mother Flora HARRIS; Hugh HARRIS; ex:
bros; wits: Henry MISKELL, Hugh HARRIS.

- Travers DOWNMAN, Farn. Par., will; 5 Apr 1728, 1 May 1728
  bro. William land in Stafford Co. containing 1272 ac,
  and he is to pay to William and Rawleigh DOWNMAN (sons
  of my bro. Rawleigh) 20 pounds sterling at age 21;
  William DOWNMAN (son of my bro. William) land lying in
  the fork of the Totuskey which was left to me by my
  bro. Robert DOWNMAN, if he has no heirs, to Travers
  DOWNMAN (son of my bro. William); kinsman John GLASCOCK
  all land left to me by my father being on the head of
  the branches of Totuskey, if he has no heirs, to my bro.
  William; kinsman William GLASCOCK a silver-hilted sword;
  kinsmen George and Thomas GLASCOCK; sisters Million
  GLASCOCK, Elizabeth PINKARD, and Priscilla HEALE; ex:
  bro. William; wits: Thomas DEW, Alexander CLARK,
  Alexander [BUTHARAN].

- John HILL, inv; 1 May 1728.

p.98 - Thomas [MILLS], f.inv; 1 May 1728.

- Richard BRANHAM, inv; 5 Jun 1728.

p.99 - Travers DOWNMAN, inv. pres. by William DOWNMAN; 5 Jun 1728.

p.101 - Ishmael DEW, inv; 5 Jun 1728.

p.102 - Gilbert CROSSWILL, will; 12 Jun 1725, 5 Jun 1728
  eld.son Gilbert half of land in Rich. Co., other half
  to son William; mentions that eld. dau. Anne is dec'd;
  no ex; wits: William THOMAS, William GARNER, Timothy
  CUNNINGHAM.

- John MOLONY, inv; 5 Jun 1728.

p.103 - Thomas GRAY, f.inv; 3 Jul 1728.

- Hannah TALBUT's husband, f.inv; 3 Jul 1728.

p.104 - Gilbert CROSSWILL, inv. signed by Mary CROSSWILL; 3 Jul 1728.

- David BOYD, inv; 6 Nov 1728.

p.105 - Capt. John MORTON, inv; 6 Nov 1728; mentions servant Hannah
  CHARLETON. [Hannah CHARLETON bound her son James
  WILLIAMS and her dau. Hannah WILLIAMS as apprentices
  and servants to Marmaduke BECKWITH, 7 Jul 1726. AB1,
  p.4.]

p.110 - Willoughby BRERETON, inv; 6 Nov 1728.

p.111 - William SMITH of the Hills in Rich. Co, planter, will; 31
  Aug 1728, 6 Nov 1728
  sons William and Elias; dau. Anne JACKSON; wife Anne;
  no ex; wits: Gilbert METCALFE, Elizabeth SMITH.

- James MERRITT, NFP, will; 30 Sep 1727, 6 Nov 1728
  wife; son John FLINT; ex: son; wits: Peter GRIMSTEAD,
  William LEWIS.

p.113 - Catharine GWYNN, will; 20 [Sep] 1728, 6 Nov 1728
  grdau. Catharine FAUNTLEROY (dau. of son Griffin);
  grson. John SMITH; dau. [?] SMITH; land to be div.
  between eld. daus. of my several sons and daus.; ex:
  sons Moore, Griffin, and William FAUNTLEROY and s-i-l
  John TAYLOE; wits: Andrew WADE, David [NOKES].

- William SMITH of the Hills, inv; 4 Dec 1728.

p.115 - William OLDHAM, NFP, will; 17 Oct 1728, 4 Dec 1728
    wife Priscilley; child wife now goes with; ex: bro.
    Samuel; wits: Joseph RUSSELL, Charles RUSSELL.
    [William OLDHAM mar. Priscilla McLAUGHLIN ca. 1727;
    he d. around Nov 1728; his only child, William, was
    b. 3 Nov 1728. MRC, p.150.]

- Madam Catharine GWYNN, inv; 4 Dec 1728.

p.121 - John METCALFE, will; 8 Nov 1728, 4 Dec 1728
    mother Anne BARROW; John and Anne RUST (chil. of
    Benjamin and Sarah RUST); Anne BAILEY (dau. of Elizabeth
    BAILEY); kinsman William BROCKENBROUGH; ex: b-i-l
    Benjamin RUST and William BROCKENBROUGH; requests
    Marmaduke BECKWITH and bro. Gilbert METCALFE advise
    the ex; wits: Elizabeth DOZIER, Thomas TEMPLEMAN,
    Sarah DYE.

p.123 - Edward GLADMAN, inv; 4 Dec 1728.

- James MERRITT, inv; 4 Dec 1728.

p.124 - William OLDHAM, inv; 1 Jan 1728/29.

- John METCALFE, inv; 1 Jan 1728/29.

p.126 - Simon TAYLOR, will; 18 Aug 1728, 4 Feb 1728/29
    son John the plant. whereon I now live, if he has no
    heirs, to son George; son William the old plant, if
    he has no heirs, to son Thomas; son Septimus the plant.
    on which Patrick [DOREEN] now lives, if he has no heirs,
    to son George; dau. Sarah JESPER; grdau. Elizabeth
    JESPER; ex: sons John, William, and Septimus; wits:
    Robert BURTEN, Mary [SCURLOCK], John HAMMOND. [Simon
    TAYLOR mar. Elizabeth LEWIS ca. 1690. MRC, p.206.]

p.127 - William BAILEY, Sitt. Par., will; 26 Feb 1728/29, 5 Mar
    1728/29
    son John 200 ac. of land, if he has no heirs, to dau.
    Frances; dau. Frances 100 ac. of land; son John to go
    to Avery DYE and remain with him until 21; ex: Thomas
    [BREID]; wits: Avery DYE, John NEWMAN, George NEWMAN.
    [William BAILEY mar. Charity McMILLION, 1710. MRC, p.6.]

p.128 - Henry BURDICK, f.inv; 5 Mar 1728/29.

- Simon TAYLOR, inv; 5 Mar 1728/29.

p.129 - William BAILEY, inv; 2 Apr 1729.

p.132 - Phillip LONG, inv; 2 Apr 1729.

p.133 - Thomas LAWSON, will; 18 Dec 1728, 7 May 1729
    son Richard; dau. Elizabeth; daus. Rebeccah, Anne;
    sons Daniel, Thomas, John, William; wife Mary; ex:
    wife; wits: William HODGKINSON, Daniel JACKSON Jr.

p.134 - Robert GRIGGS, inv; 4 Jun 1729.

- Thomas BEALE, NFP, will; 22 Feb 1728, 4 Jun 1729
    wife; daus. Anne and Elizabeth; sons Thomas and William;
    four youngest sons Taverner, Charles, Richard, and
    Reuben to eq. div. land above the falls, but not during

the life of my wife unless she gives them leave to do
so; son John the land purchased by my grfath. of Henry
CLARK containing 400 ac; wife; after wife's decease,
land belonging to the plant. I now live on to go to
son Thomas; ex: wife, sons Thomas and William; wits:
Gilbert HAMILTON, William HODGKINSON, Andrew SPREULL,
Mary HODGKINSON.

- Elizabeth BEALE, NFP, 17 Mar 1728, 4 Jun 1729
     sons Thomas, William, and John; daus. Anne and Elizabeth;
     four youngest sons Taverner, Charles, Richard, and
     Reuben; ex: sons Thomas and William; wits: Gilbert
     HAMILTON, Robert TOMLIN, Andrew SPREULL.

p.136 - Martin HAMMOND, will; 25 Apr 1729, 4 Jun 1729
     son Martin plant. and all land; ex: son Edward; wits:
     William TARPLEY, Mary TARPLEY.

  - Samuel WEATHERS, inv; 4 Jun 1729.

p.137 - Thomas LAWSON, inv; 4 Jun 1729.

p.138 - Thomas BEALE, inv; 2 Jul 1729.

  - Mrs. Elizabeth BEALE, inv; 2 Jul 1729.

p.144 - Martin HAMMOND, inv; 6 Aug 1729.

p.145 - Hannah TALBUTT, inv; 1 Oct 1729.

p.146 - Thomas THORNTON, planter, Sitt. Par., will; 28 Jun 1729,
     1 Oct 1729
     wife; ex: wife; wits: Solomon RYAN, John GREEN,
     Elizabeth GOLDEN, Mary LONG.

  - John METCALFE, f.inv; 1 Oct 1729.

p.147 - Thomas THORNTON, inv; 5 Nov 1729.

p.148 - Joseph SEAMANS, NFP, will; 20 Nov 1729, 4 Feb 1729/30
     sons Moses and Aaron all land which William HIGES now
     lives on; son Ephraim land where I now live; son John
     land which lies part in King George Co. and part in
     Stafford Co.; mentions five young sons (all under 21)
     Aaron, Ephraim, Micajah, Obediah, and Jeremiah; dau.
     Assenath; ex: son Moses; wits: Joseph RUSSELL, Richard
     ALDERSON.

p.149 - Amy RANSDELL, Sitt. Par., will; 17 Jan 1729/30, 4 Feb 1729/
     1730
     dau. Mary MOXLEY; sons John KELLY, Matthew KELLY, and
     Alexander KELLY; ex: fr. James WILSON; wits: Anne
     WILSON, James WILLIAMS, William JORDAN.

p.150 - Samuel COOK, Sitt. Par., will; 23 Mar 1724, 4 Mar 1729/30
     sons Samuel and Daniel each to receive a gun, Samuel
     to have the longer; eld. dau. Elizabeth; daus. Mary
     and Rachel; wife Anne; no ex; wits: Sarah HINTON,
     Jude. MONDEY, Thomas MOSELEY.

  - Amy RANSDELL, inv; 4 Mar 1729/30.

p.151 - William KILBEE, inv; 4 Mar 1729/30.

p.152 - Richard MEEKS, will; 29 Jan 1729/30, 4 Mar 1729/30
        daus. Elizabeth WALKER 225 ac. in Stafford Co, Anne
        SISSON 250 ac. in Stafford Co., and Mary; son Richard
        remaining land in Stafford Co; s-i-l Henry SISSON; ex:
        wife Anne; wits: Thomas LEWIS, Tobias PURCELL, William
        DEGGES.

      - Samuel COOK, inv; 1 Apr 1730.

p.153 - Dr. Robert TAYLOR, inv; 6 May 1730.

      - Richard MEEKS Sr., inv; 6 May 1730.

p.155 - John TAYLOR, inv; 6 May 1730.

      - William HAMMOCK, Farn.Par., will; 3 Jul 1730, 5 Aug 1730
        wife use of plant. during her natural life and she to
        maintain my three grchil. William, John, and Mary
        HAMMOCK which now live with me until age 21 or day of
        marriage; son Benedict the land where I now live after
        wife's death; if he has no heirs, to son Robert; grson.
        John HAMMOCK 30 ac. of land which I gave to my son
        Benedict joining the lands of SWILLIVAN and CRALLE,
        if he has no heirs to son Benedict; son Robert all the
        land where my son Benedict now lives, if he has no heirs,
        to son Benedict; ex: sons Benedict and Robert; wits:
        Thomas BARBER, Alexander CLARK, John ELMORE.

p.156 - Roger THORNTON, inv; 5 Aug 1730.

      - Job TILLERY, will; 25 Jun 17[19], 5 Aug 1730
        dau. Winifred; all land to sons William and Henry; wife
        Mary; other sons Thomas and Job; cousin Richard TILLERY;
        ex: wife; wits: Job TILLERY, Richard TILLERY, William
        BARBER. [Job TILLERY mar. Mary COLWICK by 1719. MRC,
        p.215.]

      - William OLDHAM, f.inv; 2 Sep 1730.

p.157 - Job TILLERY, inv; 8 Oct 1730.

p.158 - Elizabeth HALL, inv; 8 Oct 1730.

p.159 - William HAMMOCK, inv; 8 Oct 1730.

p.160 - John WELLS Sr., Sitt.Par., will; [nd.], 3 Mar 1730/31
        wife Milou; son George all land after wife's death;
        if he has no heirs, to son Thomas; sons Barnaby and
        John; no ex; wits: Edward EIDSON, Willoughby FIELDING.

p.161 - John HENDERSON, Sitt. Par., will; 1 Feb 1729/30, 3 Mar 1730/
        1731
        Elizabeth HENDERSON (dau. of James and Melinda HENDER-
        SON); plant. to John (son of James and Melinda HENDER-
        SON; Martha (dau. of James and Melinda HENDERSON); ex:
        Melinda HENDERSON; wits: Charles SPOE Jr, John BROWN,
        Alexander BADGEN.

p.162 - Thomas TAYLOR, Farn. Par., will; 5 Jan 1730/31, 3 Mar 1730/31
        Anne JESPER (dau. of Thomas and Sarah JESPER); Richard
        Taylor JESPER and Simon JESPER; bros. John, William,
        Septimus, and George; ex: bro. Septimus; wits: Thomas
        TAYLOR, Thomas JESPER, George HENDERSON.

      - Easter [MERCHANT], inv; 3 Mar 1730/31.

- John WELLS Sr., inv; 7 Apr 1731.

p.163 - Thomas TAYLOR, inv; 7 Apr 1731.

p.164 - John HENDERSON, inv; 7 Apr 1731.

- Henry THRELKELD, NFP, will; 12 May 1731, 2 Jun 1731
  est. to be eq. div. between wife Eleanor and son
  George; ex: wife; wits: Robert TOMLIN, Anne SMITH.
  [Henry THRELKELD mar. Eleanor SHORT, 15 Jan 1728.
  MRC, p.214.]

- Christopher PRIDHAM, NFP, will; 22 Nov 1729, 2 Jun 1731
  son Christopher Jr. all land at the courthouse which
  goes by the name of the Ordinary, if he has no heirs,
  to son Edward and son William and the child wife now
  goes with; son Christopher all plant. and land whereon
  Thomas BRISTELL lives; son Christopher to pay 2000 lbs
  of tobacco to child wife now goes with when it reaches
  21; son Edward 50 ac. of land; son William; son John;
  daus. Anne FRESHWATER and Elizabeth HOPWOOD; ex: wife
  Mary and fr. Robert TOMLIN; wits: Thomas NASH Jr,
  Richard GWILLAM. [Christopher PRIDHAM was the son of
  Christopher and Bridget PRIDHAM of Rapp. Co. He mar.
  Mary LEWIS ca. 1700. WRC, p.116; MRC, p.162.]

p.165 - Nathaniel NORTON, inv; 2 Jun 1731.

p.166 - Christopher PRIDHAM, inv; 4 Aug 1731.

- Henry THRELKELD, inv; 4 Aug 1731.

p.167 - William [McCAINE], inv; 1 Sep 1731.

- George RUSSELL, Farn. Par., will; 11 Apr 1728, 3 Nov 1731
  ex. John HILL and wife Mary to look after children
  George, Lucy, and Barbary; all est to be div. between
  wife Mary and three children; land to go to son George;
  wits: Michael KEADY, Richard APPLEBEE, Robert BOUFORD.

p.168 - George RUSSELL, inv. pres. by Mary RUSSELL; 1 Dec 1731.

p.169 - Mary SPOE, wid. of Charles SPOE, nunc. will
  On 26 Dec 1731, she died in the space of 24 hours from
  the time she first complained and not having opportunity
  to have her will made in writing, did desire by words
  of her mouth that if she should die of that sickness
  that Charles SPOE, the son of Charles SPOE her dec'd
  husb. should be heir of what she had and that should
  by right belong to her by his father's est. all which
  she desired she being at the time in perfect sense in
  the presence of Edmund COLLINSWORTH, Alexander WAREING,
  and Mary BARKER; prov. 5 Jan 1731/32.

- Mary BRAGG, inv. pres. by Joseph and Charles BRAGG ex; 5
  Jan 1731/32.

p.170 - Charles SPOE Sr., Sitt. Par., will; 1 Sep 1725, 2 Feb 1731/
  1732
  wife Mary; son Charles; dau. Elizabeth FOUSHEE; ex:
  wife and son Charles; wits: Richard CLAYTON, John R.
  [HEARLE], Edmund COLLINSWORTH.

p.171 - John PYCRAFT, inv. pres. by Winifred PYCRAFT adm; 2 Feb
  1731/32

68

[John PYCRAFT d. 3 Dec 1731. NFPR, p.148. His wid.
mar. Thomas WILLIAMS, 8 Jun 1732. NFPR, p.154.]

p.172 - Charles SPOE, inv; 1 Mar 1731/32.

p.173 - John BRUCE, inv; 1 Mar 1731/32.

p.174 - Edward BRUCE, inv; 5 Apr 1732.

- Giles WEBB, will; [nd.], 3 May 1732
son John Spann WEBB his choice of the plant. whereon
I now live on the lower side of Richard's Creek and
the main swamp; son Giles; son Isaac land given by
Robert BAYLIS; son Cudburth all my Beaver Dam plant;
daus. Betty, Mary, and Winifred; Winifred [LUCAS];
no ex; wits: John GARZIA, Samuel SAMFORD, Daniel
HORNBY. [Giles WEBB, the son of John and Mary WEBB,
was b. 15 Apr 1677. NFPR, p.195. He mar. Elizabeth
SPANN of Northumberland Co. MRC, p.226.]

p.175 - Thadeus McCARTY, inv; 3 May 1732.

p.176 - Thomas BECKHAM, will; 17 Feb 1731, 3 May 1732.
wife Anne; chil. George Tomlin and Hannah Anne; dau.
Hannah Anne to receive land bought of John HINSON
joining upon Marmaduke BECKWITH; ex: wife; wits: Richard
BARNES, William DICKSON, John DEANE.

p.177 - Thomas BECKHAM, inv; 7 Jun 1732.

p.179 - Giles WEBB, inv; 7 Jun 1732.

p.180 - John DAVIS, inv; 7 Jun 1732.

p.181 - William HANKS, NFP, will; 24 Apr 1732, 7 Jun 1732
son William land and plant. I now live on containing
100 ac, if he has no heirs to Richard HANKS; son John
land and plant. whereon William ERISKEAN now lives
containing 90 ac, if he has no heirs, to go to Edward
and James HANKS; I give to William DOWNMAN 1 ac. of
land on the north side of the Briery Swamp in NFP which
land I obtained by order of court to build a mill on,
he, the sd. DOWNMAN, paying all charges that shall
arise thereon; chil. to remain and work for their
mother; wife Hester; ex: wife and son William; wits:
James NEAL, Thomas [?], Penelope [ERISKEEN]. [William
and Hester HANKS also had at least two daus. Hannah
b. 1717 and Sarah b. 1720. NFPR, p.85.]

p.182 - William HANKS, inv; 6 Sep 1732.

p.184 - Joshua SINGLETON, Lun. Par., will; 28 Dec 1732, 5 Feb 1732/33
sons Robert and Stanley all land in Pr.William Co.
lying on the branches of Occoquan; son Joshua the plant.
where I now live in Rich. Co; three sons to be kept at
school til they are perfect readers in the Holy Bible
and capable of writing a good, legibile hand and pro-
ficient in arithmatic as far as the rule of three; dau.
Sarah to have one whole year's schooling; ex: wife
Anne; requests fr. Benjamin RUST to take care of chil.
est; wits: John SPENDERGRASS, Thomas DICKENSON, Mary
THORNTON.

- Edward EIDSON, will; 24 Oct 1732, 5 Feb 1732/33
son Joseph all land I bought of Capt. SPICER known by

the name of the Old Courthouse, if he has no heirs,
land to go to son Boyse; wife Penelope; daus. Sarah,
Hannah, and Betty to receive all the money I now have
in England; dau. Sarah to receive an orphan girl named
Catharine; ex: wife and son [sic]; wits: W. JORDAN,
James WILSON, John DEANE.

p.185 - Thomas BEALE, will; 7 Sep 1732, 5 Feb 1732/33
sis. [Eleanor]; [son] and little brothers and sisters,
that is John, [Taverner], Charles, Richard, Reuben, Anne,
and Elizabeth BEALE until youngest bro., Reuben BEALE,
reaches 18; ex: bro. William and Capt. Robert TOMLIN;
wits: Joseph BELFIELD, Elizabeth TOMLIN.

p.186 - Humphry THOMAS, Lun. Par., will; 24 [Jan] 1732, 5 Feb 1732/
1733
wife Jane all real or personal est; seven chil. [not
named]; ex: wife; wits: John NEWPORT, Edward BRYANT,
Clark SHORT.

- Joshua SINGLETON, inv; 2 Apr 1733.

p.188 - Benjamin MILNER, inv; 2 Apr 1733.

p.189 - Humphry THOMAS, inv; 2 Apr 1733.

- John BRICKEY, inv; 2 Apr 1733.

p.190 - John SPENDERGRASS, will; 19 [Jan 1732/33], 2 Apr 1733
all lands to son James; dau. Mary; my will is if my
wife do marry and by that marriage my chil. should be
abused, that then my will and desire is that my fr.
Robert TOMLIN, if he pleases, do alter the same by
making use of such means as he shall think proper to
prevent such usage; ex: wife Elizabeth; wits: Robert
TOMLIN, John DOZIER. [John SPENDERGRASS mar. Elizabeth
CRIBIN, 2 Dec 1728. MRC, p.193.]

p.191 - Edward EIDSON, inv; 2 Apr 1733.

p.192 - William NASH, NFP, will; 16 Oct 1732, 2 Apr 1733
wife Anne; sons Jeremiah, William, George, and Joseph;
ex: wife; wits: Thomas LEWIS, John McKENNE, Abraham
HANCOCK.

p.193 - Thomas WHITE, NFP, will; 6 Jan 1732, 2 Apr 1733
Anne WHITTLE; Henry [KAIM], Thomas PERFIT; George
SMITHER; Abraham DALE; desires that his smith John
FAITHFUL with his smith's tools be sold; Jeremiah
GREENHAM to assist wife; John WOODBRIDGE; half of
personal est. to wife Elizabeth; rest of personal est.
to bro. John WHITE his eld. son to whom I also give
my real est. after my wife's decease; ex: wife,
John WOODBRIDGE, Jeremiah GREENHAM; wits: Caran
BRANNAN, Eleanor CHAPMAN. [A division of the est. of
Thomas WHITE between his relict, Elizabeth, and his
bro., John WHITE, of Great Britain was made in 1733.
AB1, p.63.]

p.194 - James WOODROOF, inv; 3 Apr 1733.

- Thomas NASH, NFP, will; 7 Aug 1732, 4 Jun 1733
son Thomas all land; Thomas BARBER; Charles DOBYNS;
grson. Thomas NASH; my violin to grson. William DOBYNS;
daus. Sarah DOBYNS and Anne BARBER; ex: wife and sons;

wits: Gabriel ALLOWAY, John HAMMOND.

p.195 - Thomas BEALE, inv; 4 Jun 1733.

p.197 - Thomas SOSBURY, inv; 4 Jun 1733.

- William NASH, inv; 4 Jun 1733.

p.198 - John SPENDERGRASS, inv; 4 Jun 1733.

p.199 - Edward BARROW, NFP, will; 19 Oct 1732, 4 Jun 1733
son John; daus. Margaret and Elizabeth; est. in
Virginia and England to be eq. div. among chil; ex:
fr. Nicholas MINOR Sr. and Nicholas MINOR Jr.; wits:
Humphrey POPE Jr, William BERTRAND, Susannah BERTRAND.
[Edward BARROW, the son of Edward and Anne (STONE)
BARROW, mar. Elizabeth MINOR. MRC, p.11.]

- Thomas GRIFFIN, NFP, will; 7 Sep 17[32], 4 Jun 1733
wife Elizabeth; dau. Winifred (wife of Capt. Samuel
PEACHEY); daus. Alice Corbin, Sarah, and Anne; grson.
William PEACHEY; ex: wife and son Leroy; wits: John
GARZIA, John HOBSON, Thomas BROOM. [Thomas GRIFFIN,
the son of Leroy and Winnifred GRIFFIN, was b. 20
Sep 1684. The births of the following chil. of Thomas
and Elizabeth GRIFFIN are recorded in the NFPR: Leroy
(1711), Elizabeth (1714), Sarah (1716), and Anne (1718).
NFPR, p.73.]

p.201 - Thomas WHITE, inv; 4 Jun 1733.

p.202 - Edward BARROW, inv; 2 Jul 1733.

p.204 - Henry FENN, inv; 2 Jul 1733.

p.205 - William JENNINGS Sr., Lun. Par., will; 26 May 1733, 2 Jul
1733
son William all land on which I now live bounded between
the mill path and White Marsh Branch and Charles SPOE's
line; son John all land between the mill path and spring
branch; son Willoughby; dau. Mary; son Augustine the
remainder of land and plant; wife Mary; ex: wife and
son Augustine; wits: Cyprian ANDERSON, Charles SPOE.

p.206 - Robert PALMER, NFP, will; 25 Feb 1732, 2 Jul 1733
sons Parmenas, Truman, Thomas, William, Reuben, and
George; dau. Prudence a rug now at William ERRESKIEN's
when she is 18 or marries; dau. Elizabeth WEBB; grdau.
Sarah GLASCOCK; all land to son Joseph; ex: son Joseph;
wits: Henry MISKELL, Thomas HIGHTOWER. [Robert PALMER
apparently mar. twice. By his first wife, Prudence, he
had: Elizabeth (b.1699), Esther (b.1701), and Joseph
(b.1704) and by his second wife, Martha, he had: twins
Parmenas and Prudence (b.1719), Truman (b.1721),
William (b.1723), Thomas (b.1725), and William (b.1726/
1727). Robert PALMER d. 12 Mar 1732/33. NFPR, pp.142,143.]

p.207 - Leonard DOZIER, inv; 2 Jul 1733.

- William BRYANT, inv; 2 Jul 1733.

p.208 - John BRICKEY, f.inv. by his wife Sarah BRICKEY; 2 Jul 1733.

- Thomas NASH, inv. pres. by Anne NASH ex; 2 Jul 1733. [The
inv. included a servant named John DAVIS.]

p.211 - William JENNINGS, inv; 6 Aug 1733.

p.212 - Thomas GRIFFIN, inv; 7 Aug 1733.

p.214 - Matthew BURROWS, inv; 1 Oct 1733.

p.215 - Robert PALMER, inv; 5 Nov 1733.

- John FOUSHEE, Lun.Par., will; 4 Nov 1733, 7 Jan 1733/34
  son John all land and plant.; wife Meelin; mentions
  but does not name other chil; ex: son John; wits:
  Thomas PETTY, Charles SPOE.

p.216 - William JENNINGS, Lun.Par., will; 2 Dec 1733, 7 Jan 1733/34
  wife all land and plant., after her death to go to son
  William and if he has no heirs, to go to son John; ex:
  wife Anne; wits: Margaret TAYLOR, Charles SPOE.

p.217 - John FOUSHEE, inv; 4 Feb 1733/34.

p.218 - William JENNINGS, inv; 4 Feb 1733/34.

p.219 - Edward BARROW, f.inv; [4 Feb 1733/34].

- William BROCKENBROUGH, NFP, will; 19 Apr 1730, 4 Feb 1733/34
  mother Mary DALTON; bro. Newman BROCKENBROUGH to have
  the authority of my plant; Henry MISKELL; ex: bro.
  Newman; wits: [none given].

p.220 - Job TILLERY, Farn.Par., will; 8 Jan 1733, 4 Feb 1733/34
  sis. Elizabeth TILLERY; John HAMMOND (son of Martin
  HAMMOND); no ex; wits: Rebecca HUDSON; Gabriel ALLOWAY.

- Job TILLERY, inv; 16 Feb 1733/34.

p.221 - Thomas DEW, NFP, will; 8 Jan 1733, 4 Mar 1733/34
  Hugh WILLIAMS (son of John WILLIAMS); godson Thomas
  WILLIAMS; sisters Mary LAWSON and Elizabeth SYDNOR;
  ex: Anthony SYDNOR, John LAWSON; wits: Henry MISKELL,
  William LYELL, Thomas TUNE.

- Thomas WILLIAMS, will; 24 Jul 1732, 4 Mar 1733/34
  Mary SHORT my plant. commonly called the Settle Plant.
  on the fork of the [Herening] Creek; Thomas WILLIAMS;
  wife Winifred; ex: wife; wits: John FOUSHEE, Winifred
  WEBSTER, Winifred FOUSHEE. [Thomas WILLIAMS mar. Winifred
  PYCRAFT, wid., 8 Jun 1732. MRC, p.232. In Aug 1734,
  Winifred WILLIAMS deeded property to her grchil. James
  and Elizabeth FOUSHEE (chil. of John and Winifred
  FOUSHEE). AB1, p.74.]

p.222 - William BROCKENBROUGH, inv; 4 Mar 1733/34.

p.223 - Thomas WILLIAMS, inv; 1 Apr 1734.

p.225 - Robert MATHIS, NFP, will; 25 [?] 1734, 1 Apr 1734
  sons Newman, Griffin, Robert, and William all land in
  Prince William Co; wife Sarah; ex: wife and James
  OLDHAM; wits: Richard SEEBREE, Thomas VANLANDINGHAM.

- Thomas DEW, inv; 1 Apr 1734.

p.227 - William BAILEY, f.inv; 1 Apr 1734.

- Peter DUDLEY, inv; 1 Apr 1734 [This inv., signed by Joyce
DUDLEY, included a servant woman named Christian
FORMAN and a servant girl named Sarah JOHNSON.]

p.229 - Robert MATTHEWS, inv; 6 May 1734.

p.231 - Michael BURROES, inv; 6 May 1734.

p.232 - Thomas ASBURY, will; 24 Mar 1733/34, 6 May 1734
son Henry all the plant. where Nicholas STEVENS lives
and the plant. next to it, also the mill at Nomini; if
he has no heirs, to son Thomas, and, if he has no heirs,
to son Walker; son Thomas the plant. whereon he now
lives; son Walker 100 ac. at [Elletick] Run in Prince
William Co, it being one moiety of 200 ac., also half
my land in Appomatox; dau. Elizabeth remainder of land
in West. Co. and 75 ac. at [Elletick] Run in Prince
William Co., if she has no heirs, to dau. Mary; dau.
Mary all plant. and land where Mary HOPWOOD now lives
near Garner's Mill in West. Co., if she has no heirs,
to dau. Elizabeth; Ursley SAUNDERS 50 ac. in Prince
William Co; wife Anne; ex: wife and son Henry; wits:
John BARNETT, William JOHNSON, John WRIGHT.

p.233 - George NEWMAN, Lun.Par., will; 4 Mar 1733, 6 May 1734
bro. John NEWMAN; godson George NEWMAN (son of John
NEWMAN); d-i-l Patience FORD all her mother's wearing
clothes; ex: John FORD; wits: Avery DYE, Mary LONG,
Elizabeth WELSH.

p.234 - Thomas ASBURY, inv. pres. by Anne and Henry ASBURY; 3 Jun
1734.

p.235 - George NEWMAN, inv; 27 May 1734.

p.236 - Arthur McMAHAN, inv; 3 Jun 1734.

p.237 - Anne JENNINGS, Lun.Par., will; [28 May 1734], 3 Jun 1734
sons Edward, William, John, and Calathan; dau. Martha;
ex: Augustine JENNINGS bro. to dec'd husb; wits: Thomas
JACOBS, Richard [HEKS].

- ASBURY's f.inv; 1 Jul 1734.

- Anne JENNINGS, inv; 1 Jul 1734.

p.238 - Abraham GOAD, will; 7 Mar 1733, 1 Jul 1734
grson. William (son of William GOAD dec'd) the plant.
where Mary GOAD now lives; son John and his wife all
the land above the north fork of the Briery Swamp;
son Abraham all the land on the south side of my spring
branch, if he has no heirs, to son Peter; [son] Peter
land on the north side of spring branch, if he has no
heirs to son Abraham; son William; daus. Hannah PHILLIPS,
Elizabeth DODSON, and Alice DODSON; wife Catharine; ex:
son John; wits: Elizabeth LAWSON, Winifred MISKELL,
Henry MISKELL.

p.239 - Anne SINGLETON, Lun.Par., nunc.will;9 Apr 1734, 1 Jul 1734
est. and chil. to the care and management of fr. Benj.
RUST and that he let them remain on my plant. and em-
ploy my cousin, Mary THORNTON, to look after them;
wits: Henry WEBSTER, Mary THORNTON, Mary Ann WEBSTER.

p.241 - Abraham GOAD, inv. pres. by John GOAD; 5 Aug 1734.

- Anne SINGLETON, inv; 5 Aug 1734.

p.242 - Thomas HAMMOND, inv; 5 Aug 1734.

- James BRYANT, will; 3 Jun 1734, 2 Sep 1734
    eld. dau. Margaret NASH; dau. Mary NASH; son John; wife
    Mary; no ex; wits: Edward TOLBURT, Ruth JONES.

p.243 - Anne COOK, inv; 2 Sep 1734.

p.245 - James BRYANT, inv; 4 Nov 1734.

- Anne COOK, f.inv; 4 Nov 1734.

p.246 - Robert MATHEWS, f.inv; 4 Nov 1734.

- James SUGGITT, inv; 2 Dec 1734.

p.247 - Peter OLDHAM, inv; 6 Jan 1734/35.

p.249 - Anne SINGLETON, f.inv; 6 Jan 1734/35.

- Thomas JENNINGS, inv; 3 Feb 1734/35.

- Mary DALTON, NFP, will; 18 Sep 1734, 3 Feb 1734/35
    dau. Mary (the wife of Jonathan LYELL) the plant. where-
    on they now live; grson. Marmaduke STANDFIELD 100 ac.
    which his father Thomas STANDFIELD formerly agreed with
    me for; dau. Winifred (the wife of Henry MISKELL) the
    plant. where they now live; no ex; wits: John WILLIAMS
    Jr, Metcalf DICKENSON, Elizabeth CONWAY.

p.250 - John WADE, Farn.Par., will; 4 Feb 1734, 3 Feb 1734/35
    son John my land and plant., if he has no heirs, to
    son Joseph, if he has no heirs, to dau. Frances; wife
    Jean; other dau. [not named]; ex: wife; wits: John
    BRYAN, Joseph SANDERS, Richard WOOLLARD.

p.251 - Martin HAMMOND, inv. pres. by George HAMMOND the adm; 3
    Mar 1734/35.

p.252 - John WADE, inv; 3 Mar 1734/35.

- George DAVENPORT, NFP, will; 22 Sep 1734, 3 Mar 1734/35
    s-i-l John TILLERY and Margaret his wife 150 ac. of
    land, after their deaths, plant. to go to grson. George
    TILLERY; remaining land to grson. William STONUM;
    grdau. Winifred RICE; Sarah MITCHEL (dau. of Robert
    MITCHEL); wife Ruth; no ex; wits: Robert MITCHEL, John
    STONUM, Daniel SCURLOCK. [George DAVENPORT was the
    son of John and Margaret DAVENPORT of Lanc. Co. WLC,
    p.64.]

p.253 - Mr. William BAKER, inv; 3 Mar 1734/35.

p.255 - ASBURY's f.inv; 7 Apr 1735.

- George DAVENPORT, inv; 7 Apr 1735.

p.257 - William WOODCOCK, inv; 7 Apr 1735.

- Thomas JENNINGS, f.inv; 7 Apr 1735.

74

         - Thomas CLAYTON, inv; 7 Apr 1735.

p.258 - Thomas DURHAM, Farn.Par., will; 30 Nov 1734, 5 May 1735
            wife Mary; Dominick NEWGENT and Margaret his wife;
            son Joseph; six small chil. Thomas, John, Mary, Susanna,
            Catharine, and Millicent; dau. Sarah; Jeremiah GREEN-
            HAM to have the use of the land and plant. whereon he
            now lives during his natural life; ex: wife and Jere-
            miah GREENHAM; wits: Elizabeth HALE, William HUGHS,
            William WALKER. [Thomas DURHAM was the son of Thomas
            and Dorothy DURHAM; he mar. Mary SMOOT ca. 1710. MRC,
            p.61. Jeremiah GREENHAM was apparently his step-
            father. MRC, p.81.]

p.260 - Thomas DURHAM, inv; 3 Jun 1735.

p.261 - Alvin MOTHERSHEAD, Lun.Par., will; 3 Jan 1734/35, 3 Jun 1735
            godson George MORTON (son of William MORTON) all land
            which I bought of Thomas SIMS, John DOYLE, and James
            DOYLE containing 360 ac, if he has no heirs, to go to
            his bro. Jeremiah MORTON; John MORTON (son of William
            MORTON) all the land I bought of William MORTON his
            sd. father, if he has no heirs, to his sis. Sarah
            MORTON; Elijah MORTON (son of William MORTON); Anne,
            Elizabeth, and Jane (daus. of William MORTON); bro.
            John MOTHERSHEAD and fr. William MORTON; wits: William
            JORDAN, Arjalon PRICE, Matthew KNIGHT. [Alvin MOTHERS-
            HEAD was a son of John and Elizabeth MOTHERSHEAD of
            West. Co. WWC, p.93.]

p.262 - Thomas DRAPER, inv; 7 Jul 1735.

p.264 - Alvin MOTHERSHEAD, inv; 7 Jul 1735.

p.265 - Peter OLDHAM, inv; 4 Aug 1735.

p.267 - Philip HARRIS, will; 27 Jan 1734/35, 6 Oct 1735
            son John all the land that belongs to me; eld. dau.
            Sarah DODSON; dau. Anne TUNE; son William my gun when
            he is 21; wife Anne; daus. Betty, Winifred, and Mary;
            ex: son John and wife; wits: William EFFORD, Richard
            BROWN, Edward ALLGOOD.

p.268 - Philip HARRIS, inv; 3 Nov 1735.

p.269 - Robert MATHEWS, f.inv; 3 Nov 1735.

         - William MARKES, [Lun.Par.,] will; 4 Aug 1735, 3 Nov 1735
            daus. Anne MARKES, Frances MARKES, and Elizabeth DEANE;
            sons John and Elias; ex: fr. Elias [FENNEL] and John
            DEANE; wits: William DICKSON, Edmund HAZLE, Creighton
            DAVIS.

p.270 - William MARKES, inv; 1 Dec 1735.

p.272 - Robert DAVIS, Lun.Par., will; 14 Nov 1735, 2 Feb 1735/36
            daus. Jane, Elizabeth, and Winifred; wife Susanna; son
            Robert; ex: wife; wits: John DOZIER, Gabriel ALLOWAY,
            Richard BRAMHAM. [Robert DAVIS, a son of William and
            Elizabeth DAVIS, mar. Susanna JACOBUS. His wid. mar.
            (2) John DOZIER. MRC, p.51. See also: AB1, p.102.]

         - Samuel BARBER, Lun.Par., will; 20 Dec 1735, 2 Feb 1735/36
            wife land where I now live near Totuskey Creek opposite
            the house where Mr. William COLSTON lives; son Samuel

land where his grfath., Samuel BAILEY, lived after
wife's death; three sisters [unnamed]; son John land
where father lived; ex: wife, Gilbert METCALFE, and
Mrs. Susan METCALFE; wits: Thomas [BERBER], Thomas
NASH, Archibald MITCHELL. [Samuel BARBER mar. Anne
FOSTER, 30 Nov 1727. He was the son of Capt. William
BARBER and Joyce (BAILEY). Gilbert METCALFE was the
stepfather of Anne (FOSTER) BARBER. MRC, p.9.]

p.273 - Robert DAVIS, inv; 5 Apr 1736.

p.274 - Stanley GOWER, NFP, will; 27 Oct 1732, 5 Apr 1736
son John 100 ac. at the head of the tract of land
whereon I now dwell, including the 40 ac. I purchased
of Capt. Robert TOMLIN; dau. Catharine GOWER tract of
land near Totuskey Ferry which I had in exchange with
Mr. Joshua SINGLETON for that where he now lives; dau.
Frances SISSON tract of land formerly taken up by my
father in Essex Co. on Hoskins Creek; son Stanley the
plant. whereon I now dwell; dau. Anne SINGLETON; ex:
fr. Robert TOMLIN and s-i-l Joshua SINGLETON; wits:
Samuel BARBER, John DOZIER, Nathaniel THRIFT.

p.276 - Nathaniel THRIFT, Lun.Par., will; 21 Feb 1735/36, 5 Apr
1736
son Job all land after the death of my wife Elizabeth,
if he has no heirs, to son John, if he has no heirs,
to son Charles, if he has no heirs, to son Jeremiah,
and, if he has no heirs, to son George; ex: wife and
son Job; wits: Robert TOMLIN, John DOZIER.

      - John WARRENER (=WARNER), Lun.Par., will; 10 Dec 1735, 5
Apr 1736
whole est. to be eq. div. among my cousins Jacob,
Richard, John, William, James, Mary, and Henrietta
SUTTON; est. to be in the hands of wife Mary during
her natural life; ex: bros. Richard SUTTON and Jacob
SUTTON; wits: John DEANE, Thomas [BRADNER], Robert
[HINSON].

p.277 - John BAILEY, inv; 3 May 1736.

p.278 - John WARNER, inv; 3 May 1736.

p.279 - Thomas MATTHEWS, inv; 3 May 1736.

p.280 - Nathaniel THRIFT, inv; 3 May 1736.

p.281 - William KING, NFP, will; 15 Jan [1735], 3 May 1736
James WILSON; grson. William MITCHELL; grdau. Frances
MITCHELL; dau. Mary MITCHELL; wife Mary; ex: s-i-l
John MITCHELL; wits: Henry MISKELL, Thomas SCURLOCK.

      - William KING, inv; 7 Jun 1736.

p.282 - Mary GOAD, inv; 7 Jun 1736.

p.283 - Stanley GOWER, inv; 7 Jun 1736.

p.284 - John OGLEBY, inv; 7 Jun 1736.

p.285 - John WRIGHT, inv; 7 Jun 1736.

p.286 - Richard EVANS, inv; 5 Jul 1736.

76

p.287 - Samuel BARBER, inv; 5 Jul 1736. [includes a smith named
        James JARVIS and his tools.]

p.291 - KING's f.inv; 5 Jul 1736.

      - Samuel STEEL, inv; 2 Aug 1736.

p.292 - Samuel SAMFORD, will; 13 Dec 1735, 4 Oct 1736
        sons Thomas, James, William, and John; son Samuel land
        I bought of Richard KING; dau. Elizabeth BOGUS;
        Winifred WEBB; ex: Samuel SAMFORD; wits: John Spann
        WEBB, Isaac WEBB. [Samuel SAMFORD mar. (1) Elizabeth
        KEENE ca. 1687 and (2) Isabella LANGHEE, 1707. MRC,
        p. 177.]

p.293 - Samuel SAMFORD, inv; 1 Nov 1736.

      - Anne BECKHAM, Lun.Par., will; 22 Oct 1736, 6 Dec 1736
        son George Tomlin; dau. Hannah Anne; chil. left in the
        care of William SMITH and William BRUCE, the boy to be
        kept to his learning until he has attained perfect
        vulgar arithmatic and such branches of the mathematics
        as is most taking to him and further my daughter's
        education to be this to learn to read, write, and
        cipher and the use of the needle; ex: William BRUCE
        and William SMITH; wits: Francis WILLIAMS, Thomas
        BRADNER.

p.295 - Samuel SAMFORD, f.inv; 6 Dec 1736.

      - Edward BRYAN, Lun.Par., will; 12 Oct 1736, 3 Jan 1736/37
        sons Jeremiah, Thomas, and John; wife Mary half of
        land and a white boy named John DAILEY; mentions white
        boy named Edward DRYAS and a servant named Sarah HUDSON;
        son John to stay with wife until he is of age, if wife
        dies before he comes of age, Christopher PRIDHAM to
        take son to his est; ex: wife; wits: Joseph RUSSELL Jr;
        John JACKSON, Susannah JACKSON.

p.296 - William WALKER, inv; 3 Jan 1736/37.

p.297 - Anne BIRKHAM, inv; 3 Jan 1736/37. [included a servant
        named Mary FOLLON.]

p.299 - John TARPLEY Jr. Gent., inv; 7 Feb 1736/37. [included a
        servant named Appleby SEARL,]

p.301 - Edward BRYAN, inv; 7 Feb 1736/37.

p.302 - Anne RAYNOLDS, will; 18 Apr 1735, 7 Mar 1736/37
        grson. Thomas HUTCHINSON; grdau. Susannah LONGWORTH;
        son Andrew HUTCHINSON; s-i-l John DEBORD; William
        COWARD may take his dau. that is bound to me; no ex;
        wits: Robert GWILLAM, Robert SMITH, John ALDERSON.

p.303 - Henry WILSON, Lun.Par., will; 28 Feb 1736/37, 4 Apr 1737
        wife Winifred; son John the plant. whereon I now live
        and all the land, 200 ac; son Elias the plant. whereon
        he now lives with 100 ac; son Henry 100 ac of land
        adjoining the land bequeathed to son Elias; son George
        100 ac. of land adjoining the land bequeathed to son
        Henry; son Thomas 100 ac. of land adjoining the land
        bequeathed to son George; son George to be bound after
        next Christmas as an apprentice to learn the trade of
        a joiner; dau. Susan; s-i-l Alexander KELLY; s-i-l

Edward EIDSON to receive servant named Richard MOSS
that I bought this year; s-i-l John DOZIER to receive
servant named Richard WIGMORE; ex: son John; wits:
William JORDAN, James WILSON.

p.304 - Anne RAYNOLDS, inv; 4 Apr 1737.

p.305 - Henry HARFORD, Lun.Par., will; 30 Oct 1736, 4 Apr 1737
son John land I hold on the north side of the swamp;
sons Henry, Thomas, William lands on the south side
of the swamp; ex: wife; wits: William GARLAND Jr.,
Arch. MITCHELL, Steven GUPTON.

  - Charles NEAL, inv; 4 Apr 1737.

p.306 - Stephen LUCAS, inv; 4 Apr 1737.

  - George HILL, inv. pres. by Jane HILL adm; 4 Apr 1737.

p.307 - Anne BECKHAM, f.inv; 4 Apr 1737.

  - Gilbert METCALFE, will; 21 Jul 1736, 4 Apr 1737
wife Susanna dwelling plant. and 300 ac. binding upon
Mr. BEALE's and HAMILTON's line and my mill branch
taking in John HOW's plant; sis. Jane METCALFE;
nephew Lindsie OPIE to receive servant named George
VAUGHN; niece Susanna KENNER; godsons Moore (the son
of Maj. Moore FAUNTLEROY) and William (the son of
William FAUNTLEROY); ex: wife and Lindsie OPIE; wits:
John TAYLOE, John TAYLOE Jr, Charles [PHILLYOUNG].
[Gilbert METCALFE was the son of Richard and Elizabeth
METCALFE; he mar. Susanna (CAMMACK) FOSTER by 1716.
MRC, p.131.]

p.308 - Charles NEAL, f.inv; [2 May 1737].

  - Henry WILSON, inv; 2 May 1737.

p.312 - John YEATMAN, inv; 2 May 1737. [includes servant named
Richard WOOD.] [John YEATMAN mar. Hannah LEWIS. MRC,
p.237.]

p.314 - Samuel COOK, Lun.Par., will; 22 Nov 1737, 2 May 1737
bros.-in-law Simon GRANTER and John GORDING; ex: John
GORDING; wits: J.W. BELFIELD, Christopher COLLINS,
Richard KILLBOURN.

p.315 - Hendrie HEARTFORD, inv; 2 May 1737.

  - [Malachi] DUNAWAY, inv; 6 Jun 1737. [Malachi DUNAWAY mar.
Elizabeth NELL 23 Jan 1726/27. MRC, p.61.]

p.316 - William GRADY, inv; 6 Jun 1737.

p.317 - Samuel COOK, inv; 6 Jun 1737.

  - LUCAS' f.inv; 1 Aug 1737.

  - WYATT's inv; 1 Aug 1737.

p.318 - Gilbert METCALFE, inv; 1 Aug 1737.

p.319 - Anne WELDEN, inv. pres. by Nicholas MINOR adm; 3 Oct 1737.

78

p.320 - Edmond HAZELL, will; 18 Jun 1737, 3 Oct 1737
godson John DEAN all lands in Rich. Co. and 400 ac.
in Orange Co; John FAUNTLEROY; goddau. Mary LONG;
Winifred and Frances DAVIS; Thomas DUNTON, blacksmith
and servant to me, if he serves my ex. to the term of
five years from the time I first bought him...he shall
have all my blacksmith tools excepting the great vise;
ex: John DEAN; wits: William FAUNTLEROY Gent; Mary
AUSTIN, Jane [CROWLER].

p.321 - John WRIGHT, nunc. will; pres. in court by Mary AUSTIN,
3 Oct 1737
John WRIGHT gave all his clothes to one of his ship-
mates named Peter DEACON and what wages he had due
to him from the ship "Greyhound" and 20 shillings
which some of the men owes him, he gave to Mary AUSTIN.

    - Edmond HAZELL, inv; 7 Nov 1737.

p.323 - Robert THORNTON, inv; 16 Mar 1737/38.

p.324 - James O'NEAL, inv; 1 May 1738.

    - Fortunatus DODSON, inv; 5 Jun 1738. [Fortunatus DODSON
      mar. Ellis GOAD, 9 Sep 1726. MRC, p.56.]

p.325 - Joseph BELFIELD, Lun.Par., will; 16 Jul 1736, 5 Jun 1738
son Thomas Wright; wife Elizabeth; son Joseph half of
est, if he dies before age or marriage, his est. to
go to grchil. [unnamed]; ex: wife and son Joseph; wits:
Thomas DOZIER, Richard DOZIER Jr, Sarah DOZIER.
[Joseph BELFIELD mar. (1) Frances WRIGHT ca. 1704,
(2) Mary (LANE) WILSON, 1707, and (3) Elizabeth
DOZIER. MRC, p.15.]

p.326 - Winifred WILSON, inv; 5 Jun 1738.

p.327 - William NASH, inv; 5 Jun 1738.

    - Joseph BELFIELD, inv; 3 Jul 1738.

p.329 - James WILSON, Lun.Par., will; 31 Jul 1738, 3 Oct 1738
wife Martha the plant. whereon I now live and the land
belonging to it, that is all the land which I bought
of Hannah PORT to be added thereto out of the land
which I bought of Joseph MORTON near [Chonomun] Swamp
also the land which I bought of John WELLS, at her
death, land to go to son James, if he has no heirs,
then to sons Elias and Morton; wife also to receive
a tract of land bounded by the main road, the road
leading to West. Co., and the lines formerly belonging to BRADLEY's and JEFFEREY's land containing 25
ac., after her death, land to go to daus. Marth[a]
and Elizabeth Mountjoy (both are under 21); tract of
land devised to me by my father in his will containing 250 ac. and adjoining the lands of William DIXON
and Joseph BRUCE to go to son Elias; son William all
land bought of Joseph MORTON, if he has no heirs, to
go to son Morton; son Morton all land I bought of
William CRASK, if he has no heirs, to go to son
William; all part of lands formerly belonging to my
two dec'd bros. Elias and John WILSON to my two daus.
Martha and Elizabeth Mountjoy WILSON; fr. William
JORDAN to be guardian to son William until he is 21;

ex: wife and sons Elias and James; wits: William
JORDAN, Alvin MOUNTJOY, Robert SOMERVILL

p.331 - James WILSON, inv; 6 Nov 1738.

p.335 - James RONEY, inv; 5 Feb 1738/39.

- Charles NICHOLDS, 2 Apr 1739.

p.336 - Christopher PRIDHAM, will; 24 Jan 1738/39, 2 Apr 1739
wife Elizabeth and dau. Sarah (under 16) all land;
mother Mary BRYAN; ex: wife; wits: John RAYNOLDS,
William WALKER.

p.337 - Christopher PRIDHAM, inv; 7 May 1739.

p.338 - John TARPLEY, NFP, 23 Nov 1738, 7 May 1739
wife Anne; youngest grson. John TARPLEY plant. whereon
I now dwell, if he has no heirs, then to grson. James
TARPLEY; grson. Travers TARPLEY my mill called the New
Mill standing on Constable's Run at the head of Farnham
Creek; eld. dau. of grson. Travers TARPLEY, Betty;
grson. [Fortius] Quintus TARPLEY; wife to live in my
dwelling house with my grson. John during her widowhood or otherwise if she should think fit, she should
have my plant. at the head of Moratico which I bought
of Mr. LAWSON; desires est. to be div. by Col. Charles
GRIMES and Capt. Leroy GRIFFIN; ex: grsons. Travers
and John TARPLEY; wits: Thomas BLUETT, Eleanor BLUETT,
Rebecca CLOSINGTON. [John TARPLEY mar. Anne GLASCOCK,
Jan 1712/13. MRC, p.204. Anne TARPLEY relinquished
her legacy in this will, 7 May 1739. AB 1, pp. 134,146.]

p.339 - Eli READ, Lun.Par., will; 28 Oct 1739, 5 Nov 1739
all est. to wife Mary; ex: wife; wits: Elizabeth SUTTLE,
Sarah WINDER, Jonathan BECKWITH. [Eli READ mar. Mary
RANDALL, 20 Aug 1729. MRC, p.167.]

p.340 - Elias FENNIEL, will; 26 Oct 1739, 7 Jan 1739/40
wife Penolopha all lands on this side of the main road
whereon I now live and all that land on that side of
the coach road joining to Richard BARNES; rest of land
to John MARKS, if he has no heirs, to Anne DOZIER and
Frances THORNTON; Francis DAVIS a young grey mare now
in Mulberry Island; Boyce EIDSON; servant David MAN;
ex: wife; wits: Richard BARNES, William BROCKENBROUGH,
David TIVINDALE.

p.341 - Eli READ, inv; 7 Jan 1739.

- Edward JONES, memorandum
On 2 Sep 1739, Mr. Edward JONES of NFP, being near his
death at his own house, said in the presence of the
witnesses who were called as evidence thereto did speak
these words, that is to say, that he had sometime before
made a will, but desired it should not stand because he
had sold lands and a negro out since the making thereof
and that would breed confusion and after desired his
wife and chil. should live peaceably together and each
of them to have an equal share of his lands and living
(that he had seven negros and six chil. and a mother)
and if, please God, the negroes lived and did well,
there would be each of them one. In testimony whereof
...5 Sep 1739, /s/ Anna SPICER

Pres. in court by Isaac JONES and prov. by Isaac JONES,
Edward JONES, and Anna SPICER; 7 Jan 1739/40. [Edward
JONES Jr. mar. Margaret WHITE (possibly nee OVERTON,
the wid. of William WHITE) in Dec 1714. MRC, pp.107,
230. The births of the foll. chil. are recorded in
the NFPR: Isaac (1715), Edward (1717), Elizabeth
(1720); Margaret JONES d. 16 Dec 1722. NFPR, pp.106-07.]

p.342 - Elias FENNEL, inv; 3 Mar 1739/40. [Includes servants David
MAN, shoemaker, Philip THOMAS, and William WOODBERN.]

p.344 - John RAWLINS, inv; 3 Mar 1739/40.

   - Edmund NORTHEN, inv; 3 Mar 1739/40.

p.345 - Richard BRAMHAM, Lun.Par., will; 12 Dec 1739, 3 Mar 1739/40
[portion of page mutilated] wife Alice; son John to
receive plant. and land on which I now dwell; son
Benjamin the forest plant; dau. Eleanor; ex: wife;
wits: Robert DAVIS, [Sus]anna DOZIER, John DOZIER.

p.346 - [portion of page mutilated]

   - Moore FAUNTLEROY, Lun.Par., will; 10 Apr 1739, 3 Mar 1739/
1740
wife Margaret; son Moore the manor plant. whereon I
now live; dau. Elizabeth BROCKENBROUGH's son William
Fauntleroy BROCKENBROUGH and his heirs bearing the name
of FAUNTLEROY; daus. Catharine, Mary, and Sarah Griffin;
360 ac. in Lun.Par. bought of John HARFORD to be eq.
div. among three daus; dau. Margaret to receive tract
of land whereon Samuel CUMMINGS lives also the lands
bought of David CAVENDER and Thomas WILLIAMS and Francis
SUTTLE and Stephen WELLS; dau. Judith; sis. Elizabeth
TAYLOE; bros. Griffin and William; wife to receive the
chariot and horses; son Moore to receive the silver
tankard with the coat of arms on it; ex: b-i-l John
TAYLOE Esq., Paul MICOU, and John MICOU; wits: John
DEAN, Ambrose ARMSTRONG, Samuel CUMMINGS. [Maj. Moore
FAUNTLEROY mar. Margaret MICOU ca. 1715. MRC, p.68.
Margaret relinquished her legacy in the above will, 3
Mar 1739/40. AB 1, p.147.]

p.348 - Elizabeth JENKINS, Lun.Par., will; 28 Jun 1736, 3 Mar 1739/
1740
sons John, Mansfield, and James all land, 150 ac; son
Herman; daus. Elizabeth, Sarah STORY, and Mary CARPENTER;
grson. Edward DAVIS; ex: sons John, Mansfield, and James;
wits: William JORDAN, John WRIGHT, William McDONALD.
[Elizabeth JENKINS was the wid. of William JENKINS who
d. in 1720. She was the dau. of Herman SKELDERMAN. MRC,
pp. 104-105.]

p.349 - Edward JONES, inv. pres. by Isaac JONES an adm; 3 Mar 1739/
1740.

p.351 - Richard BRAMHAM, inv; 7 Apr 1740. [Included a servant named
Anne HARDEN.]

p.353 - Elizabeth JENKINS, inv; 7 Apr 1740.

p.354 - Tobias PHILLIPS, will; 19 Sep 1739, 7 Apr 1740
son George; daus. Elizabeth, Hannah, Frances DALE;
William DALE the younger; wife Hannah the use of my
servants Joseph [PECTON] and Thomas LAWRENCE; son

George to pay Thomas LAWRENCE 500 lbs. of tobacco for his freedom dues; the care of son George's est. and his tuition shall be to my ex; ex: wife and William GLASCOCK; wits: Godfrey WILCOCKS, William FORRESTER, Mary HOWARD.

- Thomas RAWLINS, inv; 7 Apr 1740.

p.355 - Thomas GLASCOCK, will; 16 Feb 1739/40, 7 Apr 1740 mother Million GLASCOCK all est; ex: bros. William and George; wits: Robert DOWNMAN, John GLASCOCK, Joseph PALMER.

p.356 - Maj. Moore FAUNTLEROY, inv; 7 Apr 1740.

p.361 - Thomas GLASCOCK, inv; 5 May 1740.

- Tobias PHILLIPS, inv; 5 May 1740.

p.363 - James OLDHAM, will; 12 Apr 1740, 5 May 1740 son John piece of land in North.Co; son James land in Rich. Co; daus. Mary Anne and Jude; ex: wife [Juney] and son John; wits: George OLDHAM, Moses OLDHAM.

p.364 - Edmund NORTHEN, f.inv; 5 May 1740.

- John BONIVAL, NFP, will; 17 Apr 1740, 2 Jun 1740 all est. to dau. Anne; ex: fr. Henry MISKELL; wits: John WOODBRIDGE, Elizabeth BRYANT, William DENTON. [Anne BONEWALL, dau. to John and Elizabeth, was b. in 1724, NFPR, p.17.]

p.365 - James OLDHAM, inv. pres. by Junepet OLDHAM and John OLDHAM ex; 2 Jun 1740.

p.366 - Thomas GEFFERYS, NFP, will; 10 May 1734, 7 Jul 1740 wife Mary the plant. whereon I now live; daus. Elizabeth, Winifred, Easter, Margaret, Anne, Mary, and Priscilla; sons William and Thomas; ex: wife; wits: Henry MISKELL, William OSGRIFFIN. [Thomas GEFFERYS mar. twice; by his first wife, Elizabeth, he had Betty (b.1710), Winnifred (b.1712), Hester (b.1714), and William (b.1716). By his second wife, Mary, he had Margaret,(b.1722), Anne (b.1724), Thomas (b. ?), Mary (b. ?), Priscilla (b.1732), and Travers (b.1735). NFPR, p.67, AB 1, p.166.]

p.367 - John BONIVAL, inv; 7 Jul 1740.

p.368 - James PALMER, will; 15 Oct 1736, 7 Jul 1740 Moses DAWKINS...if he lives, to have schooling; William ALLGOOD all land, if he has no heirs, to George BROWN; ex: William ALLGOOD; wits: Henry OLLARD, Edward ALLGOOD, William HARDING.

- James PALMER, inv; 4 Aug 1740.

p.369 - Thomas GEFFERYS, inv; 4 Aug 1740.

p.370 - Abraham DALE, inv; 4 Aug 1740. [Abraham and Winifred DALE had the foll. chil: Rubin (b.1721), Abraham (b.1724), Isaac (b.1727), Robert (b.1730 ?), and Thomas (b.1730). NFPR, pp.37-38.]

p.371 - Andrew MURROW, Lun.Par., will; [?], 4 Aug 1740
        wife Deborah; chil. Mary, Anne, John, William,
        Jeremiah, and Sarah; ex: wife; good fr. John BRAMHAM
        to aid wife; wits: Thomas LEWIS, Alec. BRAMHAM.
        [Andrew MURROW, bricklayer, mar. Deborah SHERLOCK,
        11 Oct 1728. MRC, p.138.]

    -- Andrew MURROW, inv; 1 Sep 1740.

p.372 - Richard BRAMHAM, f.inv; [6] Oct 1740.

    - Charles SPOE, will; 29 Sep 1740, [6] Oct 1740
        I give the service due to me from William HAYS to
        William GOGGANS til he arrives at the age of 21, the
        sd. GOGGANS clearing my est. of everything due to me;
        all land and personal est. to son Charles, if he has
        no heirs, then to George the son of William GOGGANS;
        desires son to serve Thomas TURNER until he is 21;
        ex: fr. Thomas TURNER, William GOGGANS, and Richard
        JONES; wits: Joseph AMBROSE, William BOYD, Sarah BOYD.

p.373 - Charles SPOE, inv; 3 Nov 1740.

p.375 - William SCURLOCK, inv; 3 Nov 1740.

    - John STEWARD, nunc.will; 4 Nov 1740
        Mary SMITH...saith that sometime in the month of
        Aug 1740, John STEWARD, dec'd, upon going at that
        time to work at Mr. Leroy GRIFFIN's, told Mr. Thomas
        SAMFORD in this deponent's hearing that if he should
        die before he came back that William SMITH should
        have all his wearing apparel and that he gave all the
        rest of his est...unto Mary SAMFORD the dau. of
        Thomas SAMFORD.

p.376 - Richard CROUCHER, NFP, will; [nd.], 2 Mar 1740/41
        son William all land at Charles' Beaverdam, if he has
        no heirs, to dau. Catharine; wife; ex: wife and
        Billington McCARTY; wits: Billington McCARTY, Sarah
        [BOTON].

p.377 - John BRUCE, inv; 2 Mar 1740/41.

p.378 - Christopher PETTY, NFP, will; 1 Feb 1739/40, 2 Mar 1740/41
        s-i-l Alexander NELSON; grsons. George and Joseph
        NELSON; grdaus. Mary Anne and Margaret NELSON; Will-
        oughby PETTY; wife Mary; son Joseph; ex: son; wits:
        William EVERETT, James BOOTH. [Alexander NELSON mar.
        Prudence, the dau. of Christopher PETTY, 8 Jan 1729/
        1730. MRC, p.145.]

    - Thomas DODSON, NFP, will; 17 Feb 1739/40, 2 Mar 1740/41
        wife Mary; sons Thomas, George 150 ac. of land whereon
        he now lives, Greenham the tract of land bought of
        Lambarth DODSON, Elisha the plant. where I now live,
        Abraham, and Joshua; daus. Alice, Mary OLDHAM; grdau.
        [unnamed] the dau. of David DODSON; ex: wife and son
        Greenham; wits: Henry MISKELL, John HIGHTOWER, Charles
        DODSON. [Thomas DODSON mar. Mary DURHAM. MRC, p.57.]

p.380 - Thomas DODSON, inv; 6 Apr 1741.

p.381 - Christopher PETTY, inv; 6 Apr 1741.

p.382 - Catharine STEEL, inv; 6 Apr 1741.

p.383 - Owin JONES, inv; 6 Apr 1741. [Owin JONES mar. Jane
        WILKERSON, 19 Jan 1730. MRC, p.109.]

      - John SPENDERGRASS, f.inv; 6 Apr 1741.

      - Richard CROUCHER, inv; 4 May 1741.

p.384 - Henry MEDFORD, inv; 4 May 1741.

p.385 - Gabriel PACKETT, inv; 1 Jun 1741. [Gabriel and Kathrine
        PACKETT had at least two daus., Mary (b.1727) and
        Kathrine (b.1730). NFPR, p.142.]

p.386 - Christopher PETTY, f.inv; 6 Jul 1741.

      - Elizabeth KING, NFP, will; 21 Dec 1739, 6 Jul 1741
        sons Edward MORRIS and William ELDER; daus. Mary
        MORRIS and Elizabeth; ex: William ELDER and Mary
        MORRIS; wits: John MILLNER, Richard MEEKS, Luke
        MILLNER.

p.387 - Thomas DODSON, f.inv; 3 Aug 1741.

      - Elizabeth KING, inv; 3 Aug 1741.

p.388 - William DOWNMAN, will; 15 Feb 1738/39, 3 Aug 1741
        son Robert the plant. whereon I now live including all
        the land on this side of the branch of Col. GRIMES'
        mill; son James all land in Farnham Neck; son William
        all land in the fork of Totuskey; son Travers land
        lately purchased of John WHITE; son Rawleigh land
        purchased of James ROBINSON in Prince William Co;
        son Jabes land purchased of Robert BATES in Prince
        William Co; dau. Elizabeth; ex: Maj. James BALL and
        Jesse BALL; wits: William GLASCOCK, John GLASCOCK,
        Winifred GEFFREYS.

p.389 - William THORNTON, inv; 5 Oct 1741.

p.390 - John TAYLOR, inv. pres. by Hannah TAYLOR adm; 5 Oct 1741.
        [John and Hannah TAYLOR had the foll. chil: Simon
        (b.1728), Elizabeth (b.1731), Harrison (b.1735), and
        Richard (b.1738). NFPR, pp.182-183; AB 1, p.177.]

p.391 - William DOWNMAN, inv; 2 Nov 1741.

p.393 - John STEWARD, inv. pres. by Thomas STEWARD adm; 2 Nov 1741.

      - William HILL Jr., NFP, will; 6 Jul 1741, 1 Feb 1741/42
        son Hull Chissell my forest plant; bro. Thomas Suggitt,
        in case he returns here, my riverside plant, in case
        he does not personally return to take possession of
        the sd. plant., then son Thomas Suggitt to have it;
        son Jesse; ex: wife and Daniel HORNBY; wits: Travers
        COLSTON, Winifred WEBB, Anne WEBB.

p.394 - Edward JENKINS, inv; 1 Mar 1741/42.

p.395 - Thomas BRYANT, will; 17 Feb 1741/42, 1 Mar 1741/42
        whole est. to Samuel ALGER; no ex; wits: Nathaniel
        MASON, Hugh MACKVEY, William JEFFRIES.

      - William DOWNMAN, f.inv; 1 Mar 1741/42.

84

     - Thomas BRYANT, inv; 5 Apr 1742.

p.396 - Hopkins THORNTON, inv; 5 Apr 1742.

p.397 - Elizabeth THORNTON, will; 6 Apr 1742, 3 May 1742
son Jesse all est; desires him to be under the guardian-
ship and tutorage of fr. Richard LAWSON until age 15
and then to be bound out to some good trade agreeable
to his fancy; ex: fr. Richard LAWSON; wit: Wharton
RANSDELL.

p.398 - Moses SEAMONS, Lun.Par., will; 24 Aug 1741, 3 May 1742
all land on this side of the branch to son Joseph;
wife Alice; dau. Mary; son William; all land on the
northwest side of the branch adjoining the land of
Richard GWILLAM and Edward MINTY to be sold; ex: wife;
wits: Benjamin RUST, Ephraim SEAMONS, Aaron SIMONS.

     - Joseph DURHAM, inv. pres. by William HANKS adm; 3 May 1742.

p.399 - James TUNE, inv; 7 Jun 1742.

p.400 - Elizabeth THORNTON, inv; 7 Jun 1742.

     - Moses SEAMONS, inv; 7 Jun 1742.

p.401 - Newman BROCKENBROUGH, NFP, will; 7 May 1742, 5 Jul 1742
wife plant. whereon I now live, all land between
Totuskey and Richardson's Creeks in the Folly and
within the Great Pasture Gate, and one third part of
the profits of my mill; dau. Winifred one dozen silver
spoons that were her grmother's, the late Mrs. GWYNN;
account between Mr. Luke MILLNER and myself of 8 Jan
1740 to be canceled; sis. BECKWITH; good fr. the Hon.
John TAYLOE Esq., Mr. Samuel PEACHEY, Mr. William
BROCKENBROUGH, and Mr. Luke MILLNER; son William; ex:
son William, wife, and fr. John TAYLOE Esq, Samuel
PEACHEY, and William BROCKENBROUGH Gent. ex. in trust
to see my sd. will performed; wits: Thomas SAMFORD,
Charles HAMMOND, Thomas JESPER.

p.402 - John DEANE, will; 28 Apr 1742, 5 Jul 1742
daus. Elizabeth and Asenath; all land to son John;
wife Jane; ex: wife and fr. Thomas BRADNOR; wits:
Andrew BRUCE, Thomas GREENSTREET, Rachel GREENSTREET.
[John and Jane DEANE had five chil.: John, Elizabeth,
Asenath, Agatha, and Susannah. MRC, p.70.]

p.403 - Newman BROCKENBROUGH Gent., inv; 4 Oct 1742. [Included
servant Robert PHILLS.]

p.409 - Thomas BRADNOR, inv; 4 Oct 1742. [Includes servant Walter
FERREL.]

p.410 - John HUGHLETT, will; 24 Aug 1742, 6 Dec 1742
son William the water mill and all land adjoining to
it; son Leroy George all land on the north side of the
road that goes through the plant.; grson. John HUGHLETT
remainder of the land on the south side being the plant.
whereon I now live; wife Mary; grdau. Anne Nash HUGHLETT;
[wife and s-i-l George WALKER named as ex. in a cod.];
wits: Tellif ALDERSON, William PENLEY; [wits. to cod:
George CLARK, William KENNAN, Anne CLARK.]

p.411 - John LYELL, inv; 7 Dec 1742.

p.412 - John DEANE, inv; 7 Dec 1742.

p.413 - John TUNE, will; 17 Aug 1742, 7 Dec 1742
          all land to son Mark; dau. Mary; sons Anthony and
          Harris; wife Phebe; ex: wife and son Harris; wits:
          Charles HINDS, Joshua HIGHTOWER, Frances MAHAN.

p.414 - James SAMFORD, Farn.Par., will; 9 Nov 1740, 7 Dec 1742
          wife Mary; daus. Anne, Betty, Frances, and Winifred;
          ex: wife and Isaac WEBB; wits: William BARBER,
          Robert BUFORD, Isaac WEBB. [James SAMFORD mar. Mary
          BARBER, 20 Sep 1728. MRC, p.176.]

      - Thomas HERTFORD, Lun.Par., will; 12 Nov 1736, 7 Dec 1742
          bro. Henry; nephew John (son of bro. Henry); Henry
          HERTFORD Jr; Stephen GUPTON; neice Elizabeth HERTFORD;
          no ex; wits: Archibald MITCHELL, Mary MITCHELL,
          Margaret MITCHELL.

p.415 - Thomas SUGGITT, NFP, will; 7 Sep 1740, 8 Dec 1742
          fr. William HILL, whom I have empowered my attorney,
          to keep my est. together for 16 years in case I
          should not return or be heard of in that time; plant.
          and all land to cousin Thomas Suggitt HILL and his
          heirs, if he should die before age 21, land to go to
          cousin John (son of John HILL), and, if John die,
          land to go to cousin Jesse (son of William HILL);
          cousins Winifred, Betty Anne, Hull, Susannah, and
          Jesse (chil. of William HILL), Sarah, John, and
          William (chil. of John HILL); godsons John SUGGITT
          and George WILLIAMS; Tomblin NASH; In case I should
          return anytime hereafter, then this will to be void;
          ex: William HILL and John HILL; wits: Roger WILLIAMS,
          William LYELL, Thomas NASH.

      - John TUNE, inv; 3 Jan 1742/43.

p.416 - Thomas HERFORD, inv; 3 Jan 1742/43.

p.417 - John HUGHLETT, inv; 3 Jan 1742/43.

p.418 - James SAMFORD, inv; 7 Feb 1742/43.

p.420 - John TUNE, f.inv; 7 Feb 1742/43.

p.421 - Samuel CUMMINGS, will; 19 Feb 1742/43, 7 Mar 1742/43
          William GARLAND Jr. my right of the plant. where
          Henry MEDFORD lived last [for] the term of nine years
          while my son Ephraim comes of the age of 21, then to
          come in Ephraim's possession; wife Mary; Eleanor
          PORTER; ex: fr. William GARLAND Jr; wits: A. ANDERSON,
          Henry HERFORD.

      - Margaret FAUNTLEROY, wid., inv; 2 May 1743.

p.423 - John HUGHLETT, f.inv; [6] Jun 1743.

      - John BRYANT, inv; 4 Jul 1743.

p.424 - John WINTER, inv; 1 Aug 1743.

p.425 - Samuel CUMMINGS, inv; 1 Aug 1743. [Included a servant
          named Sarah HILLARD].

    - Anne LAMBERT, will; 14 Mar 1742/43, 7 Nov 1743
        dau. Elizabeth ADKINS; grson. Lambert MORGAN; grdaus.
        Elizabeth MORGAN and Anne JONES; s-i-l William DUN;
        ex: dau. Elizabeth; wits: Andrew MORGAN, John MORGAN.

p.426 - Anne LAMBERT, inv. by Hugh LAMBERT, Andrew MORGAN, and
        John MORGAN; 5 Dec 1743.

p.427 - John JONES, will; 28 Jan 1741/42, 6 Feb 1743/44
        all est. to son Samford; d-i-l Mary JONES; ex: son;
        wits: James BAILEY, Robert SMITH.

    - Thomas Wright BELFIELD, Lun.Par., will; 6 Dec 1743, 6 Feb
      1743/44
        sons John and Joseph; daus. Elizabeth and Frances;
        ex: wife Mary and son John with fr. William JORDAN;
        wits: William LYNN, Charles BOREMAN, Edward HERNDON.
        [Capt. Thomas W. BELFIELD mar. Mary (MERIWETHER)
        COLSTON, 9 Mar 1723/24. MRC, p.16.]

p.428 - [Declaration of Mary BELFIELD]; 6 Feb 1743/44
        Mary BELFIELD, wid. and relict of Thomas W. BELFIELD,
        dec'd, declares that she will not stand to her sd.
        late husband's will, but claims to herself all the
        benefits which the law shall allow out of his est;
        wits: Avery DYE Jr, Edward PRICE.

p.429 - James WILSON, Lun.Par., will; 29 Jul 1743, 6 Feb 1743/44
        wife Elizabeth to receive lease land in Orange Co.
        bought of Joseph MORTON; dau. Sarah; sons: Reuben and
        Richard; ex: wife; Richard DOZIER Jr., and Alvin
        MOUNTJOY; wits: William WILSON, John KELLY, Morton
        WILSON.

p.430 - Capt. Thomas Wright BELFIELD, inv; 5 Mar 1743/44.

p.436 - Thomas W. BELFIELD, inv. in Orange Co.; 5 Mar 1743/4.

p.442 - James WILSON, inv; 5 Mar 1743/44.

p.443 - James WILSON, inv. in Orange Co.; 5 Mar 1743/44.

p.444 - John JONES, inv; 5 Mar 1743/44.

p.445 - Dr. Abraham BARNES, inv; 5 Mar 1743/44.

    - Richard WOOLLARD, inv; 5 Mar 1743/44.

p.446 - Elizabeth BRYANT, NFP, will; 16 Feb 1739/40, 5 Mar 1743/44
        son Charles who took care of her in her advanced age;
        ex: son Charles; wits: Thomas BROWN, Almoreen BRYANT,
        Anne GEFFERY.

p.447 - Evan THOMAS, Lun.Par., will; 5 Dec 1741, 5 Mar 1743/44
        wife Elizabeth all land and plant. whereon I now live;
        son William land and plant. after wife's death; son
        Evan land near Charles Beaverdam; daus. Elizabeth,
        Mary JONES, and Bridget [BRUCE]; s-i-l John PETTY
        who mar. dau. Anne; ex: wife; wits: Elias DAVIS,
        Youell DAVIS, William JACKSON.

p.448 - William SMITH, NFP, will; 16 Sep 1742, 5 Mar 1743/44
        wife Mary the plant. that I leased and the land be-
        longing to it; son David land after wife's death, if

he has not any land of his own, if he has land, then
to son William; son Samuel; ex: wife; wits: John
BROUGHTON, John WADE, George SANDERS.

- John POLLEY, will; 18 Jan 1743/44, 5 Mar 1743/44
all land to son John; dau. Betty; ex: wife, Daniel
LIGHTFOOT, and Isaac WEBB; wits: Samuel ALGER, Robert
BLUFORD, Thomas SAMFORD.

p.449 - John POLLEY, inv; 4 Jun 1744.

p.450 - William SMITH, inv; 4 Jun 1744.

p.451 - Elizabeth BRYAN[T], inv; 4 Jun 1744.

p.452 - Col. Charles GRIMES, inv; 4 Jun 1744.

p.453 - Charles GRIMES, Gent., inv; 4 Jun 1744.

p.456 - John PHILLIPS, NFP, will; 16 Jan 1743/44, 4 Jun 1744
wife Elizabeth to have all est. for her own proper
use without molestation during such time as she shall
remain a widow, and at the time of her marriage...
then it shall be eq. div. between her and the chil.
that William TUNE shall at that time [have] by my
sis. Joannah, only note that my meaning is that she
have half and the other half be div. between the
aforementioned chil; ex: wife and Thomas DUDLEY; wits:
Rawleigh CHINN, William DALE, Thomas DALE, Dominick
NEWGENT.

p.457 - Evan THOMAS, inv; 4 Jun 1744.

p.458 - Fielding NASH, NFP, will; [5] Apr 1743, 4 Jun 1744
wife Hannah the use of my plant. during her widowhood or until my son is 21; son William; my desire is
that my loving wife shall, at her own proper cost and
charge, find my child good, decent clothing and sufficient meat, drink, and lodging and to put him
constantly to school from 10 years old until 15, and
then my desire is that he be bound to a good tailor
of honest repute til...20; b-i-l Josiah MUSE; ex:
wife and fr. William SMITHER; wits: Eleanor SMITHER,
William JOHNSON, D. NEWGENT.

p.459 - John PHILLIPS, inv; 2 Jul 1744.

p.460 - George SISSON, inv; 2 Jul 1744.

- Jonas WILLIAMS, will; 12 Jun 1744, 2 Jul 1744.
all est. to wife Elizabeth; grdau. Elizabeth KENSON;
son Morgan; daus. Frances KENSON and Elizabeth
WILLIAMS; ex: wife; wits: Henry WILSON, Henry KING.

p.461 - Jonas WILLIAMS, about an hour or an hour and a half before
his death, told Mary EVANS and Anne KING that he had
made a will and that he had not left his clothes to
his son Morgan and he desired now that he might have
his coat, waistcoat, breeches, shirt, and hat; prov.
by the oaths of Mary EVANS and Anne KING; 18 Jun 1744.

- Jonas WILLIAMS, inv; 6 Aug 1744.

p.462 - William CRASK, will; [30] Apr 1744, 6 Aug 1744
son John the plant. whereon I now live and 100 ac.

of land adjoining, if he has no heirs, then to go to
son James; son William the plant. whereon I formerly
lived; daus. Elizabeth, Rebecca, Martha; ex: Alvin
MOUNTJOY; wits: Ellen MOUNTJOY, John BURROSS, Elias
WILSON. [William CRASK mar. Rebecca THORNTON by 1726.
MRC, p.46.]

p.463 - Fielding NASH, inv; 6 Aug 1744.

p.464 - Alexander CLARK, inv; 6 Aug 1744.

p.465 - William CRASK, 3 Sep 1744.

p.466 - John MISKELL, inv; 3 Sep 1744.

- John MILLER [=MILLNER], will; 7 Oct 1744, 5 Nov 1744
son Luke; grson. Benjamin [MILLNER]; ex: Benjamin
[MILLNER]; John WOOLLARD and Charles JONES to be
trustees over the est. and to have care of grson.
until he is 18; wits: John WILLIAMS Jr., John
HAMMOCK.

p.467 - John MILL[N]ER, inv; 3 Dec 1744. [Included an inv. of
Benjamin MILLNER, 5 Feb 1732 and a deed of gift from
Frances MILLNER to her son dated 5 Nov 1733.]
[Benjamin MILLNER mar. Frances GLASCOCK, 13 Jul 1730;
John MILLNER was the father of Benjamin. MRC, pp.
132, 133.]

- James BLACKERBY, NFP, will; 13 Jan 1743/44, 4 Feb 1744/45
wife Frances; son William all land in Northumberland
Co; son Thomas all land in Rich. Co; sons James and
Joseph; Eleanor (wife of son James); daus. Hannah
and Sarah; ex: wife and son Thomas; wits: [George]
HUNT, Daniel SCURLOCK.

p.468 - Anne DRAKE, wid; will; 3 Oct 1743, 4 Feb 1744/45
s-i-l Thomas JAMES; dau. [Hester]; daus. child now
called Jemima JAMES; mulatto boy William DEACONS;
Clapon DRAKE; godson Thomas CLAYTOR; ex: dau; wits:
Gabriel JOHNSON, Anne FLETCHER.

p.469 - Archibald MITCHELL, will; 12 Sep 1744, 4 Feb 1744/45
wife Mary the plant. I now live on; dau. Margaret
(the wife of William BROWN); son Archibald my plant.
in Lun. Par. containing 90 ac., if he has no heirs,
to go to dau. Mary; dau. Mary to have the plant. I
now live on after her mother's death, if she has no
heirs, to go to son Archibald; mentions money due
from Edward LEWIS and William GARLAND; no ex; wits:
wits: Isaac JONES, Otho PEATURS.

p.470 - On 4 Feb 1744/45, Isaac JONES and Otho PEATURS, being
evidences to a certain will of Archibald MITCHELL,
made oath...that Archibald MITCHELL's desire in
relation to the legacy left to his dau. Margaret
BROWN was that his wife and dau. Mary [might] pay
yearly to his dau. Margaret...250 lbs. of tobacco.

p.471 - Anne DRAKE, inv; 4 Mar 1744/45.

- James BLACKERBY, inv; 4 Mar 1744/45.

p.473 - Archibald MITCHELL, inv; 5 Mar 1744/45.

p.475 - Andrew BRUCE, inv; 1 Apr 1745.

p.476 - Henry WILLIAMS, NFP; will; 13 Apr 1745, 6 May 1745
son Abraham the plant. whereon I now live; dau.
Judith (under 18); ex: Isaac WOOLLARD (son of John
WOOLLARD; wits: John WOODBRIDGE, Dorothy [CROUCHER],
Anne LACY.

p.477 - Henry WILLIAMS, inv; 3 Jun 1745.

p.479 - Robert BEAUFORD, will; [nd.], 3 Jun 1745
Jeremiah BEAUFORD the plant. whereon I now live, if
he has no heirs, to his bro. John BEAUFORD, if he
has no heirs to my cousin Robert BEAUFORD, and, if
he has no heirs, to his bro. John BEAUFORD; mother
to remain on plant. during her life; cousins Robert
and Jeremiah should pay their bro. John 1000 lbs.
of tobacco when he is 21; ex: cousin Robert; wits:
John Spann WEBB, Isaac WEBB; Cod. gives a gray mare
to his s-i-l Elizabeth BEAUFORD.

- John and Mary WINN, inv; 1 Jul 1745.

p.480 - Billington McCARTY, NFP, will; [nd.], 1 Jul 1745
wife to live on plant. as long as she remains a wid.
and as mistress of my family to keep my chil. together
in the same order and decorum as if I was living;
within the space of a year or as soon as may be after
my death, [my] trustees are to buy 500 ac. of land
for each of my youngest sons; son Billington the land
I now live on; ex: wife; wits: William HENDREN,
William TILLERY, Anne MUSE. [Billington McCARTY mar.
Anne BARBER 16 Jun 1732. MRC, pp.122, 123. The
births of their following chil. are recorded in the
NFPR: Daniel (1733), Billington (1736), Thaddeus
(1739), Charles Barber (1741). NFPR, p.122.]

p.481 - Archibald MITCHELL, f.inv; 1 Jul 1745.

- Thomas W. BELFIELD, Gent., inv. ret. 9 Apr 1744, rec. 5
Aug 1745.

p.482 - Billington McCARTY, inv; 5 Aug 1745.

p.484 - Richard APPLEBEE, inv; 2 Sep 1745.

- Thomas [SORRILL], inv; 2 Sep 1745.

p.485 - Edward MINTY, Lun.Par., will; 27 Apr 1745, 2 Sep 1745
wife Margaret to have land during her life, after her
death, to be eq. div. between daus. Abigail NORTHEN
and Margaret PURCELL; s-i-l John PURCELL; ex: wife,
William NORTHEN, and John PURCELL; wits: John LANDMAN,
Tobias PURCELL.

p.486 - Mrs. Catherine BROCKENBROUGH, inv; 2 Sep 1745. [Included
a servant named Robert PHILLIPS.]

p.489 - [Division of slaves belonging to the est. of Mrs. Catherine BROCKENBROUGH; half went to Billy and the other
half went to Winnie BROCKENBROUGH, his sister.]

p.490 - Mrs. Catherine BROCKENBROUGH, will; 20 Jun 1745, 5 Aug 1745
She sent for Mrs. Mary SMITH and myself [Thomas BARBER]
and did declare this to be her last will in the words

following: I desire you to take notice that my desire is that Winnie, meaning her dau., should have
my chaise and all the [?] belonging to it [?]
this est. and all my clothes and the cash which I
have delivered her already and the rest of my est.
to be div. as the law directs; wits: Thomas BARBER,
Mary SMITH. [Catherine BROCKENBROUGH was the wid.
of Newman BROCKENBROUGH who d. 15 May 1742. NFPR, p.21.]

p.490 - Robert BEAUFORT, inv; 7 Oct 1745.

p.491 - Edward MINTY, inv; 7 Oct 1745.

p.492 - Joan MILLER, will; 23 Sep 1745, 7 Oct 1745
Isaac DALE, being first sworn, saith on oath that he
is now, as he is informed, in the 17th year of his
age and being at the house of Peter GOAD on Wednesday
the 18th day of the current September month where
Joan MILLER had resided about five months and then
and there lying sick but in perfect sense, he heard
Alice FOWLER ask the said Joan MILLER if she wanted
Peter GOAD or any other person sent for to settle her
business; she answered she wanted nobody sent for.
The said Alice FOWLER asked her if she wanted to speak
to anybody to say [if they would surely...tell them.]
She said she did not want to speak to any other person
but to those who were present and then said she gave
to Anne GOAD her hat and calico petticoat and all the
chest of her things to be eq. div. between the said
Alice FOWLER, Anne GOAD, and Frances DALE if she died
in that sickness and that she had money enough to bury
her; upon which the said Isaac DALE, this deponent, was
called as an evidence and the words repeated to her,
the said Joan MILLER, upon which she answered they were
and upon the 21st day of the same month she died at the
said Peter GOAD's house.

p.493 - John SEARGANT, inv. pres. by Elizabeth SEARGANT; 4 Nov 1745.
[Elizabeth SERJANT, wid., mar. Roger WILLIAMS, Feb 1744
(sic). MRC, p.232.]

p.495 - John POWELL, inv; 4 Nov 1745.

      - Edward MINTY, f.inv; 4 Nov 1745.

p.496 - Joan MILLER, inv; 2 Dec 1745.

      - Elizabeth SERJANT, inv; 6 Jan 1745/46.

p.497 - John ROE, inv; 6 Jan 1745/46.

p.498 - William HEADLEY, 15 Dec 1745, 3 Mar 1745/46
all land to son Andrew; daus. Anne, Susan, Elizabeth
REAMY, Mary BAKER; Anne REYNOLDS; ex: son Andrew;
wits: Thomas HUTCHINSON, William BROWN.

      - Gabriel ALLOWAY, will; 23 Jan 1741/42, 3 Mar 1745/46
wife Elizabeth the plant. I now live on; son Gabriel
land below the plant; grson. William HAMMOND all land
up to the swamp; grsons. Absolom and John HAMMOND; son
Alexander the brandy still; ex: sons Alexander and
Gabriel; wits: Archibald MITCHELL, William LAWSON.
[Gabriel ALLOWAY mar. Elizabeth HINDS by 1695. MRC, p.
3. They had the foll.chil: John (b.1695/96), Judith
(b.1703), Alexander (b.1706), Gabriel (b.1713). NFPR,
pp.3,4.]

p.499 - Peter BRYANT, NFP, will; 28 Feb 1745/46, 7 Apr 1746
wife Elizabeth; daus. Alice, Betty, Sarah; child wife
is now with; ex: wife; wits: Joshua STONE, Charles
BRYANT.

p.500 - James WILSON, NFP, will; 5 Mar 1745/46, 7 Apr 1746
cousins Moses, John, Sarah Anne, and Mary WILSON; ex:
bro. John WILSON; wits: William DAVENPORT, James Booth.

    - William HEADLEY, inv; 7 Apr 1746.

p.501 - John TILLERY, NFP, will; 5 Mar 1743/44, 7 Apr 1746
wife Margaret; sons Rawleigh 50 ac. of land in Totuskey,
Samuel, and George; four daus. [unnamed]; after the
decease of Mr. John SHAPROW, all that est. to be eq.
div. between three sons; ex: son George and William
STONUM; wits: Thomas SCURLOCK, William DAVENPORT,
Alexander SCURLOCK. [John and Margaret TILLERY had
the foll. chil: George (b.1715), Elizabeth (b.1717),
Maryanne (b.1720), and Joannah (b.1725) according
to the NFPR, p.187.]

p.502 - Gabriel ALLOWAY, inv; 7 Apr 1746.

p.504 - William PENLEY, inv; 7 Apr 1746.

p.505 - James WILSON, inv; 5 May 1746.

p.506 - John TILLERY, inv; 5 May 1746.

p.508 - Peter BRYANT, inv; 5 May 1746.

p.509 - William OSGRIFFIN, inv; 5 May 1746.

p.510 - Mary BACHELDER, Lun.Par., will; 5 Apr 1744, 2 Jun 1746
Sarah DAVIS (the dau. of Mary MINOR); dau. Anne MORTON;
ex: bro. William QUISENBERRY and William HEART; wits:
Edmund BULGER, Thomas JAMES, James GLOVER.

    - George HAMMOND, inv; [2 Jun 1746].

p.511 - Luke MILLNER, will; 6 Apr 1746, 7 Jul 1746
wife land during her widowhood; each child to have a
suitable education; son John land at Totuskey known
as Namond's Plant. and Bow Neck and all land in
Brunswick Co. bought of William REYNOLDS; son Luke
the plant. I now live on and all land as far as the
branch called Gravelly Branch; son Mark remainder of
land from the bounds of Luke MILLNER's land where
John THRIFT and John HOWELL live and the place Thomas
BRANNAN seated as also the other half of my water
grist mill with his bro. Luke; daus. Elizabeth and
Anne land in Brunswick Co. bought of Capt. Clement
READ; nephew Benjamin MILLNER; children to receive
legacy at 21 and not before; ex: wife; John WOODBRIDGE,
Henry MISKELL, Epaphroditus SYDNOR, Martin SHERMAN to
see will performed and to help with the care of the
children; wits: Catharine HANKS, Daniel LIGHTFOOT,
Thomas McMAHAN. [Luke MILLNER mar. Mary MEEKS in 1731.
MRC, p.133.]

p.514 - Mary BACHELDER, inv; 7 Jul 1746.

p.515 - Luke MILLNER, inv; [4] Aug 1746.

p.516 - Elizabeth TAFF, will; 6 Mar 1741, [?]
         eld. dau. Bridget LOVELACE; Anne DEW; youngest dau.
         Elizabeth GIBSON; ex: son John; wits: John ROE,
         Bridget CREEL, Mary JOBSON.

     - John SLATER, inv; 2 Feb 1746/47.

p.517 - Martin DYE, inv; 2 Feb 1746/47.

p.518 - Mrs. Elizabeth TAFF, inv. pres. by John TAFF; 2 Feb 1746/
         1747.

p.519 - Moses THOMAS, inv; 2 Mar 1746/47.

p.520 - Thomas FRANKLIN, inv; 2 Mar 1746/47.

     - William GARLAND, will; 3 Feb 1746/47, 6 Apr 1747
         son William; daus. Magdalen GUPTON, Mary JONES,
         Frances RUST, Anne WHITE; grsons. George HARDWICK
         and Robert MIDDLETON; Isabel TAVER; wife Haney Ritta;
         ex: son William; wits: Jeremiah BROWN, William HASTIE,
         Joseph RUSSELL Jr.

p.521 - William McKENNIE, inv; 6 Apr 1747.

p.522 - Samuel JACKSON, inv; 4 May 1747.

p.523 - William GARLAND, inv; 4 May 1747.

p.524 - Susannah METCALFE, wid., will; 2 Feb 1746/47, 4 May 1747
         desires ex. to purchase, of William BAKER, the tract
         of land to him belonging which is adjacent to the land
         given and devised to my grson. John BARBER after the
         death of his mother Anne BARBER, which said tract of
         land is to be purchased I do hereby give and bequeath
         to my dau. Anne BARBER; grsons. Samuel and John BARBER;
         ex: dau. Anne BARBER and Capt. William BROCKENBROUGH;
         wits: Gilbert HAMILTON, James [FENDLEY], Thomas LAWSON,
         Charles BEALE. [Susannah was the wid. of Gilbert
         METCALFE, d.1737. MRC, p. 131.]

p.525 - Joseph BRAGG Sr., Lun.Par., will; 26 Feb 1746/47, 4 May
         1747
         sons Joseph, Newman, Thomas, Moore the plant., William,
         Benjamin, and Richard; daus. Elizabeth and Catharine;
         sons Moore and Newman to have three years schooling;
         ex: wife; wits: Richard LAWSON, William LAWSON, Ingoe
         DOZIER. [Joseph BRAGG Sr. had two wives and 12 chil;
         by his first wife he had: Joseph, Thomas, Mary,
         Catharine, and Elizabeth, and by his second wife,
         Elizabeth, he had: William, John, Benjamin, Moore,
         Newman, Joseph Jr., and Reuben. MRC, p.22.]

p.526 - Joseph BRAGG, inv; 1 Jun 1747.

p.527 - Thomas WALKER, will; 10 Nov 1746, 1 Jun 1747
         arms to be sold to pay Jeremiah BROWN; smith's tools
         to sons Thomas and Samuel upon proviso they stay with
         their mother as long as she stays single; son William;
         wife Mary to receive land, after her death, to son
         William; ex: wife and John REYNOLDS; wits: George
         BERRICK, William FORSTER.

     - Susannah METCALFE, inv; 1 Jun 1747.

93

p.529 - Thomas FRANKLIN, f.inv; 6 Jul 1747.

- Thomas WALKER, inv; 6 Jul 1747.

p.530 - Frances HOPKINS, Lun.Par., will; 8 Sep 1745, 3 Aug 1747
        s-i-l Avery DYE Sr. and his wife Catharine; parcel
        of land I now live on to be eq. div. between Avery
        DYE Sr. and Avery DYE Jr; ex: Avery DYE Sr.; wits:
        Martin DYE, Thomas NEWMAN, Catharine DYE. [Frances
        was the wid. of (1) John MACKMELLION (d.1706), (2)
        John WILSON (d.1709), and (3) George HOPKINS (d.1721).
        MRC, p.97. Her est. was div. among Avery DYE, Benj.
        BRUCE, and William BAILEY (son of John BAILEY), 5
        Oct 1747. AB 1, p.281.]

- Frances HOPKINS, inv; 7 Sep 1747.

p.531 - Elizabeth TAYLOR, will; 11 May 1747, 7 Sep 1747
        wearing apparel to be eq. div. between two daus.
        Dorothy CROUCHER and Sarah ELLATE; greatgrdaus. Betty
        LEE, Anne LEE, and Sarey LEE and greatgrson. Richard
        LEE (all chil. of grson. William LEE); ex: grson.
        William LEE; wits: William BARBER, William TILLERY.

p.532 - William HILL, inv; 5 Oct 1747.

p.533 - Catharine LANDMAN, inv; 2 Nov 1747.

- John TAYLOE, will; 31 Jan 1744/45, 2 Nov 1747
        wife use of whole tract of land containing about 1200
        ac. whereon I now live in Rich. Co; daus. Betty CORBIN
        and Anne Corbin TAYLOE; bro. William; fr. and kinsman
        Col. Thomas LEE; son John several tracts of land:
        4000 ac. at [Kelockpon] Mountains in Fairfax or Prince
        William Co., 2146 ac. in the same co., 1200 ac. upon
        Goose Creek purchased of Benjamin GRAYSON, 5000 ac.
        in Prince William Co. upon which the furnace stands,
        and other lands after wife's death; ex: wife, son
        John, and kinsman Col. Thomas LEE; wits: William KAY,
        Andrew ANDERSON, Muh°. McGINNIS, John McDONALD.
        Cod. 300 pounds current money to the vestry of Lun.
        Par; money to fr. and relation Thomas LEE Esq. of
        Stratford in West. Co. and Col. Henry LEE of West.
        Co; mentions the late Mrs. GWYNN (grmother of his
        dau. Betty CORBIN); bro. William of Lanc. Co; desires
        son to provide and pay for, in times of necessity, a
        physician for his aunt BROCKENBROUGH and to assist
        her; fr. Maj. John CHAMPE of King Geo. Co.; desires
        son to employ William PEIRCE of West. Co. who has
        lived sometime with him; fr. Col. Thomas LEE, son
        John, and s-i-l Richard CORBIN to be guardians of
        dau. Anne Corbin TAYLOE; wits: Gilbert HAMILTON,
        David KER, William PEIRCE.

p.537 - Mr. Chichester CHINN, inv; 7 Mar 1747/48. [Chichester
        CHINN mar. Agatha THORNTON, 26 Oct 1739 in Lanc. Co.;
        MRC, pp. 35,36.]

- Edmund NORTHEN, Lun.Par., will; 10 Jun 1743, 7 Mar 1747/48
        wife Elizabeth; son William the plant. whereon he now
        lives with half the land I now possess, if he has no
        heirs, land to be eq. div. among grchil., that is, the
        chil. of my dau. Sarah NELMS; grson Edmund Northen
        NELMS the plant. whereon I now live and half the lands,

if he has no heirs, to be eq. div. between his sisters;
b-i-l Solomon NORTHEN; ex: son William and s-i-l Joshua
NELMS; wits: Thomas LEWIS, Thomas SMITH, Robert SMITH.

p.538 - James BARTLETT, will; 29 Nov 1747, 7 Mar 1747/48
nephew; Mary BUCKEY; wife Mary; all children [nfi.];
ex: wife and bro. Thomas BARTLETT; wits: Henry SUTTLE,
Thomas BARTLETT Jr, William BARTLETT.

p.539 - George THRELKILL, Lun.Par., will; 5 Oct 1747, 7 Mar 1747/48
bro. William DAVIS of West. Co.; sis. Elizabeth DAVIS
of West. Co. all money due me in the hands of Mr.
William GARLAND; ex: William THRIFT and John REYNOLDS;
wits: Thomas HUTCHINSON, Joseph HULL, John PURCELL.
[William and Elizabeth DAVIS were the half-bro. and
sis. of George THRELKILL. See MRC, p.214.]

p.540 - Septimus TAYLOR, inv; 4 Apr 1748. [Septimus TAYLOR and
his wife Bridget had the foll. chil: Sarah (b.1733),
Anne (b.1735), Charles (b.1737), Kathrine (b.1740),
John (b.1742), and Septimus (b.1745). NFPR, pp.182,183.]

p.541 - John DOZIER, inv; 4 Apr 1748. [John DOZIER was probably
a son of the immigrant, Leonard DOZIER. He mar. (1)
Sarah WILSON and (2) Susannah (JACOBUS) DAVIS, wid.
of Robert DAVIS, by May 1740. He had at least two
chil., William (b.1723/24) and John (b.1732). MRC,
p.59; NFPR, p.53; DB 10, p.6.]

p.542 - Edmund NORTHEN, inv; 4 Apr 1748.

p.544 - James BARTLETT, inv; 4 Apr 1748.

p.545 - George THRELKILL, inv; 4 Apr 1748.

     - George TAYLOR, Lun.Par., will; 16 Feb 1747/48, 4 Apr 1748
George Taylor MEGGE the plant. where I now live;
Elizabeth MEGGE (sis. of George Taylor MEGGE); Mary
MEGGE to live on the plant. with her chil. if she and
George T. MEGGE can agree, and, if not, she is to
have one bed and furniture and to leave the plant;
sis. Catharine BRUCE and her husband should have the
first 30 ac. of land I bought of Thomas TAYLOR during
their life, and at their death, to return to George T.
MEGGE; Thomas TAYLOR; ex: George T. MEGGE and fr.
William BARBER; wits: John RAINES, Joshua SINGLETON,
Thomas TAYLOR.

p.546 - William GREENWAY, inv; 22 Jun 1748.

p.547 - The Hon. John TAYLOE Esq., inv; 19 Aug 1748.

p.553 - John McKENNY, inv; 19 Aug 1748.

p.554 - George TAYLOR, inv; 19 Aug 1748.

     - Elizabeth DOZIER, inv; 19 Aug 1748.

p.555 - Robert DAVIS, inv; 19 Aug 1748.

p.556 - Joseph BROOKS, inv; 19 Aug 1748.

     - Simon SALLARD, inv; 19 Aug 1748.

p.558 - Elizabeth DOZIER, LUN.Par., will; 7 May 1748, 4 Jul 1748
chil. James, John, Leonard, Mary JONES, Elizabeth
THORNTON, Sarah JETER, Peggy BAKER, and Susannah
BRAGG; grdau. Elizabeth DOGGETT; ex: sons Leonard
and James; wits: Robert HALL, Richard LAWSON.
[Elizabeth DOZIER, the dau. of John INGO, was the
wid. of (1) Thomas ASCOUGH and (2) Leonard DOZIER.
MRC, p.59.]

- Robert DAVIS, will; 6 Mar 1746, 4 Jul 1748
land to be eq. div. between sis. Elizabeth HAMMOND
and Winifred JARRETT; Liddy STEEL (dau. of Elizabeth
STEEL); part of est. received from father-in-law John
DOZIER to be eq. div. between two sis; John HAMMOND
(at whose house DAVIS has been sick); ex: John HAMMOND;
wits: William GARLAND, Catharine STEEL. [John DOZIER
was the second husband of Susannah (JACOBUS) DAVIS
and the step-father of Robert DAVIS. MRC, p.51.]

p.559 - John McKENNEY, Lun.Par., will; 25 Apr 1748, 5 Jul 1748
John NASH, Anne NASH, Mary NASH, Joseph NASH; John
and Mary [CORROLAS]; dau. Rebecca 2000 lbs. of tobacco which John ANDERSON owes me; I set Charles TOOL
free [on the] 25th day of Dec next; I give him a pair
of shoes and stockings and two shirts, a country cloth
waistcoat, an upper cloth waistcoat, and one hat provided he demands no other freedom dues; remainder of
est. to be eq. div. between two daus. Elizabeth and
Rebecca after William NASH's children's est. be paid
off; ex: John LANDMAN and Jeremiah BROWN; wits:
Margaret SMITH, James LANDMAN, Mary [CURLIS].

- BARTLETT's f.inv; 31 Oct 1748.

p.560 - Joseph RUSSELL the Younger, will; 15 Aug 1748, 3 Oct 1748
I give and bequeath to my dear father, of the Province
of Maryland, my lands and all household furniture; sis.
Mary; mother; bros. William, Solomon, and Daniel; Mrs.
Mary GARLAND; sis. Lydia [BUSH]: ex: fr. John GARLAND;
no wits; prov. by John McDONALD and John WHITEHILL;
John McDONALD, aged 50 years and upward...deposeth
that upon a Sunday in August he had discovered that
Joseph RUSSELL the Youngest, who is since dead, was
going to fight a duel with one Capt. [EWART] and that
he informed Col. TAYLOE, with whom the said RUSSELL
lived, of it, who thereupon gave the said RUSSELL some
writing to keep him employed and ordered him not to go
to the appointment, that the day following, the said
RUSSELL told him he had made his will in order to
fight the duel but the Col. had stopped that; then
the said RUSSELL produced the will he said he had made
and read it to this deponent and this deponent saith
by the words read to him in the will produced...that
it was the same which the said RUSSELL had before read
to him and that he has sworn at times since seen and
heard the said RUSSELL read the said will to himself
and others and that GARLAND mentioned in the will was
always his intimate friend and that if he had ten times
as much he should not begrudge to leave it to him and
further this deponent saith not; 20 Sep 1748

p.561   Deposition of James WHALEY, aged 60 years or thereabouts...on Friday 16 Sep 1748, Joseph RUSSELL, the
Youngest, came to his house and there told him that

he should never discover the illness he then had on
him and signified to him to take notice that he had
made a will some time ago...20 Sep 1748.

Deposition of John WHITEHILL, aged 23...20 Sep 1748.

p.562 - Thomas JESPER, NFP, will; 1 Jan 1747/48, 3 Oct 1748
son Thomas the plant. where he now lives and all the
lands on the east side of the swamp that divides the
land he lives on from the land I now live on; son
Richard Taylor the plant. where I now live, on the
west side of the swamp, if he has no heirs, to go to
son John; daus. Elizabeth, Mary CONNOR, Anne [HENDRON],
and Sarah; grson. Thomas CONNOR; wife Sarah; son Simon;
ex: wife and son Richard; wits: Isaac JONES, Thomas
NASH Jr, Alexander DUDLEY. [Thomas JESPER mar. Sarah
TAYLOR, March 1710/11. MRC, p.106.]

p.563 - Thomas JESPER, inv; 30 Nov 1748.

- Joseph BROOKS, f.inv; 3 Dec 1748.

p.564 - William HODGKINSON, Lun.Par., will; 26 Mar 1746/47, 5 Dec
1748
Betty HOW (dau. of John HOW); Aaron SIMONDS, Elias
YEATS, Anne MURPHY, godson Marmaduke BECKWITH Jr;
Marmaduke BECKWITH Sr; ex: wife Mary; wits: John
YEATMAN, Joseph YEATMAN, Elizabeth DOZIER.

- Anne HARRISON, NFP, will; 2 Nov 1748, [?]
sons Samuel, George land bought of William ESKRIDGE;
son Benjamin the other part of the land bought of
ESKRIDGE; grdau. Anne HARRISON; Anne (the wife of
Jeremiah HARRISON); Ellen (the wife of Benjamin
HARRISON); Joyce WEBSTER; sons Matthew and James;
ex: sons George, Matthew, and James; wits: William
HARTLEY, Edward GOLDSBY, Jane GOLDSBY.

p.565 - Elizabeth DOZIER, f.inv; 31 Mar 1748/49.

- William HODGKINSON, inv; 1 Apr 1749.

p.567 - Anne HARRISON, inv; 3 Apr 1749.

p.569 - Bernard GAINES, will; 18 Nov 1747, 3 Apr 1749
wife the plant. whereon I now live; son the plant.
known as "The Indian Neck"; land in Albemarle Co. to
be sold by my ex. in joint with the Rev. Mr. Robert
ROSE and Mr. John HARVIE and the money used to pay
debts; three daus; ex: wife and William JORDAN; wit:
James FINDLAY. [Bernard GAINES mar. (1) Martha TAYLOR
and (2) Elizabeth (?). MRC, p.74.]

- Isaac WOOLLARD, NFP, will; 11 Feb 1748/49, 3 Apr 1749
bro. Joseph; father John; wife Catharine; est. bequeathed to wife, after her remarriage or death, to
go to bros. or sisters being of the whole blood to
myself to be eq. div; father to be ex; also asks
father to take upon him the care and execution of the
will of Henry WILLIAMS late of Rich. Co. dec'd whereof he was ex; wits: John WOODBRIDGE, Charles HINDS,
Thomas ROLLINS.

p.570 - John McDANIEL, inv; 20 Apr 1749.

97

- Bernard GAINES, inv; 20 Apr 1749.

p.571 - Thomas JESPER, f.inv; 20 Apr 1749.

p.572 - Know all by these presents that I, Mary McGUIRE of Rich.
         Co., having been sickly for these eight years and un-
         able to maintain and support myself for the world
         without the service and assistance of somebody to be
         with me to provide my necessaries, and my dau. Sarah,
         laboring under many and great hardships to perform the
         same, and knowing the pains she took, and seeing her
         dutiful behavior towards me, determined to pay her
         (rather than a stranger) the 250 lbs. of tobacco per
         annum which was the wages I must have given to another,
         which wages now amount to 2000 lbs. of tobacco and I
         being unable to pay the same without selling my est.
         which consists of the things hereafter mentioned...
         I, the sd. Mary McGUIRE, for and in consideration of
         the above-mentioned services and towards the discharge
         of the above sd. 2000 lbs. of tobacco which I do here-
         by acknowledge to have been received, have bargained
         and sold unto my dau., Sarah BRUMBELOW, and do by these
         presents bargain, sell, and forever make over all and
         singular of the sd. goods and household stuff...to
         her my sd. dau. Sarah BRUMBELOW...23 Jun 1749; wits:
         Edward OGLEBY, [William ROBERTSON], Jean OGLEBY.
         Note. This deed was recorded in this book by mistake.

       - Joseph RUSSELL of the Province of Maryland, will; 26 Nov
         1748, 5 May 1749
         dau. Lydia [BEECH]; sons Solomon, Daniel, and William;
         dau. Mary; in case beloved wife Sarah will return into
         the Colony of Virginia within three months after my
         decease, and there dwell during her natural life, it
         is my will and desire that she shall have full possess-
         ion and use of all my est. which I have bequeathed to
         my three chil. Mary, Daniel, and William...but, if
         she refuses and neglects to return to Virginia within
         the time aforesaid and there dwell...in that case, I
         hereby revoke and make null and void the aforementioned
         bequest to her; desires sons Daniel and William to be
         bound to the joiner's trade until 21 unto William
         JAMES in Richmond; ex: wife and bro. Charles; wits:
         James MUNCASTER, Matthew FRAZIER. [Joseph RUSSELL Jr.
         mar. Sarah the wid. of Francis ARMISTEAD by Nov 1722.
         MRC, p.175.]

p.573 - Elizabeth HAMMOND, inv; ord. 3 Apr 1749.

       - Thomas NASH, will; 26 Nov 1748, 3 Jul 1749
         son Thomas 50 ac. next to the land of William DUDLEY;
         wife Agatha; dau. Anne; ex: wife; wits: Richard T.
         JESPER, John JESPER, William DUDLEY.

p.574 - Joseph RUSSELL, inv; [nd.]

       - Isaac WOOLLARD, inv; ord. 3 Apr 1749.

p.575 - Thomas LEWIS, inv; ord. 5 Jun 1749.

       - William HODGKINSON, f.inv; [nd.]

       - Thomas NASH, inv; ord. 3 Jul 1749.

p.579 - Thomas SMITH, inv; ord. 7 Aug 1749.

p.580 - Thomas PLUMMER, NFP, will; 29 Aug 1744, 2 Oct 1749
        wife Betty; son John land in Gloucester Co; other
        child [unnamed]; ex: Capt. John SMITH, Capt. John
        WOODBRIDGE, and wife; wits: Leroy GRIFFIN, John Spann
        WEBB, John [CROFFIELD].

      - William HODGKINSON, f.inv; 12 Oct 1749.

p.581 - Thomas PLUMMER, inv; completed 11 Oct 1749.

p.587 - Solomon REDMAN, Lun.Par., will; 11 Jun 1740, 7 Nov 1749
        all boys [unnamed] to be of age at 18; dau. Winifred;
        wife Mary; ex: wife; wits: Robert HALL, Richard LAWSON,
        Mary READ. [Solomon REDMAN mar. Mary STEWART by May
        1711. MRC, p.167.]

p.588 - Jeremiah EDMONDS, now of Essex Co., will; 26 Apr 1749,
        7 Nov 1749
        est. to be eq. div. between wife Anne and dau. Sarah;
        wife to take care of dau. Elizabeth and young child
        not yet christened; dau. Sarah to be bound by the
        county court of Essex to Miss Susannah [BROOME] of
        the aforesaid county to serve her if she, the sd. Miss
        [BROOME] shall live so long until dau. is 19; ex: fr.
        Richard BARNES of Rich.Co; wits: Richard [SRINGLE],
        Samuel DAVIS Jr, Edward BULLOCK.

      - Thomas SETTLE, Lun.Par., will; 15 May 1747, 1 Jan 1749/50
        grdau. Catharine BURRAS; greatgrson Tarpley BRAGG
        otherwise SETTLE; ex: Henry SETTLE and Richard LAWSON;
        wits: Joseph AMBROSE, Judith AMBROSE, John RYAN.

p.589 - Solomon REDMAN, inv; ord. 6 Nov 1749.

p.590 - Jeremiah EDMONDS, inv; taken 30 Nov 1749.

      - Stephen GUPTON, will; [nd.], 5 Mar 1749/50
        wife Magdalene to receive servant man [Urruch
        Christopher THEATILLA]; eld.dau. Anne; eld. son
        Stephen; son William Garland; youngest son Vincent;
        ex: wife and fr. William GARLAND; wits: Charles
        HAMMOND, Anne WHITE, William WHITE. [Stephen GUPTON
        mar. (1) Margaret COWARD in 1729 and (2) Magdalene
        GARLAND. NFPR, p.75.]

p.591 - Thomas SETTLE, inv; ord. 1 Jan 1749/50.

      - Thomas CANNAN, NFP, will; 4 Feb 1749/50, 6 Mar 1749/50
        I give to George LEWIS, being the man I do now live
        with, all my clothes with my saddle and bridle and
        1-1-8 cash with my crop of tobacco after Mr. Travers
        COLSTON's account is paid; ex: George LEWIS; wits:
        Joseph HULL, William LAMBERT, Edward DAVIS.

p.592 - Daniel HORNBY, NFP, will; 13 Oct 1749, 2 Apr 1750
        Travers COLSTON Jr. all est., if he has no heirs, to
        Rawleigh COLSTON, and, if he has no heirs, to William
        BEALE Jr; est. to be in the care of Capt. William
        BEALE and Mr. Travers COLSTON during the minority of
        Travers COLSTON Jr; asks that William NASH and wife
        be allowed to live at dwelling plant. or at the ferry;
        Taverner BEALE one diamond ring of 20 pounds sterling
        value whereon shall be engraved "Be true to your
        trust"; Capt. Travers TARPLEY and his son Samuel
        Travers TARPLEY; Robert TOMLIN Jr; Winifred BEALE;

It is my will that Travers COLSTON Jr. be suitably
maintained and educated out of the profit of my est.
and that there be a Latin master employed at the rates
of 20 pounds sterling a year for the space of five
years against he is 10 years old, which master shall
have his residence at my now dwelling house during the
sd. term and shall be obliged to teach 10 scholars and
to take no more at any one time during the sd. term,
one of which shall be, if Mr. William BEALE pleases,
his son William who shall be accomodated with the sd.
Travers and master at the expense of my sd. est. and
likewise Mr. COLSTON's son William shall be another
when he is fit to be put to the Latin and shall be
accomodated as aforesaid. The remainder shall be made
up by this neighborhood by such as will put their chil.
to learn Latin, particular Mr. Thomas SAMFORD, the two
Mr. WEBBs, and Mr. Edgecomb SUGGITT whom I desire may
have the preference of making up the vacancy with sons
that are fit to be taught Latin from time to time during
the sd. five years; Charles COLSTON; Thomas BEALE (son
of Capt. BEALE); Capt. William BEALE; William BEALE Jr.
(son of Capt. William BEALE); ex: Capt. William BEALE
and Mr. Travers COLSTON; wits: Richard GWILLIAM, Mary
GWILLIAM, Elizabeth GWILLIAM. [Daniel HORNBY mar.
Winifred TRAVERS in 1741; she d. 10 Aug 1749 and he
d. 14 Feb 1749/50. NFPR, p.97, MRC, p.98.]

p.595 - George KIRK, will; 24 Jan 1749/50, 2 Apr 1750
wife Mary; sons James and Isaac; dau. Millie; ex:
f-i-l William SMITH; wits: Hugh LAMBERT, Argeland
SHURLEY, William HARTLEY.

p.596 - Samford JONES, NFP, will; 29 Mar 1750, 2 Apr 1750
wife all goods and chattels; daus. Sarah, Winifred,
and Lisha; child wife is now with; ex: Henry MISKELL
and John WOOLLARD; wits: James McKILDO, John SAMFORD,
William HAMMOND. [The fourth child was Jane (b.1750).
NFPR, p.108.]

    - Mrs. Mary MITCHELL, nunc.will; prov. 2 Apr 1750
[Depositions by Catharine ALLOWAY and Marget STANLEY]
Catharine ALLOWAY saith that on Friday the 16th day
of this instant March, she this deponent asked the
late Mrs. Mary MITCHELL, who was then sick, who she
intended to leave her est. to if she died; she said
she gave it all to her dau. Elizabeth HARRINGTON.
[Marget STANLEY made essentially the same deposition]
18 Mar 1749/50.

p.597 - John HOW, inv; ord. 5 Mar 1749/50.

p.598 - William MORGAN, inv; ord. 5 Mar 1749/50.

    - Anthony MORGAN, inv; ord. 5 Mar 1749/50. [An Anthony
MORGAN mar. Anne DUNKIN in 1711. MRC, p.137.]

p.599 - Griffin DOBBYNS, inv; ord. 5 Mar 1749/50. [Griffin and
Mary Anne DOBBYNS had the foll. chil: Betty (b.1731/
1732), Mary Anne (b.1733), Drury (b.1735), Samuel
(b.1740), and Griffin (b.1743); Griffin d. 10 Feb
1749/50 and Mary Anne, his wife, d.12 Feb 1749/50.
NFPR, p. 45.]

p.600 - Stephen GUPTON, inv; ord. 5 Mar 1749/50.

p.601 - Elizabeth ROLLINS, inv; ord. 5 Mar 1749/50.

p.602 - James HOWARD, NFP, will; [nd.], 7 May 1750
        wife all est; sons William, Thomas, Spencer, and
        James (all under 21); ex: wife; wits: Thomas BROOME,
        Griffith WILLIAMS. [James HOWARD mar. Mary SCURLOCK
        in 1729. MRC, p.98. They had the foll. chil: William
        (b.1730), Thomas (b.1731), Travers (b.1733-d.1734),
        Nanny (b.1735), Sarah (b.1736), Spencer (b.1739),
        Patty (b.1741), and James (b.1743). NFPR, pp.98,99.]

     - Joseph PALMER, NFP, will; 21 Mar 1749, 7 May 1750
        plant. and land to son Rawleigh after his mother's
        decease or widowhood; rest of est. to be eq. div.
        among chil; ex: wife; fr. John WOODBRIDGE to advise
        and direct her; wits: Charnock HIGHTOWER, James
        FORRESTER. [Joseph and Anne PALMER had the foll. chil:
        Rawleigh (b.1733), Isaac (b.1738), John (b.1741),
        William (b.1745), and Robert (b.1748). NFPR, p.143.]

p.603 - Samuel ALGAIR, NFP, will; 3 Mar 1749/50, 7 May 1750
        s-i-l ROBINSON; daus. Elizabeth and Mary; three eld.
        chil. Thomas, Alicia LIGHTFOOT, and Anne ROBINSON;
        plant. and land to eld. son Thomas after wife's death
        or remarriage; rest of est. to wife Mary and the chil.
        I had by her to be eq. div; s-i-l Daniel LIGHTFOOT to
        assist wife; no ex; wits: William HANKS, Thomas SAMFORD.

p.604 - John FOWLER, will; 13 Apr 1750, 7 May 1750
        plant. and land to wife Alice, after her death to son
        William; ex: wife; wits: D. NEWGENT, Reuben DALE,
        Joseph BRANNAN. [N.B. There were apparently other
        chil. not mentioned in the will.]

     - Downing HOWELL, will; 28 Mar 1750, 7 May 1750
        George RUSSELL; Thomas RUSSELL; Job THOMAS; desires
        John HOWELL and George DAVIS to div. the remainder of
        the seven hogsheads between whom they shall think fit;
        bro. John HOWELL to take care of my son John and bring
        him up in the fear of God; wife Alice; it is my desire
        that my child shall live with his mother without my
        bro. John can [show] some lawful occasion to take him
        from her; ex: John HOWELL and George DAVIS; wits:
        Thomas RUSSELL, Patrick KENDRICK.

p.605 - Thomas EWERS, NFP, will; 17 Mar 1749/50, 7 May 1750
        Thomas [HOLLIS] alias RAINBOW (the son of Mary RAIN-
        BOW) all my est; fr. Mary RAINBOW; asks William
        GLASCOCK to see that the child's est. is not wasted;
        no ex; wits: Thomas SAMFORD, Lewis HAMMOND.

p.606 - Samford JONES, inv; ord. 2 Apr [1750].

p.607 - Thomas CANNAN, inv; returned 28 Apr 1750.

     - Solomon REDMAN, f.inv; [nd.]

     - George KIRK, inv; ord. 30 Apr 1750.

p.608 - Mary MITCHELL, inv; ord. 2 Apr 1750.

p.610 - William ERSKIEN, inv; ord. 2 Apr 1750.

p.612 - George TAYLOR, inv; ord. 2 Apr 1750.

p.613 - James WHALEY, Lun.Par., will; 4 Jan 1749/50, 4 Jun 1750
        sons Thomas, William, and James; I give and bequeath
        to William WHALEY, my younger son, 4000 lbs. of tobacco
        received for the negro named Kate of Valentine GARNER
        and to be left in Col. John TAYLOE's hands while the
        child comes of age, if he dies, tobacco to go to son
        Thomas; my dau., I cut her off with a shilling; ex:
        son William; wits: David HILMAN, Daniel BENTLEY.
        [Elizabeth, the wid. of James WHALEY, mar. John FINDLEY
        in 1754. MRC, p.69.]

p.614 - John JACKSON, will; 7 Apr 1750, 4 Jun 1750
        son Joseph land and plant. where I now live; son
        Joseph left to Edward FRANKLIN until age 21; ex;
        Edward FRANKLIN; wits: William WHALEY, Richard HILMAN.

     - James WEBB, will; 5 Apr 1750, 4 Jun 1750
        wife Betty use of half the land; daus. Anne, Sarah,
        Mary, and Judy; sons John, James; land and plant. to
        son Joseph; ex: Robert DOWNMAN, John WEBB, and Joseph
        WEBB; wits: Christopher CHINN, Travers DOWNMAN.

p.616 - John FOWLER, inv; ord. 7 May 1750.

p.618 - Joseph PALMER, inv; taken 2 Jun 1750.

p.619 - Downing HOWELL, inv; ord. 7 May 1750.

p.620 - Caran BRANNAN, will; 8 Feb 1749/50, 4 Jun 1750
        wife Margaret use of land and plant., after her death
        to son James; sons Caran, Joseph, and Thomas; William
        CROUCHER and his wife Eleanor; dau. Eleanor CROUCHER;
        ex: wife and son Joseph; wits: John DURHAM, James
        HOWARD.

p.621 - Hull Chissell HILL, inv. at the house of Thomas BROOME;
        ord. 7 May 1750.

     - Elizabeth WILLIAMS, inv; ord. 1 Apr 1750.

p.622 - Samuel ALGAR, inv; ord. 7 May 1750.

p.624 - Thomas EWERS, inv; ord. 7 May 1750.

p.625 - Charles BOWLES, [account of sales]; [nd.] [A Charles
        BOWLES d. 10 Jan 1749/50. NFPR, p.18.]

p.626 - Thomas HUTCHINSON, inv; ord. 4 Jun 1750.

     - Stephen GUPTON, f.inv; [nd.]

p.627 - John JACKSON, inv; ord. 4 Jun 1750.

     - Samford JONES, f.inv. pres. by Mary JONES, [nd.]

     - George KIRK, f.inv; received 25 Jun 1750.

p.628 - Thomas CANNAN, f.inv; [nd.]

     - James WEBB, inv; ord. 4 Jun 1750.

p.629 - Richard BROWN, inv; 4 Jun 1750.

p.631 - Caran BRANNAN, inv; [nd.]

102

p.633 - Leroy GRIFFIN, will; 8 Apr 1749, 6 Aug 1750
Being at this time free from aches and ills either of
body or mind; my body is to be deposited in the earth,
its natural mother, in the foll. manner: so soon as my
coffin can be prepared, I desire that six of the neigh-
boring gentlemen, my intimate acquaintances, may convey
me to the place appointed for my reception and the
minister perform the burial service without sermon and
for this service I give a mourning ring of 20 shillings
value to the minister and each of the six gentlemen that
perform the last office of friendship to me; [I'll] have
no ceremonious pomp but a dinner prepared by the gentlemen and they to be entertained in the same manner as if
myself was present, and I ernestly forbid that any expense be made as to mourning except for my wife because
I look upon it as a needless and very extraordinary
charge in a large family; now, as to temporals: Imprimus.
I think no method which I can fall upon can provide so
well for my loving woman, Mary Anne GRIFFIN, as the
provision which the law has made in that case and that
she, my sd. wife, may not be in any manner obligated
to her child., I desire her thirds of my est. may be
allotted so soon as may be after my decease...; after
wife's decease, her one third to be div. among all
surviving chil. and not to rescind to heir at law; son
Thomas Bertrand part of land at the head of Farnham
Creek; son Leroy riverside tract; dau. Elizabeth small
part of my forest land that includes my plantations
where Thomas BROOME, James BRANNAN, and Jane OSGRIFFIN
now live; son Corbin all the remainder of my land in
Rich. Co; now, as an inference may be fairly drawn,
from my disposal of my lands as aforesaid, that Thomas
Bertrand, my eld. son, will inherit that seat of land
whereon Mr. William BERTRAND of Lanc. Co. now lives as
being entailed on his heirs and having none other child
at present except my wife; however, should it unluckily
happen that by a wife hereafter the sd. William BERTRAND,
Gent. should have heirs, to deprive my sd. wife and son
from inheriting, so that the land be lost from my family,
then my will is that my homeland be eq. div. between my
sons, Thomas Bertrand and Leroy, that my son Corbin has
1000 ac. of my forest land in one piece where he pleases,
and that the residue of my forest lands, except my dau's
before given, be eq. div. between my two sons, Thomas
and Leroy, but if that tract of land descends to us, as
I hope it will, my lands to be as above given; son
William tract in Prince George Co. bought of Isham
EPPES containing 750 ac. and his choice of any two of
the lots in Blandford Town; desires his ex. to purchase
a tract of good land not under 500 ac. and not above
50 miles from Bolling's Point to give to son William;
son Samuel tract in Prince George Co. bought of Thomas
WILLIAMS containing 800 ac. and the remaining lot of
land in Blandford Town; tract of 200 ac. in Prince
George Co. bought of Thomas WILLIAMS to be eq. div.
between sons William and Samuel; son Cyrus 1292 ac. in
Brunswick Co to go with lot of land in Petersburg Town;
ex: wife, Samuel and William PEACHEY, William GLASCOCK,
and John TARPLEY; "And this my last will, I pray ye
fulfill, exactly as I have designed it; that quarrels
mayn't rise, on this present devise, because in plain
words you will find it." Wits: A. ANDERSON, John HILL
Jr, Robert FORRESTER.
Cod., 30 May 1750, child wife now goes with to receive
1880 ac. in Prince William Co. purchased of Mr. JONES

dau. Elizabeth, to receive the plant. whereon Samuel
ROLLINS now lives; wits: James CRAIG, Robert FORRESTER,
Anne DODSON. [Col. Leroy GRIFFIN mar. Mary Anne BERTRAND
in 1734. MRC, pp.81,82. William BERTRAND apparently
did not have any other children. WLC, p.16.]

p.635 - Leroy GRIFFIN, inv; ord. 6 Aug 1750.

p.640 - James WHALEY, inv; ord. 6 Aug 1750.

- Samuel PEACHEY, NFP, will; 12 Dec 1748, 5 Nov 1750
land in Essex Co. bought of ADCOCK together with the
land adjoining that descended to me from my mother to
go to son Samuel, if he dies without heirs, to go to
son William; son William the land which I now live on
pursuant to my grandfather PEACHEY's will, if he has
no heirs, to go to son Samuel; sons Thomas Griffin
and Leroy; dau. [unnamed] (the wife of John EUSTACE);
daus. Phoebe, Winnie Griffin, and Anne; dau. FLOOD;
grdau. Catharine FLOOD; son Thomas Griffin's godfather
Capt. BROCKENBROUGH; desires son William to find nails
and build one 16' x 20' dwelling house and one 20' x
32' tobacco house on each of two youngest sons' land
to be purchased for them and to give his bro. Samuel,
when he comes of age, as much timber from Piscataway
as will serve to build him a dwelling house and sufficient outhouses on his land; ex: fr. Col. Leroy
GRIFFIN and son William; son is not to act without the
advice of GRIFFIN until 21; wits: Adam MENZIES,
Andrew MANNEN, Isaac BRIZENDINE. [Samuel PEACHEY mar.
(1) Winifred GRIFFIN and (2) Judith (STEPTOE) LEE;
his dau. Alice Corbin mar. John EUSTACE in 1743. MRC,
pp. 155, 65, 66.]

p.643 - Dudley BENNEHAN, NFP, will; 12 Mar 1749, 5 Nov 1750
son Alexander the plant. whereon I now live; son
Dominick the land and plant. I bought of Dominick
NEWGENT; wife Rachel; ex: wife and William DAVENPORT;
wits: D. NEWGENT, Godfrey WILCOX, James HINDS.

p.644 - Millian GLASCOCK, will; 5 Nov 1747, 3 Dec 1750
sons George and John; grsons. George (son of George),
William Jr., and Thomas to receive the mill; grdaus.
Judith, Millian, Winnie, and Priscilla; ex: son John;
wits: John DURHAM, George PHILLIPS, Gregory GLASCOCK.

p.645 - Manly BROWN, will; 5 Mar 1749, 3 Dec 1750
wife; sons James and Richard; ex: b-i-l Lewis LAMKIN
and wife; servant boy John HELAND to be sold and not
appraised; wits: George LAMKIN, John BROWN, Mary
LAMKIN. [Manly and Mary BROWN had the foll. chil:
James (b.1741), Richard (b.1745), and Hannah (b.1751)
sic. NFPR, p.23.]

- Thomas SCOTT, will; 14 Jun 1750, 3 Dec 1750
wife Mary all est. during her life; after her decease,
to be eq. div. among chil. [unnamed]; no ex; wits:
William HUNT, Christopher COLLINS.

p.646 - Mr. Dudley BENNEHAN, inv; taken 28 Nov 1750.

p.648 - John WADE, inv; ord. 5 Nov 1750.

p.649 - John LANDMAN, Lun.Par., will; 20 Oct 1750, 4 Feb 1750/51
wife Elizabeth the plant. I now live on joining the

land of Tobias PURCELL and going as far as the swamp
called Sisson's; if wife is with child, as I believe
she is, the land to fall to that child; remaining
land to dau. Margaret; bros. William and George; ex:
James LANDMAN and wife; wits: Jere. BROWN, John PURCELL,
Elizabeth PUGH.

- Manly BROWN, inv; ord. 3 Dec 1750.

p.651 - James HOWARD, inv. pres. by Mary HOWARD; ord. 7 May 1750.

p.652 - Mrs. Mary BELFIELD, nunc. will; 8 Oct 1750, 4 Feb 1750/51
Alexander PARKER, Doctor of Physic, aged 60 years or
thereabouts of the Co. of Essex...deposeth...that he
did attend Mrs. Mary BELFIELD, late of this co., in
her last illness and that the sd. Mary did to wit on
the 5th day of this present October declare to him...
her desire of making her last will and testament...
and did desire him to commit the same to writing in
the words following: whereas my son, John BELFIELD,
my daus., Mary SMITH and Elizabeth BELFIELD, and my
grdau., Frances MORTON, being provided for already,
I give all my est. unto my dau. Frances BELFIELD and
her heirs...and that the sd. Mary BELFIELD was at
that time in her perfect sense and memory.

- Henry KING, Lun.Par., will; 8 Feb 1750/51, 4 Mar 1750/51
bro. William; wife Anne; wife's sisters Hannah
MOZINGO and Elizabeth TAYLOR; no ex; wits: Thomas
NEWMAN, Peter EVANS.

p.653 - Million GLASCOCK, inv; [nd.]

p.654 - Mrs. Mary BELFIELD, inv; ord. 4 Feb 1750/51.

p.655 - Betty PHILLIPS, inv. pres. by Thomas DUDLEY adm; ord. 4
Feb 1750/51.

- John LANDMAN, inv; ord. 4 Feb 1750/51.

p.656 - Richard BROWN, inv; ord. 4 Feb 1750/51.

p.657 - Joseph HULL, inv; ord. 4 Feb 1750/51.

p.658 - Thomas SCOTT, inv; ord. 3 Dec 1750.

p.659 - John WILLIAMS, NFP, will; [nd], 1 Apr 1751
Henry WILLIAMS all the land between Griffin DOBBYN's
line and High Field Swamp to him and his son John
and 40 ac. of land adjoining the plant. running down
to the swamp; son John all land from Bates' Spring
Branch to William DEW's line; son Samuel land and
plant. whereon I now live; son Thomas all land on
Nottoway River below Rocky Run; son Luke plant. on
Nottoway River and the land above Rocky Run; daus.
Betty LYELL and Sarah LAWSON; grdaus. Anne LYELL and
Winifred JONES; son Hugh; sons-in-law Roger WILLIAMS
and Edward JONES; ex: wife; wits: Epaphroditus SYDNOR,
Thomas TUNE, Mary SYDNOR.

p.660 - John BROWN, will; 25 Feb 1750/51, 1 Apr 1751
son Jeremiah all land and plant; grson. Jeremiah
(son of dau. Mary); grson. John BROWN (son of son
Jeremiah); daus. Nanny, Christian SULLIVANT, and
Susannah LEWIS; son Jeremiah to receive four pistols

of Richard BROWN, my s-i-l, that he owes me; ex: wife
and son Jeremiah; wits: William GARLAND, Elijah FEEN.

p.661 - John BAILEY, nunc.will; 31 Jan 1750/51, 2 Apr 1751
Deposition of Thomas SAMFORD...saith that on Tuesday
the 29th day of this instant January, the late John
BAILEY, who was then sick, desired him to take notice
of these words, that he gave his est. to be eq. div.
and that one bro. should not have it all;
Judith NASH saith the same.

p.662 - William WALKER, inv; ord. 4 Mar 1750/51.

p.663 - John DAVIS, inv; ord. 4 Mar 1750/51.

p.664 - John BAILEY, inv; ord. 1 Apr 1751.

     - John WILLIAMS, inv; ord. 1 Apr 1751.

p.666 - [John] WILLIAMS, div. of est., on 27 Apr 1751, among:
Henry WILLIAMS, John WILLIAMS, Luke WILLIAMS, Thomas
WILLIAMS, Samuel WILLIAMS, Jane WILLIAMS in behalf
of Elizabeth LYELL, and Christian LAWSON.

p.668 - John BROWN Sr., inv; ord. 1 Apr 1751.

     - Luke DEMERRETT, will; 13 Jan 1750/51, 3 Jun 1751
all land to wife Jean; son John; mentions, but does
not name, all children; ex: wife; wits: John RAYNOLDS,
Willoughby HARRISON. [According to MRC, p.53, and NFPR,
p.44, a Luke DEMERRETT mar. Judith WIN in 1728/29, and
they had two daus. Elizabeth (b.1729) and Mary (b.1731).]

p.669 - George TILLERY, NFP, will; 16 Jan 1750/51, 5 Aug 1751
whole est. to wife Judith, after her death to son
George; all chil. (nfi.); ex: wife and Dennis CONWAY;
wits: Willoughby ROUTT, Gabriel SMITHER. [George and
Judith TILLERY also had a dau. Elizabeth (b.1739).
NFPR, p.188.]

p.670 - Daniel HORNBY Gent., inv; taken 11 Apr 1750.

p.673 - Samford JONES, f.inv; 5 Aug 1751.

p.674 - Thomas WRIGHT, inv; ord. 3 Jun 1751.

     - Samuel PEACHEY Gent., inv; [nd.]

p.679 - George TILLERY, inv; ord. 5 Aug. 1751.

p.680 - Luke DEMERRITT, inv; ord. 2 Sep 1751.

p.681 - Charles HAMES, inv; ord. 2 Sep 1751. [Charles and Lucresy
HAMES had a dau., Anne, b. in 1743. NFPR, p.78.]

     - Thomas JACKSON, inv; ord. 2 Sep 1751.

p.682 - Mrs. Betty PLUMMER, nunc.will; 17 Mar 1749/50, 6 Mar 1751
Deposition by Roger WILLIAMS, his wife Elizabeth,
Mary GWILLIAMS, Betty Anne HILL, Dorothy CROUCHER,
and Catharine LANDMAN.
Roger WILLIAMS saith that on Thursday night between
the 15th and 16th day of this instant March, the late
Mrs. Betty PLUMMER, who was then sick, called to him
and his wife and said to them that she wanted to make

her will and desired them not to disclose or make the
same known til her death and told them that she left
Diana, the house wench, to James LANDMAN and Kate to
Edward SMITH (her bro. Capt. John SMITH's son), and
the rest of her negroes to be div. between James
LANDMAN and her sd. bro's son, but if James LANDMAN,
who was then sick, should die and not recover, then
she gave all her negroes to her sd. bro's son Edward
SMITH.

p.683 - John LANDMAN, inv; [nd.]

- Edmund COLLINSWORTH, Lun.Par., will; 14 Apr 1751, 3 Feb
1752
eld. son John the plant. whereon I now live, if he
has no heirs, then to two daus. Hannah and Sarah; sons
Edmund and James; dau. Eleanor; ex: Mr. William JORDAN,
Capt. Alvin MOUNTJOY, and son John; wits: William
SANDERS, Christopher COLLINS.

p.684 - John PURCELL, will; 13 Jan 1752, 3 Feb 1752
James ENGLISH, Andrew ANDERSON; son John; prov. by
deposition of Jeremiah BROWN, 15 Jan 1752, Jeremiah
BROWN, aged 32 years or thereabouts,...saith that he
was sent for to the house of John PURCELL, dec'd, on
Monday the 13th of this instant January, and was
desired by the sd. John PURCELL to write his will...
and that he read every paragraph to him as he wrote
it but that the sd. John departed this life before it
was signed, to wit, near upon dark on the sd. 13th
instant.... Deposition of George BERRICK, aged 47
years or thereabouts [essentially the same.]

p.685 - Simon JESPER, NFP, will; 7 Feb 1752, 2 Mar 1752
bros. Richard Taylor and John; Michael CONNELL; Mary
CONNELL; sisters Elizabeth FRESHWATER and Sarah
WILLIAMS; cousins Anne TAYLOR, Jude HINES (under 12),
and Winnie CONNELL; no ex; wits: John HILL, Thomas
DUDLEY, John NASH.

p.686 - Philemon BIRD, NFP, will; 2 Jan 1752, 2 Mar 1752
land and all appurtenances to wife Mary, after her
death, to son John, if he has no heirs, to dau. Betty,
if she has no heirs, to dau. Joannah, if she has no
heirs, to eld. dau. Sarah BRUCE, and, if she has no
heirs, to go to Job TILLERY's proper heir at law; my
sd. land above given to my dau. for want of my son
his having issue, I value to be worth 4000 lbs of
tobacco, I therefore order that whichever of my four
daus. shall happen to enjoy my sd. land...she so
inheriting is hereby obliged to pay her sisters their
proper shares of the value I have set upon the land;
ex: wife; wits: Daniel JACKSON, Thomas SAMFORD, Job
TILLERY. [Philemon BIRD mar. Mary MACKGYAR, 25 Feb
1727/28. MRC, p.18.]

p.687 - Edmund COLLINSWORTH, inv; ord. 3 Feb 1752.

p.688 - John PURCELL, inv; ord. 3 Feb 1752.

p.689 - John DOUCHER, will; 18 Jan 1752, 6 Apr 1752
fr. Willoughby NEWTON and his heirs all the tract of
land I now live on which I bought of John GUPTON and
all other est; ex: Willoughby NEWTON; wits: John
NEWTON, Nathaniel ROWE, Thomas CARPENTER.

p.690 - Joseph AMBROSE, will; 8 Feb 1752, 6 Apr 1752
wife Judith all est; daus. Mary, Anne, and Judith;
ex: William SANDERS and wife; wits: George SANDERS,
John BARBER.

p.691 - Harris TUNE, NFP, will; 5 Mar 1752, 6 Apr 1752
sis. Mary BLINCOE; bros. Mark and Anthony; cousin
Travers TUNE; ex: good fr. Christopher LAWSON; wits:
Thomas TUNE, Mary McINDREE, Sarah LAWSON.

p.692 - James BRANNAN, nunc. will; 9 Mar 1752, 6 Apr 1752
Deposition of Thomas DUDLEY...on Wednesday the 26th
of February last, James BRANNAN, who was then sick,
called to him...and told him he was sure he should
die in a little time and said he desired after his
death, the land he then lived on should be sold to
raise money to pay for the land he had purchased in
Nottoway and, if the land should sell for any more
money than paid for the Nottoway land, he gave it to
be eq. div. amongst his wife and chil. and desired
his wife might have his est. inventoried and appraised
and then his chil. would get their parts;
Hannah LINDSEY made essentially the same deposition.
[James and Wilmoth BRANNAN had the foll. chil: Mary
(b.1743), William (b.1745), and Betty (b.1748). NFPR,
p.21.]

     - Joseph BRANNAN, will; 20 Feb 1752, 6 Apr 1752
bro. Thomas the bed and furniture which my father left
me after my mother's decease; bros. James and Caran;
ex: bro. James; wit: Hannah LINDSEY; pres. in court
by Wilmoth BRANNAN [his sister-in-law].

p.693 - John BURROS, inv; ord. 2 Mar 1752.

p.694 - Philomon BIRD, inv; ord. 2 Mar 1752.

p.695 - Dr. John DOUCHER, inv; [nd.]

p.696 - George Tomlin BECKHAM, inv; ord. 6 Apr 1752.

     - Thomas WRIGHT, f.inv; [nd.]

p.697 - James BRANNAN, inv; ord. 6 Apr 1752.

p.698 - Joseph AMBROSE, inv; ord. 6 Apr 1752.

     - Simon JESPER, inv; [nd.]

p.699 - Luke DEMERRIT, f.inv; 4 May 1752.

     - Richard FLYNT, Lun.Par., will; 23 Feb 1752, 6 Jul 1752
wife Mary; son William 20 ac. adjoining Moore FAUNT-
LEROY's Mill, when he is 18, if he has no heirs, to
go to sons John and Richard; eld. sons John and Richard
all the land and plant. I now live on, if either dies
without heirs, his part to go to son David; grdaus.
Anne and Elizabeth MUSE; son William to be kept at
school until 15; ex: sons John and Richard; wits:
Augustine SANFORD, James J. BARKER.

p.701 - William DUDLEY, NFP, will; 21 Dec 1751, 7 Jul 1752
wife Mary the manor part of my plant. whereon I now
live; sons William, Richard, Thomas, and Alexander;
money to be raised out of the drink which is made on

this plant. any time within five years to pay for the
building of a house 12' x 16' which my will and desire
is for my son William to have; daus. Wilmoth BRANHAM,
Winnifred SMITH, Anne, and Catharine; ex: wife; wits:
Simon JESPER, John JESPER, Isaac JONES.

p.703 - Harris TUNE, inv; ord. 6 Apr 1752.

- Thomas BARBER, weaver, inv; ord. 4 May 1752.

p.704 - David TIVENDALE, inv; [nd.]

- Joseph BRANNEN, inv; ord. 1 Jun 1752.

- Samuel RUST, inv; ord. 4 May 1752.

p.705 - Richard FLYNT, inv; ord. 6 Jul 1752.

p.707 - William DUDLEY, inv; ord. 7 Jul 1752.

p.708 - Samuel RAMEY, inv; ord. 4 May 1752.

p.709 - William CROUCHER, inv; ord. 7 Jul 1752.

p.710 - George GLASCOCK, NFP, will; 2 Jun 1749, 2 Oct 1752
       son George all land bought of Thomas YOUNG and Reuben
       DALE; son William all land bought of David FOWLER,
       John FOWLER, and Thomas BRYAN; dau. Judith; no ex;
       wits: William HANKS, Richard HANKS, Thomas HANKS;
       pres. in court by Judith GLASCOCK, 18 Sep 1752.

- William CARTER, inv; [nd.]

p.711 - Simon JESPER, f.inv; [nd.]

p.712 - Edward MORRIS, NFP, will; 5 May 1751, 2 Oct 1752
       dau. Dorcas TUNE and her son Anthony; son Jesse (under
       18); wife Elizabeth tract of land adjoining George
       SANDERS until son Jesse is 18; daus. Winifred and
       Anne; sons Hammond and John; ex: wife; wits: Charles
       DOBYNS, John THRIFT, Henry MISKELL. [Edward MORRIS
       mar. Elizabeth HAMMOND, 25 May 1727. MRC, p.138.]

p.713 - William BRUCE, inv; ord. 4 Aug 1752.

- Edward HUGHES, inv; ord. 3 Aug 1752.

p.714 - Gregory GLASCOCK, inv; ord. 13 May 1752.

p.716 - George GLASCOCK, inv; taken 4 Oct 1752, pres. by Judith
       GLASCOCK.

p.717 - Edward MORRIS, inv; ord. 2 Oct 1752.

p.718 - Jeremiah GREENHAM, will; 28 May 1751, 1 Jan 1753
       John DURHAM my great bible; wife; Christopher HARE
       (now in England); ex: William GLASCOCK and his son
       William; wits:James BOOTH, John WILLIAMS,
       Thomas PENLY. [Jeremiah GREENHAM mar. (1) Dorothy
       DURHAM and (2) Mary [?]. MRC, p.81.]

p.719 - Jeremiah GREENHAM, inv; ord. 1 Jan 1753.

p.720 - John WHITEHILL, nunc.will; 19 May 1753, 2 Jul 1753
       Deposition of Thomas SIMPSON, aged 24,...saith that

John WHITEHILL, an inhabitant of Rich., departed this
life at his usual dwelling house on Friday the 18th of
this instant, and that, about 14 days before his death,
this deponent went to visit him as a neighbor and that
the sd. WHITEHILL told this deponent it was his desire
to make his will, whereupon this deponent sent for one
George BERRICK and his wife to be wits. to the same
and that the sd. WHITEHILL desired this deponent to
take notice that he desired Capt. John SMITH to take
his est. into his management for the payment of his
just debts and that after such payment, the residue
of his est., if any remained, he desired it should be
given to William [HASTIE] and further...that the sd.
WHITEHILL told him that he had sometime before given
the sd. [HASTIE] all his tools and implements as a
perruche maker and further saith not;
George and Elizabeth BERRICK made the same deposition.

p.722 - William DODSON, will; [nd.], 6 Aug 1753
          bro. James; Alice FOWLER; nephew Samuel DODSON; nieces
          Anne and Alice DODSON; wife Hannah; ex: Charles and
          Samuel DODSON; wits: Rawleigh CHINN, Thomas LAWRENCE,
          Hannah LINDSEY.

       - Richard Taylor JESPER, NFP, will; 15 Jan 1753, 6 Aug 1753
          sis. Sarah WILLIAMS and her husband John WILLIAMS a
          gun and sword; cousin Anne TAYLOR who now lives with
          me; ex: bro. John; wits: Isaac JONES, Thomas NASH,
          Davi[d] CONNELL.

p.723 - John WHITEHILL, inv; appraised 19 Jul 1753.

WILL BOOK 6, 1753-1767

p. 1 - Billington McCARTY, inv; ord. 4 Jun 1753.

p. 4 - William DODSON, inv; 6 Aug 1753.

p. 5 - Richard Taylor JESPER, inv; 6 Aug 1753.

p. 6 - Edgcomb SUGGITT, NFP, will; 5 Jan 1753, 1 Oct 1753
          wife plant. and land where I now live until the chil.
          come to age (the boys at 21 and the girls at 18 or
          when married); chil. Jemima, John, Edgcomb, William,
          Elizabeth, Lucy, and the youngest daus. Sarah and
          Susannah; ex: Mr. John WOODBRIDGE and wife; wits:
          William NASH, Roger WILLIAMS, John HAMMILTREE.

p. 9 - William PHILLIPS, NFP, will; 22 Feb 1753, 2 Oct 1753
          son Joshua; wife Anne; dau. Elizabeth BRUMLEY; no ex;
          wits: Charles NICHOLS, William LEE, Richard LEE.

p.10 - William PHILLIPS, inv; 11 Oct 1753.

p.12 - John YEATMAN, inv; [nd.]

p.13 - Benjamin BRUCE, inv. by Elizabeth BRUCE; 1 Oct 1753.

p.14 - William HAMES, NFP, will; 11 Dec 1752, 7 Jan 1754
          wife Elizabeth; chil. William, John, Elizabeth JONES,
          Charity HARRIS, Mary Anne ALLGOOD; chil. of Mary Anne
          ALLGOOD; ex: wife; wits: William CLARK, Richard LITTRILL,
          William HARRIS.

p.15 - Luke MILNER, nunc.will; 30 Jan 1754, 4 Feb 1754
Monday, the 7th day of this instant January...[he]
wished his est. to be eq. div. between his mother,
bros, and sisters, and amongst his little sisters
also, meaning the two girls his mother had by James
McINDREE at the time he was living in the house of
James McINDREE; prov. by the oaths of Thomas WILLIAMS
and Daniel LIGHTFOOT.

p.16 - William HAMES, inv; 29 Jan 1754.

p.17 - Leonard HART, inv; [nd.]

p.18 - William JONES, nunc.will; prov. 1 Apr 1754
Winifred WHITE saith that on Monday the 11th day of
this instant March, the late William JONES, who was
sick, called to her who was then at the looking
glass putting on her cap, and desired her to bring
him the glass that he might look at himself; and after
he had done so, was surprised and said he had fell
away in his flesh very much and this deponent replied to him that he then looked ten times as well as
he did last week and said you don't think how bad you
have been, do you remember you made your will when
you was so bad; he said he did; she asked him how he
had disposed of his est.; he replied that he had left
it among you, meaning his two bros., Isaac and Edward
JONES, and said he gave his negro man named Robin to
Edward JONES and his horse and saddle to Isaac JONES.
Sworn to 15 Mar 1754 by Winifred WHITE and Barbary
JONES.

p.19 - Charles BRYANT, NFP, will; 28 Jan 1754, 1 Apr 1754
chil. Thomas, Anne, Betty, John, and Peggy (all under
age); ex: James and William FORRESTER; wits: John
TARPLEY, Joshua STONE, Faunt. BRYAN.

p.20 - James HARRIET, nunc.will; 2 Dec 1753, 1 Apr 1754
whole est. to George SANDERS and Mary MEEKS; no ex;
wits: H. MISKELL, William BARBER.

- Edward MOZINGO, Lun.Par., will; 10 Nov 1753, 1 Apr 1754
sons: John, Edward part of my land up to the tobacco
house, remainder of land to son George; if George
HARRISON and Margaret, his wife, thinks fit, they
shall live on the sd. lands seven years, yielding and
paying rent yearly 450 lbs. of tobacco; daus. Margaret,
Sarah CHANDLER; d-i-l Hannah; ex: sons Edward and
George; wits: Robert HALL, Daniel MILNER, Susannah
Newman MOSES.

p.21 - [Matthew] WILSON, Lun.Par., will; 20 Nov 1751, 1 Apr 1754
sons Morton and William; ex: sons; wits: John WILSON,
Crask THORNTON, Julius HUNT.

p.22 - Benjamin RUST, Lun.Par., will; 19 Feb 1754, 1 Apr 1754
dau. Hannah all my riverside tract it being 750 ac.
in the lieu of the Totuskey land which was settled on
her by a deed of gift; grdau. Sarah VASS tract of
land on Totuskey; grdau. Anne LOWREY; dau. Sarah
LOWREY; dau. Hannah to have the care of grdau. Sarah
VASS's est. until she reaches 18 or marries; negro
girl Lettis and all her future increase should have
liberty to chose their master or mistress at every
New Year's Day as long as any of them shall be alive

so that it is in any of my family; to my namesake,
Benjamin RUST (the son of John and Sarah RUST) 600
ac. lying in Fairfax Co. adjoining to the land of
John RAINES; bro. Peter RUST; Thomas TAYLOR, William
ANDERSON; William BARBER; ex: dau. Hannah, bro. Peter,
and kinsman Samuel RUST (the son of Peter RUST); wits:
H. MISKELL, John LOWREY, Wm. BARBER, Winifred MORGAN.

p.25 - Capt. George BALL, inv; [nd.]

p.28 - Thomas BARBER, Lun.Par., will; 8 Dec 1753, 6 May 1754
          land and plant. whereon I now live to wife, upon her
          death to son Thomas; land at the head of Totuskey
          Creek together with the land leased to John CHAPRON
          to be sold at public auction; daus. Betty, Anne,
          Frances, Catharine, and Lucy; ex: wife, son Thomas,
          Arjalon PRICE, and Samuel BARBER; wits: Joshua
          SINGLETON, William DENTON, William BARBER.

p.29 - James OLDHAM, will; 4 Feb 1754, 6 May 1754
          son William land whereon I now live, for want of any
          heirs, to my dau. Tabitha, then to my son James
          OLDHAM otherwise called James HEYDON; b-i-l John
          BROWN; ex: wife Leannah and John BROWN; wits: George
          BROWN, Rawleigh TILLERY, A. HOBSON.

p.30 - John EFFORD, NFP, will; 30 Nov 1752, 6 May 1754
          sons William and John; dau. Elizabeth WOOLLARD; wife
          Frances; no ex; wits: Ellis [WADE], George SANDERS,
          H. MISKELL.

p.31 - John YEATMAN, f.inv; [nd.]

        - Benjamin RUST, inv; ord. 1 Apr 1754.

p.34 - Charles BRYAN, inv; ord. 1 Apr 1754.

        - William JONES, inv; taken 24 Apr 1754.

p.37 - William YEATS, inv; ord. 1 Apr 1754.

p.38 - Edward MOZINGO, inv; ord. 1 Apr 1754.

p.39 - James OLDHAM, inv; ord. 6 May 1754.

p.40 - John EFFORD, inv; 23 May 1754.

        - John CONNELLY, inv; ord. 1 Mar 1754.

p.41 - Edgcombe SUGGITT, inv. by John WOODBRIDGE ex; ord. 1 Oct
          1753.

p.43 - Capt. Thomas BARBER, inv; ord. 6 May 1754.

p.46 - Matthew WILSON, inv; ord. 1 Apr 1754.

p.47 - Philip HILLIARD, inv; ord. 6 Jun 1754 [Philip, the son of
          Philip and Eleanor HILLIARD, was b. 10 Aug 1753.
          NFPR, p.95.]

p.48 - Alexander KELLY, Lun.Par., will; 25 Jan 1754, 7 Oct 1754
          dau. Susannah THORNTON; sons James and Alexander; ex:
          bro. Matthew KELLY; wits: William WILSON, Sarah KELLY,
          Powel BEELAND.

p.49 - William WALKER, Lun.Par., will; 15 Apr 1750, 7 Oct 1754
       wife Jane the plant. I now live on and all the land
       belonging thereto, at her death, to son William, and
       if he has no heirs, to son John; wife Jane to receive
       the plant. purchased from Moses HOPWOOD, and, after
       her death, to sons Thomas and Solomon to be eq. div.
       between them, if they have no heirs, then to son
       Samuel, on proviso my son Solomon should contract
       marriage with any of the BILLINGS, I desire the land
       last mentioned be eq. div. between my sons Thomas and
       Samuel; son Thomas all my shoemakers tools; son
       Samuel all my coopers tools; wife Jane to have the
       still; ex: wife and son Thomas; wits: Thomas LEWIS,
       Eliz. WALKER, George FRESHWATER.

p.51 - George SANDERS, Lun.Par., will; 6 Apr 1754, 4 Nov 1754
       son William the lower portion of my land where he
       now liveth after my wife's decease; son George the
       upper part of my land where he now liveth after my
       wife's decease; dau. Judith AMBROSE; wife Anne; ex:
       sons William and George; wits: Jonathan BAYL,
       Christopher COLLINS.

p.52 - John FRESHWATER, inv; ord. 7 Oct 1754.

     - James HARRIOT, inv; ord. 1 Apr 1754.

p.53 - William WALKER, inv; ord. 7 Oct 1754.

p.54 - Alexander KELLY, inv; ord. 7 Oct 1754.

p.55 - William JONES, inv; ord. 5 Aug 1754, appraised 17 Oct 1754.

p.57 -- George HARDWICH, Lun.Par., will; 14 Jun 1754, 6 Jan 1755
       bro. Aaron; Gilbert and Anne BALDERSON; Haney Ritta
       BALDERSON; bro. William; ex: bro. Aaron; wits: William
       GARLAND, Richard NEALE.[George HARDWICH or HARDWICK
       was the son of James and Henrietta (GARLAND) HARDWICK
       of West.Co. WWC, p.103.]

p.58 - William ELDER, NFP, will; 24 Apr 1754, 3 Feb 1755
       chil. Elizabeth GLASCOCK, Peter, William, Sarah,
       Anne; son John; son Thomas 200 ac. of land being part
       of a patent of 400 ac. in Dinwiddie Co. whereon he
       now liveth; sons Edmund and Joseph the remainder of
       the sd. tract in Dinwiddie Co; son Ephraim; dau.
       Maryann; son Charles the land whereon I now live;
       wife Anne; dau. Winifred; no ex; wits: John WOOD-
       BRIDGE, Joshua STONE, James FORRESTER.

p.59 - Alexander ALLOWAY, NFP, will; 27 Jan 1753, 3 Feb 1755
       son John the plant. and land I now live on, if he
       has no heirs, to my three cousins William HAMMOND,
       John HAMMOND, and Isaac ALLOWAY; ex: b-i-l John
       HAMMOND; wits: William GARLAND, Lewis HAMMOND,
       Newman MISKELL.

p.60 - George SANDERS, inv; 22 Feb 1755.

     - George HARDWICH, inv; [nd.]

p.61 - William ELDER, inv; ord. 3 Feb 1755.

p.62 - John BRAMHAM, Lun.Par., will; 28 Mar 1754, 8 Apr 1755

son Richard; dau. Nelly to have one year's schooling
and then to be left in the care of my bro. Benjamin
BRAMHAM; wife Catharine; bro. Benjamin to take the
lease of my ordinary on his own account discharging
my wife from any trouble concerning it; ex: bro.
Benjamin and William GARLAND; wits: Jane STEELE,
Alexander ALLOWAY.

p.63 - Mansfield JENKINS, Lun.Par., will; 1 Nov 1754, 7 Apr 1755
wife Patience all that tract of land whereon I now
live, then to be div. between sons John and Mansfield;
sons James, William, Thomas, and Jeremiah; dau. Elizabeth; son Jesse and the child my wife now goes with;
ex: wife, Alvin MOUNTJOY, and sons John and Mansfield;
wits: James JENKINS, Mark MERRITT, Eliz. JENKINS.

p.64 - James HINDS, NFP, will; 12 Feb 1755, 7 Apr 1755
son John all my land; rest of est. to be eq. div.
between three chil. John, Elizabeth, and Mary; ex:
Joseph WOOLLARD; wits: William JONES, Thomas SMITH,
Maryann JONES.

p.65 - David JACKSON, Lun.Par., will; 8 Sep 1753, 7 Apr 1755
daus. Catharine and Mary; ex: son Daniel; wits:
Robert HALL, Richard LAWSON.

p.66 - John CLARK, will; 4 Apr 1754, 7 Apr 1755
son John part of my land whereon he now lives lying
on the east side of a branch of the Drinking Swamp
heading up to the road that leads from Totuskey to
the coach road and on the south side of the sd.
road; dau. Mary the remaining part of the land that
I hold on the southeast side of the sd. road; son
Robert the plant. on the northwest side of the sd.
road; grson. John BENTLY; wife Elizabeth; ex: wife
and son John; wits: George CLARKE, Mary CLARKE.

p.67 - Alexander ALLOWAY, inv; ord. 3 Feb 1755.

p.68 - Margaret MINTY, Lun.Par., will; 30 Jan 1755, 5 May 1755
cousin Mathew FLEMMING; grson. William SMITH; dau.
Anne [TOOLE]; my desire is that my dau. Anne [TOOLE]
take her dau. Sarah home to live with her; grsons.
Edmund NORTHERN, Edward Minty PURCELL, William
[RUSSELL]; grdaus. Sarah SMITH, Elizabeth NORTHERN;
s-i-l William NORTHERN; Martha FLEMING; William SMITH
and his sis. Sarah SMITH; daus. Margaret PURCELL,
Abigail; ex: s-i-l William NORTHERN; wits: William
GARLAND, William ALLGOOD, John ALDERSON.

p.69 - John BRAMHAM, inv; ord. 8 Apr 1755.

p.70 - James HINDS, inv; ord. 7 Apr 1755.

p.71 - David JACKSON, inv; ord. 7 Apr 1755.

p.72 - John CLARK, inv; ord. 7 Apr 1755.

p.73 - Anthony SYDNOR, inv; ord. 7 Apr 1755.

p.74 - William TUNE, NFP, will; 27 Feb 1755, 3 Jun 1755
son Henry my land and all the appurtenances and when
my son Tarpley shall arrive to the age of 21, my son
Henry to pay my sons Samuel, William, and Tarpley,

if living, five pounds; dau. Leannah; wife; ex: son
Henry and fr. Henry MISKELL; wits: Daniel MISKELL,
David MISKELL.

p.75 - Mansfield JENKINS, inv; ord. 7 Apr 1755.

p.76 - Eliza[beth] WEEKS, inv; ord. 3 May 1755.

p.77 - Margaret MINTY, inv; ord. 5 May 1755.

p.78 - William TUNE, inv; ord. 3 Jun 1755.

p.79 - Jeremiah PETTS, inv; ord. 7 Jul 1755.

      - Jeremiah WALKER, inv; ord. 4 Aug. 1755.

p.80 - Edward TOMLINSON, Lun.Par., will; 2 Jan 1754, 6 Oct 1755
          dau. Sarah WANLESS whom I brought up from a child;
          ex: fr, Benjamin WANLESS; wits: Thomas WATSON, James
          GOULDIE.

      - Daniel LIGHTFOOT, will; 25 Mar 1755, 6 Oct 1755
          wife Alicia; chil. [unnamed]; ex: wife, John JESPER,
          and Henry MISKELL; wits: Charles HAMMOND, James
          DOWNMAN, Anne [HASTY]. [Daniel LIGHTFOOT mar. Alicia
          ALGAR, dau. of Samuel and Mary ALGAR, ca. 1740. MRC,
          p.119.]

p.81 - [Edward] TOMLINSON, inv; [nd.]

p.82 - Daniel LIGHTFOOT, inv; [nd.]

      - Thomas FRESHWATER, Lun.Par., will; 5 May 1754, 1 Mar 1756
          son Thomas plant. where I now live; son George one
          shilling to prevent him coming in for any of the rest
          of my est; dau. Anne, if she should be alive, likewise
          one shilling; rest of est. to be sold and money div.
          between chil. Reuben and Mary; William WHITE should
          have my son Reuben until he arrives at 21; ex: wife
          [Elizabeth] and John JESPER; wits: Samuel BARBER,
          William BARBER.

p.83 - FRESHWATER's Gift to his wife
          The last will of Thomas FRESHWATER declared by him to
          his wife, Elizabeth, on Saturday night between the 6th
          and 7th days of this present instant December in the
          presence of Mary McGEE and her son George TAYLOR.
          [Thomas FRESHWATER was the son of Thomas and Mary
          (HUDSON) FRESHWATER. MRC, p.74.]

      - Thomas FRESHWATER, inv; ord. 1 Mar 1756.

p.85 - Samuel GRAY, inv; ord. 1 Mar 1756.

p.86 - Anthony SYDNOR, f.inv; ord. 1 Mar 1756.

      - Epaphroditus SYDNOR, will; 20 Feb 1756, 3 May 1756
          wife Mary; chil. John, William, Betty, Epaphroditus,
          Isaac, Winnie, Anthony, and Giles; son William the
          tract of land I now live on; son Isaac tract of land
          I bought of Richard TAYLOR lying in Amelia Co; I
          desire that my children's parts of my est. be kept
          together and, as they come of age, to receive their
          proportion; ex: fr. John SMITH and son John of this
          county; wits: William M'KAY, H. MISKELL, Samuel
          WILLIAMS, William DEW.

p.87 - Epaphroditus SYDNOR, inv; ord. 3 May 1756.

p.88 - John GLASCOCK, will; 27 May 1756, 5 Jul 1756
nephew William GLASCOCK (son of bro. William) tract
of land I bought of William ROUGHT; nephew George
GLASCOCK (son of bro. George); nephew William GLAS-
COCK (son of bro. George); nieces Judy and Winnie
GLASCOCK; Samuel and Winnie PEACHEY; nephew Thomas
GLASCOCK; ex: William GLASCOCK (son of William) and
Thomas GLASCOCK; wits: George PHILLIPS, Charles
LOVELACE, Isaac PROCTOR.

p.89 - John GLASCOCK, inv; [nd.]

p.91 - John Span WEBB, inv; ord. 5 Jul 1756. [John Span WEBB
mar. Sarah ALDERSON ca. 1740; their only child was
William. MRC, p.226.]

p.92 - William REID, inv; ord. 6 May 1756.

p.93 - Charles LOVELACE, will
wife Bridget the plant. I now live on, formerly called Rich Neck with 150 ac. of land, upon her death or
remarriage, the land to return to Charles LOVELACE;

At a court held for Rich. Co. the 2d day of August
1756, this writing was pres...by the within named
Bridget LOVELACE as the last will of her husband,
Charles LOVELACE dec'd, and failing to prove the
same to be wrote by the sd. Charles LOVELACE and not
being signed, it is the opinion of the court the same
should not be admitted to record; whereupon Charles
LOVELACE, eld. son and heir-at-law to the aforesaid
Charles LOVELACE dec'd, personally appeared in court
and prayed that the sd. writing should be recorded
as the last will of his father aforesaid and the same
is ordered accordingly. [Charles LOVELACE Sr. (1696-
1755) married, by 1741, Bridget (McLAUGHLIN) JOBSON
dau. of Manus and Elizabeth (WOODBRIDGE) McLAUGHLIN.
MRC, p.121.]

- Charles LOVELACE, inv; ord. 2 Aug 1756.

p.94 - Anne BRYAN, inv; ord. 1 Nov 1756.

p.95 - William LONGWORTH, inv. on 9 Sep 1756 by John LONGWORTH
adm.

p.96 - James HARRISON, Farn.Par., nunc. will; 27 Dec 1756, 3
Jan 1757 [at the home of his bro. Matthew HARRISON]
bros. George, Benjamin, and Matthew; goddau. Martha
[MOOR]; ex. bro. Matthew; no wits.

- Thomas BARBER Gent., inv; ord. 3 Jan 1757 [mentions Thomas
BARBER, Betty BARBER, Anne BARBER, Francis BARBER,
Catharine BARBER, and Lucy BARBER.]

p.97 - James HARRISON, inv. by Matthew HARRISON ex; ord.3 Jan 1757.

p.98 - Avery DYE, Lun.Par., will; 24 Oct 1756, 4 Apr 1757
wife Katharine; grson. Martin DYE (when 21); sons
Avery, William, George, and Fauntleroy (when 21);
ex: wife, son Avery, and Thomas NEWMAN; wits: John
NEWMAN Jr., [?], Thomas NEWMAN. [Avery DYE Sr.
mar. Katharine MACKMILLION dau. of John and Frances
MACKMILLION. MRC, p.62.]

p.99 - Francis EFFORD, NFP, will; 10 Jan 1757, 4 Apr 1757
all est. to be eq. div. between four chil: Betty
POLLY, John POLLY, George EFFORD, Esackariah EFFORD;
ex: Thomas JESPER Jr; wits: Isaac JONES, Alicia
JONES, Mary JONES.

- John ALDERSON, inv; ord. 7 Mar 1757.

p.101 - Francis EFFORD, inv; ord. 4 Apr 1757.

- Avery DYE, inv; ord. 4 Apr 1757.

p.102 - William JORDAN, Gent., inv. by John Morton JORDAN; [nd.]
[mentions servants Samuel JANNIS and Elizabeth
KENHILL.] [William JORDAN mar. (1) Mary (MOUNTJOY)
MORTON, wid. of John MORTON Jr., and (2) Anne
(FOSTER) BARBER, wid. of Samuel BARBER; John Morton
was the only child of the first marriage. MRC, p.110.]

p.103 - Jesse GLASCOCK, inv. by William GLASCOCK adm.; ord. 2
May 1757.

p.104 - George TAYLOR, Lun.Par., will; 19 Jul 1756, 1 Aug 1757
mother Mary McGEE all my land, after her death, to
my sis. Elizabeth McGEE; Rachel TAYLOR to have two
years schooling at the charge of my mother and sis;
ex: mother and sis; wits: Thomas BARBER, Daniel
JACKSON, Anne BARBER.

- John ELMORE, NFP, will; 20 Jun 1757, 3 Oct 1757
wife Anne entire est., after her death or remarriage,
to return to chil; son George plant. I now live on,
he lacking heirs, to go to son John; son Travers;
sons Charles and Travers to have two years schooling;
ex: wife and Daniel EVERETT; wits: John GIBSON, John
BOOTH, Gabriel SMITHER. [John ELMORE mar. Anne
RAYNOLDS, 29 Nov 1728. NFPR, p. 59.]

p.105 - George TAYLOR, inv; ord. 1 Aug 1757.

p.106 - William BARKER, inv; ord. 3 Oct. 1757.

- John ELMORE, inv; ord. 3 Oct 1757.

p.108 - Dr. James FENDLAY, inv; ord. 3 Jan [1757].

p.109 - Thomas SCURLOCK, NFP, will; [28] Feb 1756, 7 Nov 1757
wife Anne use of my whole est., at her death, to go
to son Alexander, if he has no heirs, land to go to
son [Michael]; daus. Mary DODSON and Elizabeth GRIGGS;
grchil. Joshua and Sarah SCURLOCK (chil. of my son
William); chil. of my son James to receive one
shilling each in full to debar them from any other
part of my est; ex: wife; wits: [Newgent] George
ROUTT, James BOOTH.

p.111 - William FAUNTLEROY, Lun.Par., will; 26 Oct 1757, 5 Dec 1757
the lands I bought of Emmanuel CLEAVES, Matthew
THORNTON, Hopkins THORNTON, and Col. John TAYLOE...
lying between Rappahannock Creek and Doctor's Creek
to my son William; lands bought of Capt. John SPICER,
Capt. Daniel McCARTY, Matthew DAVIS, and the courthouse land which I bought of the county...and makes
the tract I now live on to my son William; lands I
bought of Mr. Edward BARRON, James HEARNE, and Jane

McCLINCH to my son Moore; tract of land called
Quintanoake, which was given by grfather GRIFFIN
to Moore FAUNTLEROY; George Hale FAUNTLEROY (son of
Moore FAUNTLEROY);the lands I bought of Mr. Thomas
Wright BELFIELD, Mr. James SKELTON, Mrs. Mary BELFIELD,
and Daniel DALEY lying in Essex Co. to my son John;
all lands in Caroline Co. to three sons William, Moore,
and John; daus. Sarah GRAY (and her chil.), Hannah
ROBINSON, Apphia DANGERFIELD, Catharine LEWIS, Mary
BROOKE, Anne [PETTIT]; grson Henry ROBINSON (son of
dau. Hannah); grchil. Mary, Martha, Lucy, and Leroy
DANGERFIELD (chil. of dau. Apphia); grson. Robert
BROOKE (son of dau. Mary); ex: kinsman The Hon. John
TAYLOE Esq. and three sons William, Moore, and John;
wits: Thomas NEWMAN, Sam. ROCK, John HORTON.

p.114 - Charles BROWN, inv; ord. 7 Nov 1757.

p.115 - Thomas SCURLOCK, inv; ord. 7 Nov 1757.

p.116 - Richard ALDERSON, will; 23 May 1753, 6 Mar 1758
son John all land; son Richard; ex: son John; wits:
John RAYNOLDS, James LUTTRELL.

p.117 - Moore FAUNTLEROY, will, 12 Nov 1754, 6 Mar 1758
all lands to eld. son Moore; son John and the child
my wife is now big with; ex: fr. and relations Col.
Landon CARTER, Col. John TAYLOE, William BROCKENBROUGH,
and Charles BEALE; wits: Charles MORTIMER, Robert
JORDAN.
Cod. As John had a son named William, since the making
of this will, who died, it is my desire that what was
intended him by this will may be given...to my youngest
child which is a girl named Susannah; 21 May 1756.

p.118 - Mary CUMMINS, will; 20 Feb 1758, 7 Mar 1758
Willoughby HARRISON; Joseph PARK; Anne NASH (wid.);
unnamed grdau.; son Edward PRIDHAM; grson Christopher
PRIDHAM; ex: neighbors John RUSSELL and William
GARLAND; wits: Mary FRESHWATER, Mary WALKER.

p.119 - Edward GOLDSBY, Lun.Par., will; 7 Feb 1758, 3 Apr 1758
wife Jane; if wife should remarry, est. to be div.
among chil. [unnamed]; ex: wife; wits: Wm. THRIFT,
Anna THRIFT, Richard [FRYER].

p.120 - Richard ALDERSON, inv; ord. 6 Mar 1758.

p.121 - Mary CUMMINGS, inv; ord. 6 Mar 1758.

p.122 - Elizabeth BRAGG, inv; ord. 6 Mar 1758.

p.123 - Edward GOLDSBY, inv; ord. 3 Apr 1758.

p.124 - William HAMMOND, inv; ord. 3 Apr 1758.

       - Joseph EIDSON, inv. by John EIDSON adm; ord. 1 May 1758.

p.126 - Maj. Moore FAUNTLEROY, inv; ord. 7 Mar 1758.

p.129 - Robert MITCHELL, Lun.Par., will; 2 Jan 1758, 3 Jul 1758
wife Hannah; son William; all chil. including the one
my wife is now big with; ex: wife, bro. Richard
MITCHELL, and Moore FAUNTLEROY; wits: John BELFIELD,
Henry FRANKS, Wm. ROBINS, Peter EVANS. [Robert MITCHELL

was the son of Robert (1684-1748) and Susannah
MITCHELL of Lanc. Co. He mar. Hannah BALL, dau. of
Col. William BALL on 7 Sep 1746. WLC,p.157, MRC, p.134.]

p.130 - Joshua PHILLIPS, NFP, will; 16 May 1758, 3 Jul 1758
dau. Anne (under 18); son William (under 19) all
carpenter's and cooper's tools; wife; mother Anne
PHILLIPS to have the care of my dau; ex: wife,
Samuel BRUMLEY, and George DAVIS; wits: Charles HINDS,
Charles NICHOLS, [A.] DANIEL.

- James BLAKERBY, inv; ord. 6 Mar 1758.

- Robert MITCHELL, inv; ord. 3 Jul 1758.

p.133 - William FAUNTLEROY, inv. [in margin: N.B. the division
is recorded in the Book of Orphans]; 7 Aug 1758.
[Included est. in Caroline Co.]

p.140 - Phillis BOWLES, will; 15 Jun 1758, 4 Sep 1758
dau. Elizabeth HUMPHRIES; Dinah GLASCOCK (wife of
Travers GLASCOCK); ex: Travers GLASCOCK; wits:
George DAVIS, Anne DAVIS.

- Job HAMMOND, will; 18 Oct 1758, 6 Nov 1758
sons Samuel, [Jarvis], Job, Thomas; daus. Susannah,
Elizabeth, Mary, Amadine; ex: son Thomas; wits: John
HAMMOND, Anthony TUNE, Darcos TUNE. [Job HAMMOND mar.
Amadine BAYLIS, dau. of Thomas and Catharine BAYLIS,
by 1 Sep 1703. MRC, p.86.]

p.141 - William JONES, will; 6 Oct 1758, 6 Nov 1758
son Charles (when 21); wife and other chil. (unnamed); ex: William GARLAND, Bradley GARNER, Eleanor
JONES, and wife; wits: John HORTON, Thomas CALLIS.

p.142 - Margaret DOWNMAN, NFP, will; 13 Sep 1758, 6 Nov 1758
[son] William; sons Rawleigh, Charles, Christopher,
and Elijah; grson Rawleigh DOWNMAN; grdau. Margaret
DOWNMAN; ex: son Christopher; wits: Charles DODSON,
Thomas HOWARD, Thomas DALE, Dominick NEWGENT.
[Margaret was the wife of Rawleigh DOWNMAN (1680-
1719) of Lanc. Co. and the dau. of Capt. William BALL
also of Lanc. Co. WLC, pp. 6, 74; MRC, p.243.]

p.143 - Job HAMMOND, inv; ord. 6 [Nov 1758].

p.145 - Joshua PHILLIPS, inv; ord. 3 Jul 1758.

p.147 - FAUNTLEROY's f.inv; [nd.]

p.148 - Edward JONES, NFP, will; 5 Oct 1756, 2 Apr 1759
wife Barbary the plant. I now live on, after her death,
to go to dau. Elizabeth JONES; daus. Winifred, Lucy,
Margaret; ex: bro. Isaac; wits: Isaac JONES, W. WHITE.
[Edward JONES mar. Barbary BAKER in 1750. MRC, p.107.]

p.149 - Mrs. Margaret DOWNMAN, inv; completed 8 Dec 1758.

p.150 - Charles BRAGG, inv; ord. 2 Apr 1759.

p.151 - John WOOLLARD, NFP, will; 9 Mar 1759, 7 May 1759
son Joseph land whereon I live; son Samuel land I
bought of William HAMMOND; son John; Joseph (son of
John WOOLLARD); Priscilla (dau. of son John); dau.

Anne SMITH; Anne SMITH (dau. of Thomas and Anne SMITH);
John SMITH (son of Thomas and Anne); wife Anne; son
William 45 pounds from Joseph and Samuel WOOLLARD;
ex: sons Joseph and Samuel; wits: Henry MISKELL, Wm.
WOOLLARD, John HANCKS.

p.153 - William JONES, inv; ord. 6 Nov 1758.

p.154 - William BAILEY, inv; ord. 7 May 1759.

p.155 - John NEWMAN, inv; ord. 2 Apr 1759.

p.156 - Thomas WALKER, will; 17 Apr 1759, 2 Jul 1759
all est. to mother Jane WALKER; ex: mother; wits:
John RAYNOLDS, William WALKER, John WALKER.

p.157 - William EVERETT, NFP, will; 18 Feb 1759, 2 Jul 1759
daus. Ruth ROUTT, Anne HAMMOND, Elizabeth WILLIAMS,
and Sarah DODSON; son Daniel half of the land whereon I now live; wife Margaret; no ex; wits: William
FORRESTER, Gabriel SMITHER.

p.158 - John WOOLLARD, inv; ord. 7 May 1759.

p.160 - Daniel BURGESS, inv; ord. 2 Jul 1759.

p.161 - Thomas WALKER, inv; ord. 2 Jul 1759.

    - William EVERETT, inv; ord. 2 Jul 1759.

p.163 - Sarah SNEADE, Lun.Par., will; 21 Jan 1758, 5 Nov 1759
grsons Charles Sneade MORTON and Thomas MORTON; dau.
Elizabeth MORTON; servant John SHAPPLEY unto s-i-l,
James MORTON, for the residue of his time of servi-
tude; nieces Anne (the wife of John EIDSON) and
Sarah (the wife of William SPENCE); ex: trusty fr.
John EIDSON and grson Charles Sneade MORTON; wits:
Valentine STURMAN, Roderick [PERRY], James MORTON,
Christopher COLLINS.

p.164 - Anthony SYDNOR, will; 27 Sep 1759, 5 Nov 1759
grson John (son of late son Epaphroditus SYDNOR)
dwelling plant; grson Anthony SYDNOR residue of land
on north side of the mill swamp...to the Drinking
Swamp...land purchased of John BROWN, Leroy and John
HUGHLETT, and part of the land I bought of CRALLE;
grson Giles SYDNOR land on south side of the mill
swamp known by the name of Mingoe's Quarter; grson
Robert SYDNOR all land on lower side of a valley...
to the mill swamp...to the mouth of Dunn's Spring
Branch...through Canterbery's Orchard to the outer-
most bounds of my land, including the land I bought
of Henry CLARK and George HILL; grson Epaphroditus
SYDNOR all my land at Moratico Quarter; wife Elizabeth;
grchil. William, Elizabeth, Isaac, Winifred, and
Susannah SYDNOR; dau. Dewannah SYDNOR plant. and
houses known as Sawney's Quarter; eight chil. of
dec'd son Epaphroditus; three chil. of dec'd son
Anthony; grchil. Anne ROUTT, John, Anthony, Sillah,
Lucy, William, Richard, and George; grdaus. E. NELMS,
Lucy ROUTT, and Elizabeth DOWNMAN; daus. Anne MITCHELL,
Lucy DOWNMAN, and Ruth BELFIELD; Mr. Travers TARPLEY;
grchil. Wilmoth SMITHER, John ROUTT, and Thomas
BELFIELD; ex: grson John SYDNOR; wits: Robert HAMMOCK,
Hugh HAMMOCK, Frances SYDNOR. [Anthony SYDNOR mar.

120

        (1) Winifred GLASCOCK and (2) Elizabeth DEW. MRC,p.
        200.]

p.168 - John WILSON, Lun.Par., will; 6 Mar 1759, 4 Feb 1760
        son Joseph (under 18) plant. whereon I now live; sons
        John, James Molden, Tarpley, and Spicer all land in
        Culpeper Co; daus. Susannah, Sarah, Anne [LAYN]; son
        John to be bound unto James KELLY when 14; ex: Wm.
        LAINE and Alvin MOUNTJOY; wits: George NEWMAN,
        Edmond YARDLEY, John BRAGG.

p.169 - Charles HINDS, NFP, will; 6 Jan 1760, 4 Feb 1760
        son Thomas all lands on north side of branch begin-
        ning at Farnham Bridge...to WILLIAMS' line, if he
        has no male heirs, to son Charles; son Richard all
        remaining lands, if he has no male heirs, to son
        Josiah; three youngest sons Richard, Charles, and
        Josiah; fr. Christopher LAWSON to bring up son Richard;
        fr. Joseph WOOLLARD to bring up youngest son Josiah;
        fr. Mr. Charles DOWNMAN to bring up son Charles; dau.
        Judith to receive the bed and furniture whereon she
        commonly lies; ex: Christopher LAWSON and Joseph
        WOOLLARD; wits: Richard LEE, Abraham WILLIAMS,
        George [GEAYDEN].

p.170 - Henry WILLIAMS, NFP, will; 20 Apr 1759, 4 Feb 1760
        son John all land; sons Daniel, Henry, and Permenus;
        dau. Sarah WOOLLARD; godson Alexander BRYANT (son of
        Alexander BRYANT); son John to keep son Permenus un-
        til 21; ex: son John and fr. Christopher LAWSON; wife
        [unnamed]; wits: John GIBSON, Bridget OWENS, Eliz.
        [MERRUE].

p.171 - Sarah SNEAD, inv; ord. 5 Nov 1759.

p.172 - Henry WILLIAMS, inv; ord. 4 Feb 1760.

p.173 - Charles HINDS, inv; ord. 4 Feb 1760.

p.174 - Anthony SYDNOR, inv; ord. 5 Nov 1759.

p.176 - George NASH, inv; ord. 4 Feb 1760.

    - Thomas JESPER Sr., NFP, will; 20 Oct 1759, 5 May 1760
        son Thomas 52 and one half ac. where he now lives
        and 50 ac. now in the possession of my bro. John,
        land that my grfath. Richard JESPER bought of Richard
        DUDLEY, if he has no heirs, to son Daniel; son Daniel
        50 ac. adjacent to Thomas JESPER's 50 ac. and the
        plant. I now live on, if he has no heirs, to son
        Thomas; if neither son has heirs, land to be eq. div.
        between two daus. Mary Anne and Betty; care of Betty
        JESPER to son Daniel if she shall like to live with
        him or under his care, if not, my desire is that she
        may choose a guardian and have her part of the est.
        out of his hands; care of Francis EFFORD's children
        and their estates to son Daniel; ex: Thomas and Daniel
        JESPER; wits: Isaac JONES, John NIXSON, George GAYDEN,
        John JESPER.

p.178 - John WILSON, inv. pres. by William LANE one of the ex;
        ord. 3 Feb 1760.

p.180 - Thomas JESPER, inv; ord. 5 May 1760.

p.183 - Henry HEADLEY, inv; ord. 5 May 1760. [Henry HEADLEY, the son of Henry and Jane HEADLEY, mar. Anne PUGH, the dau. of Lewis and Anne PUGH, ca. 1736; they had at least seven chil: Mary (b.1738), Anne (b.1741), Robert (b.1745), William (b. ca. 1749), James (b.1751), Luke (b.1754), and John (b.ca. 1757). There may have also been two other sons. NFPR, p.91.]

p.185 - Joseph WOOLLARD, inv; ord. 5 May 1760.

- Jesse HILL, Farn.Par., will; 25 May 1760, 7 Jul 1760 loving bro. Thomas Suggitt HILL all est; godson Isaac BEACHAM (son of Isaac BEACHAM), in regard to the love I bear to him, as to discharge a debt which I owe to the father of the sd. boy; aunt Susannah WEBB; sis. Winifred WILLIAMS; godson Thaddeus WILLIAMS (son of Samuel) to have 10 pounds for schooling; ex: Thomas S. HILL and Samuel WILLIAMS; wits: William NASH, John WALKER, Randal WALKER, John PLUMMER.

p.186 - Isaac WEBB, NFP, will; 19 Oct 1759, 7 Jul 1760 sons John, Isaac, James, Charles, and Cudbuth [sic]; wife Frances; dau. Nancy; seven younger chil. Cudbuth, Elizabeth, Winnie, Nancy, Percilla, Charles, Isaac; ex: wife and fr. Joshua SINGLETON; wits: Billington McCARTY, William HUNT, William WEBB. [Isaac WEBB (1709-1760), the son of Giles and Elizabeth (BARBER) WEBB, mar. Frances BARBER. MRC, p.226.]

p.190 - James BARKER, Lun.Par., will; 14 Oct 1760, 3 Nov 1760 fr. Robert SPENCE all the plant. whereon I now dwell which I bought of John JORDAN; Sarah and Elizabeth GREENSTREET; George FISHER; Vincent (son of William JENKINS and Frances his now wife); two nephews and nieces John BARKER (son of my bro. William), Joshua (son of Richard JENKINS and Sibella his now wife), and Anne SPENCE (dau. of William SPENCE and Sarah his now wife); ex: Capt. Moore FAUNTLEROY; wits: Richard FLINT, Roderick PERRY, Valentine STEARMAN, Christopher COLLINS.

p.191 - James MORTON, Lun.Par., will; 1 Apr 1760, 3 Nov 1760 wife Elizabeth; son Thomas, after wife's death, the tract of land I purchased of Jane COLE containing 50 ac; sons Charles, Snead, and Thomas; ex: wife; wits: Richard FLYNT, Christopher COLLINS. [James MORTON mar. Elizabeth (SNEAD) KEITH, wid., dau. of Charles SNEAD. MRC, p.139.]

p.192 - Gabriel ALLOWAY, will; 21 Feb 1760, 3 Nov 1760 son Isaac; wife Catran; daus. Judy and Elizabeth; ex: Isaac JONES and George CLARK; wits: Anthony [DOWTON], Mary CLARK.

p.193 - Abraham WILLIAMS, inv. of all his est. that has come into the possession of Thomas SMITH his guardian; [nd.]

p.194 - Thomas YEATMAN, inv. by Eleanor YEATMAN; ord. 7 Jul 1760.

p.195 - Anne MEEKS, Lun.Par., will; 28 Apr 1758, 2 Feb 1761 s-i-l Henry SISSON; grdaus. Judith NASH, Sarah SMITH, and Anne MEEKS; daus. Mary McINDRE and Elizabeth WALKER; ex: s-i-l Henry SISSON; wits: H. SETTLE, John JONES, William WILSON. [Anne MEEKS was the wid. of Richard MEEKS. MRC, p.187.]

p.196 - John LAWSON, NFP, will; 15 Jan 1758, 2 Feb 1761
daus. Lucy LAWSON, Anne LAWSON, Elizabeth BARBER,
Joanna HOBSON, Catharine WHITE; son Christopher; ex:
son Christopher and s-i-l Adcock HOBSON; wits: H.
MISKELL, John OLDUM, Richard HANES.

p.197 - Henry MISKELL, will; 31 Oct 1760, 2 Feb 1761
son William the plant. whereon I now live and half of
the land contained within this tract adjoining the sd.
plant; son Newman the plant. which I bought of Jonathan LYELL and half of the land contained within this
tract adjoining the sd. plant; son Daniel the plant.
whereon he now lives with the upper part of the land
from Col. John TARPLEY's plant; son David the plant.
whereon he now lives the lower half of the land to
the mill pond and pocoson; if any of the sons dies
without heirs, son Jeremiah (under 21) shall have
that one's part of land; s-i-l William DOBYNS and
Rebecca his wife the land that I bought of Thomas
DEW dec'd; daus. Rebecca DOBYNS and Rachel DOBYNS;
William BAKER all former balances of all accounts if
any such on my old books that have not been credited
to be void against him; grdau. Winifred BAKER (when
21); son Jeremiah to be bound by my ex. to Alexander
DUDLEY or Solomon REDMOND until 21 to learn either
of their trades; wife [unnamed]; ex: Travers TARPLEY,
William MISKELL, and George MISKELL; wits: William
SYDNOR, Thomas CONNALLY, John HARFORD. [Henry MISKELL
mar. Winifred DALTON, dau. of John and Mary DALTON.
MRC, p.133.]

p.199 - James MORTON, inv; ord. 3 Nov 1760.

p.200 - Elizabeth APPLEBY, will; 22 Sep 1757, 2 Mar 1761
eld. son John; dau. Tomizine; ex: youngest son Richard; wits: Anne JOHNSON, Thomas SAMFORD.

p.201 - Tobias PURCELL, will; 22 Jan 1761, 2 Mar 1761
John Purcell MURRAY (son of Mary Anne MURRAY) all the
land I have on the south side of Young's Swamp; Tobias
Purcell MURRAY (son of Mary Anne MURRAY) all my manor
plant. and the still on the north side of Young's
Swamp; daus. Elizabeth ALGOOD, Catharine PURCELL;
Winifred Purcell MURRAY, Lucy Purcell MURRAY; ex:
Mary Anne MURRAY; wits: William NORTHEN, George
WILLIAMS, Luke WILLIAMS. [Tobias PURCELL, son of
David and Belinda PURCELL, was b. in NFP 23 Dec 1691.
He mar. (1) Margaret ? ; there is some doubt
whether he mar. (2) Mary Anne MORROW. MRC, p.164.]

p.203 - Susanna GRAY, Sitt.Par., will; 15 Jan 1761, 2 Mar 1761
dau. Ellen ROBINS; grdau. Mary Ellen ANDERSON, ex:
dau; wits: John JENNINGS, Thos. BRUCE, Francis JEN-
NINGS.

p.204 - Anne MEEKS, inv; ord. 2 Feb 1761.

p.205 - Abraham DANIEL, inv; ord. 7 Jul 1760.

p.206 - Henry MISKELL, inv; ord. 2 Feb 1761.

p.207 - Isaac WEBB, inv; ord. 7 Jul 1760.

p.209 - Gabriel ALLOWAY, inv; ord. 3 Nov 1760.

p.211 - William DUDLEY, inv; ord. 2 Mar 1761.

p.212 - Richard BARNES, Lun.Par., will; 15 Jul 1754, 2 Mar 1761
dear bro. and friends Maj. Abraham BARNES and his two
sons, John and Richard, Col. Landon CARTER, and Col.
John TAYLOE all that plant., tract, or parcel of land
whereon I now live...adjoining on the main road and
[the land of] Edward TOMLINSON also all that plant.,
tract, or parcel of land lying at Mulberry Island on
the river side, also all that land which was Mrs.
INGO's dower and which is part of another tract of
land lying at Mulberry Island, and also all that land
I bought of John MARKS; wife Penelope; son Thomas;
daus. Mary [KELSICK], Rebecca BECKWITH, Elinor, Sarah,
and Elizabeth; ex: bro. Abraham; wits: William WILSON,
John SAMFORD, John NEWMAN, George WILSON, Henry
SISSON, William FORD;
Memorandum, 10 Jul 1757; mentions Jonathan BECKWITH
husband of dau. Rebecca.
Cod., notes that dau. Elinor mar. John Morton JORDAN.
p.245 - To all Christian people to whom these presents shall come,
I Abraham BARNES of St. Mary's Co. in the Province of
Maryland send greeting, whereas my bro. Richard BARNES
late of Richmond Co. in the Colony of Virginia, in his
lifetime duly made his last will...whereby he appointed me...his whole...ex. and whereas the sd. Richard
BARNES soon after making the sd. will died, and I the
sd. Abraham BARNES have refused to accept the said
executorship and have never acted therein. Now know
ye that I...as a further declaration thereof do by
these presents renounce and disclaim this said executorship as witness my hand and seal this 24th day of
February; wits: Ger. HOOE, Francis RANDALL.
[Capt. Richard BARNES mar. (1) Frances INGO and (2)
Penelope MANLY. MRC, p.10.]

p.246 - John LAWSON, inv; ord. 2 Feb 1761.

p.247 - Charles DOBYNS, inv; ord. 2 Mar 1761.

p.248 - Samuel BARBER, will; 10 Oct 1760, 4 Mar 1761
aunt LEWIS; Mary BEALE (wife of Charles BEALE) and
Sarah MORTIMER (wife of Charles MORTIMER); Thomas
LAWSON; William BROCKENBROUGH; William MUIR; Samuel
KELSICK all land in NFP; fr. Younger KELSICK all land
in Lun.Par; William BROCKENBROUGH to be guardian of
Samuel KELSICK; ex: William BROCKENBROUGH, John ORR,
and Younger KELSICK; wits: A. BARNES, Francis RANDALL,
Sally BARNES, Elizabeth BARNES.

p.249 - Richard LAWSON, Lun.Par., will; 12 Feb 1759, 4 May 1761
wife; grsons Thomas Lawson REDMAN, Elijah MOORE, and
Vincent MOORE; daus. Mary REDMAN, Anne HALL; sisters
Anne MURPHY, Elizabeth DAVIS; ex: wife, bro. Thomas
LAWSON, and s-i-l John REDMAN; wits: Henry SETTLE,
Anne LAWSON, Mary BRAMHAM.

p.251 - Richard BARNES, inv; ord. 2 Mar 1761.

p.255 - William FREEMAN, inv; ord. [3] Nov 1760.

     - Susannah GREY, inv; ord. 7 Mar 1761.

p.256 - James BARKER, inv; ord. 3 Nov 1760.

p.257 - Joseph BRUCE, inv; ord. 2 Mar 1761.

p.258 - Tobias PURCELL, inv; ord. 2 Mar 1761.

p.259 - William HARPER, NFP, will; 31 Dec 1759, [1] Jun 1761
son Joshua; daus. Mary CAVENTER, Susannah; wife
Elizabeth; other chil. William, Daniel, George,
Elizabeth, Wilmoth, and Hannah; grson. James HARPER;
ex: wife and son Joshua; wits: William HARRIS,
Ambrose JONES, Peter LAMKIN.

p.260 - Robert TOMLIN Sr., will; 14 Feb 1760, 1 Jun 1761
son Robert plant. and tract of land in Lun.Par. on
the Rappahannock River; son Walker all land in North.
Co; sister-in-law Mrs. Betty WEBB; Mrs. Susannah WEBB
so long as she lives with her aunt, Mrs. Betty WEBB,
and assists her in the care and affairs of my family
and est; ex: The Hon. John TAYLOE Esq., Col. Presley
THORNTON, and Dr. Nicholas FLOOD; wits: Williamson
BALL, William SALLARD, John [FONES]. [Robert TOMLIN
was the son of Capt. Robert and Elizabeth TOMLIN.
MRC, p.217.]

p.262 - James LANDMAN, Lun.Par., will; 4 Nov 1760, 6 Jul 1761
wife Elizabeth; chil. Vincent, Catharine, Fanny; ex:
wife and bro. George LANDMAN; wits: Benjamin BRAMHAM,
William LANDMAN.

     - John RAYNOLDS, will; 9 Apr 1761, 6 Jul 1761
wife Anne the plant. whereon I now live and the land
near Mr. HAMILTON's, after her decease, to son George;
no ex; wits: Robert FERGUSON, George HOW, Jeremiah
BROWN, Andrew HEADLEY, John BROWN.

p.264 - Alvin MOUNTJOY, inv; his wid., Ellen MOUNTJOY, objected
to part of the appraisement since she possessed the
one slave from Matthew THORNTON, a former husband.
[Alvin MOUNTJOY mar. Eleanor the dau. of Capt. John
and Elizabeth (MOSS) CRASK; their only child was
Mary. MRC, p.140.]

p.266 - Richard BARNES, f.inv; ord. 4 Jun 1761.

p.267 - Elizabeth GRIFFIN, will; 28 Nov 1760, 3 Aug 1761
dau. Anne TARPLEY; grdaus. Elizabeth TARPLEY, Alice
TARPLEY, Winnie TARPLEY, Mrs. Phoebe MENZIES, Mrs.
Alice EUSTACE, Mrs. Elizabeth ADAMS, Miss Betty
COLSTON; grson. Griffin [PERT]; fr. Col. William
PEACHEY and John TARPLEY; ex: fr. John TARPLEY; wits:
Travers TARPLEY, Joanna STEPTOE, Nancy STEPTOE.

p.269 - John BYRD, Farn.Par., will; 14 Jul 1761, 3 Aug 1761
parcel of land consisting of 88 ac. between Job
TILLERY and Samuel BARBER to be eq. div. between
John LISLE, David JONES, Joanna BYRD, and Sarah
BRUCE (lawful daus. of Thomas BRUCE and Sarah his
wife); crop of corn and tobacco to John LISLE except
that part I agreed to let William CAVANNER have;
sis. Joanna; John BRUCE (son of Thomas BRUCE); Wm.
JONES (son of David JONES); four sisters [unnamed];
fr. John LISLE to be ex. to my sisters Joannah and
Sarah BRUCE; wits: John HAMMOND [Younger], Job
TILLERY.

p.271 - James LANDMAN, inv; ord. 6 Jul 1761.

p.272 - Thomas DUDLEY, inv; [nd.]

p.275 - Jeremiah PACKETT, inv; ord. 2 Mar [no year given].

     - Robert TOMLIN Gent., inv; returned 1 Aug 1761.

p.278 - Anne MEEKS, f.inv; ord. 2 Feb 1761.

     - Richard LAWSON, inv; ord. 4 May [1761].

p.280 - John RAYNOLDS, inv; ord. [6] Jul 1761.

p.283 - Elizabeth APPLEBY, inv. and sale; [nd.]

p.285 - John BYRD, inv; 3 Aug 1761.

     - Sarah BURROWS, inv; [nd.]

p.287 - By an ord. of Rich. Court at the request of Thomas
        GRIFFIN, guardian to his brother's orphans, we,...,
        have valued the foll. goods presented to us at the
        Lancaster Quarter; 25 Sep 1761.

p.290 - Samuel BARBER Gent., inv; 11 Sep 1761.

p.292 - Sarah EFFORD, inv; [nd.]

p.293 - John WILLIAMS Sr., NFP, will; 8 May 1761, 1 Feb 1762
        daus. Anne MISKELL, Lucy, Elizabeth, Jane, and
        Margaret; sons Jonathan, Rawleigh, and John (under
        12); John and Jonathan (sons of Anne MISKELL); wife
        Elizabeth; ex: fr. Samuel and Luke WILLIAMS and
        Daniel EVERETT; wits: William [DEW], George WILLIAMS,
        Luke WILLIAMS.

p.294 - John BRICKEY, NFP, will; 19 Feb 1762, 1 Mar 1762
        wife's son Jerem[iah] WARD one gun and the other
        necessaries befitting a soldier and, when he shall
        reach 21, my desire is that he have a sufficient
        horse, bridal, and saddle and suit of wearing apparel
        befitting a person of his circumstances on condition
        he remain with his mother and be obediant an assistant
        to her; Temperance LASEY; cousin John BRICKEY and his
        son Gerrard; cousin Darcas BRICKEY; ex: wife Mary;
        wits: Hugh THOMAS, James BALEY Jr., Hugh THOMAS Jr.

p.296 - John WILLIAMS, inv; ord. 1 Feb 1762.

p.297 - Robert TOMLIN, inv; ord. 1 Feb 1762.

     - Edward JONES, inv; ord. 2 Apr 1759 [mentions "somethings
        never div. between Isaac JONES and his bro. Edward
        JONES], recorded 1 Feb 1762.

p.299 - John BRICKEY, inv; 5 Apr 1762.

p.300 - Mary EVANS, inv. by Peter EVANS adm; ord. 1 Mar 1762.

     - Mary HOW, will; 21 Nov 1761, 7 Jun 1762
        grson. Thomas LUTTRELL; grdau. Mary LUTTRELL; dau.
        Elizabeth LUTTRELL; ex: dau; wits: Jeremiah BROWN,
        William LUTTRELL, Presley LUTTRELL.

p.301 - John HARRIS, NFP, will; 5 Mar 1762, 7 Jun 1762
        wife Charity all est; sons Hugh and John; other est.

to be div. between chil. after wife's death or remarriage; ex: wife and good friends Luke WILLIAMS
and John SYDNOR; wits: David MISKELL, Wm. OSGRIFFIN.

p.302 - James DOWNMAN, NFP, will; 26 Nov 1761, 7 Jun 1762
I devise that all my negroes and other personal est.
may be kept together until all my chil. shall be well-
educated and raised; son Travers to have 50 pounds to
purchase land also a tract of land on Farnham Creek
which I purchased of Mr. John MILLNER; child that
wife is now going with; plant. and land, containing
about 450 ac., I now live on to wife until son
Rawleigh shall reach 21; ex: wife and friends Capt.
Robert DOWNMAN, Richard MITCHELL, and Maj. Travers
TARPLEY; wits: John WOODBRIDGE, Anne ROUT.

p.304 - James LUTTRELL, inv; ord. 9 Jun 1762.

p.305 - Mary HOW, inv; ord. 9 Jun 1762.

     - John GOWER, inv; ord. 7 Jun 1762.

p.306 - William HARPER, inv; ord. 1 Jun 1761, appraised 5 Jul 1762.

p.307 - John HARRIS, inv; ord. 7 Jun 1762.

p.308 - James DOWNMAN, inv; ord. 7 Jun 1762.

p.310 - Elizabeth GLASCOCK, inv; ord. 7 Jun 1762.

p.311 - Thomas THORNTON, inv; ord. 7 Feb 1763; rec. 9 May 1763.

     - Charles NICHOLES, inv; ord. 2 Aug.1762, rec. 9 May 1763.

p.312 - The Rev. Joseph SIMPSON, inv; ord. 1 Mar 1762, rec. 11
May 1763. [The Rev. SIMPSON was a curate in Rich. Co.
and King George Co. He mar. Mary SKINKER in 1749,
and they had at least four chil: John, Joseph,
Thomas, and Elizabeth. MRC, p.187.]

p.313 - Mary ALGER, NFP, will; 16 Oct 1762, 6 Dec 1762
est. to be div. between all chil; dau. Winifred
EFFORD; ex: Joshua SINGLETON; wits: [Harris] WOOLLARD,
Winifred EFFORD, Samuel ALGER, Richard APPLEBY, John
EFFORD.

p.314 - Betty WEBB, Lun.Par., will; 16 Mar 1761, 4 Oct 1762
nephews John WEBB (son of Isaac WEBB dec'd), John
WEBB (son of Giles WEBB), William SYDNOR (son of
Epaphroditus SYDNOR dec'd), Walker TOMLIN (son of
Robert TOMLIN dec'd), and Robert TOMLIN (son of
Robert TOMLIN dec'd); nieces Lucy and Elizabeth WEBB
(daus. of Giles WEBB), Betty SYDNOR (dau. of Epaphroditus SYDNOR dec'd), Winnie WEBB, and Winnie SYDNOR;
cousin Susannah WEBB; ex: nephew Robert TOMLIN and
fr. Williamson BALL; wits: William [SALLARD], John
JONES.

p.315 - Thomas SAMFORD, NFP, will; 7 Jul 1762, 1 Nov 1762
the desk, the great glass, and six leather chairs in
the hall together with the brandy still and a 20 gal.
iron kettle go to my proper heirs at law and are to
be entailed on the plant. I live on, provided my sd.
heirs at law pay 20 pounds current money into my est.

to be div. as hereafter directed; dau. Mary CHILTON
(wife of John CHILTON); other chil. James, Thomas,
Elizabeth, and John Ames; ex: fr. John WOODBRIDGE;
wits: Joshua SINGLETON, Giles SAMFORD, Anne SAMFORD,
[Stanley GOWER]. [Thomas SAMFORD was b. in 1688; he
mar. Frances ? , who d. in 1750. MRC, p.177.]

p.317 - John OLDHAM, will; 29 Jan 1762, 6 Sep 1762
grson. John HARFORD land and plant. on Glascock's
Mill Pond at the place called [Strumbles]; daus.
Anne BROWN, Margaret CONNALLY, Jean HIGHTOWER, Mary
TARPLEY, Wilmoth BRIGSBEY; ex: fr. Luke WILLIAMS
and William DOBYNS; wits: George BROWN, John LOVE-
LACE, Leannah LOVELACE.

p.318 - William DEGGE, Lun.Par., will; 26 Feb 1761, 1 Nov 1762
wife Doratha; land to son John after wife's death;
chil. William, Robert, Mary, and Anne; ex: wife and
sons John and Robert; wits: John BEALE, Richard NEALE,
Henry ALLISON.

p.319 - William DEGGE, inv; ord. 1 Nov 1762, rec. 17 May 1763.

p.320 - Thomas SAMFORD, inv; ord. 1 Nov 1762, rec. 17 May 1763.

p.326 - Mary ALGER, inv; ord. 6 Dec 1762, rec. 10 May 1763.

p.327 - John OLDHAM, inv; ord. 6 Sep 1762, rec. 16 May 1763.

p.328 - Almorean BRYANT, NFP, will; 16 Jun 1762, 1 Nov 1762
wife Margaret; sons Thomas, John, William, Dennis
Connor, and Peter; ex: wife, John [BLAND], and
William FORRESTER; wits: Jesse BRYANT, Rawleigh
BRYANT, Gabriel SMITHER.

p.329 - Robert SPENCE, Lun.Par., will; 21 Sep 1762, 7 Mar 1763
wife Sarah; son Robert tract of land and plant.
devised to me by James BARKER and for which I paid
to Mr. John JORDAN; grson. Robert Spence McKILDO;
ex: son Robert; wits: Christopher COLLINS, [?].

p.330 - Jonathan BAYES, Lun.Par., will; 10 Jan 1763, 7 Mar 1763
wife Mary; Elizabeth YATES (dau. of my sd. wife);
ex: wife and fr. John EIDSON; wits: John [BAYLIS],
John RYALS.

p.331 - John GIBSON, NFP, will; 2 Mar 1763, 4 Apr 1763
chil. William, Rawleigh, Anne HOWARD, Mary, Priscilla,
and Winnie; ex: s-i-l Thomas HOWARD and son Rawleigh;
wits: Alexander DALE, Gabriel SMITHER. [John GIBSON
mar. Elizabeth CALL in NFP on 7 Aug 1729; the births
of their chil. are rec. in the NFPR. NFPR, p.68.]

p.332 - Robert SPENCE, inv; ord. 7 Mar 1763, rec. 20 May 1763.

p.334 - Jonathan BAYES, inv; ord. 7 Mar 1763, rec. 2 May 1763.

p.335 - Almoreen BRYANT, inv; ord. 7 Mar 1763, rec. 20 May 1763.

p.336 - John GIBSON, inv; ord. 4 Apr 1763, rec. 21 May 1763.

p.337 - Elizabeth PINKARD, NFP, will; 26 Apr 1762, 6 Jun 1763
sis. Mrs. Priscilla CHINN; kinsman Robert Porteus
DOWNMAN; mentions tract of land belonging to Travers

DOWNMAN of North. Co; kinsmen Capt. Robert DOWNMAN,
William DOWNMAN of Rich. Co., Rawleigh DOWNMAN of
the Kingdom of Great Britain, George HEALE, John
CHINN, and Mrs. Betty LEE of Lanc. Co; [Jabas]
DOWNMAN of Prince William Co; goddau. Miss Elizabeth
GLASCOCK (dau. of William GLASCOCK of Rich. Co.);
Mrs. Elizabeth McCARTY (wife of Billington McCARTY
of Rich. Co.); chil. of the late dec'd Maj. George
GLASCOCK; chil. of the late dec'd James DOWNMAN;
ex: friends and relations Mr. William GLASCOCK,
William DOWNMAN, Robert DOWNMAN of Rich. Co. and Mr.
George HEALE of Lanc. Co; wits: John MILNER, Jeremiah
NEASOM, Thomas HOWARD, Spencer HOWARD. [Elizabeth
DOWNMAN mar. Thomas PINCKARD in NFP, 22 Apr 1727.
MRC, p.159.]

p.339 - Walter WALLACE, nunc. will; 9 May 1763, 6 Jun 1763
declared to Anne SCURLOCK and her son [Myal] SCURLOCK
on 21 Apr last past at the house of the deponents,
being then much indisposed and having come there
[with] as they understood for that purpose being
about to enter into a course of...[WALLACE mentioned
his son George; wife and dau; and a payment to Dr,
ROBINSON]; Walter WALLACE departed this life yesterday at his own habitation; sd. will reduced to writing on this 9th of May 1763; wits: Anne SCURLOCK,
[Myal] SCURLOCK. [Walter and Margaret WALLACE of
NFP had at least three chil: George (b.1737),
Elizabeth (b.1739), and a second Elizabeth (b.1751).
NFPR, p.193.]

  - Tarpley TUNE, inv.; 20 Jul 1763. [Tarpley TUNE , the son
of William and Joannah TUNE, was b. in 1741, and d.
of small pox at the home of his bro. Samuel in 1763.
NFPR, p.190; AB 1, p.503.]

  - Anne BARBER, inv; ord. 6 Jun 1763, rec. 22 Jul 1763.

p.340 - Walter WALLACE, inv; 23 Jul 1763.

p.341 - Samuel BAILEY, NFP, will; 10 Feb 1763, 5 Sep 1763
son John; chil. Betty and Charles; bro. William; ex:
bro. William, b-i-l James KENYON, and fr. Joshua
SINGLETON; wits: William BARBER, Charles BARBER,
Mary BARBER.

p.342 - John FORD, Lun.Par., will; 8 Mar 1756, 6 Feb 1764
my will is that all my people be kept together as
they now are upon my plant. for this present year;
wife Jane all plant. and land...from Cheiftuxen Swamp
except 40 ac. of woodland on the lower line; sons
John and Thomas; five young chil. by wife Jane; son
John to be under the care of son William until 21;
ex: son William and Mr. John BELFIELD; wits: John
JENKINS, Thomas BRUCE, Peter EVANS. [John FORD mar.
Jane DEANE, the wid. of John DEANE who d. in 1742.
MRC, p. 70.]

p.343 - Thomas BRUCE, Lun.Par., will; 20 Jan 1764, 6 Feb 1764
dau. Sarah one trunk and all her mother's wearing
clothes; wife all the rest of the est; no ex; wits:
Wm. ROBINS, Wm. BRUCE, Wm. HALL. [Thomas BRUCE mar.
(1) Sarah BIRD, dau. of Philemon and Mary BIRD, sometime between 1752 and 1759. MRC, p.27; his second
wife was Elizabeth ? .]

p.344 - At a court held for Rich. Co. the 2nd day of Apr 1764,
        Elizabeth BRUCE, the wid. of Thomas BRUCE dec'd,
        disclaimed all her right to any portion of her hus-
        band's est. under his will.

      - Thomas LAWSON, inv; ord. 3 Oct 1763, rec. 5 May 1764.

p.346 - John FORD, inv; ord. 6 Feb 1764, rec. 3 May 1764.

p.347 - John JENNINGS, inv; ord. 7 Feb 1764, rec. 4 May 1764.

p.348 - John FEAGINS, will; [nd.], 2 Apr 1764
        all est. to wife Wilmoth; son Alexander G.; younger
        son Samuel (under 18); ex: wife and son Alexander G.;
        wits: Thomas BROWN, John FEAGINS.

      - William KENNON, inv; ord. 6 Feb 1764, rec. 23 May 1764.

p.350 - Isaac JONES, NFP, will; [21 Sep 1754], 2 Apr 1764
        bro. Edward; sis. Winifred WHITE; ex: bro.; wits:
        Thomas JESPER, Thomas NASH, John JESPER.

      - John FEAGINS, inv; ord. 2 Apr 1764, rec. 21 May 1764.

p.351 - Joseph THRIFT, inv; ord. 2 Apr 1764, rec. 24 May 1764.

      - Isaac JONES, inv; ord. [2] Apr 1764, rec. 26 May 1764.

p.353 - [Notation in margin] NASH's inv. at the time of the
        division; 28 May 1764.

p.354 - Daniel SCURLOCK, Lun.Par., will; 31 Mar 1762, 7 May 1764
        sons John and George; dau. Anne BLACKERBY; wife Mary;
        ex: son George; wits: Rawleigh DAVENPORT, Fortunatus
        DAVENPORT.

p.355 - [Bridget] LOVELACE, inv; ord. 7 May 1764.

      - Daniel SCURLOCK, inv; ord. 7 May 1764.

p.356 - The Rev. Joseph SIMPSON, f.inv; [nd]

p.357 - David MISKELL, inv; ord. 6 Jun 1764.

p.358 - Joseph BRYANT, inv; ord. 4 Jun 1764.

p.359 - Mary DUDLEY, inv; ord. 5 Jun 1764.

p.360 - Thomas SAMFORD, nunc. will; 19 Apr 1764, 7 May 1764
        The deposition of Mr. Joshua SINGLETON of NFP, sent
        for by Mr. Thomas SAMFORD Sunday night the 15th day
        of this instant April at about 9 or 10 o'clock; he
        saw Thomas SAMFORD at the house of Mr. James SAMFORD
        where Thomas was then sick...Thomas SAMFORD told this
        deponent that he left his est. to his bros. James and
        John, and his sisters Elizabeth and Mary. Brought
        to court 7 May 1764 by John S. CHILTON. [Thomas SAMFORD
        (1741-1764) was the son of Thomas and Frances SAMFORD.
        MRC, p.261.]

p.361 - James FORRISTER, Farn. Par., will; [3] Jan 1764, 6 Aug 1764
        land and plant., after the death of Samuel DOBYNS and
        his wife Winifred, my loving dau., to go to my grson.
        William Forrister DOBYNS; wife [unnamed]; ex: Samuel
        DOBYNS; wits: Thomas BRYANT, Anne BRYANT, Griffin
        DOBYNS.

- William LEE, inv; ord. 2 Jul 1764.

p.362 - William HAMMOND, inv; ord. 2 Jul 1764.

p.363 - Sarah WOOLLARD, Farn.Par., will; 25 Jun 1764, 7 Aug 1764
        chil. Richard, William, and Betty Anne WARNER; grdau.
        Sarah WARNER; grson. William TILLERY; William WARNER;
        no ex; wits: Thomas W. SAUNDERS, John HANKS, William
        EFFORD. [Sarah was the wid. of Richard WOOLLARD.
        NFPR, p.205.]

p.364 - Charles LOVELACE, inv; ord. 7 May 1764.

p.365 - John JESPER, NFP, will; 9 Jun 1764, 3 Sep 1764
        wife Mary the plant. whereon I now live, after her
        death or remarriage, to son Thomas, if he has no
        heirs, to son Richard; daus. Anne and Sally; John
        LISLE, godfather to son Richard, to have him in
        possession after the space of six years to put to
        any trade or vocation he shall think proper for him
        to get a living; ex: wife and John LISLE; wits:
        Thomas [Williams] SAUNDERS, [Lisha] LIGHTFOOT, Joanna
        BIRD.

p.366 - Sarah WOOLLARD, inv; ord. 7 Aug 1764.

p.367 - George GAYDEN, Farn.Par., will; 1 Jun 1764, 5 Sep 1764
        all lands, being about 100 ac., to son George, if he
        has no heirs, to son John; dau. Elizabeth NIXSON; ex:
        Charles TAYLOR; wits: Charles JONES, John HAMMOCK.

p.368 - Fauntleroy BRYANT, NFP, will; [?] May 1764, 1 Oct 1764
        wife; grson. Thomas HENDREN; sons Merryman and Moses;
        ex: son Merryman; wits: Samuel DOBYNS, Thomas BRYANT.
        [Fauntleroy BRYANT and his wife Elizabeth had at least
        four chil: Million (b. 1737), Winifred (b. 1741),
        Merryman (b. 1746), and Moses (b. 1751). NFPR, pp.26-
        27.]

      - Charles BEALE, will; 22 May 1760, 1 Oct 1764
        wife and child, should they both live; if son Charles
        should die before he arrives to full age in the life-
        time of his mother, I give the lands whereon I now
        live and half of all my slaves to my dear wife and
        her heirs; several grchil. and nephews Thomas BEALE,
        Susannah BEALE, Anne HAMILTON, John Eustis BEALE,
        and Charles BEALE (son of bro. Taverner); bro. Richard
        BEALE and nephews Thomas BEALE and Austin BROCKENBROUGH,
        and son Charles, when at proper age, to be ex; bros.
        William BEALE, Richard BEALE, and William BROCKENBROUGH
        to be guardians of son during his minority; wits:
        Robinson DAINGERFIELD, John LANDMAN, Sophia JACKSON,
        William BROCKENBROUGH;
        Memorandum dated 9 Mar 1763 states that son Charles
        BEALE is old enough to be an ex.

p.370 - John JESPER, inv; [nd.]

p.371 - George GAYDEN, inv; ord. 5 Sep 1764; rec. 2 May 1765.

      - Charles BEALE, inv; ord. 1 Oct 1764.

p.375 - Daniel JACKSON, inv; taken [4] Feb 1765.

      - Charles BEALE, f.inv; est. in Orange Co. appraised; 23
        Oct. 1764.

p.377 - Mary HODGKISSON, Lun.Par., will; 14 Jul 1764, 6 May 1765
         niece Anne SANDY all Westmoreland land; Winifred
         SANDY (dau. of Anne SANDY) land in West. Co; Mary
         SANDY (dau. of Anne SANDY); Margaret TEMPLEMAN (dau.
         of John TEMPLEMAN, dec'd) my now dwelling plant. and
         all my land in Rich. Co; sis. Charlotte TEMPLEMAN
         (when 18 or married); [Williammoley] (dau. of niece
         Mary SANDY); John SANDY (husband of Mary SANDY); son
         John SANDY; John POTTER (son of James and Lucresey
         POTTER); Joseph SUTTON (son of fr. Richard SUTTON);
         two negroes Omar and Tom to have liberty to choose
         whom they would live with amongst my kindred; niece
         Betty SANDY; niece Anne SANDY and friends William
         TEMPLEMAN and Richard Hutson TEMPLEMAN should have
         the care of Margaret TEMPLEMAN's est. until she is
         18 or marries; ex: Anne SANDY; wits: Richard SUTTON,
         Thomas YEATMAN, Frances YEATMAN.

p.378 - William DOWNMAN, inv; ord. 3 Jun 1765.

p.380 - Robert ESKRIDGE, inv; ord. 15 Sep 1764.

p.381 - Agatha DISKINS, inv; ord. 4 Mar 1765.

      - Mary INGLISHBY, will; 23 Feb 1765, 4 Mar 1765
         chil: Mary, Betty, Judy [JONES]; ex: fr. James SAM-
         FORD; wits: Keen SAMFORD, Mary DOWTINE.

p.382 - Jeremiah [MURRAH], Lun.Par., will; 11 Mar 1762, 6 May 1765
         uncle Benjamin BRONHAM land and plant. whereon John
         LANDMAN now lives; Aile BROMHAM, Samuel BROMHAM, John
         BROMHAM; ex: uncle Benjamin BRONHAM; wits: Catherine
         BRONHAM, Thomas THORNTON, George MURPHY.

p.383 - Samuel ALGER, will; 23 Jun 1764, 7 Mar 1765
         sis. Winifred EFFORD 40 ac. in Rich. Co. adjoining
         Richard APPLEBY's land; rest of land to bro. William
         ALGER; ex: fr. John EFFORD; wits: William SMITHY,
         Keen SAMFORD, John SMITH Jr.

      - Edward JONES, inv; ord. 6 May 1765.

p.384 - Mary HODGKISSON, inv; 1 Jun 1765.

p.385 - William CRASK, will; 16 Mar 1765, 3 Jun 1765
         wife Martha; sons James and William; ex: John CRASK
         and Francis RANDALL; wits: George NEWMAN, William
         BRUCE, Francis RANDALL, Anne HINSON.

      - [Joannah] BIRD, inv; 3 Jun 1765.

p.386 - John RUSSELL, will; 8 Nov 1763, 1 Jul 1765
         wife [unnamed]; no ex; wits: William GARLAND, John
         DEMERITT.

      - Thomas LYNE, Lun.Par., will; 13 Mar 1762, 1 Jul 1765
         son Robert all the plant. and land whereon I now live,
         if he has no heirs, to son James reserving one half
         for wife Mary during her widowhood; son Thomas land
         and plant. purchased of Henry HAUGHES, George WELLS,
         and James JENKINS, if he has no heirs, to son James;
         son James tract of land I agreed to purchase of Hen.
         WILSON; daus. Susannah SETTLE, Mary, Bathia, Anne,
         and Elizabeth; ex: wife and son Robert; wits: Hen.
         FRANCKS, Rich. FLINT, John JENKINS, Christopher
         COLLINS.

132

p.388 - William CRASK, inv; ord. 3 Jun 1765.

p.389 - Jane OSGRIFFIN, inv; [ord. 16 May].

- Garland MOORE, will; 5 May 1762, 3 Jun 1765
wife Anne; sons Robert, Garland, and Peter; dau.
[Mathir] MOORE; ex: wife and fr. William GARLAND;
wits: Mary BRICKEY, Alse [HARRISON], Sarah DUNKIN.

p.390 - Thomas LYNE, inv; ord. 1 Jul 1765.

p.391 - William WEBB, will; 8 Nov 1764, 7 Oct 1765
wife Winifred est. real and personal until the child
she is now going with shall arrive to the age of 18
years or day of marriage; ex: wife and fr. John
TARPLEY; wits: Alice TARPLEY, Leroy PEACHEY. [William
WEBB mar. Winifred Griffin TARPLEY in 1763; he was
the only son of John S. and Sarah (ALDERSON) WEBB.
William and Winifred had one child, Wilalmira. MRC,
p.226-227.]

p.392 - Jane WILLIAMS, NFP, will; 24 May 1764, 7 Oct 1765
grdaus. Winifred JONES, Leanna LYALL, Sarah LYALL,
Elizabeth LAWSON, and Anne BENNEHAN; grson. John
WILLIAMS (son of John WILLIAMS dec'd); dau. Sarah
LAWSON; sons Luke, Thomas, and Samuel; ex: son
Samuel; wits: Thomas SMITH, Anne SMITH, Elizabeth
[DANIEL]. [Jane WILLIAMS was the wid. of John
WILLIAMS; they had at least five chil: Luke and Sarah
(b.1722), Thomas (b.1724), Jane (b.1725), and Samuel
(b.1728). NFPR, p.200.]

p.393 - John RUSSELL, inv; ord. 1 Jul 1765.

p.394 - Memorandum of Mr. Fauntleroy BRYANT's est; [nd.]

p.396 - Henry PUGH, will; 5 Aug 1765, 2 Jun 1766
dau. Margaret; son Lewis; wife Sarah; ex: wife and
William WEBSTER; wits: George LANDMAN, Jeremiah
BROWN.

- Mary COLLIER, will; 6 Nov 1760, 2 Jun 1766
Thomas PUGH; John BILLINS (son of John BILLINS);
Elizabeth BILLINS; Margaret PUGH; Mary BILLINS;
Liddy BILLINS (dau. of John BILLINS); Elizabeth
BILLINS' dau. Sarah PUGH; ex: Henry PUGH; wits:
Jeremiah BROWN, Henry PUGH Jr.

p.397 - Capt. Charles BEALE, inv. and division of est; ord. 1
Dec 1766, completed 14 Jan 1767.

p.400 - [List of people who purchased items from BEALE's est;
17 Jan 1767.]

p.403 - Godfrey WILLCOX, inv; ord. 2 Jun 1766.

p.404 - Garland MOORE, inv; taken 17 Oct 1765.

p.405 - Henry PUGH, inv; 7 Jun 1766.

p.406 - Tobias PURCELL, inv; returned 2 Feb 1767.

p.408 - John PEARSON, inv; taken 15 Jan 1767.

- William DRAPER, inv; ord. 5 May 1766.

p.409 - William GARLAND, will; 25 Aug 1766, 3 Nov 1766
son George tract in the upper part of the county
near the beaver dams; son William all my lands in
the fork of Totuskey; surveyor's instruments to son
Griffin; son Jeremiah 1000 ac. in the county of
Buckingham after it is cleared out; son Vincent the
land I now live on; if any additional land be recovered in Buckingham Co. it is to be eq. div. between sons Jesse and Travis; daus. Annaretta,
Henrietta, and Mary; wife Mary; it is also my desire
that William WEBSTER be not removed so long as he
chooses to stay where he now lives and pay annually
300 lbs. of tobacco; ex: wife and sons George and
William; wits: Henry ALLISON, John PURSELL, Robert
DEGGES.

p.411 - Ellen YEATMAN, inv; ord. 5 May 1766.

p.412 - Robert HALL, Lun.Par., will; 19 Mar 1766, 3 Nov 1766
wife Anne; chil. [unnamed]; ex: wife; wits: Moore
BRAGG, Mary ESKRIDGE, Elizabeth WRIGHT.

p.413 - Robert HALL, inv; ord. 3 Nov 1766.

    - Roger WILLIAMS, NFP, will; 4 Jan 1767, 2 Mar 1767
daus. Elizabeth DAMERON and Sarah; sons George,
Hukey; son Luke all my land except 30 ac. that I
purchased of Michael CONNEL adjoining the land that
I purchased of Owen BRADY; chil. of son John; Capt.
Leroy PEACHEY; wife Priscilla; ex: son Luke; wits:
Samuel WILLIAMS, Luke WILLIAMS, Jesse MORRIS, Rich.
BROWN Jr. [Roger WILLIAMS mar. Anne WILLIAMS 5 Aug
1728; Anne d. 31 Dec 1744. NFPR, pp. 200, 201.]

p.414 - Elizabeth TAYLOR, inv; ord. 7 Sep 1747.

p.415 - Joseph JACKSON, will; 26 Mar 1767, 6 Apr 1767
all land joining to Col. John TAYLOE Esq. to be sold
to the highest bidder; Benjamin BRAMHAM; William
RAYNOLDS; Frances DOWNTON; Betty DAVIS (dau. of
Elizabeth DAVIS); William SUTTON; Thomas FRANKLIN
to have all my working tools except my whipsaw; John
REDMAN; ex: Benjamin BRAMHAM and John REDMAN; wits:
John ESKRIDGE, John [KIRK], Thomas FRANKLIN, Vincent
REDMAN.

p.416 - Joseph JACKSON, inv; ord. 6 Apr 1767.

p.417 - William JONES, inv; ord. 16 Apr 1767.

    - Roger WILLIAMS, inv; ord. 2 Mar 1767, returned 4 Jul 1767.

p.419 - William ROCHESTER, will; 16 Sep 1766, 3 Aug 1767
wife all land and plant. whereon I now live; chil.
[unnamed]; ex: wife Elinor and friends Bradley
GARNER and John ROCHESTER; wits: John DEMERITT,
Richard YEATS, Burgess LONGWITH. [William ROCHESTER
mar. (1) Mary ASBURY and (2) Elinor JONES, 1764. MRC,
p. 172.]

p.420 - Robert RANDALL, inv; ord. 4 May 1767.

    - Alice FOWLER, will; 27 Aug 1767, 7 Sep 1767
daus. Anne CORNELIUS and Alice DALE; sons Richard
and John; ex: George GLASCOCK and son John; wits:

134

George GLASCOCK Jr., Rawleigh GIBSON, George HANKES.

p.421 - John RICHARDSON, will; 2 May 1767, 7 Sep 1767
wife Mary; ex: wife; wits: John HART, Matthew [DEAT-
ERLY], C. THORNTON.

- Matthew HARRISON, NFP, will; 13 Oct 176[4], 7 Sep 1767
son George all land; son Matthew; dau. Anne Rust;
other chil. Elizabeth, Mary, Benjamin, and the child
my wife is now with; sons George, Matthew, and
Benjamin to have two, four, and five year's schooling
respectively; daus. Elizabeth and Mary to have three
year's schooling each; child wife is now with, if a
boy, to have five year's schooling, if a girl, to
have three year's; ex: wife Alice; wits: Garland
MOORE, Isaac PROCTOR, Abraham PROCTOR, Wm. HARTLEY.
Cod. 29 May 176[?], wife has given birth to another
child besides that above-mentioned unborn; son
Benjamin to have the still given to Matthew; land
purchased of Alice MIDDLETON to be in the possession
of Alice and Leasure MIDDLETON during their natural
lives then to go to William and Thomas MIDDLETON
(sons of Leasure), if there are no heirs, to son
Matthew [HARRISON]; wits: Robert MOORE, Peter MOORE,
William HARTLEY.

p.424 - John BEALE, Lun.Par., will; 22 Dec 1766, 3 Aug 1767
wife Elizabeth; daus. Anne, Sarah, Winifred,
Eustice, Elizabeth, and Charlotte; ex: John Eustice
HANCOCK and Richard EDWARDS; wits: William BUCK-
LAND, Job THOMAS, Job THOMAS Jr.

p.425 - Thomas ASBURY, inv; ord. 4 Jan 1767.

WILL BOOK 7, 1767-1787

p. 1 - William KENNAN, inv; ord. 4 Aug 1767.

p. 2 - Robert KENNAN, inv; ord. 4 Aug 1767.

- John GRIFFIN, inv; ord. 3 Aug 1767.

p. 3 - Isaac PROCTOR, inv; ord. 3 Aug 1767.

p. 4 - Matthew HARRISON, inv; ord. 7 Sep 1767.

p. 6 - William ROCHESTER, inv; ord. 3 Aug 1767.

p. 7 - Alice FOWLER, inv; appraised 30 Sep [1767].

- Gilbert HAMILTON, Lun.Par., will; 31 Aug 1765, 1 Feb 1768
all est. to wife Anne; no ex; wits: John BEALE,
Robert FERGUSON. [Gilbert HAMILTON mar. Anne BEALE,
4 Nov 1732. MRC, p.85.]

p. 8 - William WEBB, inv; [nd.]

p. 9 - William HENDRON, NFP, will; 11 Nov 1765, 2 May 1768
sons William, Dowden Howell, Robert, and John; daus.
Lydia, Anne, Sally OSGRIFFIN, and Mary GLASCOCK; son
William my right of the plant. whereon I now live by
lease from Col. John TARPLEY; wife [Annarah]; ex:
son William; wits: John MILNER, Judith BRYANT,
William ALGAR. [William and Honor HENDREN had the

fol. chil: Sally (b.1737), Winifred (1739-1740), Mary
(b.1741), Roseanna (b.1743), William (b.1744), Lidya
(b.1746), Anne (1749-1749), Anne (b.1749), Downing
Howell (b.1754), and Robert (b.1756); William HENDREN
Sr. d. 2 Feb 1768. NFPR, pp. 92-93.]

p. 10 - John SAMFORD, Farn.Par., will; 1760, 2 May 1768
wife Sarah; son Giles; Sarah [Dowten CARAH]; dau.
Anne; ex: wife and son Giles; wits: Keene SAMFORD,
John HAMMOCK, Winne SAMFORD.

p. 11 - Travers TARPLEY, NFP, will; 18 Feb 1768, 6 Jun 1768
wife Betty dwelling plant. with all houses and lands
which I bought of Charles McCARTY; daus. Fanny, Lucy,
Betty PEACHEY, Winnie McCARTY, Milly, and Nancy; Mary
STOTT; [grand]sons William Travers PEACHEY and
Bartholomew McCARTY; mentions money due from brother
Col. John TARPLEY; ex. to be guardians of two young-
est daus. Milly and Nancy; ex: John BELFIELD and
Richard MITCHELL; wits: Corbin GRIFFIN, Burgess SMITH,
John SYDNOR, Billington McCARTY. [Travers TARPLEY
mar. Betty SYDNOR. MRC, p.204.]

p. 13 - Maj. Travers TARPLEY, inv; ord. 6 Jun 1768.

p. 16 - John SAMFORD, inv; ord. 2 May 1768.

p. 18 - Reuben DALE, inv; taken 6 Jun 1768.

- Robert SMITH of Rich., for fatherly love to his dau.,
Margaret INGRAM, and for the sum of 35 pounds, sells
slaves to her; [nd.]

p. 19 - John RICHARDSON, inv; ord. 7 Sep 1767.

- William HENDREN, inv; [nd.]

p. 20 - Bryant STOTT, NFP, will; 11 May 1768, 7 Aug 1768
wife Mary; land to be eq. div. between two sons
Robert and Rawleigh; dau. Tabitha; ex: sons; wits:
Dennis CONWAY, James LITTRELL.

p. 21 - Bryant STOTT, inv; ord. 7 Aug 1768.

p. 22 - Thomas TUNE, will; 30 Feb 1762, 6 Mar 1769
sons Travers, Kester; daus. Elizabeth DAVIS, Sarah
MILNER, Anne BARNES; ex: son Kester; wits: Luke
WILLIAMS, Cobham GAYTHINGS, William WILLIAMS.
[Thomas TUNE mar. Anne HARRIS, 24 Jun 1727; they had
the fol. chil: Elizabeth (b.1729), Travers (b.1731/32),
Thomas (b.1734), Sarah (b. 1735), Anne (b. 1737),
Duannah (b.1743), NFPR, pp. 189-190.]

p. 23 - Mary LAWSON, wid., will; 26 Nov 1768, 6 Mar 1769
all est. to dau. Anne HALL, wid.; ex: dau.; wits:
Richard PARKER, Lettice [PILLION].

- Charles JONES, will; 13 Dec 1768, 6 Mar 1769
daus. Alicia BRYANT, Mary DOWTEN, Leanner, and Anne;
all land to son Samford; ex. not named; wits: John
HAMMOND Jr., Anthony DOWTEN.

p. 24 - Anthony COOKE, inv; [nd.]

p. 25 - Henry ALLISON, inv; ord. 7 Nov 1768.

136

p. 26 - James CLARK, inv; [nd.]

p. 30 - Samuel RUST, will; 21 Apr 1766, 3 Apr 1769
         eld. son Benjamin all est. in Rich. Co. and tract
         in Yeocomico Neck in West. Co. known as Ball's
         Tract; all other lands to son Peter; ex: friends
         Col. William BROCKENBROUGH and William GARLAND; wits:
         Henry ALLISON, Stanley GOWER, John S. CHILTON.
         [Samuel RUST mar. Hannah RUST, 1755. MRC, p. 175.]

p. 31 - Nathaniel JACKSON, will; 23 Oct 1768, 3 Apr 1769
         wife plant. and all lands; son Vincent; dau. Eliza-
         beth; ex: fr. Solomon REDMAN, son Vincent, and wife;
         wits: William BROCKENBROUGH, Elizabeth ROBINSON.

p. 32 - Thomas TUNE, inv; ord. 6 Mar 1769.

p. 33 - Charles JONES, inv; ord. 6 Mar 1769.

p. 34 - Nathaniel JACKSON, inv; ord. 3 Apr 1769.

p. 36 - William BARNES, inv; 18 Jan 1769 [sic].

p. 37 - Samuel RUST, inv; 18 Jan 1770.

p. 38 - Nicholas McGINNISS, inv; 18 Jan 1770.

p. 39 - John JONES, inv; 19 Jan 1770.

p. 40 - Robert DOWNMAN, inv; 20 Jan 1770.

p. 45 - William FORRESTER, inv; ord. 5 Jun 1769.

p. 47 - William FORRESTER, NFP, will; 2 May 1769, 5 Jun 1769
         desires whole est. to be kept together for 10 years;
         wife Amoney to have the land whereon her mother now
         lives; upon wife's death, land to go to son William;
         son William all land in Rich. Co; son Thaddeus all
         land in North. Co; [third child unnamed]; ex: wife,
         William STONUM, and Samuel DOBBYNS; wits: Thomas
         COLEMAN, William FORRESTER Jr., Samuel BARNES.

p. 48 - Robert DOWNMAN, NFP, will; 11 Jun 1769, 3 Jul 1769
         son William 500 ac. in Dinwiddie Co. where he now
         lives being part of a tract I purchased of Burnal
         CLAYBURN and half of a tract in Amelia Co. that I
         bought of [Mr] Thomas BALL; s-i-l Thomas BALL and
         his wife Mildred; grdaus. Elizabeth Porteus BALL and
         Anne BALL; son Robert Porteus the land I now live on
         and land on the south side of the main road leading
         from Glascock's Warehouse up by Read's Old Field
         commonly called Read's Race Ground; dau. Elizabeth
         all land on the north side of the sd. road including
         the race ground; son Rawleigh tract of land in
         Dinwiddie Co. which I purchased of William HANCKS
         and 250 ac. adjoining being part of a tract whereon
         my son William now lives which was purchased of [Mr]
         Burnel CLAYBURN and half of a tract in Amelia Co; ex:
         friends Richard MITCHELL and William STONUM with son
         Robert; wits: Thomas GLASCOCK, James ALDERSON, Rawleigh
         DOWNMAN, Jeremiah NEASUM. [Robert DOWNMAN mar. Eliza-
         beth PORTEUS before 1744. MRC, p.59; NFPR, pp. 52,53.]

p. 49 - Nicholas McGINNIS; Ebenezer BALDERSON, Zachariah WHITE,
         and Sileicia WHITE appeared before Justice John

BELFIELD and made oath that Nicholas McGINNIS, who
died yesterday, did in his last sickness in his own
house give his son, Richard McGINNIS, all his working tools and the timber in his shop...29 Mar 1769,
rec. 5 Jun 1769.

p. 50 - Samuel RUST, inv; 24 Jan 1770.

p. 51 - Elizabeth PINCKARD, inv.; 14, 15 Jun 1763, rec. 25 Jan 1770.

p. 54 - William DEW, will; 18 May 1769, 6 Nov 1769
daus. Lucy, Joannah BOOTH; sons Alexander, Samuel,
Thomas; Samuel LYELL (son of Millian LYELL); wife;
son Thomas one shilling and no more, he, as well as
Benjamin NEASUM, who mar. my dau. Sarah, having already had their full parts of that they could expect
from my est; ex: fr. Christopher LAWSON; wits: James
BOOTH, Jonathan WILLIAMS, Jehu PULLEN, Rawleigh NEWGENT.

p. 56 - Alexander BENNEHAN, inv; 15 Feb 1770.

- Simon SALLARD, Lun.Par., will; 23 Nov 1769, 5 Mar 1770
mother Blanche SALLARD the use of 100 ac. of land,
half of a tract left me by my father, Simon SALLARD,
sd. land to be taken from the river upwards; wife
Elizabeth remaining land; son Simon land after wife's
death and also tract purchased of Joshua SINGLETON;
dau. Jane to be brought up and educated; bro. John
SALLARD; ex: wife, Avery DYE, Thomas KIBERT; wits:
George H. FAUNTLEROY, William BUCKLAND, John WALKER.

p. 58 - Mary Anne GRIFFIN, will; 15 Nov 1769, 5 Mar 1770
dau. Elizabeth ADAMS; son Leroy; grdau. Anne Corbin
GRIFFIN; ex: son; wits: William PEACHEY, Charles
FORRESTER.

- William DEW, inv; 14 Mar 1770.

p. 60 - John WOODBRIDGE Gent., inv. pres. to our view in Fairfax
Co., 20 Sep 1769, rec. 15 Mar 1770.

p. 61 - William GARLAND, inv; ord. 3 Nov 1766, rec. 16 Mar 1770.

p. 64 - Judith GLASCOCK, NFP, will; 19 Sep 1766, 7 May 1770
sons George and William; dau. Judith; ex: son William;
wits: Sarahann BRYANT, Reuben BRYANT, Samuel BRYANT.

p. 65 - Agnes ANDERSON, inv; 19 Jun 1770.

p. 66 - John WOODBRIDGE Gent., inv; 28 Aug 1770.

p. 72 - George H. FAUNTLEROY, Lun.Par., will; 12 Apr 1770, 6 Aug
1770
wife piece of land named Mangorite in Rich. Co. and
675 and a half ac. in Lanc. Co.; if wife should have
any children by me, sd. lands to be eq. div. among
them; servant boy Adam; George SYDNOR a silver watch;
no ex; wits: Henry TODD, Apphia TODD; pres. in court
by the wid. Sarah FAUNTLEROY. [Dr. George Heale
FAUNTLEROY mar. his first cousin, Sally FAUNTLEROY,
in 1768. MRC, p. 68.]

p. 73 - Samuel ALGAR, inv; 19 Sep 1770.

138

- John SANDY, Lun.Par., will; 19 Aug 1769, 4 Sep 1770
    wife Mary; daus. [William] Moley, Betty, and Nanny
    Murfey; sons Mason and Thomas; daughter's aunt Mary
    HOSKINS dec'd; ex: wife; wits: Charles KNIGHT, John
    LYALL, George RUSSELL.

p. 74 - Bartholomew BELCHER, NFP, will; 20 Aug 1770, 1 Oct 1770
    son Abraham; bro. John in Warsher Town, Staffordshire,
    England; Beck the mother of my son; fr. James SAMFORD
    to receive such as my crop of corn and tobacco for
    the trouble of his house and burying of my corpse; ex:
    fr. Richard FOSTER; wits: Jonathan WILLIAMS, [blank]
    LIGHTFOOT, John HEFORD.

p. 76 - George BERRICK, will; 1 Aug 1770, 6 Nov 1770
    wife Betty land and plant. whereon I live; five chil.
    John, David, George [remaining chil. unnamed]; ex:
    sons David and George; wits: [Cate] WEBSTER, Richard
    NEALE.

p. 77 - John SANDY, inv; 24 Nov 1770.

p. 78 - John HAMMOND, will; 12 Feb 1771, 4 Mar 1771
    son Thomas my glebe land and adjoining land; son
    Absolom; dau. Susannah CONNELL; grsons. Charles and
    John HAMMOND; William DUDLEY; John DUDLEY; dau. Jean
    LEE; Judith, Elizabeth, and Caty (daus. of son William);
    Anne LEE (dau. of Jean LEE); daus. Anne, Maryanne,
    Betty, and Caty; ex: son Thomas; wits: Charles HAMMOND,
    William ENGLISH, Daniel BROWN.

p. 79 - Crask THORNTON, Lun.Par., will; 23 Jan 1771, 1 Apr 1771
    William and Mary YEATMAN; wife [Susannah]; Sebella
    YEATMAN; no ex; wits: William WILSON, Jos. [AMBROSE].

p. 80 - Joan RUSSELL, nunc. will prov. by Richard HOLIDAY, John
    SELF, and John LAMBERT;
    On the 8th of this instant Nov, the wits. were all at
    the dwelling house of Joan RUSSELL...she said that she
    gave her still worm to her dau. Elizabeth WALKER; 13
    Nov 1770; pres. in court by John WALKER, 4 Feb 1771.

p. 81 - George H. FAUNTLEROY, inv; 29 May 1771.

p. 83 - John HAMMOND, inv; 29 May 1771.

p. 84 - John LINDSEY, inv; 29 May 1771.

p. 85 - [Esial] William HENDREN, inv; 29 May 1771.

p. 86 - Billington McCARTY, NFP, will; 15 Mar 1771, 6 May 1771
    wife Elizabeth; sons Daniel, William, Thaddeus, and
    Dennis; daus. Nancy, Elizabeth DOWNMAN; ex: wife and
    bros. Thaddeus and Charles; wits: William PEACHEY,
    Betty MISKELL, James WEBB. [Billington McCARTY mar.
    Elizabeth DOWNMAN in 1756. MRC, p. 123.]

p. 89 - Anthony DOWTIN, NFP, will; 7 Mar 1771, 3 Jun 1771
    dau. Winifred; Sarah Dowtin CARY; wife Mary; ex: wife
    and Joshua SINGLETON; wits: Giles SAMFORD, Winnie
    DOWTIN, Sarah Dowtin CARY.

p. 90 - Crask THORNTON, inv; 1 Jul 1771.

p. 91 - Joan RUSSELL, inv; 8 Aug 1771.

p. 92 - Mrs. Joan THORNTON, sale of est; [nd.]

p. 93 - John PLUMMER, will; 3 May 1771, 7 Oct 1771
        son Thomas all lands, if he has no heirs, to be eq.
        div. between four daus. Mary, Elizabeth, Sarah, and
        Rebecca Willoughby; wife; plant. called Sisson's to
        be rented or leased until son Thomas is 21; ex: good
        friends John SMITH Jr. and Thomas Suggitt HILL and
        wife; wits: Sally JONES, Thomas JONES, Catesby JONES.
        [John PLUMMER mar. Sarah SMITH, 7 May 1756. MRC,p.159.]

p. 95 - Simon SALLARD, inv; 7 Oct 1771.

p. 96 - John KING, inv; 7 Oct 1771.

p. 97 - Anthony DOWTEN, inv; 7 Oct 1771.

p. 99 - Thomas THORNTON, Lun.Par., will; 31 Oct 1771, 2 Dec 1771
        wife Rebecca Sisson entire est., if she should re-
        marry, est. to be div. amongst wife and two chil.
        Francis Sisson and Elizabeth; ex: wife and fr. Benj.
        BRAMHAM; wits: Daniel LAWSON, Anne THOMPSON, Rebecca
        LAWSON. [Thomas THORNTON mar. Rebecca Sisson LAWSON,
        Feb 1769. MRC, p. 214.]

p.100 - James LEWIS, NFP, will; 4 Jan 1771, 6 Jan 1772
        son John Lewis TILLERY tract of land bought of Job
        TILLERY; other chil: Mary Anne HARRINGTON, Leannah
        Lewis TILLERY, Betty Lewis TILLERY, and William Lewis
        TILLERY; dau. Mary Anne HARRINGTON tract of land
        bought of Alexander ALLOWAY whereon Samuel HARRINGTON
        now lives; ex: William MISKELL, Samuel HARRINGTON;
        wits: John BEELAND, Peter NORTHEN, George NORTHEN;
        Cod., 4 Jan 1771; mentions three ac. of land on
        Accaceek Point in Lun.Par; William NORTHEN to have
        liberty of this land for fishing and his sons after
        him.

p.103 - Matthew KELLY, Lun.Par., will; 5 Jan 1772, [2] Mar 1772
        son John; daus. Sarah BRAGG (wife of Moore BRAGG),
        Elizabeth BRAGG, [no first name given] DYE, and Anne
        DYE; ex: son John and s-i-l Moore BRAGG and Fauntle-
        roy DYE; wits: John EIDSON, William BEVER, Christopher
        COLLINS.

p.105 - Henry DUNKIN, Lun.Par., will; 21 Jan 1771, 2 Mar 1772
        wife Charity; sons Charles, George, Henry, and Coleman;
        son Henry to be schooled out of est; dau. Frances
        TARRENT 5 pounds for six years of schooling of her
        chil. if she remains without a husband; ex: son Coleman,
        John McLANAHAN, Thomas [WRITE]; wits: William CONOLEY,
        James McLANAHAM, Frances TARRENT. [Henry DUNCAN mar.
        (2) Charity MITCHELL, 1766. MRC, p. 61.]

p.107 - Matthew KELLY, inv; 13 Apr 1772.

p.108 - William DAVENPORT, NFP, will; 11 Jul 1771, 11 May 1772
        wife Elizabeth; sons William the plant. whereon I now
        live containing 160 ac., Fortunatus the land where he
        now lives to the main swamp, Rawleigh 200 ac. in Lanc.
        Co. formerly belonging to Mr. John HEALE dec'd, and
        Opie (when he comes of age); daus. Judith GEORGE and
        Elizabeth TUNE; grson. William OLIVER; ex: wife and
        sons William and Fortunatus; wits: Gabriel SMITHER,
        John POPE Jr., George SCURLOCK;

Cod., As I have already given my son George all that
I ever intended, it is my will that none of his heirs
shall inherit any more of my est. hereafter. [William
DAVENPORT was the son of William and Rachel DAVENPORT
of Lanc. Co.; he mar. Elizabeth HEALE, 26 Nov 1728.
WLC, p. 64; MRC, p. 49.]

p.111 - Alexander SCURLOCK, inv; 7 May 1772.

p.113 - Henry DUNKIN, inv; 8 May 1772.

p.115 - Rawleigh STOTT, will; 27 Feb 1772, 1 Jun 1772
bro. Robert; ex: bro. Robert; wits: Benjamin VILLAN-
DINGHAM, James LITTRELL.

p.116 - George MISKELL, will; 23 Oct 177[1], 3 Aug 1772
sons William and George; wife Magdalen; dau. Magdalen;
ex: William MISKELL [Senior] and son George; wits:
Luke WILLIAMS, John SYDNOR.

p.117 - Henry SETTLE, Lun.Par., will; 16 Oct 1770, 3 Nov 1772
wife Anne; sons Bailey and Reuben; daus. Jemima
GEARY, Keziah HUTCHINSON, Anne BARTLETT, Elizabeth
BRAGG; grsons. Henry (son of Reuben) and Thomas
PRITCHETT; grdaus. Bathsheba HUTCHINSON (dau. of
Jeremiah and Keziah HUTCHINSON), Joannah BARTLETT,
Anne FLEMING, Anne PRITCHETT; dau. [Jemima] to be in
the care of son Reuben; ex: son Bailey; wits: John
EIDSON, Henry SISSON Jr., Christopher COLLINS;
Cod. mentions grdaus. Jemima FRANKLIN and Anne PRITCHETT.

p.119 - John SUGGITT, NFP, will; 17 Nov 1771, 2 Nov 1772
land in North. Co., known as Perring's, to be sold;
Elizabeth GIBSON alias SUGGITT (dau. of Priscilla
GIBSON) an education and maintenance; mother Eliza-
beth; wife Hannah; dau. Judith [Payne]; ex: [named
in a memorandum] friends Richard MITCHELL and Thomas
Suggitt HILL; wits: Williamson BALL, Cuthbert WEBB,
James WEBB, Thomas Suggitt HILL.

p.121 - Christopher LAWSON, will; 17 May 1772, 7 Sep 1772
whole est. to wife; it is my will that my chil. such
as is unmarried to live all together with her in the
same manner and subjection to her as they are now to
me, and more especially my son Epaphroditus, if he
should behave ill-natured and undutiful to his mother
in any respect, that she may turn him away or either
of them that will not behave humble and dutiful to
her as such chil. should do to their parent; lands
and plant. to son Epaphroditus; son John; daus. Betty
DIGGS, Joannah, Katy, and Lucy; ex: wife, William
MISKELL, George REYNOLDS; wits: Elizabeth BARBER,
Charles McCARTY, William BARBER Jr.

p.123 - William STONE, will; [nd.], 7 Dec 1772
wife Anne; bro. Benjamin; no ex; wits: Thomas DOBYN[S],
Thomas STONE, Betty WILLIAMS. [William STONE mar. Anne
HARRISON; she d. in 1774. MRC, p. 196.]

p.124 - Thomas DALE, inv; 27 Feb 1773.

p.125 - George BERRICK, inv; 1 Mar 1773.

p.126 - Rawleigh STOTT, inv; 1 Mar 1773.

p.127 - Ambrose CALLIS, inv; 2 Mar 1773.

- Christopher LAWSON, inv; 22 Apr 1773.

[no pages numbered 130, 131, or 132]

p.133 - Billington McCARTY, inv; 22 Apr 1773.

p.137 - William DAVENPORT, inv; 23 Apr 1773.

p.140 - James ENGLISH, inv; 23 Apr 1773.

p.141 - Thomas THORNTON, inv; 23 Apr 1773.

p.143 - George MISKELL, inv; 23 Apr 1773.

p.144 - John PALMER, inv; 23 Apr 1773.

p.145 - William STONE, inv; 23 Apr 1773.

p.146 - Elizabeth FRESHWATER, will; 5 Sep 1772, 2 Nov 1772 [sic]
        grson. Abner DOBYNS (son of Sarah DOBYNS); s-i-l Henry
        DOBYNS; bro. John JESPER; sis. Sarah WILDY; ex: dau.
        Sarah DOBYNS and s-i-l Henry DOBYNS; wits: George
        GARLAND, Judith HAMMOND. [Elizabeth (JESPER) FRESH-
        WATER was the second wife of Thomas FRESHWATER who
        d. in 1755. MRC, p. 74.]

p.147 - Joshua SINGLETON, will; 17 Aug 1772, 3 Mar 1773
        land in Lunenburg Co. to son Joshua when he is 21
        (in the year 1779), if he has no heirs, to son Frederick;
        land in Lun.Par. in Rich. Co. to son Frederick when
        he is 21; dau. Anne McCarty; sons James and Samuel;
        eld. son Robert the plant. and land whereon I now live;
        on or about 25 Dec 1779, desires all negroes, stocks
        of all kinds, and other movables to be eq. div. amongst
        chil; ex: friends William MISKELL, Charles McCARTY,
        Thomas S. HILL, and son Robert; wits: John HAMMOND,
        Cuthbert WEBB, Charles WEBB. [Joshua SINGLETON mar.
        Anne SAMFORD in 1749. MRC, p. 187.]

p.150 - John REDMAN, inv; 17 Nov 1773.

p.150a- Joshua SINGLETON, inv; 18 Nov 1773.

p.152b- John SUGGITT, inv; 19 Nov 1773.

p.153 - William THOMAS, inv. pres. by Ellender THOMAS adm.; 9 Feb
        1774.

p.154 - Joshua SINGLETON, [f.] inv; 10 Feb 1774.

- Thomas DURHAM, inv; 10 Feb 1774.

p.155 - Elizabeth FRESHWATER, inv; 24 Feb 1774.

p.156 - Stanley GOWER, inv; 3 Mar 1774.

p.158 - James LEWIS, inv; 4 Mar 1774.

p.160 - James FRARY, inv; 4 Mar 1774.

- Chloe CONWAY, will; 18 Sep 1770, [nd.]
        father Dennis CONWAY; ex: father; wits: Thomas
        CONWAY, Maryann HARRIS, John HARTLEY. [Note by Clerk
        of the Court] This will ought not to have been recorded.

142

p.161 - Anne STONE, will; 26 Feb 1774, 7 Mar 1774
           est. I got by my husband, William STONE, to go to
           Elizabeth WILLIAMS for her own use and not to be
           applied to the use or command of Abraham WILLIAMS;
           Thomas STONE (son of William STONE); bro. Jeremiah
           HARRISON; sis. Hannah GILBERT; mentions est. of her
           father Samuel HARRISON; ex: bro. Jeremiah and William
           GILBERT; wits: Sarah HINDS, Betty WILLIAMS, Winnie
           WILLIAMS.

p.162 - Alexander DUDLEY, NFP, 23 Nov 177[3], 8 Mar 1774
           land lately sold in Frederick Co. to Cornelius LIVING-
           STON to whom I give my bond; chil. [unnamed]; ex: wife,
           Winifred, and friends Benjamin BRAMHAM and George
           GARLAND; wits: George ROBINSON, Isaac ALLOWAY, William
           BARBER Jr.

p.163 - Rawleigh GIBSON, nunc. will; 9 Nov 1773, 7 Mar 1774 and
           6 Jun 1774.
           James ALDERSON and Sarah Anne ALDERSON came to court
           and made oath that Rawleigh GIBSON departed this life
           last night sometime after midnight...They were to see
           the sd. Rawleigh the day before his death when he said
           in their presence that the will which he had made...
           some time before his present sickness was not agreeable
           to his mind or desire and bid them take notice that
           [he wished his est.] to be div. into three parts be-
           tween Anne HOWARD (the wife of Thomas HOWARD), Absolom
           CREEL, and Priscilla GIBSON; Priscilla GIBSON to have
           choice of the three divisions and to be ex.

p.164 - Robert Porteus DOWNMAN, NFP, will; 26 Jan 1774, 4 Apr 1774
           wife Elizabeth; daus. Fanny Porteus and Elizabeth
           Porteus; land between the lands of Rawleigh DOWNMAN of
           Lanc. Co., the heirs of Alexander BENNEHAN, and myself,
           including 400 ac., to dau. Fanny, remaining land to dau.
           Elizabeth; bro. Rawleigh; ex: wife and friends Richard
           MITCHELL and Robert SYDNOR; wits: John SYDNOR, Charles
           McCARTY, Judith GLASCOCK. [Robert P. DOWNMAN mar.
           Elizabeth SYDNOR in Jul 1770. MRC, p. 59.]

p.166 - John EIDSON, Lun.Par., will; 6 Nov 1773, 4 Apr 1774
           daus. Frances, Caty, Rebecca, Anne, Lucy, and Mary;
           sons Lawrence and George; wife Anne; ex: wife and fr.
           Christopher COLLINS; wits: George NEWMAN, James KELLY,
           Joseph SCATES, John MARKS.

p.168 - Anne STONE, inv; 2 Apr 1774.

      - [William BRAGG], inv; 28 Apr 1774.

p.169 - Richard WOOLLARD, inv; 29 Jun 1774.

p.170 - John EIDSON, inv; 4 Jul 1774.

p.172 - Robert P. DOWNMAN, inv; 7 Jul [1774].

p.176 - Rawleigh GIBSON, inv; 10 Oct 1774.

p.177 - Thomas BROWN, inv; 10 Oct 1774.

p.179 - Thomas BROWN, will; 2 Jan 1772, 1 Aug 1774
           wife Eleanor plant. and land purchased of cousin Thomas
           BROWN and lease purchased of Winifred WEBB; if wife
           marries or dies, land to go to son Christopher, if he

has no heirs, then to son Thomas, and, if he has no
heirs, to son James; other chil. Charles, Daniel,
Rachel, Ellen, Hannah, Elizabeth; ex: wife and son
Charles; wits: Hudson MUSE, James MUSE, Rawleigh
DOWNMAN Jr, William THOMAS, Willoughby TILLERY, James
ABERCROMBIE.

p.181 - Jane SMITH, Lun.Par., will; 23 Mar 1774, 4 Jul 1774
sis. Winnie FONES; Mary ANDERSON; sons James, Benjamin,
Jeremiah, William, and Reuben ALDERSON; ex: sons
William and Reuben; wits: Robert SMITH, John WALKER,
Mary WATTS. [Jane SMITH was the wid. of Benjamin SMITH
and John ALDERSON. MRC., p. 189.]

p.182 - Henry SISSON, will; [nd], 6 Mar 1775
wife Anne the plant; son John; grsons. Henry and John
SISSON; grdaus. Elizabeth Stuard SISSON and Sarah
REDMAN; ex: Solomon REDMAN; wits: John LYELL, Thomas
FRANKLIN, Bailey SETTLE. [Henry SISSON mar. Anne MEEKS
by 1729. MRC, p. 187.]

p.183 - Edward PRIDHAM, Lun.Par., will; 5 Nov 1773, 8 Nov 1774
sons Christopher and Edward; daus. Betty DAVIS, Frances,
and Mary Anne MOORE (wife of Sampson MOORE); wife
Frances; ex: wife and son Christopher; wits: William
RIGMAIDEN, Burgess LONGWITH, John LAMBERT.

p.185 - William CREWDSON Sr., Lun.Par., will; 2 Dec 1774, 3 Apr
1775
wife Eleanor; sons James and William (to receive two
silver casters marked "IMB" and one silver mug marked
"MB"); dau. Mary FRARY; ex: sons James and William,
and friends James KELLY and Nathaniel MOTHERSHEAD;
wits: Gilbert BALDERSON, William OLIFF, Thomas PLAYLE.

p.186 - Josiah HINDS, NFP, will; 3 Dec 1774, 3 Apr 1775
godson Richard Hinds STEEL; bro. Thomas HINDS; cousin
Anne HINDS; ex: bro. Thomas and fr. Thomas SMITH;
wits: Samuel WOOLLARD, Abraham SELF.

p.187 - William CARTER, Lun.Par., will; 30 Aug 1774, 7 Nov 1774
son John CARPENTER land whereon I now live; wife;
ex: wife; wits: William DODD, Henry DRAKE, Jane
CARPENTER.

p.188 - George CLARK Sr., will; [nd.], 8 Nov 1774
son Robert all the ordinary and houses and lands be-
ginning at the road; son George remainder of houses;
rest of est. to be eq. div. among other chil. Catharine,
Thomas, Robert, Jane, George, Richard, and William;
ex: sons Thomas and Robert; wits: Jane STEELE, Leroy
OLDHAM.

- Alexander DUDLEY, inv; 15 Jun 1775.

p.190 - George CLARK, inv; 15 Jun 1775.

p.191 - Jane SMITH, inv; 15 Jun 1775.

p.192 - David GEORGE, inv; 15 Jun 1775.

- Ebenezer BALDERSON, inv. pres. by Gilbert BALDERSON the
adm; 15 Jun 1775. [Ebenezer BALDERSON, the immigrant,
was apparently brought into Virginia by Landon CARTER
prior to 1738. He mar. Frances the dau. of James and

              Henrietta HARDWICK. They had possibly three chil:
              Gilbert, Anne, and Henrietta. OB 10 and OB 11.]

p.193 - Edward PRIDHAM, inv; 15 Jun 1775.

      - William CARTER, inv; 15 Jun 1775.

p.194 - Jeremiah WROE, inv; 15 Jun 1775.

p.195 - Memorandum of Henry PRESCOAT's est; 15 Jun 1775.

      - Robert CLARK Jr., nunc. will
           Will of Robert CLARK Jr. who departed this life yes-
           terday morning, the 5th instant October, made in the
           presence of William LAMBERTH on Monday night the 3rd
           instant; "I give my land to Bob and the rest of my
           est. may be eq. div. between Molly and Johnny."
           What, to your brother John?" replied LAMBERTH. He
           answered, "no, no." "Or do you mean to little Johnny?"
           He answered again, "yes" "And, if my land is entailed,
           so that Bob can't have it, I desire he may have an
           equal share of all my other est. with Molly and Johnny
           and I desire that Richard shall have one year of his
           time as he has been trusty. I have told William
           HEARTLEY and Samuel DUNAWAY the same I have told you
           and don't doubt that Mr. HEARTLEY has wrote it down
           or will do it." Sworn to in court by William LAMBERTH,
           6 Oct 1774.
           [According to the deposition of William HEARTLEY dated
           6 Oct 1774, Robert CLARK said if his land was not en-
           tailed, he desired Bob, the son of John CLARK, might
           have it. Molly was the sis. of Robert CLARK.]
           Pres. in court 7 Nov 1774 by Thomas CLARK Jr. who was
           granted administration.

p.197 - Robert CLARK, inv; 15 Jun 1775.

p.198 - Henry SISSON, inv; 15 Jun 1775.

p.199 - Mary GARLAND, will; 9 Feb 1774, 6 Jun 1774 and 1 Aug 1774
           sons Jesse, Travis, and Griffin; daus. Mary, Anne
           GARNER, and Henrietta; ex: son Griffin and Richard
           NEALE; wits: Richard GARNER, Mary BELL.

p.200 - James WEBB, will; 8 Sep 1774, 1 May 1775
           mother Frances WEBB; bros. Charles, Cuthbert, Isaac,
           and John; sisters Elizabeth HARRISON, Winnie WEBB,
           Nancy EDMONDSON, and Drucilla WEBB; ex: bro. John;
           prov. by the oaths of William MISKELL and Charles
           McCARTY.

p.202 - Joshua STONE, will; 15 Feb 1774, 8 Nov 1774 and 3 Jul 1775
           sons Joshua, Benjamin (100 ac. of land purchased of
           William GRIFFIN), Thomas, and John; grson. [?] STONE;
           ex: sons Benjamin and Thomas; wits: John YEARBY, Moses
           BRYANT, Judith YEARBY, John STONE. [Joshua STONE mar.
           Wilmoth BRYANT, 22 Nov 1738. MRC, p. 196.]

p.203 - William CREWDSON, inv; 3 Aug 1775.

p.205 - Josiah HINDS, inv; 3 Aug 1775.

      - John YEARBY, NFP, will; 28 Jun 1772, 3 Jul 1775, 6 May
      1776

mother Elizabeth YEARBY; sons Thomas land in Rich.
Co., George Woodbridge land in Lanc., Dinwiddie, and
Brunswick Cos; s-i-l. William GIBSON land and plant.
known as the Brick House; land in Fairfax Co. contract-
ed for with David BOYD of North. Co. should be made
good to him; remaining land on Pohick Run in Fairfax
Co. to be sold; daus. Sarah and Betty Woodbridge; ex:
Richard MITCHELL, David BOYD, and George YEARBY; wits:
James KIRK, Isaac JAMES, George YEARBY.

p.207 - Charles DODSON, will; 19 Aug 177[2], 4 Sep 1775
sons Charles and Solomon; dau. Margaret [ELLETT]; wife
Mary; ex: wife and Thomas HOWARD; wits: Thaddeus
JACKSON, William FLEMING, Rodham PRITCHETT.

p.208 - George BARNES, nunc. will pres. by Robert NEWSOM, Alexander
DALE, and Thaddeus BRYANT
They say that George BARNES wished his wife to have his
whole est; after her death, to be div. between his
three chil. [unnamed]; ex: Charles BARNES, Edward
DOBYNS, and Spencer HOWARD; will certified 8 Apr 1775.

p.209 - Robert HEADLEY, will; 13 Jun 1775, 4 Sep 1775
all lands to eld. son George, if he has no heirs, to
son Henry, if he has no heirs, to son John, and, if
he has no heirs, to youngest son not yet baptised;
four sons to have two years schooling each; ex: George
TALBOT, Elizabeth HEADLEY, and Peter [HATTEN]; wits:
Cuthbert WEBB, Charles WEBB. [Robert, the son of
Henry and Anne (PUGH) HEADLEY, was b. 24 May 1745.
NFPR, p. 91.]

p.210 - Mary CLARK, nunc. will; certified 24 Aug 1775, pres. 4
Sep 1775
John CLARK, Robert CLARK, and Richard HAMLIN of Rich.
Co...made oath that Mary CLARK, dec'd, just before
she departed this life, called on them to witness that
it was her will...that Rebecca CLARK should have her
bed and the rest of her est. be eq. div. between the
chil. of the sd. Rebecca CLARK except the side saddle
and that she gave to Elizabeth, the wife of Thomas
CLARK.

      - Edward OGLEBY, NFP, will; 25 Oct 1771, 2 Oct 1775
wife Jeane whole est; fr. John HAMMOND; ex: wife and
John HAMMOND; wits: Benjamin BRAMHAM, Joshua SINGLETON,
Lewis HAMMOND.

p.211 - Leroy GRIFFIN, will; 26 Oct 1775, 4 Dec 1775
eld. dau. Anne CORBIN all negroes in West. [Co.]; daus.
Elizabeth and Judith; all my right, title, and interest
in and to my claim of land under His Majesty's proclaim-
ation to be vested in youngest dau. Judith; ex: wife,
bro. Thomas B., Col. James BALL, and William PEACHEY;
wits: James [SELDEN], Thomas BEALE, John LELAND Jr.,
Joseph DALE.

p.213 - William THRIFT, Lun.Par., will; 24 Apr 1775, 4 Mar 1776
dau. Anne GARLAND and her sons Griffin and William;
sons Jesse, Thomas, and Nathaniel; daus. Sarah,
Winifred STOREY, and Esther CRITCHER; son Benjamin
to have 50 pounds on condition that he has an heir
lawfully begotten of his own body, but, if he should
die without such heir, then money to be eq. div. among
my three ex; son William; dau. Mary DOWNTON; ex: sons

William, Jesse, and Thomas; wits: Richard WAGSTAFF,
George THRIFT, Daniel LAWSON Jr.

p.214 - Henry HARFORD, will; 7 Jan 1776, 6 May 1776
wife Mary the land and plant. I live on; eight chil.
[unnamed]; son William; ex: wife; wits: Richard NEALE,
William WEBSTER.

p.215 - Anthony TUNE, NFP, will; 3 May 1776, 5 Aug 1776
sons Anthony, John, and Jesse; dau. Betty; ex: Hudson
MUSE of Farnham Par; wits: Samuel DOBYNS, John [STONE].
[Anthony TUNE mar. Dorcas MORRIS in 1749. MRC, p.219.]

p.216 - Robert SMITH, Lun.Par., will; 7 Aug 1776, 2 Sep 1776
goddau. Elizabeth ALDERSON (dau. of William ALDERSON);
cousin John SMITH (son of Thomas SMITH); godson John
REYNOLDS (son of George REYNOLDS); fr. Benjamin
BRAMHAM; bro. Thomas SMITH; Catharine PURCELL; nephew
John SMITH (son of Thomas SMITH); Joseph SMITH (son
of Thomas SMITH); ex: friends Benjamin BRAMHAM and
George GARLAND; wits: David BERRICK, Peter NORTHEN,
George BERRICK, Abigail NORTHEN, Sary NORTHEN.

p.218 - James MITCHELL, Lun.Par., will; 18 Feb 1776, 2 Sep 1776
wife Lucy; chil. John and Frances; ex: wife, John
BELFIELD, Richard ROUTT, and bro. Richard MITCHELL;
wits: Christopher COLLINS, Hannah COLLINS, Richard
MITCHELL. [James MITCHELL mar. Lucy ROUTT in Dec 1770.
MRC, p.134.]

p.219 - Richard JONES, planter, Lun.Par., will; 13 Aug 1775, 2
Sep 1776
bros. Griffin and John; sisters Elizabeth TURNER and
Abigail LUNN; Anne CLAXTON, if she should die before
Jeremiah CLAXTON and Elizabeth CLAXTON, her part to
be div. eq. between them; rest of est. to Jeremiah
CLAXTON; ex: Jeremiah CLAXTON; wits: William [DODSON],
Daniel BUTLER, Joshua HINSON.

p.220 - Eleanor MOUNTJOY, Lun.Par., will; 12 Dec 1771, 2 Dec 1776
grsons. Joseph PIERCE (son of William PIERCE), William
YEATMAN; niece Martha HART (wife of John HART)·; grdaus.
Ellen and Mary PIERCE (daus. of William PIERCE), and
Sybella and Mary YEATMAN (daus. of Thomas YEATMAN);
ex: s-i-l. William PIERCE; wits: Henry DUNKIN, John
HART, Christopher COLLINS.

p.221 - Sarah RUSSELL, will; 27 Dec 1774, 2 Jan 177[5]
s-i-l. John REYNOLDS; dau. Betty REYNOLDS; ex: dau.
and s-i-l.; wits: John YEATMAN, George REYNOLDS, Job
THOMAS.

p.222 - James MITCHELL, inv; 27 Jan 1777.

p.223 - Edward OGLEBY, inv; 27 Jan 1777.

p.224 - Leroy GRIFFIN, inv; 27 Jan 1777.

       - William THRIFT, 28 Jan 1777.

p.226 - John NORWOOD, inv; ord. 5 Dec 1774, rec. 28 Jan 1777.

p.227 - Thomas GLASCOCK, inv; 28 Jan 1777.

p.229 - Anthony TUNE, inv; 28 Jan 1777.

p.230 - Joshua STONE, inv; 28 Jan 1777.

p.231 - James WEBB, inv; 28 Jan 1777.

p.232 - Mary CLARK, inv; 28 Jan 1777.

    - John PHILLIPS, inv; 29 Jan 1777.

p.233 - Richard JONES, inv; 5 Feb 1777.

p.234 - Blanch SALLARD, inv; ord. Mar 1774, rec. 5 Feb 1777.

p.235 - Leroy GRIFFIN, inv; 5 Feb 1777.

p.239 - Dr. Nicholas FLOOD, inv; taken 27, 28, and 31 May 1776,
rec. 8 Feb 1777. [Includes a long list of medicines.]

p.270 - Thomas GLASCOCK, will; 26 May 1772, 2 Oct 1775
wife; two chil. [unnamed]; no ex; wit: William CONNER;
pres. by Mary GLASCOCK the wid.

p.271 - John PHILLIPS, NFP, 26 Feb 1763, 4 Sep 1775
wife Elizabeth; sons Joseph, John, Bryant, and George;
child wife is now bearing; ex: wife and fr. William
STONUM; wits: D. NEWGENT, Jehu. PULLEN, William SMOOT.
[John PHILLIPS was apparently first mar. to Mary [?]
who was the mother of Joseph (b. 1753). His second
wife was Elizabeth [?]. The child she was bearing
at the time the will was written was Milly (b. 4 Apr
1763). NFPR, p.148.]

p.272 - Thomas MORTON, will; 10 May 1776, [nd.]
dau. Elizabeth; sons James, Charles Snead, and John;
wife Anne; ex: wife; wits: John ESKRIDGE, Thomas
PLAYLE, William YATES, Mary [ARIDAL].

p.273 - Samuel WILLIAMS, NFP, will; 2 Nov 1776, 8 Apr 1777
wife Betty Anne; tract of land in Halifax Co. to be
sold and the money div. between three daus; it is my
will and desire that my old hopping negro man, Guy,
be at liberty on the 20th day of every Dec, so long
as he shall live, to chose a master or mistress from
among my wife and chil. whom he shall serve the suc-
ceeding year; five chil. [not specified]; son Thaddeus
land and plant. whereon I now live; son David tract
of land bought of William SYDNOR; ex: wife and Col.
William PEACHEY; wits: [John] SYDNOR, Richard GLASCOCK,
Charles McCARTY, William MISKELL, Charles BARBER,
Robert PALMER. [Samuel WILLIAMS mar. Betty Anne HILL
in 1751. MRC. p.232. They had the following chil:
Winifred (b.1752), Sarah Suggitt (b.1754), Thaddeus
(b.1756), Samuel (b.1759), David (b.1762), Cyrus (1765-
1770), Betty Anne (b.1769), Rebecca (b.1774). NFPR, p.
202.]

p.275 - Samuel WILLIAMS, inv; 14 Apr 1778.

p.278 - Francis RANDALL, will; 17 Nov 1776, 3 Feb 1777.
dau. Anne Hill Chloe and her chil. Milly, Rose, and
Rachel; grson. Francis HILL; sons George, Thomas, and
William; son Thomas HILL and his heirs in the same
manner I formerly gave them by deed in Spotsylvania
Office but not recorded; mentions his right to a
slave now in the possession of his mother as heir to
Robert and Alice Davis RANDALL; daus. Betsy, Molly,

Sally, and Fanny; asks son George to take care of
his sister Anne HILL and children during her widowhood;
ex: son George; wits: Lawrence POPE, Powell BURLAND,
James CREWDSON.

p.279 - Francis RANDALL, inv; 14 Apr 1778.

p.280 - John HARDIDGE, will; 12 Feb 1776, 2 Jun 1777
wife; son Joseph plant. in North. Co; son John plant.
in Rich. Co; dau. Barbary; s-i-l. Abraham EILIS; ex:
son John; wits: Stuart REDMAN, Vincent JACKSON,
William HABRON.

p.281 - John HARDIDGE, inv; 14 Apr 1778.

p.282 - Charles BROWN, will; 4 Mar 1777, 6 Oct 1777
land to be eq. div. between two sis. Elizabeth and
Margaret BROWN; ex: fr. John SYDNOR; wits: [Betty
DAMERON], Frances SYDNOR, John SYDNOR; pres. in
court by Eleanor BROWN.

p.283 - Charles BROWN, inv; 15 Apr 1778.

- Betty TARPLEY, will; 14 Aug 1777, 1 Sep 1777
to be buried by the side of my dear husband in Farnham Churchyard; dau. Nancy; surviving chil. and the
chil. of dec'd dau. Betty PEACHEY; ex: s-i-l. Capt.
Charles McCARTY; wits: Samuel COLSTON, Leroy PEACHEY.
[Elizabeth TARPLEY was the wid. of Maj. Travers
TARPLEY who d. 1768. MRC, p.204.]

p.284 - Mrs. Betty TARPLEY, inv; 15 Apr 1778.

p.286 - David THORNTON, will; 24 Feb 1776, 4 Aug 1777
daus. Mary Anne MOORE, Betty CLARK, and [Ezbell]
THORNTON; son Robert; wife Betty; ex: wife, Benjamin
BRAMHAM, and Andrew MORGAN; wits: William GARLAND,
Anne GARLAND.

p.287 - David THORNTON, inv; 15 Apr 1778.

p.289 - John KENNER, will; 27 Jul 1776, 2 Jun 1777
est. to be kept together for the support of my wife
and chil. until William is 21, then to be eq. div.
between wife and five chil: Mary, Sarah, William,
Elizabeth, and Frances; land and plant. to son
William; ex: wife Sarah and John SYDNOR; wits:
William HARTLEY, Anthony SYDNOR, Francis Spelman
CRALLE.

p.290 - John KENNAN [sic], inv; 15 Apr 1778.

p.291 - Christopher BROWN, NFP, will; 8 Feb 1776, 2 Jun 1777
bro. Charles; sis. Margaret and Elizabeth; Peter
ENGLISH; Thomas WILLIAMS, wife Rachel; ex: Thomas
WILLIAMS; wits: William HARTLEY, John KENNAN.

p.292 - Christopher BROWN, inv; 15 Apr 1778.

p.293 - Elizabeth DEW, NFP, will; 21 Nov 1777, 2 Mar [1778]
grchil. Alexander and Joannah DEW (chil. of Thomas
DEW); grson. Obediah WILLIAMS; son Alexander; ex:
William MISKELL; wits: Thaddeus WILLIAMS, John
WILLIAMS.

- Thomas HAMMOND, Lun.Par., will; 16 Oct 1777, 5 Jan 1778
wife Rebecca Sisson whole est; wife's child Frances
Sisson THORNTON which she had by her former husband
to be brought up and given schooling as my own; my
two chil. Elizabeth and Lucy; ex: wife and Daniel
LAWSON; wits: Vincent GARLAND, George HOWE Jr., Mary
Anne HAMMOND. [Thomas HAMMOND mar. Rebecca Sisson
(LAWSON) THORNTON wid. of Thomas THORNTON. MRC,p.86.]

p.294 - Thomas HARFORD, will; 3 Sep 1776, 2 Jun 1777
sis. Anne all land and plant., if she dies, to nephew
Henry HARFORD (son of dec'd bro. Henry), if he dies
before age 21, land to go to nephew William HARFORD
(son of dec'd bro. Henry); no ex; wits: Richard NEALE,
William WEBSTER.

p.295 - Joseph BRANN, Lun.Par., will; 6 Jan 1778, 2 Mar 1778
sons Joseph and Andrew; daus. Mary, Anne WILLIAMS;
ex: Morton WILSON and Joseph WILSON; wits: Joseph
WILSON, Morton WILSON, John KELLY.

p.296 - William MITCHELL, Lun.Par., will; 7 Nov 1775, 2 Feb 177[?]
all est. to bros. Robert and Richard; Jennings BECK-
WITH; sisters [unnamed]; ex: bros. Robert and Richard;
proved to be the handwriting of William MITCHELL by
Moore BRAGG.

p.297 - Winifred HAMMOND, will; 30 Jan 1777, 2 Jun 1777
cousin Charles BAILEY; sis. Katy BAILEY; Betty Brunton
SMITH; godson John HAMMOND (son of John HAMMOND) of
this county; cousin Betty BAILEY; no ex; wits: Susanna
DAVIS, John HAMMOND, Elizabeth HAMMOND.

p.297 - Jesse THRIFT, Lun.Par., will; 4 Feb 1777, 7 Apr 1777
bro. Thomas money to pay for the land I bargained for
in Gloucester likewise the land to be his property;
bro. William; sisters Mary [DOWNTIN] and Sarah McKENNY;
ex: bro. William; wits: George BERRICK, Mary WATTS,
Anne ALLGOOD.

p.298 - John PURCELL, inv; 16 Apr 1778.

p.299 - Robert HEADLEY, inv; ord. 4 Sep 1775, rec. 16 Apr 1778.

p.300 - Susannah EIDSON, inv; 16 Apr 1778.

- William FEAGINS. inv; 17 Apr 1778.

p.301 - William CONNELLY, inv; 17 Apr 1778.

p.302 - George BARNES, inv; 17 Apr 1778.

p.303 - Lucy DOWNMAN, NFP, will; 24 Sep 1775, 6 Jul 1778
daus. Anne, Fanny, and Priscilla; other chil: Betty,
Rawleigh, and [Susannah]; girls to have twice as
much as the boys; ex: friends Richard MITCHELL, John
SYDNOR, and Charles McCARTY; wits: Thomas SMITH,
Richard APPLEBY, Sarah APPLEBY.

p.304 - Elizabeth SYDNOR, NFP; will; 25 Aug 1777, 6 Jul 1778
s-i-l. Richard MITCHELL; grsons. John SYDNOR, Anthony
SYDNOR, Sydnor BENNETT; daus. Dewanna, Lucy DOWNMAN,
Ruth BELFIELD, and Anne MITCHELL: chil. of dec'd dau.
Betty TARPLEY; ex: s-i-l. Richard MITCHELL and grson.
John SYDNOR; wits: Travers DOWNMAN, Priscilla DOWNMAN.

150

p.305 - George REYNOLDS, NFP, will; 23 Jun 1777, 4 May 1778
        chil. John, William, George, Epaphroditus, Frances,
        Anne, and child wife is now big with; ex: wife Frances
        and friends Hudson MUSE, John HAMMOND, and Charles
        McCARTY. [George REYNOLDS mar. Frances BARBER in 1759.
        MRC, p.167.]

p.306 - William BROCKENBROUGH, will; 16 Oct 1777, 6 Jul 1778
        eld. son Austin; Lucy (dau. of son Austin); William
        (eld. son of son Austin); son John the plant. I now
        live on; grson. John (son of Dr. John BROCKENBROUGH);
        son Moore land called [Barrows] and mill; grson.
        William (son of Moore); all books to son Newman;
        Elizabeth FAUNTLEROY (dau. of son Newman); son Thomas;
        ex: sons Moore and Newman; wits: Robert W. CARTER,
        Vincent GARLAND, Daniel LAWSON Jr., George HOW Jr.

p.308 - William BEALE, will; 9 Mar 1776, 6 Jul 1778
        sons Thomas, William tract of land in Rich. Co.
        purchased of William COLSTON occupied by Samson
        MARMADUKE, Reuben all lands in Culpeper, Richard,
        and Robert; daus. Susannah, Sarah, and Mary; William-
        son BALL (who mar. dau. Anne); I give my Negro man,
        Dick, for his faithful service and care in watching
        on me, liberty of choosing every Christmas Day his
        master or mistress amongst all my chil. for the fol-
        lowing year; other chil. John, Elizabeth, Winifred,
        and Travers; ex: sons Thomas, John, William, and
        sons-in-law Richard PARKER and Robert Wormley CARTER;
        wits: Harrison RANDOLPH, Landon CARTER Jr., Thomas
        PARKER.

p.310 - John BROWN, NFP, will; 22 Jan 1777, 6 Jul 1778
        wife Anne; chil. [unnamed]; ex: wife and William
        OLDHAM Sr; wits: Con. ROCK, Vincent BROWN, John FRANCE.

      - Nicholas FLOOD, NFP, will; [nd.], [nd.]
        In my 63rd year, having entered in on the 2nd day of
        Aug last, New Style; if I happen to die in America,
        I desire to be buried at the east end of North Farnham
        Church on the right hand of dau. Catharine McCALL who
        d. in 1767; parcel of wool cards, cotton cards, spin-
        ning wheels, and other implements of domestic industry
        equal to the expense of the marble monumental stone
        which I have desired to be erected to be disposed of
        among the poor...of industrious housekeepers in NFP
        according to their want of such implements; wife;
        land in Essex Co. bought of George CLAYTON and Merri-
        wether SMITH to be sold; dwelling plant. and all lands
        in Rich. Co. to grdau. Elizabeth McCALL, if she has no
        heirs, to grdau. Catharine McCALL, if she has no heirs,
        to nephew Nicholas FLOOD (2nd son of late bro. William);
        lacking heirs, to go successively to: nephew William
        [Pinkstant] FLOOD (eld. son of late bro. William),
        Walter Flood JONES (eld. son of fr. Dr. Walter JONES),
        William JONES (2nd son of Dr. Walter JONES), Elizabeth
        FLOOD (2nd dau. of bro. William), Thomas Griffin
        PEACHEY (2nd son of fr. and b-i-l. Col. William PEACHEY),
        William Travers PEACHEY (3rd son of Col. William
        PEACHEY), William PEACHEY (eld. son of fr. Maj. Leroy
        PEACHEY), Leroy PEACHEY (2nd son of Maj. Leroy PEACHEY);
        Cetera desunt; the undersigned believe that this is
        the will of Dr. Nicholas FLOOD: George McCARTY, Chas.
        McCARTY, George YERBY, Benjamin BRAMHAM, Robert
        TOMLIN, Charles HAMMOND. [Dr. Nicholas FLOOD mar.

Elizabeth PEACHEY; they had one dau., Catharine
who mar. Archibald McCALL in 1761. RCV, p.196.]

p.323 - John RYALS, Jr., inv; 7 Nov 1778.

p.324 - Thomas MORTON, inv; 7 Nov 1778.

p.325 - Elizabeth DEW, inv; 7 Nov 1778.

- Jesse THRIFT, inv; 7 Nov 1778.

p.326 - Jospeh BRANN, inv; 8 Nov 1778.

p.327 - John McCAVE, inv; 8 Nov 1778.

p.328 - Capt. William BEALE, inv; 8 Nov 1778.

p.331 - William BEALE, inv. in Culpeper Co.; 8 Nov 1778.

- Robert SMITH, inv; 8 Nov 1778.

p.332 - John JONES, Lun.Par., will; 13 Aug 1778, 5 Oct 1778
sons Griffin, Richard half of est; daus. Sarah and
Mary; grsons. William and Jonathan JONES other half
of est. to be eq. div; ex: wife; wits: John ESKRIDGE,
John HALL, Moore BRAGG.

p.333 - Jesse THORNTON, inv; 12 Jan 1779.

- Mrs. Winifred HAMMOND, inv; 12 Jan 1779.

p.334 - [William] BEALE's Memorandum: Whereas the [sullion] girl,
Nanny, given in my will to my dau. Mary has never had
any chil., as a recompense for her not breeding, I do
hereby give my sd. dau., Mary, a negro girl named
Nancy, dau. of Nell; 1 Jun 1777; wits: William BEALE,
Will BEALE Jr; proved: 2 Nov 1778.

- Newman BARNES, NFP, will; 24 Aug 1778, 1 Feb 1779
land and plant. whereon I live to son Newman, if he
has no heirs, to son Morton, and, if he has no heirs,
to dau. Lucy; Newman BARNES, the illegitimate son of
Susannah TEAGUE, 100 pounds to be put out at interest;
ex: Thomas JONES, Walker TOMLIN, William MORTON,
William MISKELL; wits: John HAMMOND, Richard MITCHELL,
Peggy MISKELL, Newman MISKELL.

p.335 - Daniel JESPER, will; 8 Nov 1778, 1 Feb 1779
son Thomas the plant. I now live on provided he makes
his bro., Daniel--or, in case of his death--his next
elder bro. that shall be living, a good right to the
plant. that came by his mother; if Thomas has no heirs,
plant. to go to son Daniel, and, lacking heirs, to go
successively to sons William, George, and Edward; ex:
wife Catharine, Edward SAUNDERS, and John HAMMOND,
wits: Thomas JESPER, George MISKELL, Robert JESPER.

p.336 - Landon CARTER of Sabine Hall, will; 4 Sep 1770, [1] Feb 1779
son Robert Wormley to have half of my slaves except
those hereafter given to George CARTER, my grson., and
to Robert HAMILTON; the other half...to be eq. div. between sons Landon and John (friends Mr. Nelson BERKELEY,
Mr. Robert BEVERLY, the Hon. John TAYLOE, and Mr.
Richard PARKER to div. the slaves); son Robert W. all
lands in York, Charles City, King and Queen, Lancaster,

152

Northumberland, Richmond, Westmoreland, King George,
and Stafford cos. as also all my lands upon Shenandoah
River as well as those in the county of Frederick as
that tract on the Blue Ridge or the Virginia side of
the Shenandoah River, as it is called by the upper
inhabitants, which includes the Blue Ball Mountain
excepting always tract called Summer Duck Run which
I have hereinafter given to Robert HAMILTON in case
that tract may happen to lie in King George, Stafford,
or Prince William co; both of my Bull Run tracts to
be eq. div. between sons Landon and John; son Landon
half of the lands on Goose Creek, that is, such of
them as are situated in Loudon, Fairfax, Prince William,
or Fauquier cos; the other half of sd. lands on Goose
Creek to son John; having paid my dau. BERKELEY her
full fortune long ago and also given her her mother's
gold watch, now new[ly] fitted up and with a new gold
chain to it, I only give her 20 pounds; daus. Maria
BEVERLEY (wife of Mr. Robert BEVERLEY), Lucy, and
Judith; I intended to have given Robert HAMILTON (son
of the late Gilbert HAMILTON) that tract of land which
I purchased of Tobias PURCELL...on Summer Duck Run,
in whatsoever counties it may be, together with six
young working slaves...I say I intended this legacy...
but having seen every good purpose...of my intention
in great danger of being defeated through the weakness
of his mother in keeping him at home only to loiter
and misspend his time without the least chance of
improving himself, to take care of (perhaps) all that
he will have to live upon, I will now attempt to take
care of him, I now direct sd. land and slaves to go to
him at the age of 21; reflecting with a grateful as
well as a brotherly concern that the name of George
would be lost in my family, from whom I received a
very considerable part of my est., and, being persuaded
that through my means, my son Robert W. had a child...
by the name of George...land adjoining Leesburgh to
be called Georgia and go to grson. George CARTER; ex:
sons Robert, Landon, and John; wits: Walker TOMLIN,
John BEALE, William BEALE Jr.
Cod., 4 Sep 1770; dau. Judith has mar. Reuben BEALE;
therefore, bequest to her is revoked, but est. is to
go to her after her husband's death, if she survive
him; revokes bequest to Robert HAMILTON and land and
slaves to go to son Robert; wits: William BEALE Jr.,
Thomas PARKER.
Cod., 6 Oct 1778; all bequests of watches revoked;
Summer Duck Run to go to grson. George; having suf-
ficiently forgiven dau. Judith, now the wife of Mr.
Reuben BEALE, for everything that could look like a
disobedience, I have told her and her sd. husband
and her bros. that I had altered my intentions re-
specting her and therefore order that my three sons
pay her the same fortune that I have given to my dau.
Lucy, now Lucy COLSTON; my desire to reward the de-
serving compels me to take note of my coachman, Nat,
and my wench mulatto, Betty, therefore, I direct that
on every Christmas Day they shall have liberty to
make choice of which one of my children they shall
desire to live with and both Nat and Betty shall have
an annuity of 10 pounds per annum paid to them; wits:
David BOYD, Edward Minty PURCELL. [Landon CARTER's
dau. Maria mar. Robert BEVERLEY of Essex Co. in 1763.
MRC, p.18.]

p.345 - Jesse BRYANT, NFP, will; 22 Oct 1778, 3 Nov 1778
son Thaddeus plant. whereon I live, if he has no heirs,
to son Richard; John NASH to care for chil. at 10
pounds [per year] and to have use of their [est.] at
6 pounds per year until the heirs shall arrive at
maturity; ex: fr. Rawleigh BRYANT and George NASH;
wits: Jonathan BRYANT, Gabriel SMITHER.

- James WEBB, inv; ord. 7 May 1775, rec. 1 Apr 1779.

p.346 - John JONES, inv; 3 Apr 1779.

- Jesse BRYANT, inv; 24 Apr 1779.

p.347 - Cobham GATHINGS, inv; 24 Apr 1779.

- Daniel JESPER, inv; 17 May 1779.

p.348 - Fortunatus DAVENPORT, will; 22 Jan 1773, 7 Jun 1779
wife Elizabeth; child. Joseph, George, Betty Heale,
Rachel, and Fortunatus; son Joseph to have land and
plant. whereon I now live after wife's death or remarriage; ex: wife, bro. William, and fr. John POPE
Jr.; wits: John HUNTON, George SCURLOCK, John POPE Jr.

p.349 - George OLIFF, Lun.Par., will; 11 May 1778, 5 Jul 1779
sons James, George Steward, and William; daus. Jemima,
Rebecca, Mary CARR, and Anne FISHER; ex: son William
and s-i-l. John FISHER; wits: James NEWMAN, John COATS.

p.350 - Joshua SINGLETON, inv. in Lunenburg Co., returned 23 Jun
1773.

- Robert MOORE, will; [?] Jun 1779, 4 Oct 1779
wife Anne all est. during her widowhood; land to be
sold when all children come of age and money to be
eq. div. among them; ex: wife; wits: William GARLAND,
George HOW.

p.351 - John DRAPER, inv; ord. Aug 1779.

p.352 - John DRAPER, NFP, will; 2 Jul 1779, 2 Aug 1779
wife Leanner; child. Caty, Betty, William, John, and
Fanny; ex: fr. John HAMMOND; wits: Samuel TUNE,
William MISKELL, Cuthbert WEBB.

p.353 - Andrew HEADLEY, Lun.Par., will; [nd.], 7 Feb 1780
land to wife, after her death, to be eq. div. between
two sons William and John; daus. Dorcas GOLDSBY,
Molly SELF, Elizabeth, and Sally; ex: wife and son
William; wits: John HOW, Elizabeth HOW. [Andrew
HEADLEY's wife was Sarah, probably the dau. of
Elender PORTER of West. Co. WWC, p.171.]

p.354 - John TAYLOE, Lun.Par., will; 22 May 1773, 5 Jul 1779
desires to be buried near parents with decent church
burial without any of the usual pagentry; wife; godson John Tayloe CORBIN 100 pounds sterling; goddau.
Lucy PAGE 100 pounds sterling; John Tayloe THORNTON
100 pounds sterling; cousin John SMITH all interest
due on his bond; minister and vestry of Lun. Par.
500 pounds sterling in trust for the use of the poor-
est inhabitants of the sd. par., being honest people,
to be let to interest on good land security or otherwise so laid out that the interest or better profits

154

thereof be distributed with equity and justice...every
year at the lower church of the sd. parish on Restor-
ation Day when I hope the incumbent will give them
prayers and sermon, not mentioning this bequest; this
legacy to continue forever; Margaret GARRETT 20 pounds
sterling per annum for the tender care of my children;
faithful servant Mr. Thomas LAWSON; daus. Elizabeth
and Rebecca; son John; all est. in Prince William Co.
also all est. in Baltimore Co. in the Province of
Maryland...and all sloops, schooners, boats, and
vessels with all the tackle to be kept together as
one entire est. to be worked as heretofore in making
of pig iron; if wife should be pregnant and bear a son,
son to be named Gwynn Williams and to have Occoquan
est. and all lands in Loudon Co; ex: The Hon. Richard
CORBIN Esq., Mann PAGE Esq.,of Mansfield, the Hon.
George PLATER Esq., b-i-l. John Tayloe CORBIN, Mann
PAGE Jr. (son of Mann PAGE), Warner LEWIS Jr. (son of
Warner LEWIS), nephews, sons-in-law Edward LLOYD,
Francis Lightfoot LEE, and the Hon. Ralph WORMSLEY
Esq. with fr. Col. William BROCKENBROUGH and Mr.
Thomas LAWSON my iron agent; no wits. [For an account
of the TAYLOE family, see: MRC, p. 267. As of 1976,
there was about $18,000 in the fund which John TAYLOE
set up for the poor of Lun.Par. RCV, pp.391-392.]

p.358 - Moses BRYANT, Pittsylvania Co., will; 23 Oct 1778, 6 Sep
1779
all land and slaves and every other individual of est.
both in Pittsylvania and Rich. Cos. to be sold and the
money arising to go to sister's son Thomas HENDREN of
Rich. [Co.]; ex: Joshua STONE; wits: Joshua STONE,
Mary STONE, J. STONE.

p.359 - Caty BAILEY, will; 5 Jul 1779, 7 Aug 1780
son Charles lands and plant. whereon I now dwell; dau.
Betty; ex: son Charles and fr. Col. William PEACHEY
and Capt. William SMITH; wits: Alexander BRYANT;
Susannah [...]IGUE, Mary SMITH.

p.361 - Catharine HANKS, inv; ord. 1 Feb 1779.

p.363 - Anne HILL, inv; [nd.]

- John TAFF, will; 17 Jan 1780, 7 Feb 1781
dau. Winnie 65 ac. out of the 150 ac. where I now live;
son Samuel remaining land; Thomas and Rawleigh TAFF
(sons of Susannah TAFF); the third part of John
WOODBRIDGE's whole land and negroes that my brother,
Thomas TAFF, promised to me, if it is recovered, to
go to Thomas and Rawleigh TAFF, dau. Winnie, and son
Samuel; ex: son Samuel; wits: Sylvester [?], Joseph
[ELDER], Molly TAFF.

p.364 - George OLIFF, inv; ord. 5 Jul 1779.

p.365 - John BAILEY, Lun.Par., will; 14 Apr 1780, 1 May 1780
mother, Sarah BRAGG, 15 ac. that Capt. George RANDAL
has leave of Rich. Court to build a mill on; b-i-l.
James BRAGG the remaining 185 ac; ex: father-in-law
Moore BRAGG; wits: William HALL, Keziah BRAGG, William
BRAGG.

p.366 - John BAILEY, inv; ord. 1 May 1780.

- George BROWN, Farn. Par., will; 28 Jul 1775, 7 Aug 1780
    sons Thomas, Vincent 100 ac. of land known as Spain
    to be eq. div; ex: sons John and Charles and bro.
    Vincent; wits: Samuel BARNES, Luke HEADLEY, Dudley
    DALE.

p.368 - Joseph PHILLIPS, NFP, will; 21 Feb 1777, 7 Aug 1780
    sis. Leah CORNELIUS to have land during her life, after
    her death to go to her son William [?] CORNELIUS;
    Joseph WILLIAMS all my part of my father's household
    furniture; godfather Caran BRAMHAM; mentions wages for
    the year 1776 due from Richard NASH; ex: Caran BRAMHAM;
    wits: Anne BRAMHAM, Eleanor BRAMHAM, Barbara BRAMHAM.

p.369 - William COLSTON, will; 5 Oct 1780, 5 Jan 1781
    wife Lucy; son William Travers my manor plant. includ-
    ing the lands purchased of the late Mr. PLUMMER and
    Mr. HILL; daus. Susannah and Elizabeth; ex: Col.
    William PEACHEY and Col. Robert W. CARTER; wits: Leroy
    PEACHEY, James COX. [William COLSTON mar. Lucy CARTER
    in 1775. MRC, p.42.]

p.370 - Charles DOBYNS, will; 30 Oct 1780, 1 Jan 1781
    son Daniel land and plant. where I now live, if he has
    no heirs, to dau. Caty, if she has no heirs, to dau.
    Sarah, if she has no heirs, to dau. Nancy; dau. Lucy;
    bro. William to care for dau. Lucy and be her guardian;
    ex: bros. William, Daniel, Samuel, and Abner; wits:
    Leroy DOBYNS, Merryman THRIFT, Edward DOBYNS. [Charles
    DOBYNS mar. Lucy ELDER in 1762. MRC, p.54.]

p.372 - George DOWNMAN, Farn. Par., will; 15 Nov 1780, 5 Feb 1781
    wife Frances Spelman; dau. Elizabeth BALL; ex: wife
    and William DOWNMAN Sr; wits: John WROE, Peter WROE.

p.373 - George BARRICK, NFP, will; 20 Nov 1781, 2 Apr 1782
    wife and children [unnamed]; ex: fr. Henry DOBYNS and
    William HAZARD; wits: William MISKELL, Cuthbert WEBB,
    Joshua SINGLETON.

p.374 - Samuel DOBYNS, NFP, will; 29 Dec 1781, 4 Feb 1782
    sons William F. and Samuel; ex: William F., Edward,
    and Abner DOBYNS; wits: William BAKER, Daniel DOBYNS.

p.375 - Benjamin BURRISS, Lun.Par., will; 19 Jun 1779, 5 Feb 1782
    son Josiah; wife Elizabeth; youngest son Benjamin;
    daus. Elizabeth and Anne; ex: George NEWMAN and James
    CREWDSON; wits: Powell BEELAND, James DIGMAN, Jeremiah
    JENKINS.

p.376 - Christopher COLLINS, will; [nd.] 1781, 5 Nov 1781
    son Christopher all land in Rich. Co. lying on Honey
    Run purchased of Col. James BALL of Lanc. Co.; son
    Thomas the plant. whereon I live; dau. Angelica;
    Margaret RICHARDSON wife of Isaac; John and Christopher
    (sons of Joseph WILSON); Elizabeth (dau. of Joseph
    WILSON); ex: sons Christopher and Thomas; no wits.

p.378 - George DAVIS, will; 22 Apr 1780, 3 Sep 1781
    son John all land adjoining the tract he now lives on
    together with the mill, millstones, and ironwork;
    daus. Sally and Betty; son George; wife Elizabeth;
    ex: wife, sons John and George, and friends William
    and Leroy PEACHEY; wits: James COX, William JENKINS,
    Jonathan TEAGUE. [George DAVIS mar. Elizabeth TUNE
    in 1759. MRC, p.50.]

156

p.381 - Cuthbert WEBB, will; 25 Jan 1781, 2 Apr 1782
mother Frances WEBB; sisters Winnie WEBB and [Priscilla]
SINGLETON; bros. Charles and Isaac; godsons James
Cuthbert SINGLETON, John HILL, and John EDMONDSON;
nephew George HARRISON, niece Frances HARRISON, goddau. Priscilla WEBB; ex: bros. Charles and Isaac and
fr. Robert SINGLETON; no wits. [Cuthbert WEBB, a son
of Isaac and Frances WEBB, was b. 1 Jun 1745. NFPR,
p.196.]

p.382 - James LUTTRELL, St.Stephen's Par., North. Co., will; 27
Apr 1780, 1 Oct 1781
wife Frances plant. in Rich. Co. during her life, then
to dau. Betty; son Leroy the plant. whereon I now live
in North. Co., if he has no heirs, to dau. Betty;
Eleanor FRANCE; ex: wife, son Leroy, Rice COOKMAN,
Richard GRINSTEAD; wits: Richard GRINSTEAD, James
VANLANDINGHAM, William GRINSTEAD.

p.383 - Benjamin BURRAS, inv; 1 Apr 1781, rec. 2 May 1782.

p.384 - Andrew HEADLEY, inv; 9 Feb 1780, rec. 3 May 1782.

p.385 - John TAFF, inv; 3 May 1782.

p.386 - William COOK, inv; 3 May 1782.

p.387 - John KENNAN, inv; 3 May 1782.

p.388 - George REYNOLDS, inv; ord. 6 Jul 1778, rec. 3 May 1782.

p.391 - Samuel DOBYNS, inv; 9 Oct 1782.

p.392 - William WARNER, inv; 9 Oct 1782.

p.393 - William COLSTON, inv. pres. by Robert Wormley CARTER the
ex; 4 Jan 1783.

p.395 - John SALLARD, NFP, will; 11 Apr 1782, 3 Jun 1782
desires that the boy, George, that now lives with
him to be freed and to be clothed and schooled out of
his est. until he is able to be put to a trade;
nephew Thomas GLASCOCK; bro. William SALLARD; ex:
fr. Benjamin BRANHAM, Walker TOMLIN, and George SISSON;
wits: Charles BARBER, John BAKER.

p.396 - George REYNOLDS, will; 19 Jul 1781, 6 Aug 1781
dau. Jane; wife Anne; ex: fr. Spencer GILL and Eliz.
REYNOLDS; wits: William DAVIS, Anne JONES, Joseph
REYNOLDS.

p.397 - Nathaniel WROE, NFP, will; 17 Feb 1782, 6 May 1782
sons John, George, and William the plants. whereon
they have settled; wife and dau. Jane the plant. whereon I now live, after their decease, to son Thomas;
ex: son John; wits: William BEARCROFT, Robert STOTT,
Samuel CRALLE.

- Thomas SMITH, NFP, will; 9 May 1771, 1 Jul 1782
son Thomas all lands bought of William WEBB, William
DENTON, and John SMITH Gent; son John lands bought of
Betty HILL and William ALGER; mentions dec'd father-
in-law John WOOLLARD and dec'd b-i-l Joseph WOOLLARD;
son Joseph Woollard SMITH all lands bought of Daniel
JESPER and John HAMMOND; daus. Anne DAVIS, Caty,

Betty (afflicted with fits, to be cared for by her
bro. Thomas), Jane, and Sally; Elizabeth DANIEL; ex:
Col. William PEACHEY, John PLUMMER, Samuel WILLIAMS,
Samuel WOOLLARD, and son Thomas; wits: Daniel JESPER,
Joseph SAUNDERS, John DANIEL.

p.401 - George REYNOLDS, inv; 7 Feb 1783.

p.402 - Nathaniel WROE, inv; 7 Feb 1783.

      - John JENNINGS, inv; 7 Feb 1783.

p.403 - William ROBINS, Lun.Par., will; 25 Aug 1781, 6 May 1782
        wife Ellen one moiety of land and mansion house during
        her widowhood; son John the other moiety of land;
        daus. Isabel, Marina, and Ellen; ex: wife and son
        John; wits: Jennings BECKWITH, William CREWDSON,
        Christopher COLLINS. [William ROBINS mar. Ellen
        THORNTON. MRC, p.171.]

p.404 - William ROBINS, inv; 12 Feb 1783.

p.405 - Edmond NORTHEN, inv; ord. 1 Jul 1782, rec. 12 Feb 1783.

p.406 - William BAKER, NFP, will; 26 Jan 1780, 7 Oct 1782
        son Samuel; dau. Winifred HARFORD; other chil. John,
        Lucy, Nancy, Caty, Betty, Billington, Barbara, and
        Milly; ex: Daniel and Abner DOBYNS; wit: Winnie
        DOBYNS.

p.407 - William LAMBERT, inv. pres. by John LAMBERT adm.; ord.
        Sep 1777, rec. [18] Feb 1783.

p.408 - Mrs. Elizabeth WILLIAMS, inv; 18 Feb 1783.

      - William BAKER, inv; taken 24 Oct 1782, rec. 19 Feb 1783.

p.409 - Charles DOBYNS, inv; 19 Feb 1783.

p.410 - Thomas HAMMOND, inv; taken 23 Jan 1778, rec. 19 Feb 1783.

p.411 - Edward JONES, will; 7 Oct 1781, 2 Sep 1782
        I being in perfect health, of a right mind and good
        memory, knowing that death are [sic] everywhere and
        that life are uncertain and I am going where I never
        may return, I have a desire to put it out of the
        power of all human nature to interrupt or disturb the
        peace or welfare of my loving wife and child which I
        leave behind; my desire is, if I never return, that
        during her widowhood, she shall dispose of everything
        that I am worth, after my debts are paid, at her will;
        if she remarries, I leave unto the child everything
        but what the law allows her; if the child should die
        before it be of age or without heir, whether she marry
        or no, it shall be all hers; I acknowledge this my
        hand and seal in the presence of Richard CLAUGHTON,
        Henry SPENCE, Christopher [DEATNY]. Pres. in court
        by Patty JONES, the wid. and relict.

      - Edward JONES, inv; 20 Feb 1783.

p.412 - Frances PRIDHAM, will; 17 Apr 1782, 6 May 1782
        son Christopher all my right and title to the slaves
        mentioned in my husband, Edward PRIDHAM's, will that
        was to be div. between my son Edward and my dau.

158

Frances...son Edward being now dead and I being his
heir; ex: Vincent GARLAND and William REYNOLDS; wits:
Burgess LONGWITH, Peter DAVIS, Mary Anne MOOREMAST.

- Robert SINGLETON, NFP, will; 2 Sep 1781, 5 Aug 1782.
    wife Priscilla; son James Cuthbert; bros. James, Joshua,
    and Samuel; ex: wife and friends John SYDNOR and Robert
    TOMLIN; wits: William BARBER, Anne HAMMOND, Robert
    TOMLIN.

p.414 - George BARRICK, inv; 25 Feb 1783. [Mentions his wid. Anne.]

p.415 - Maurice BRENT, will; 27 Jan 1782, 7 Oct 1782
    wife Sinah whole est; son Hugh est. after wife's death;
    ex: William BRENT and Charles [P.] McCARTY; wits: Eppy
    TILLERY, John PULLEN, John BROWN.

- Richard BURRELL, will; 9 May 1781, 6 May 1782
    Mr. Samuel WOOLLARD to have the care of all worldly
    affairs for to sell them and pay all my debts and him-
    self for his trouble and whatever is over, be it little
    or much, my desire is that a negro woman belonging to
    him, named Betty, may have it for her own property;
    wits: Luke JACKSON, Susannah TEAGUE, William ENGLISH,
    John WOOLLARD.

p.416 - Hannah CORBIN now living at Mrs. Elizabeth McFARLANE's in
    West. Co., will; 20 Oct 1781, 7 Oct 1782
    youngest dau., a Baptist, Martha HALL, half of my
    house at Woodberry, that is: my lodging chamber, the
    nursery closets of each side, the chimney adjoining,
    half the garden, and half the orchard joining that
    side of the garden and the plant. at Peacock's while
    she remains unmarried, but, should she marry before
    my death, then this bequest is to be void; mentions
    slaves deeded to dau. by Dr. HALL; only son Elisha
    HALL all land at Woodberry and Peacock's in Rich. Co.
    and all est. at Jenningses in West. Co. except what
    I have given to his Baptist sister; dau. Martha
    TURBERVILLE to be sole heir of all that belongs to
    me in Fauquier and King George Cos; no ex; wits:
    Robert WILLESS, Francis McTHANY, Mary PRATT;
    Cod., 20 Oct 1781, son Elisha to have all profits of
    the est. the year I die; will pres. in court by
    George TURBERVILLE. [Hannah CORBIN was the wid. of
    Gawin CORBIN of West. Co. and a dau. of Col. Thomas
    LEE of Stratford. She lived with Dr. Elisha HALL
    at Woodberry without benefit of a legal marriage.
    WCW, p.144; RCV, p.148.]

p.417 - Mary JACKSON, NFP, will; 19 Feb 1783, 3 Mar 1783
    sons Daniel and Luke; daus. Betty Dudley FLINN and
    Lucy; ex: son Daniel; wits: Job TILLERY, Elizabeth
    EFFORD, John FLINN.

p.418 - George EDWARDS, Lun.Par., will; 8 Jan 1783, 3 Mar 1783
    wife Sarah; dau. Frances; at wife's death, her third
    of the est. to be eq. div. between children William,
    John, Janey Wildy; ex: fr. Benjamin BRAMHAM, John
    HOW, Vincent GARLAND, and wife; wits: William BEALE
    Jr., Thomas BRO[R]CKE.

p.419 - Job THRIFT, will; 6 Feb 1781, 7 Apr 1783
    son George land and plant.; daus. Winifred, Nancy,
    and [Mary Thrift MORGIN]; ex: son George; wits: Edmond

NORTHEN, John WORTHER, Betty NORTHEN, Wm. NORTHEN.

p.420 - George EDWARDS, inv; 12 Apr 1783.

p.421 - Thomas SMITH, inv; 14 Apr 1783.

p.423 - Frances PRIDHAM, inv; 14 Apr 1783.

- Joseph DAVIS, inv; 14 Apr 1783.

p.424 - Cuthbert WEBB, inv. at the house of Mrs. Frances WEBB,
        19 Apr 1783.

- WEBB's inv; 10 May 1783.

- Priscilla WILLIAMS, will; 6 May 1783, 2 Jun 1783
        grsons. William OLDHAM the plant. whereon I now live
        containing 150 ac, and Samuel OLDHAM; fr. James HOWARD
        to have the above land until grson. comes to age 21;
        grchil. Sillah JENKINS, Pressy HENDREN, Mary GREENLOW,
        Nancy OLDHAM, Betty OLDHAM, Milly WELLDON, Caty OLDHAM,
        and Sally OLDHAM; ex: James HOWARD; wits: Charles
        MISKELL, Lewis HAMMOND, John BARRICK. [Priscilla
        WILLIAMS was the wid. of (1) William OLDHAM and (2)
        Henry WILLIAMS, whom she mar. in 1729/30. MRC, p.231.
        She and her first husband had one child, William
        (b.1728); by her second husband she had Sarah (b.1730),
        John (b.1733), and Isaac (b.1735). NFPR, p.200-201.]

p.425 - Edward MOZINGO, carpenter, Lun.Par., will; 30 Jan 1783,
        2 Jun 1783
        sons John, Absolom, Thomas, Richard, and William;
        wife Hannah; daus. Elizabeth and Hannah; ex: Presley
        NEALE, Joshua HINSON, and John MOZINGO; wits: Joshua
        HINSON, William DEAKINS.

p.426 - Jane FORD, inv; 18 Jun 1783.

p.427 - John BROWN Sr., Farn. Par., will; 10 Jan 1775, [nd.]
        sons William the land whereon he now lives, Rawleigh
        the land whereon he now lives, and Spencer; wife
        Catharine; dau. Sarah HAZARD; ex: sons John and
        Rawleigh; wits: J. ROBINSON, Thomas BLACKBERRY,
        William BROWN.

p.428 - Robert FORRESTER Sr., Farn. Par., will; 28 Oct 1780, 4
        Aug 1783
        wife Bridget; daus. Alice LEWIS, Fanny, and Bridget;
        grchil. Robert and Nancy FORRESTER; after wife's
        death, land to be eq. div. among four sons: Charles,
        James, Robert, and Griffin; ex: wife and sons James
        and Robert; wits: Vincent BROWN, Sarah BROWN, Charles
        NORWOOD.

- John WROE, Lun.Par., will; 14 Jun 1783, 4 Aug 1783
        sons-in-law Joshua RAMEY, James COATS; wife Sarah;
        daus. Anne RAMEY, Eleanor COATS; ex: wife; wits:
        John WRIGHT, Presley NEALE, Henry SISSON.

p.429 - Samuel BRYANT, will; 25 Nov 1782, [nd.]
        wife Winnie; desires that Eleanor MACKDANIEL have a
        year's schooling; Samuel BRYANT (son of Rawleigh
        BRYANT); ex: fr. Rawleigh BRYANT and Thomas COLEMAN;
        wits: James HOWARD, Charles MISKELL, Rawleigh DALE.

p.430 - John LAMBERT, inv; 7 Aug 1783.

    - Edward MOZINGO, inv; 8 Aug 1783.

p.431 - Ambrose JONES, will; 2 Nov 1776, 6 Oct 1783
        wife whole est. during her life; sons William, John,
        and Charles; ex: sons William and John; wits: John
        SYDNOR, Thomas HAYDON, James [NATT].

p.432 - Thomas BARTLETT, Lun.Par., will; 6 Dec 1767, 6 Oct 17[83]
        wife Catharine; son John all land and plant. whereon
        I now live after wife's death; sons James, Joseph,
        Thomas, and [Elisha]; daus. Anne JONES, Mary [SCOTT],
        Bathsheba FONES, and Sarah SCATES; ex: wife and son
        Charles; wits: John EIDSON, Daniel JACKSON, Morton
        WILSON, Christopher COLLINS.

p.433 - Catharine TALBERT, will; 3 Jun 1783, 6 Oct 1783
        Elizabeth WILKEY to have whole est; ex: Elizabeth
        WILKEY; wits: Spencer GILL, William WILKIE, George
        HEADLEY.

    - John BROWN, inv. at the home of Anne BROWN; 21 Oct 1783.

p.434 - William FORD, inv; 22 Oct 1783.

p.435 - Robert FORRESTER, inv; 14 Sep 1783.

p.436 - Mrs. Hannah CORBIN, inv. at Woodberry in Rich. Co; 15 Nov
        1783.

p.439 - Daniel DOBYNS, NFP, will; 15 Jan 1784, 3 May 1784
        son Daniel land and plant. when 21 also a brandy still
        which Mr. Thomas SYDNOR is to furnish on or before 10
        Jun next; s-i-l. Joseph DAVENPORT; ex: fr. Griffin
        FAUNTLEROY, bro. Abner DOBYNS, and s-i-l. Joseph
        DAVENPORT; wits: Daniel MISKELL, John DAVIS, Leroy
        DOBYNS, Richard PACKETT. [Daniel DOBYNS appears to
        have been mar. twice. By his first wife, Winifred,
        he had: Frances (b.1760), Charles (b.1761), and
        Winifred (b.1764); he mar. his second wife, Elizabeth
        SYDNOR, in 1765, and they had: Anna (b.1767), Betty
        (b.1769), and Daniel (b.1771); his dau. Frances mar.
        Joseph DAVENPORT in 1782. NFPR, pp.46-47; MRC, pp.
        49, 54.]

p.441 - John JENKINS, inv; ord. 6 Aug 1783.

    - George STONUM, inv; ord. 3 Nov 1783.

p.442 - Robert CLARK, NFP, will; 5 Jan 1784, 6 Apr 1784
        daus. Alice and Frances; ex: Thomas CLARK; wits:
        Daniel BROWN, George NORTHEN.

p.443 - Ambrose JONES, inv; 25 May 1784.

p.444 - William JONES, inv; 25 May 1784.

p.445 - Mrs. Priscilla WILLIAMS, inv; 25 May 1784.

p.446 - Job THRIFT, inv; 12 May 1784.

p.447 - George DAVIS, inv; 1784.

p.450 - Frances WEBB, will; [nd.], 6 Apr 1784
            Charles WEBB; son Isaac WEBB; daus. Winifred, Drucilla
            SINGLETON; grchil. George and Frances HARRISON;
            Deposition by Anne McCarty EDMONDSON, 12 Nov 1783...
            Mrs. Frances WEBB desired, in her last sickness, that
            an instrument of writing that John SMITH Gent., had
            which she had gave [sic] him some time ago was her
            will and that the same was still her desire;
            Deposition by Mrs. Lucy SMITH (wife of John SMITH Jr.,
            Gent., 11 Nov 1783 [substantially the same as above].
            [Frances WEBB was the wid. of Isaac WEBB who d. in
            1760. MRC, p. 226.]

p.451 - Obediah WARRICK, inv; 15 Sep 1784.

p.452 - Charles McCARTY, NFP, will; 11 Nov 1784, 4 Apr 1785
            sons Bartholomew, and Charles Travers to be continued
            with their two uncles in their present employment until
            21, and I trust that, as soon as their services are
            sufficient for their clothing and other maintenance,
            their uncles will give it to them, until that time,
            they are to be supported out of my est., and, as I,
            at this time, hold myself clear of debt, there need
            be no appraisement of my est; wife Winnie; daus.
            Fanny, Winnie, and Betty Anne; son Bartholomew choice
            of the land whereon I now live or that which I purchas-
            ed of William McCARTY; son Charles the other tract of
            land; whereas it has pleased God to afflict my sons
            Tarpley, Presley, and John so as to render them unable
            to provide for subsistence in this world, sons Bartho-
            lomew and Charles to care for them; ex: bro. Thaddeus
            McCARTY and fr. John SYDNOR; wits: John HAMMOND, John
            REYNOLDS, Charles HAMMOND, Thad. McCARTY. [Charles
            Barber McCARTY mar. Winifred TARPLEY ca. 1760. MRC,
            p. 123.]

p.454 - George HARRISON, NFP, will; 4 Sep 1784, 6 Dec 1784
            sisters Hannah and Alice; wife Betty Linton whole est;
            [mentions possible unborn child]; dau. Alice Griffin;
            Matthew HUMPHRIES (son of Betty); Benjamin Harrison
            MORGAN; Susannah LAWSON; Alice WROE; ex: wife, John
            SYDNOR, and Vincent JACKSON; wits: William GARLAND,
            Andrew MORGAN Jr., Abraham PROCTOR, William MIDDLETON.

p.456 - Thomas HAMMOND, will; 16 May 1779, 7 Mar 1785
            sons Aris, Thomas, Merryman, and William; daus. Elizabeth,
            Anne, Catharine, and Darcy; ex: son William; wits:
            William DOBYNS, Leroy DOBYNS, John FLYNN.

p.457 - Priscilla GIBSON, will; [?] 1779, 7 Mar 1785
            all est. to dau. Betty GIBSON alias SUGGITT; Frances
            Amis SAMFORD (dau. of James and Rebecca SAMFORD); chil.
            of Thomas HOWARD [unnamed]; ex: James SAMFORD, William
            FORRESTER, and Thomas SMITH Jr; wit: Benedict SHORT.

p.458 - John HART, will; 30 Dec 1784, 7 Mar 1785
            sons James, Reuben, William, and John; ex: sons John
            and William; wits: Joseph DOZIER, Gilbert BALDERSON.

p.459 - John HART, inv; 3 May 1785.

      - William GLASCOCK, NFP, will; 5 Feb 1784, 7 Mar 1785
            grdaus. Winnie ARMISTEAD, Milly SYDNOR and Elizabeth
            [the latter two daus. of Williamson BALL]; sons William,
            John, George, and Richard land and plant. whereon I

162

now live; grson. Thomas GLASCOCK; s-i-l. Rawleigh
DOWNMAN land and plant. that descended to me by the
death of my bro. John except that part which I lately
sold to my son John; daus. Priscilla HARVEY, Anne
ROBERTSON, Elizabeth DOWNMAN all my proportion of the
est. of the late Mrs. Elizabeth PINKARD; s-i-l. William
HARDING; chil. of dec'd dau. Milly HARDING; ex: son
John and fr. Charles McCARTY; wits: George YERBY,
Ben. SMITH, Thaddeus McCARTY, Milton Sims GLASCOCK.

p.462 - George NEWMAN, will; 29 Sep 1784, 6 Dec 1784
son George 400 ac. the plant. whereon I now live, if
he has no heirs, to be eq. div. among four daus. Patty,
Milly CREWDSON, Jenny, and Nancy; dau. Nancy 41 and
a half ac. the plant. whereon Edmund YARDLEY now lives;
Rebecca RYALS as much cash as will build her a house
12 feet square; ex: son George, Zachariah WHITE, James
KELLY, and bro. Thomas; wits: Morton WILSON, Thomas
SCULL.

p.464 - Daniel MUSE, Lun.Par., will; 28 Jan 1783, 6 Dec 1784
wife whole est; dau. Betty Muse MOXLEY and her daus.
Betty and Patty; Peggy MOXLEY; sons Thomas, Hudson
the home plant. after wife's death, and Daniel the
land whereon Edward MOZINGO lives after wife's death;
grson. Joseph Reynolds MUSE; dau. Peggy GRAY; ex:
sons Hudson and Daniel; wits: James KELLY, John McKAY,
Nathaniel MUSE, Daniel MOTHERSHEAD;
Cod., 20 Nov 1784; dau. Betty Muse SISSON's son James
MOXLEY to have a young grey horse; wits: Hudson MUSE,
Walker MUSE, Peggy GRAY, Daniel MOTHERSHEAD.

p.466 - William REYNOLDS, inv; ord. 6 Sep 1784.

p.467 - Harmon JINKINS, Lun.Par., will; 23 Dec 1784, 7 Mar 1785
son William Taylor; wife Hannah Anne; other chil.
[unnamed]; ex: James KELLY and Henry SISSON; wits:
William SAUNDERS Jr., [Aguth.] JINKINS.

p.468 - Elizabeth SUGGITT, NFP, will; [nd.], 6 Dec 1784
son Edgecomb; daus. Lucy LEWIS, Sarah JONES, and
Susannah COLE; John SLAUGHTER Sr; ex: son Edgecomb
and Richard APPLEBY; wits: James HILLYER, Henry BROOK.

p.469 - William RICHARDS, inv; taken 7 Mar 1785.

p.470 - Robert CLARK, inv; 13 Apr 1784, rec. 9 Jun 1785.

p.471 - John CRASK Sr., Lun.Par., will; 22 Apr 1784, 7 Mar and
5 Apr 1785
sons Vincent and Jesse; wife Sarah; ex: sons William
and Griffin; wits: Edward MARKS, Jesse CRASK, Daniel
WILSON.

p.472 - James ALDERSON, NFP, will; 2 Jun 1782, 2 May 1785
son James the plant. whereon I now live and tract of
land purchased of Mr. Stokely TOWLES called Reades;
chil. John and Elizabeth; mentions tract of land
purchased of Mr. Hudson MUSE and by him purchased of
Mr. William GRIFFIN and his bros. known to be mentioned
by the sd. GRIFFIN to be all the unleased lands sold
out of the est. of his bro., Thomas B. GRIFFIN, dec'd,
in NFP; son William tract of land at Farnham Church
bought of Mr. Hudson MUSE; son Jeremiah tract of
GRIFFIN's land purchased of Mr. Hudson MUSE and at

present known by George BARNES' lease; dau. Jane
NORTHEN plant. in Lun. Par., after her death, to go
to grson. James NORTHEN; daus. Sarah Anne STONE and
Anne Walker (under 18); wife Sarah Anne; ex: wife,
fr. Thomas YERBY, James ALDERSON, and Peter NORTHEN;
wits: Luke JACKSON, Travers DOWNMAN.

p.475 - William SMOOT, St. Stephen's Par., North. Co., will; 28
Aug 1782, 6 Dec 1784
land bought of William ELLET and Peter BESHAUGH to be
eq. div. between my two grchil. William Smoot BRYANT
and Betty BRYANT (chil. of Eleanor), the part whereon
the houses stand to Wm. S. BRYANT and that part over
the road next to Turner HANKS to Betty BRYANT; son
John plant. in North. Co; grdau. STOTT the plant.
purchased of William MASON; Lishey BRYANT to have the
use of 10 ac. in North. Co; Nancy Austin EVERITT;
Betty Brown VANLANDINGHAM my plant. in Rich. Co.
known as Luck Ordinary, if she has no heirs, to my
son John; daus. Nanny STOTT and Eleanor BRYANT; ex:
Thomas COELMAN, Thomas WALKER, and John ABBEY; wits:
John ABBEY, Thomas COELMAN, William BRYANT, John GILL.
Frances SMOOT, wid. of the sd. William SMOOT, renounc-
ed all benefit or advantage under the sd. will.

p.477 - Alexander BRYANT, NFP, will; 12 Nov 1784, 6 Jun 1785
wife Alice; daus. Nanny Alice, Mary, Caty Anne GUPTON;
son Alexander; grson. Stephen GUPTON; ex: wife and
son Alexander; wits: George BERRICK, Robert THORNTON,
Isabella BERRICK.

p.479 - William SMOOT, inv; 23 Jun 1785.

p.480 - Thomas HAMMOND, inv; 28 Jun 1785.

p.481 - Caty Anne GUPTON, will; 2 May 1785, 6 Jun 1785
daus. Nancy, Haney, and Elizabeth; ex: bro. Alexander
BRYANT; wits: Rebecca DOBYNS, George MISKELL.

p.482 - Robert CALLIS, will; [?] 1784, 2 May 1785
son Richard; wife Elizabeth; ex: Richard NEALE and
Thomas CALLIS; wits: Richard [FAVER], Francis CALLIS.
[Robert CALLIS mar. Elizabeth NEALE. MRC, p.32.]

p.483 - John MOORE, inv; ord. 6 Apr 1784, rec. 28 Jun 1785.

p.484 - William JONES, inv; 28 Jun 1785.

     - Maurice BRENT, inv; 1 Jul 1785. [Mentions Sinah BRENT's
part.]

p.486 - Henry HAZARD, NFP, will; 4 Jan 1780, 4 Jul 1785
wife Anne; sons Joseph, William, Henry, and John;
daus. Susannah, Betty, Mary, and Nancy; ex: John
HAZARD, William HAZARD, and Alexander [HINTON]; no
wits.

p.487 - Frances WEBB, inv; 8 Aug 1785.

p.488 - George DOWNMAN, inv; 9 Aug 1785.

p.489 - William GUPTON, inv; 9 Aug 1785.

p.490 - Mrs. Mary GARLAND, inv; taken 21 Oct 1774 and Jan 1775,
rec. 9 Aug 1785.

p.491 - Turner HANKS, inv; taken 25 Sep 1784, rec. 9 Aug 1785.

p.492 - Samuel TAFF, inv; 10 Aug 1785.

p.493 - James LUTTRELL, ord. 1 Oct 1731 [sic], rec. 10 Aug 1785.

p.494 - Herman JENKINS, inv; 10 Aug 1785.

p.495 - Gabriel SMITHER, NFP, will; 30 Dec 1784, 1 Aug 1785.
        sons Gabriel, Richard, and Lancelot; daus. Molly
        PRITCHETT and Betty; ex: Lancelot and Richard SMITHER;
        wits: Spencer HOWARD, Rawleigh BRYANT, Rodham PRITCHETT.

p.496 - John BROWN, inv; 11 Aug 1785.

p.497 - William HARRIS, inv; ord. 7 Nov 1769, rec. 11 Aug 1785.

p.500 - William GLASCOCK, inv; 11 Aug 1785.

p.502 - Abraham WILLIAMS, inv; ord. 1 Nov 1779, rec. 11 Aug 1785.

      - Moses BRYANT, inv; taken 7 Jan 1779, rec. 12 Aug 1785.

p.503 - Mary LYNE, Lun.Par., will; 21 Dec 1784, 7 Nov 1785
        dau. Jane ASBURY; est. of late dec'd husband, Thomas
        LYNE, to be eq. div. after my death if collected
        among all my chil. then living; son James; ex: son
        James and fr. Robert MITCHELL; wits: Thomas COLLINS,
        John WILSON.

p.505 - Gabriel SMITHER, inv; 19 Dec 1785.

p.506 - William HALL, inv; 10 Jan 1786.

p.507 - Thomas STONE Jr., NFP, will; 12 Feb 1784, 3 May 1784,
        8 Nov 1785, and 5 Dec 1785
            uncle Thomas STONE with whom I now live; ex: uncle
            Thomas STONE; wits: Thomas BRYANT, Anne WILLIAMS,
            Sarah STONE. [Pres. in court by Thomas STONE; the
            court noted that the testator was under 21; pres. on
            8 Nov 1785 by William DOBYNS, the guardian of Joshua
            STONE, the heir at law.]

p.508 - Alexander BRYANT, inv; 16 Jan 1786.

p.509 - Caty Anne GUPTON, inv; 10 Jan 1786.

p.510 - John PROSSER, inv; 16 Jan 1786.

p.511 - Robert LYNE, will; 27 Dec 1785, 6 Mar 1786
        son Thomas all plants. and lands; wife Anne; dau.
        Susannah; desires that 20 shillings a year be given
        for the maintenance and support of the ministers of
        the Gospel and the Church of God of the Baptist
        faith and order in Lun. Par; ex: wife, James KELLY,
        Christopher COLLINS, and Joseph WILSON; wits: Thomas
        STOWERS, Thomas ASBURY, James KELLY, William STOWERS.

p.513 - Thomas WHITE, will; 22 Sep 1780, 3 Apr 1786
        In case my two bros., William and Samuel, who are now
        engaged and enlisted in the war, should die and not
        survive me or should die without lawful heirs, I give
        and bequeath unto my beloved sister, Mary Anne, all
        right, title, and interest in my land in Lanc. Co;
        uncle Zachariah WHITE; ex: uncle Zachariah WHITE;

wits: Seleashea WHITE, Jesse WHITE, Mary WHITE.

p.514 - William WHITE, will; 7 Oct 1782, 3 Apr 1786
        bro. Presley WHITE all interest to land in Lanc. Co;
        three sisters Mary Anne GREEN, Sally, and Franky;
        ex: uncle Zachariah WHITE; wits: Jesse WHITE, William
        WHITE.

      - Luke WILLIAMS, will; 19 Feb 1786, 3 Apr 1786
        son William land on which I live; son Thomas; other
        chil. Butler, Roger, Anne, Lucy, Harris, Joannah,
        Sarah, Mildred DOWLIN, and Barbara; ex: fr. John
        HARFORD, George MISKELL, Thaddeus WILLIAMS; wits:
        John WILLIAMS, Susannah DAVIS, Job STUCKEY.

p.515 - Stewart REDMAN, NFP, will; 9 Jan 1786, 6 Mar 1786
        Sarah HODGES the plant. whereon I live; son Stewart
        all land in West. Co. and this plant. after the death
        of Sarah HODGES; daus. Grace, Winifred, Mary Stewart,
        and Jemimah; grson. John HARDWICK; ex: Vincent JACKSON;
        wits: George HABRON, James LAMBERT, Thomas SELF.
        [The probate material mentions Jemimah REDMAN as the
        wid. of Stewart.]

p.517 - Fortunatus DAVENPORT, inv; ord. May 1785, unadministered
        by Elizabeth, his wid., 9 May 1786.

p.518 - Robert CALLESS, inv; 9 May 1786.

p.520 - Janett McGINN, inv; ord. 6 Jun 1785, rec. 10 May 1786.

      - Stewart REDMAN, inv; ord. 6 Mar 1786.

p.522 - Betty SMITH, inv.; ord. 2 May 1785; appraised at the home
        of Mr. Thomas SMITH, 25 Nov 1785.

      - Christopher COLLINS, inv; taken 24 Nov 1781; mentions
        legacies of 150 ac. on Stony Run to Christopher
        COLLINS and 75 ac. at the Mansion House to Thomas
        COLLINS; other legatees: Angelica COLLINS, Margaret
        RICHARDSON, John WILSON, Christopher WILSON, and
        Elizabeth WILSON; rec. 7 Oct 1786.

p.525 - Sally DAVIS, will; 22 Apr 1783, 7 Jul 1783
        bros. John and George; uncle Kester TUNE; Caty Hale
        TUNE; Sally DAVIS; ex: James COX and John COLE; wits:
        James COX, John COLE, Caty DOBYNS. [Kester TUNE was
        the bro. of Sally DAVIS' mother, Elizabeth (TUNE)
        DAVIS who mar. George DAVIS. NFPR, pp. 42, 189.]

      - Samuel STOWERS, will; 24 Mar 1785, 2 Oct 1786
        wife Anne; son Thomas the plant. I purchased of Mr.
        Thomas COLLINS, if he has no heirs, land to be div.
        amongst my chil; sons William, Coleman, Richard, and
        Henry; daus. Frances and Lettess; bro. Nicholas;
        Thomas ASBURY Sr; ex: wife, sons Thomas and William;
        wits: Zach. WHITE, Henry ASBURY, William BRAGG.

p.527 - Robert HAMMACK, NFP, will; 1 Oct 1785, 2 Oct 1786
        wife Anne all land whereon I now live; son Benedict
        all land at wife's death; son Lewis; daus. Rayne
        SAMFORD, Nancy JESPER, and Christian JONES; grson.
        William SAMFORD; grdau. Elizabeth JESPER; Lewis
        HAMMACK; Robert HAMMACK; plant. where Daniel CRALLE
        lives to dau. Mary CRALLE as long as she lives; ex:

Daniel BROWN, Benedict HAMMACK, and Thomas JESPER;
wits: William HAMMACK, Thomas BROWN, Ben. HAMMACK.

p.528 - William SMITH Gent; NFP, will; 20 Jan 1786, 2 Oct 1786
In nomine Dei, Patris, Filii, et Spiritus Sancti,
Amen. Wife the lands whereon I now live purchased
from Charles BARBER and the lands purchased from the
ex. of the late Samuel PEACHEY together with the land
purchased from William SAMFORD; son William Colston
lands after wife's decease, all lands on east and
southeast side of the Folly and Totuskey Lower Warehouse Road; other chil. Betty [BRERETON], Sarah,
Catharine [GWYNN], Thomas Plummer; grson. John S.
GARLAND; son John to receive 50 pounds to spend or
game away, I give it to him for that purpose, expect-
ing no better from him; ex: bro. Benjamin SMITH, fr.
Griffin FAUNTLEROY, and son William; wits: Samuel
KELSICK, Thomas LIGHTFOOT, John SAMFORD;
[A cod. grants additional lands to son Thomas P.]

p.530 - Robert LYNE, inv; 5 Dec 1786.

p.531 - Luke WILLIAMS, inv; 1 Jun 1786.

p.532 - Priscilla GIBSON, inv; ord. 7 Mar 1785.

p.533 - John BOWDOIN, Moratico Hall, will; [?] 1786, 3 Jul 1786
desires to be buried in the yard of the Lower Church
of Lun.Par; dau. [not named], if she die without issue,
est. to be div. into eq. parts two of which to go to
sis. [not named] and one part to go to brothers and
other sisters [not named]; man Robin, my now body-
servant, to be emancipated providing it can be done
without obliging him to leave the state and he is to
be furnished with a good suit of mourning and to keep
all his clothes and other little property which he
now possesses, this I do in reward of his faithful
services; no ex; no wits;
On Wednesday, 29 Mar 1786, Mr. John BOWDOIN desired
that Mr. Thomas Griffin PEACHEY, his lady, with some
other person and myself would take notice that he
wished to make his will as he was extremely low spirit-
ed; we endeavored to take his mind off it, observing
that we hoped, as we really did, that he would be
calmer by the morning; when, as he requested me, I
would commit to writing what he had informed us on
the evening of the same day; he asked me if I had done
it; I again waived it; the business was not mentioned
to me through the next Thursday, till after Dr. JONES
came in the evening; when applying to the Doctor and
his assenting, I retired and wrote the contents of this
paper with intention to read it to Mr. BOWDOIN, have
the blanks filled up and such alterations or amendments
made thereto, as he should direct, however, the doctor
I suppose, never thought him in a proper state of mind
to execute a will and it rested as I left it on Thursday evening; he died on Monday morning, 3 Apr 1786.
Pres. in court by the Rev. Samuel McCROSKEY and Peter
BOWDOIN Gent.

p.534 - Thomas HOGAN, will; 7 May 1785, 4 Sep 1786
whole est to wife; after her death, to be eq. div.
between all my chil. and the chil. she had by me
before wedlock, Travers and Marah ERLS alias HOGANS
[sic]; son Thomas; ex: sons Thomas, Travers ERLS, and

wife; wits: Thomas DOBYNS, Christopher DEATLEY,
William DEATLEY.

p.535 - Samuel WOOLLARD, NFP, will; [?] 1786, 1 Jan 1787
wife Mary Anne; son John land I bought of Charles
HAMMOND, John SAUNDERS, and Alexander George FEAGINS;
son Samuel land I bought of my bro. John whereon
William ENGLISH now lives also my father's purchase
of William HAMMOND and the tract I bought of Jesse
MORRIS; son William Jesper land I bought of Richard
BARNES, Charles TAYLOR, and Col. John SMITH; daus.
Elizabeth SMITH, Anne, Eleanor, Mary Anne, Hannah,
and Sarah; dau. Anne to receive a negro girl, Sarah,
of that family which have brought suit for their
freedom; ex: wife, sons John and Samuel, and fr. Leroy
PEACHEY, Thomas SMITH, and Thaddeus WILLIAMS; wits:
Jonathan WILLIAMS, Obediah WILLIAMS, Thomas HINDS,
William ENGLISH.

p.538 - Sarah S. WILLIAMS, NFP, will; 1 Apr 1786, 2 Apr 1787
mother Betty A.; sisters Winifred DOBYNS and Betsy
A. WILLIAMS; bros. Thaddeus, David all right and claim
in the sale of the Halifax land; nephew Samuel WILLIAMS;
ex: bro. David; wits: Abner DOBYNS, Hannah DALE, Mary
DOBYNS, Dominick BENNEHAN.

p.539 - [page partially mutilated]

- William KIRKUM, Lun.Par., will; 11 Oct 1786, 2 [Apr] 1787
grdau. [Franky] McCAVE; dau. Caty BURGESS; sons.
Thomas and [James]; desires that neither s-i-l., John
[CREWDSON] nor John HOWELL, nor any of their chil.
should have any part of est; ex: George Lee TURBER-
VILLE; wits: Nancy Wright DAVIS, Betty Taylor
TURBERVILLE, Solomon NASH, George Lee TURBERVILLE.

WILL BOOK 8, 1787-1794

p. 1 - Thomas LYNE, inv; ord. 7 Nov 1785.

p. 2 - David JONES, NFP, will; 15 Oct 1786, 2 Apr 1787
wife Caty the land I bought of John Lewis TILLERY;
sons Abner and Spencer; dau. Mary Anne; ex: wife and
son Abner; wits: Luke JACKSON, Jonathan TEAGUE,
Susannah TEAGUE; N.B. The heir-at-law was William
JONES. [David JONES mar. Caty BAKER in 1781. MRC, p.107]

p. 3 - Thomas STONE, inv; taken 26 Nov 1785.

p. 4 - James ALDERSON, inv; taken 10 Jun 1785.

p. 7 - Samuel STOWERS, inv; ord. Oct. 1786, rec. 2 Apr 1787.

p. 9 - Robert HAMMACK, inv; 2 Apr 1787.

p. 11 - Thomas HOGAN, inv; [nd.]

p. 12 - George HARRISON, inv; ord. 6 Dec 1784.

p. 14 - John GOLDSBY, inv; rec. 8 Nov 1786.

p. 15 - William SMITH, inv; 5 Mar 1787.

p. 17 - William ELMORE, inv; ord. 17 Oct 178[6].

p. 18 - Joseph PALMER, inv; 12 Jul 1787. [Mentions Rawleigh and
William PALMER.]

p. 20 - Nathaniel NASH, Lun.Par., will; 8 Jun 1775, 4 Jun 1787
daus. Sarah [DUFF], Elizabeth DRAKE, Mary, Anne,
and Susannah; sons George, Winder, and James; grson.
Newman NASH; wife Sedwill; ex: wife and son James;
wits: William WILSON, John WRIGHT, John HART.

p. 21 - William BRUCE, Lun.Par., will; 12 Nov 1783, 4 Feb 1788
wife Betty; if sd. wife should extravagantly waste
or embezzle my sd. est., then ex. to confine her to
her dower as the law directs; son Andrew all land
after wife's death; son William; nephew James CRASK;
ex: trusty and well-beloved fr. and nephew James
CRASK; wits: John MARKS, Daniel WILSON, Andrew BRUCE,
William BRUCE.

p. 23 - John EFFORD, inv; 17 Nov 1787.

     - John LYELL, will; 14 Nov 1787, 8 Apr 1788
wife Sarah land and plant. where I now dwell, after
her death, to son John; youngest son Robert; ex: wife,
son John, and neighbor Vincent REDMAN; wits: Thomas
FRANKLIN, Mason SANDY, Joseph LYELL.

p. 25 - William BRUCE, inv; 9 Feb 1788.

p. 26 - Mrs. Hannah CORBIN, inv. at her quarter in West. Co.,
taken 21 Oct 1782 and 13 Jan 1783; George TURBERVILLE
Sr. was the adm.

p. 28 - Jeremiah SELF, inv; ord. Feb 1788.

p. 29 - Vincent BROWN, inv; 7 Jul 1788.

p. 30 - John LYELL, inv; [nd.]

p. 31 - Nathaniel NASH, inv; brought to court 5 May 1788.

p. 33 - George NEWMAN, inv; ord. 6 Dec 1784.

p. 35 - David JONES, inv; 1 Dec 1788.

p. 36 - Thomas DOBYNS, NFP, will; 8 Feb 1788, 1 Dec 1788
son Lawson land and plant. in the fork of Totuskey;
daus. Nancy OLDHAM, Milly, and Barbary; ex: friends
Col. William PEACHEY, Thaddeus WILLIAMS, and William
OLDHAM; wits: Henry DOBYNS, Frances THORNTON, George
DAVIS, Daniel DOBYNS. [Thomas DOBYNS was the third
husband of Rebecca Sisson LAWSON who had mar. (1)
Thomas THORNTON in 1769 and (2) Thomas HAMMOND.
Thomas DOBYNS mar. her in 1781. MRC., p.55. Thomas
DOBYNS was previously mar. to Rachel (?); they had
the fol. chil: Newman (b.1759), Thomas (b.1761),
Barbara (b.1767), William Henry (b.1776); Thomas and
Rebecca had at least one child, Lawson, b. in 1782.
NFPR, pp.46-47.]

p. 37 - Elizabeth WOOLLARD, NFP, will; [?] Feb 1788, 1 Dec 1788
daus. Caty, Winifred DAVIS; sons Richard, John, and
Joseph; grdau. Betty WOOLLARD; ex: fr. Thomas SMITH;
wits: William EVERITT, Elijah HANKS, Lucy WARNER.

p. 38 - Maurice BRENT, inv; taken 15 Jul 1785, pres. 26 Sep 1786.

p. 39 - Thomas DOBYNS, inv; ord. [?] Dec 1788.

p. 40 - Daniel LAWSON, Lun.Par., will; 5 Oct 1787, 2 Feb 1789
        sons Thomas, William, and Richard each 100 ac. in
        Gloucester Co.; dau. Rebecca Sisson DOBYNS a bond of
        John HOW's due me from the sd. HOW; Thomas DOBYNS
        (husband of Rebecca Sisson DOBYNS); dau. Bathsheba
        ALLISON; son Daniel all lands in Richmond Co; ex:
        son Daniel; wits: Walker TOMLIN, Daniel FITCHETT,
        Elizabeth TOMLIN, Lucy BARNES, Rebecca B. KELSICK.

p. 41 - Col. William BROCKENBROUGH, inv; 16 Jul 1788.

p. 45 - Dr. BROCKENBROUGH's negroes left at old house.

      - Newman BROCKENBROUGH's negroes left at old house.

p. 46 - [BROCKENBROUGH's inv.] at the Mill Plantation, at the
        Old House, and at the Mulberry Island Plantation.

p. 48 - The above stocks and plant. on Mulberry Island belonged
        to the est. of Col. William BROCKENBROUGH and Richard
        BARNES jointly; ord. 6 Jul 1778.

      - Anthony SYDNOR, NFP, will; 7 Oct 1781, 1 Jun 1789
        chil. James Downman, Isaac, Nancy, and unborn child;
        land in Amelia Co. to be eq. div. between two sons;
        ex: wife, John SYDNOR, Abner DOBYNS, and wife's bro.
        Rawleigh DOWNMAN; wits: Newman MISKELL, Thomas DOBYNS,
        John MISKELL. [Anthony SYDNOR mar. Elizabeth DOWNMAN
        who was probably the dau. of Robert and Elizabeth
        DOWNMAN; she was b. in 1752. NFPR, pp. 52, 180.]

p. 50 - James HILLYER, inv; 1 Jun 1789.

p. 51 - Robert SINGLETON, inv; ord. 6 Apr 1784.

p. 52 - Elizabeth SUGGITT, inv; presented 4 Nov 1788.

p. 53 - John SUGGITT, inv; ord. [?] Dec 1788.

p. 54 - Richard FRARY, will; 4 Nov 1788, 4 May 1789
        bro. James; ex: bro. and fr. Nathaniel MOTHERSHEAD;
        wits: John THOMPSON Sr., John THOMPSON Jr., William
        YATES.

p. 55 - Thomas BROWN Sr., Lun.Par., will; 11 Dec 1788, 7 Sep 1789
        son Daniel BROWN; dau. Sarah BROWN; grson. William
        COATS (son of Elizabeth COATS); wife Sarah; ex: wife;
        wits: N. MOTHERSHEAD, William YATES, Betty Burris
        MITCHELL.

p. 56 - John CARPENTER, Lun.Par., will; 4 Oct 1788, 7 Sep 1789
        nephew John CARPENTER of West. Co; ex: sis. Mary
        CARTER and Nathaniel MOTHERSHEAD; wits: Sarah CARTER,
        [Arm.] PLAYLE, William YATES.

      - William FAUNTLEROY, inv; pres. 22 Jul 1789.

p. 57 - Newman MISKELL, NFP, will; 19 Jul 1789, 7 Sep 1789
        sis. Milly MISKELL; cousin George MISKELL; ex: friends
        John SYDNOR, George MISKELL, and Epaphroditus SYDNOR;
        wits: Caster TUNE, John THORNTON.

p. 58 - Alexander HUNTON, NFP, will; 28 Apr 1789, 5 Oct 1789
            sons Robert, William, John, George, Thomas, and
            Alexander; daus. Mary, Betty, Susannah, Sally, Nancy,
            Caty, and Lucy; son Thomas my plant. whereon I now
            live as far as the road which runs through near the
            middle of my land; son Alexander the rest of my land
            from the dividing road to Moratico Branch; if dau.
            Molly should continue to be divested of her reason,
            son Thomas shall keep her and have the use of her
            est. so long as she continues in that situation;
            land in Albemarle Co. to be sold; ex: wife, sons
            Robert, Thomas, and Alexander, and fr. Thomas WILLIAMS;
            wits: Thomas WILLIAMS, James ALDERSON, Bryant PHILLIPS.

p. 60 - Benjamin NEWSON, NFP, will; 6 Oct 1789, 7 Dec 1789
            son William the tract of land I now live on; grson.
            Samuel NEWSOM; dau. Sally; son Samuel to receive chest
            of joiner's tools; William NEWSOM to build a log house
            12 feet square for his sis. Sally as long as she liveth
            single; ex: son William and George BERRICK; wits:
            George BERRICK, Thomas JESPER, Elizabeth BEARCROFT.

p. 61 - Dewanna SYDNOR, NFP, will; 22 Oct 1789, 7 Dec 1789
            nieces Dewanna SMITHER, Nancy DOWNMAN, Molly DOBYNS,
            and Winnie SYDNOR; sis. Anne MITCHELL; nephews James
            SYDNOR, John SYDNOR, Giles SYDNOR, and Travers
            DOWNMAN; ex: John and Giles SYDNOR; wits: John DAVIS,
            Anne DOWNMAN, Dewanna SMITHER. [Dewanna SYDNOR was the
            dau. of Anthony and Elizabeth (DEW) SYDNOR; she was
            b. in 1719. MRC, pp. 200-201.]

p. 62 - William GARLAND, will; 23 Nov 1788, 7 Dec 1789
            sons Griffin, William all the lands in the fork of
            Totuskey, and Valentine; daus. Mary and Anne; wife
            Anne; ex: wife and son William; wits: John ROCHESTER,
            Daniel MORGAN, John ROCHESTER Jr.

p. 63 - John THRIFT, will; 10 Sep 1789, 7 Dec 1789
            son Nathaniel 50 ac. adjoining the house he now lives
            in which I gave to him; son John rest of land; sons
            Merryman and Samuel; dau. Amandine; if dau. Amandine
            should intermarry with William POOLEY or live with
            him, it is then my will and desire that she should
            have no part of my est; ex: son John; wits: John
            SYDNOR, Giles SYDNOR, John THORNTON. [John THRIFT's
            wife was Massie (?). NFPR, p.186. There are two
            records of marriage bonds for William POOLEY: (1)
            to Elizabeth HAMMOND, 13 Sep 1787 and (2) to Annaniah
            THRIFT, 21 Sep 1789. MRC, p. 160. It is possible
            that Annaniah and Amandine were the same person.]

        - Benjamin NEWSOM, inv; 1 Feb [1790].

p. 65 - Jane BULGER, Lun.Par., will; 16 May 1785, 1 Feb 1790
            son John BULGER land I now live on which I possess
            in my own right; Thomas James (son of son John); eld.
            son Edmund BULGER; no ex; wits: George Lee TURBERVILLE,
            Mary BULGER, Gracy BULGER, Solomon NASH. [Jane BULGER
            was the wid. of John WRIGHT who d. in 1736; she mar.
            (2) Edmund BULGER by 2 Aug 1748. MRC, p.30.]

p. 66 - John MISKELL, inv; ord. [?] Jun 1789.

        - John COLE, NFP, will; 19 Aug 1789, 5 Apr 1790
            wife Susannah; ex: wife and friends John [SADLER]

and Thomas WILLIAMS; wits: Christopher CHINALT, Letty
PILLION, Rob. WARNER.

p. 67 - William ALDERSON, Lun.Par., will; 5 Dec 1787, 7 Jun 1790
wife Mary; chil. John, William, Jerry, and Rachel;
George TERRY; James HOW; ex: wife, and John and
William ALDERSON; wits: Vincent GARLAND, William
MOORE.

p. 68 - Alexander HUNTON, inv; 20 May 1790.

p. 71 - BECKWITH's inv; returned Jul 1790.

p. 74 - Edward DOBYNS, NFP, will; 12 Oct 1788, 5 Oct 1789
wife; chil. Winnie, Frederick, Edward, and Tabitha;
ex: wife; bro. Abner and fr. Charles BARNES to assist
wife; wits: Thaddeus FORRESTER, Robert NEASOM, William
ALDERSON. [Edward DOBYNS mar. Amony FORRESTER (wid.)
in 1769. MRC, p. 54.]

p. 76 - William ALDERSON, inv; 2 Aug 1790.

p. 77 - John THRIFT, inv; 6 Sep 1790.

p. 78 - George NASH, will; 23 Nov 1789, 4 Oct 1790
wife Lucy; chil. Richard, Winnifred, Hannah, and
Sally; ex: wife and bro. John NASH; wits: Thomas
WILLIAMS, Rawleigh NEWGENT, Fortunatus TILLERY.

p. 79 - John PULLEN, will; 12 May 1790, 4 Oct 1790
plant. to son Jeduthan; sons Moses and Jonathan; daus.
Sarah and Elliner; sons Thomas and William; ex: sons
Jeduthan and Jonathan; wits: Thomas WILLIAMS, Joseph
REDMAN, Joseph [GARARD] Jr.

p. 80 - William STONUM, NFP, will; 7 Sep 1789, 3 Jan 1791
grson. George Norise STONUM 100 ac. of land that I
bought of George WALLACE when 21, if he has no heirs,
then to son William STONUM; grson. William FORRESTER
my Common Prayer Book that was his father's; grdau.
Nancy DAVENPORT and her son William Hale; Nancy
CAMPBELL the woman's saddle her mother had; son
George STONUM's three chil. or the survivors of them;
Betty CAMPBELL's three chil. or the survivors of them;
ex: son William; wits: John POPE, George SCURLOCK.
[William and Susanna STONUM had the fol. chil: Sarah
(b. 1737), George (b. 1740), Anne (b. 1744), William
(b. 1752), and Fortunatus (b. 1755). NFPR, p.177.]

p. 81 - William MISKELL, inv; 1 May 1790.

p. 86 - Moore FAUNTLEROY, Lun.Par., will; 20 Jul 1790, 7 Feb 1791
dau. Ellen SYDNOR land I bought of Lindsey OPIE in
Lanc. Co. adjoining the land that I got by her mother
containing 84 acres; right to a 125 ac. tract of land
to Mr. DAVENPORT (son of William DAVENPORT); if any
land in Lanc. Co. that I had by my first wife should
be recovered by any suit...; wid. of son George Hale
FAUNTLEROY; dau. Susannah TOMLIN lands I bought of
William DAVENPORT adjoining the land she now lives
on; dau. Catharine MARSHALL; son Samuel Griffin
FAUNTLEROY tract of land I bought of Col. Robert W.
CARTER called Ring's Neck; son William tract of land
where I now live and all the lands I have purchased
in the upper part of the county, tract of land called

Quintanoak in Farnham Par. and the land I bought of
John FULKS; grdau. Catharine SYDNOR; grdau. Catharine
TOMLIN; Mary NASH (dau. of Nathaniel NASH) to receive
a tenement of land where James NASH now lives; Sarah
NASH (dau. of Mary NASH); mentions dec'd dau. Apphia
FAUNTLEROY and dec'd bro. Henry; ex: sons-in-law
Robert TOMLIN and William SYDNOR and sons Samuel and
William; wits: William FAUNTLEROY Jr, William KENDALL.
[Col. Moore FAUNTLEROY (b.1716) mar. (1) Anne HEALE
of Lanc. Co. in 1736 and (2) Elizabeth MITCHELL by
1748. MRC, p. 68.]

p. 89 - William Forrester DOBYNS, NFP, will; 1 Dec 1790, 7 Feb 1791
wife Betty Hale DOBYNS; son Samuel (under 18) land
and plant. after wife's death; dau. Betty P.; ex:
wife, Joseph and George DAVENPORT; wits: John BAKER,
Thomas TUNE. [William F. DOBYNS, the son of Samuel
and Winnie DOBYNS, was b. 17 May 1760; he mar. Betty
Hale DAVENPORT in 1782. MRC, p. 56: NFPR, p. 46.]

p. 90 - Richard PACKET, Lun.Par., will; 18 Nov 1790, 2 Feb 1791
d-i-l. Jane Willdy EDWARDS, agreeable to my wife's
desire, all her wearing apparel and one sealskin
trunk provided that she, my dearly beloved wife Sarah,
should not survive her present complaint; little
children [unnamed]; ex: fr. William YATES; wits:
Isabel [CREWDSON], Franky PACKET, Winifred [HANEY].
[Richard PACKET mar. Sarah EDWARDS in 1788. MRC, p.153.]

p. 91 - Edward WRIGHT, inv; ord. Apr 1788.

p. 92 - Mrs. Sarah WROE, inv; ord. 5 Jul 1790.

p. 93 - William DOWNMAN, will; 24 Oct 1790, 4 Apr 1791
cousin Dennis McCARTY; grdau. Elizabeth Ball DOWNMAN;
ex: Dennis McCARTY and John SYDNOR Sr; wits: Leroy
OLDHAM, John WROE, Thomas WEYMOUTH.

p. 94 - John MARKS Sr., Lun.Par., will; 23 Mar 1786, 4 Apr 1791
son James land where I now live; wife Hannah; daus.
Betty BRUCE, Frances BRAGG, Penelope CARTER, Mary
WILSON, Hannah BRUCE, Sarah CRASK. and Susannah CRASK;
sons William, John, and Elias; grdau. Jane NEWMAN
(dau. of Anne NEWMAN); grson. William MARKS; I give
and bequeath unto my grson. William MARKS one negro
boy named Will to be his property in lieu of my son
Fennell MARKS' part of my est. to be his property as
beforesaid; ex: son Elias and s-i-l. Daniel WILSON;
wits: Shelton WILSON, Griffin CRASK, James CRASK.

p. 96 - James BRANNAN, will; 3 Dec 1790, 4 Apr 1791
bro. Spencer the plant; sis. Barbary; ex: bro. Spencer
and fr. Thomas WILLIAMS; wits: Jerry NASH, Richard
NASH, Thomas WILLIAMS.

p. 97 - George NASH, inv; 4 Apr 1791.

p. 98 - Alice WEMS, late of the State of Maryland, inv. taken 6
Jan 1790.

p.100 - Philip Thomas LEE, late of the State of Maryland, inv.
taken Jan 1790.

p.101 - Edward DOBYNS, inv; 15 Feb 1791.

p.102 - William F. DOBYNS, inv; 15 Feb 1791.

p.104 - Dewanna SYDNOR, inv; 27 Apr 1791.

p.105 - Mary REDMAN, inv; ord. Jan 1791.

p.107 - Hannah CORRIE, will; 3 Apr 1790, 4 Jul 1791.
        son Peter RUST to pay out of my est. to my grdaus.
        Ailcey LEE and Lettis Lee RUST one half of the value
        of the Totuskey land settled on me by a deed of gift
        which land I joined in the sale of to one EDWARDS and
        is now in the possession of Mr. Robert TOMLIN; son
        Peter RUST to have riverside plant. known by the name
        of Islington containing by estimation 750 ac; ex: son
        Peter; wits: John WEATHERS, Rebecca B. WEATHERS.
        [Hannah RUST mar. her cousin Samuel RUST in 1755, and
        after his death, she mar. John CORRIE of Essex Co. in
        1769. MRC, p.175.]

p.108 - Rodham PRITCHET, will; 15 Nov 1790, 4 Jul 1791
        dau. Nancy SMITHER; grdaus. Peggy Fleming SMITHER,
        Nancy Garner PRITCHET; grsons. Samuel SMITHER, Gabriel
        Smither PRITCHET; wife Judith; all lands to be eq. div.
        after wife's death between sons Rodham and John; son
        Samuel Conoway; daus. Susannah and Polly; ex: friends
        Capt. Thomas WILLIAMS, Thaddeus WILLIAMS, and Thomas
        COLEMAN; wits: Christopher JACKSON, Samuel A. SELF,
        Benjamin HALE. [The births of Alesey Conway (1781)
        and Samuel Conway (1790) to Rodham PRITCHET are rec.
        in the NFPR, p.151.]

p.109 - Thomas SMITH, inv; Jun 1791. [Included a list of slaves
        entitled "Negroes that's contending for their freedom."]

p.112 - Alexander DALE, inv; ord. Feb 1791.

p.113 - John PULLEN, inv; 5 Sep 1791.

p.116 - Moore FAUNTLEROY, inv; ord. 7 Feb 1791.

p.124 - Inv. of the personal est. of John BOWDEN Jr. dec'd in
        Northampton Co.; 10 Jul 1786. [This was John BOWDOIN
        Jr., the son of John BOWDOIN (d.1755) of Northampton
        Co. MRC, p.21.]

p.126 - Mr. John BOWDOIN Jr., inv. at Moratico Hall; appraised
        Sep 1786, pres. in court 7 Apr 1788, rec. [3] Oct 1791.

p.127 - Joseph DALE, NFP, will; 11 Mar 1791, 6 Jun 1791
        wife Elizabeth; daus. Elizabeth, Nancy, Winifred, and
        Polly; youngest son Joseph (under 15); wife and other
        chil. Archelaus and Sally Williams; ex: wife and fr.
        Thomas DAVIS; wits: John FAUNTLEROY, Abner DOBYNS,
        Edward BARNES. [The births of Elizabeth (1772),
        Archelus (1774), and Polly (1781) to Joseph and Million
        DALE are rec. in the NFPR, p.39.]

p.129 - William WILLIAMS, NFP, will; 27 Sep 1791, 7 Nov 1791
        friends George MISKELL and Thaddeus WILLIAMS; sisters
        Nanny WILLIAMS and Barbary NEASOME; niece Betsy [HARIES];
        ex: George MISKELL and Thaddeus WILLIAMS; wits: Richard
        DOZIER, Mary DOZIER, Sarah P. DOZIER.

p.130 - John THORNTON Sr., will; 1 Dec 1790, 5 Sep 1791
        son John; sis. Betty THORNTON; sister's dau. Anne

REYNOLDS; ex: son John; wits: John WEYMOUTH, Nath. THRIFT.

- Moore FAUNTLEROY, f.inv. at Quintanoak; 2 Jan 1792.

p.131 - Richard PACKETT, inv. taken in West. Co. 25 Apr 1791, rec. 2 Jan 1792.

- William B. JONES, inv; 2 Jan 1792.

p.132 - William DOWNMAN, inv; 2 Jan 1792.

p.134 - William STONUM, inv; 2 Jan 1792.

p.136 - Moore BRAGG, Lun.Par., will; 20 Aug 1788, 2 Jan 1792
          wife; sons William, James, Matthew the acre of land
          I bought of Capt. George RANDALL; daus. Rebecca and
          Anne; grson. William BRAGG; after wife's death, est.
          to be sold and money eq. div. between five chil; ex:
          wife and William BRAGG; wits: John [HOLT], James
          KELLY Jr., Richard [S.] McGINNIS.

p.137 - Vincent JACKSON, will; 11 Dec 1791, 6 Feb 1792
          son William my lands and plant. and all the rest of
          my est. I desire may be eq. div. between John, Vincent,
          Tom, and Betty being the four chil. of Elizabeth
          ALLGOOD; ex: Elizabeth ALLGOOD; wits: John MUSE,
          George HABRON. [The births of Vincent Jackson (1781),
          Betsy Jackson (1788), and Tomme Jackson (1790) to
          Elizabeth ALLGOOD are rec. in the NFPR, p.3.]

p.138 - Sarah CRASK, Lun.Par., will; 1 Dec 1791, 2 Apr 1792
          sons Jesse, Vincent, and James; ex: sons Vincent and
          Jesse; wits: William YATES, Nath. [STROTHER], Peggy
          CRASK. [Sarah (WILSON) was the wid. of Vincent CRASK
          whom she mar. in 1785. MRC, p.46.]

p.139 - James BRANNAN, inv; Apr 1792.

p.140 - Hannah CORRIE, inv; Mar 1792.

p.141 - Elizabeth FLOOD, being aged and infirm, will; 18 Aug 1789,
          7 Nov 1792
          fr. Mrs. Winifred COCK (wife of Mr. John COCK) of
          North. Co; fr. Mrs. William ARMISTED; ex: bro. Leroy
          PEACHEY and kinsman Bartholomew McCARTY; wits: James
          DODSON, William ALDERSON, Elizabeth ALDERSON.

p.142 - John COLE, inv; Jan 1793.

p.144 - Moore BRAGG, inv; Jan 1793.

p.145 - Frances P. DOWNMAN, will; 3 Aug 1792, 7 Jan 1793
          sisters Elizabeth SMITH, Moriah SMITH, and Susannah
          SMITH; goddau. Frances [M. LEVY]; bros. John, William,
          Colston, Sydnor, and Benjamin SMITH; ex: friends
          Bartholomew McCA[RTY], Ezekial LEVY, and James SYDNOR;
          wits: Eppa SYDNOR, Fanny BAILEY.

p.146 - William WILLIAMS, inv; taken 10 Nov 1791, rec. Jan 1793.

p.148 - Thomas JESPER Jr., NFP, will; 17 Dec 1792, 7 Jan 1793
          land to be div. between two sons John Taylor and
          Samuel Bisco; daus. Fanny Greenwell and Molly; wife
          Johanner; ex: bro. Richard JESPER and George NORTHEN;

wits: Alex. BRYAN, John BARRICK, William NEWSUM

p.149 - John MARKS, inv; Apr 1793.

p.150 - Thomas JESPER, inv; Apr 1793.

p.151 - Moore BROCKENBROUGH, inv; 3 Jun 1793.

p.153 - Robert FERGUSSON, Lun.Par., will; 1 May 1785, 3 Jun 1793
wife; son William land and plant. at death of wife;
other chil. Robert, Mary, Margaret, Griffin, and
Jesse; ex: wife and son William; wits: Benj. N.
GARLAND, George MOORE, Mary C. GARLAND, Mary GARLAND,
Mary WATTS, James RUST.

p.154 - Zachariah EFFORD, will; 16 Apr 1792, 3 Jun 1793
wife Betty; sons John, George, and Zachariah; dau.
Franky; George MISKELL and George NORTHERN; wits:
Luke JACKSON, John JESPER.

p.155 - Moore FAUNTLEROY of Crondall, will; 14 Jan 1793, 3 Jun
1793
natural dau. Maria FAUNTLEROY (dau. of Catharine
SHORT) all landed est. in the Co. of Rich. known as
Crondall Estate; natural daus. Fanny and Florinder;
if natural dau. Maria FAUNTLEROY should die before
she arrives to the age of 21 or marries, landed est.
to fall to John MORTIMER, he taking the name of
FAUNTLEROY, but, if he refuses, then to go to relation
William FAUNTLEROY of Mile End Green, England; aunt
Mary GIBERNE; godson Moore Fauntleroy BROCKENBROUGH;
faithful servant Samuel COLE; servants Davy and Dick
to be free; ex. and guardians of dau. Maria: friends
Thomas and John BROCKENBROUGH; wits: [Mace] CLEMENTS,
John [SMAW], Yovell WILLIAMS.

p.156 - Maj. John BELFIELD, inv; taken 11 Oct 1792, rec. 3 Jun 1793.

p.157 - George YERBY, NFP, will; 23 May 1785, 3 Jun 1793
all land in Rich. Co. to be eq. div. between my two
sons George and John M.; land in Fairfax lying on
Pohick to be sold; sons also to receive lands in Lanc.
Co; daus. Sarah M., Nancy, Judith G., and Betsy; two
sons to have a good education; ex: friends William
MISKELL, John FAUNTLEROY, Abner DOBYNS, and Thaddeus
WILLIAMS; wits: Chichester TAPSCOTT, Sally KEYSER,
Ellin Ball GLASCOCK. [George YERBY mar. (2) Elizabeth
Rust GARLAND, dau. of Griffin GARLAND in 1790. MRC,
p.238.]

p.159 - John CLARK, inv; Aug 1793.

p.160 - Maj. Moore FAUNTLEROY, inv; 2 Sep 1793.

p.161 - Mary ELMORE, NFP, will; 5 Jun 1792, 3 Dec 1793
seven eldest chil. Annie, Milly, George, Mary, William,
Caty, and Richard; youngest son Charles Burton; dau.
Elizabeth; ex: dau. Elizabeth and fr. Samuel BARNES;
wits: Thomas COLEMAN, Sally COLEMAN, Anne COLEMAN,
Susanna THOMAS.

p.162 - William FAUNTLEROY of Naylor's Hole, will; 7 Oct 1793,
3 Dec 1793
slaves Tom and his wife [Ro?lana] and Roger and his
wife Nelly to have their freedom; son Moore to have

tract of land called the Old Plantation supposed to
be 1000 ac., also 100 pounds to be raised out of my
est. for his medical services to my white and black
family; son John to receive plant. after the death
of son Moore; son Griffin Murdock tract of land I
bought of William FORD adjoining Cat Point Warehouse;
son Joseph; son Robert tract called Naylor's Hole;
wife to receive the mulatto girl Betsy [or Becky];
chil. of dau. Jane TURNER: Harry, Thomas, Richard,
George, Elizabeth, Jenny, and Polly; chil. of dau.
Apphia CARTER [unnamed]; s-i-l. Capt. John C. CARTER;
natural son Alexander (son of Betsy FISHER) 287 ac.
at the crosslands which I purchased of my son Griffin;
ex: sons Moore, John, Griffin, Joseph, and Robert and
Col. Vincent REDMAN; son Robert to be guardian to
son Alexander until he is 18; wits: Richard BRUCE,
Thomas PRITCHETT.

p.163 - Anne MITCHELL, NFP, will; 3 Jun 1790, 3 Dec 1793
sis. Ruth BELFIELD tract of land I purchased of Mr.
Thomas BEALE whereon I now live; Mrs. Frances SYDNOR
(wife of nephew John SYDNOR); nephew Thomas SYDNOR;
nieces Mrs. Anne Mitchell CHINN, Mrs. DANIEL, and Mrs.
KELLINGHAM (daus. of late sis. TARPLEY); niece Sarah
SYDNOR; nephew Giles SYDNOR; nephews Rawleigh and
Travis DOWNMAN; niece Frances LEVE; niece Anne SYDNOR
(dau. of nephew Anthony SYDNOR); niece Anne FLINT;
nieces Anne DOWNMAN, Frances DOWNMAN, and Priscilla
DAVIS; ex: nephew Thomas SYDNOR and Rawleigh DOWNMAN;
wits: Robert NEASOM, William HAMMACK, Joseph TAPSCOTT,
Caty NEASOM. [Anne SYDNOR mar. Richard MITCHELL, bond
24 Aug 1752; she was the dau. of Anthony and Elizabeth
(DEW) SYDNOR; Richard MITCHELL d. in 1781; his will
was prov. in Lanc. Co. MRC, pp.134, 200, 201; WLC,
p.158.]

p.165 - Ellin BROWN, NFP, will; 11 Feb 1784, 3 Dec 1793
daus. Ellin HUNTON, Elizabeth BROWN, and Margaret
BROWN; ex: Alexander HUNTON and Richard [CLAY]TON;
wits: George NORTHEN, Sarah HAMMACK, Jemimah REDMAN.

     - Elizabeth THORNTON, Lun.Par., will; 23 Mar 1785, 6 Jan 1794
daus. Mary ALDERSON, Anne REYNOLDS; sons John and
William; daus. Frances THORNTON, Betsy and Lucy HAMMOND;
ex: fr. Benjamin BRAMHAM and John THORNTON; wits:
Ailce DEMERETT, John DEMERETT, Mary BRAMHAM. [Elizabeth
DAVIS mar. Thomas THORNTON who d. in 1763; she was the
dau. of Richard and Mary (BERRICK) DAVIS. MRC, p.214.]

p.166 - Williamson BALL, will; 26 Nov 1786, 6 Jan 1794
daus. Milly, Elizabeth, Priscilla, Judith, Lucy
HARRISON, and Margaret WILLIAMSON; son Harrison; ex:
bro. William BALL and friends Robert W. CARTER, Robert
TOMLIN, Robert MITCHELL, and Landon CARTER of Sabine
Hall; no wits. [Capt. Williamson BALL (1736-1793),
the eld. son of George BALL and Judith PAYNE, mar. (1)
(?) GLASCOCK, (2) Anne BEALE, and (3) Priscilla
(CHURCHILL) SPANN. MRC, p. 9.]

p.168 - Thomas FRANKLIN, Lun.Par., will; 5 Apr 1793, 6 Jan 1794
wife Mary; dau. Nelly; son William; other chil. Elizabeth, Thomas, Molly, and Edward; ex: wife, fr. William
PORTER, and bro. William FRANKLIN; wits: William
EDWARDS, William PORTER, Elizabeth FRANKLIN.

p.169 - Elizabeth BARRICK, Lun.Par., will; 28 Sep 1784, 3 Feb 1794
        whole est. to Griffin Garland BARRICK and he is to be
        ex; wits: Thomas FRANKLIN, Benjamin BRAMHAM, Vincent
        BRAMHAM.

p.170 - James CRASK, Lun.Par., will; 24 [Jan] 1794, 3 Feb 1794
        sons Mark and Joel; ex: friends Andrew and William
        BRUCE; wits: Daniel WILSON, Betty BRUCE, Daniel
        CONNOLLEE.

WILL BOOK 9, 1794-1822

p.   1 - Judith GRIFFIN, inv; 17 Jan 1794.

p.   2 - Thomas FRANKLIN, inv; 2 Jun 1794.

p.   3 - Richard SANFORD, inv; 2 Jun 1794.

     - Elizabeth BERRICK, inv; 2 Jun 1794.

p.   4 - Thomas HUNTON, inv; 7 Jul 1794.

p.   5 - Mary KELSICK, will; 15 Aug 1784, 7 Jul 1794
        son Robert land in Culpeper Co., but, if he should
        not return to Virginia, he being absent from hence
        several [page torn here] said land to go to Sir
        Jonathan BECKWITH and his heirs in trust to sell and
        dispose of the same [page torn here] got for it and
        the money arising from the sale thereof to be eq.
        div. between my son [page torn here] my four daus.
        Eleanor BARNES, Isabella BARBER, Elizabeth YOUNGER,
        and Rebecca BECKWITH; ex: Jonathan BECKWITH; wits:
        Frances BARNES, Richard PARKER, Jennings BECKWITH,
        Jonathan BECKWITH. [Mary BARNES, the dau. of Richard
        and Penelope (MANLY) BARNES, mar. Younger KELSICK
        ca. 1752. MRC, pp. 10, 111, 112.]

     - John WROE, will; 9 Jan 1794, 7 Jul 1794
        nine chil. Hannah MIDDLETON, Betty, Jane, Nancy, Alice,
        John, Samuel, Nathaniel, and Sarah; ex: bro. George
        and Richard STREET; wits: Samuel JACKSON, Samuel
        CRALLE, Leroy LUTTRELL, John BEELAND.

     - John SMITH, will; 13 May 1793, 1 Sep 1794
        grdau. Frances SMITH (dau. of Colston SMITH) my plant.
        I purchased of Willoughby NEWTON and my water grist
        mill also the lands I purchased of Thomas GLASCOCK
        and Jennings ROOKER, if he has no heirs, to grdau.
        Mary KELSICK; grdau. Susannah SMITH; dau. Mary KELSICK;
        fr. John SYDNOR; desires Daniel JACKSON to live at the
        mill plant. as an overseer and to look after the mill
        until Frances SMITH arrives to lawful age or marries;
        ex: friends Samuel HIPKINS, Eppa SYDNOR, Daniel JACK-
        SON, and John SYDNOR; wits: Vincent BRANN, Thomas
        STEPHENS, James SYDNOR.

p.   6 - Barbara BRANNAN, will; 9 Jan 1794, 1 Sep 1794
        bro. Spencer BRANNAN; sisters Catty DARBY and Nancy
        THOMAS; ex: bro. Spencer; wits: Richard NASH, Leroy
        STOTT, Fortunatus TILLERY.

p.   7 - Griffin M. FAUNTLEROY, Farn.Par., will; 18 Jan 1791, 1
        Sep 1794
        wife Anne; sons Belfield and Joseph; daus. Peggy YERBY,

Anne POLLY, and Elizabeth; ex: wife, bros. John and
Robert, and Thomas YERBY; no wits. [Griffin FAUNTLEROY
mar. Anne BELFIELD ca. 1770. MRC, p. 68.]

- Thomas MORSE, inv; 1 Sep 1794.

p. 8 - Zachariah EFFORD, inv; 6 Oct 1794.

p. 9 - George SAUNDERS, being very old though, thank God, in
tolerable health, will; 10 Nov 1788, 6 Oct 1794
wife Sarah; sons Thomas W. the plant. I now live on
(except the brandy still), John, Joseph, George, and
Edward; daus. Caty JESPER, Sarah, Mary, and Betty;
Daniel JESPER; ex: fr. Thaddeus WILLIAMS, son Edward,
and s-i-l. George MISKELL; wits: Abner DOBYNS, George
JESPER, Elizabeth IVES. [George SAUNDERS, the son of
John and Mary SAUNDERS, was b. 10 May 1712. He mar.
(1) Mary WILLIAMS by 1736 and they had seven chil:
Thomas Williams (b.1737), Katherine (b.1739), George
(b.1742), John (b.1744), Joseph (b.1746), Mary (b.
1749), and Elizabeth (b.1753), and (2) Sarah BRUMBELOW
in 1756 by whom he had two chil: Edward (b.1756) and
Sarah (b.1758). NFPR, pp. 163, 164; MRC, pp.177, 178.]

- Bathsheba ALLISON, Lun. Par., will; 11 Sep 1794, 6 Oct 1794
daus. Rebecca ALLISON and Catharine JACKSON; son
Thomas L.; William ALLISON; no ex; wits: William
JACKSON, Daniel LAWSON. [Bathsheba LAWSON mar. Henry
ALLISON, bond 28 Sep 1761. MRC, p. 3.]

p. 10 - William JACKSON, will; 22 Oct 1794, 1 Dec 1794
wife Catharine who is with child; ex: wife and fr.
Daniel LAWSON and Thomas L. ALLISON; wits: David
DUNGAN, Rebecca ALLISON. [William JACKSON mar.
Catharine ALLISON, bond 7 May 1792; the unborn child
was Henry Allison b. 11 Oct 1793. NFPR, p.102.]

- Charles SALLARD Sr., will; 3 Jan 1791, 1 Dec 1794
wife Anne all land in Rich. Co. on Totuskey Creek;
daus. Mary Metcalfe BAILEY, Judith HART, Rebecca
MALLORY, Anne TUCKER, Sarah SALLARD, and Peggy
CONNOLLY; son Charles land on both sides of Harricane
Creek supposed to be 1000 ac; ex: son Charles and
sons-in-law Joseph TUCKER and Zacches HART; wits:
Charles BAILEY, Rebecca PLUMMER, Wm. Colston SMITH.

p. 11 - Robert TOMLIN Jr., Lun.Par., will; 31 Mar 1794, 1 Dec 1794
wife Sarah; sis. Winifred TOMLIN; niece Eloisa Tomlin
McCARTY; wife to have one third of the money left her
by her grandmother BROWNE; ex: father Robert TOMLIN
and b-i-l. Bartholomew McCARTY; wits: Charles BROWNE,
William DUNLOP Jr.

p. 12 - George HOW, Lun.Par., will; 23 Apr 1794, 1 Dec 1794
whole est. to wife Mary; after her death to be eq.
div. among all chil: John, Caty, Winnie, George,
William, Thomas, James, and Abner; son George to
have the family bible; ex: Thomas and Mary HOW; wits:
William FLEMING, John HOW, Vincent PACKETT.

p. 13 - James BRAGG, inv; 1 Dec 1794.

- Richard Schooly McGINNIS, inv; 1 Dec 1794.

p. 15 - Richard SHACKLEFORD, Lun.Par., will; 16 Jul 1794, 1 Dec
1794
son William land and plant. in James City Co; sons
Clement and Vincent the land I purchased of Joseph
SIMMONS containing 50 ac; son Jack; grchil. John,
Nancy, Lawson, and Vincent SHACKLEFORD; grdau. Peggy
Shackleford SAUNDERS; as my land and plant. whereon
I now live came to me by my wife Peggy LANDMAN so
that her three chil. Clement, Vincent, and my. grdau.
Peggy SAUNDERS in right of her mother, will claim by
law their eq. proportion; it is my particular request
that my son Clement shall remain on the plant. with
his proportion of my est. given him and that Miss
Caty ALLGOOD be maintained thereon and live with him
so long as she remains unmarried and that my son
Jack be not taken from her; ex: sons Clement and
Vincent; wits: Charles [I.] McCARTY, Henry FRANKS
[Jr.], John BROCKENBROUGH. [Richard SHACKLEFORD mar.
Margaret LANDMAN, bond 17 Jan 1767. MRC, p.185.]

p. 16 - Peter GOAD, will; 26 Apr 1786, 1 Dec 1794
acquaintance Col. George GLASCOCK all my carpenter's
and cooper's tools; acquaintance Miss Sarah GLASCOCK
all my land that I got of my bro. Abram GOAD, that is
the tract lying between Capt. Thomas WILLIAMS and
Turner HANKS dec'd, the land whereon Hanner DALE now
lives; ex: fr. Col. George GLASCOCK; wits: Judith
GLASCOCK, Catharine GLASCOCK.

- Thomas BROCKENBROUGH, will; 27 Jun 1794, 5 Jan 1795
servant David CARRINGTON to be set at liberty at my
death and to be paid one pound per year for five years;
Patty, a dau. of Old Frank and Bess, and all her chil.
to be set at liberty and be paid 10 pounds a year
during her life and to be well supported out of my
est. until the girl Betty is of age sufficient to be
hired out to trade and the boys also at the discretion
of my ex. to such occupation as their genius most
inclines; fr. Sydnor BELFIELD; whole est. real and
personal to bros. John and Newman; ex: bros. John and
Newman BROCKENBROUGH; no wits.

p. 17 - Mrs. Betty Anne WILLIAMS, inv; 5 Jan 1795.

p. 18 - Mary ELMORE, inv; 2 Feb 1795.

- Thomas PRITCHETT, appraisement; 2 Feb 1795.

p. 19 - Robert TOMLIN, Lun.Par., will; 18 Dec 1794, 5 Jan 1795
wife Susannah land and plant. whereon I now live and
land and plant. known as Raines, after her death, to
go to son Moore Fauntleroy TOMLIN, if he dies before
he arrives of age, marries, or has no lawful issue,
land to go to dau. Elizabeth McCARTY; dau. Elizabeth
McCARTY to receive one half of profits of lands in
the fork of Totuskey in NFP, the other one half of
the profits for the use and benefits of my wife and
unmarried chil; other daus. Kitty, Apphia, Nelly,
and Susannah; ex: bro. Walker TOMLIN and s-i-l.
Bartholomew McCARTY; wits: Walker TOMLIN, David
BARRICK. [Robert TOMLIN was the son of Robert and
Winifred (WEBB) TOMLIN; he mar. Susannah FAUNTLEROY
ca. 1770. MRC. p.217.]

- Charity DUNCAN, will; 24 Jan 1793, 5 Jan 1795
  grson John MITCHELL the plant, land, and tenements
  whereon I now live, if he has no heirs, land to be
  sold and the money to be div. between three chil:
  Thomas COLEMAN, Richard MITCHELL, and Hannah LUTTRELL;
  grdaus. Sarah WALKER, Sarah COLEMAN, Frances KIRK;
  ex: sons Thomas and Richard; wits: George CONNOLLEY,
  George WALKER, Betty CONNOLLY. [Charity MITCHELL mar.
  Henry DUNCAN, bond 29 Oct 1766. MRC, p.61.]

p. 20 - Robert THORNTON, inv; 2 Feb 1795.

p. 22 - John LEWIS, inv; 2 Feb 1795.

p. 23 - Charles JONES, will; 21 Nov 1794, 2 Feb 1795
  daus. Barbary, Mary PULLEN; son Charles; grson. Wm.
  STANLEY; ex: son Charles and fr. Richard DOZIER;
  wits: Jonathan BRYANT, John THRIFT, John BRYANT Jr.

  - Charles SALLARD, inv; 2 Feb 1795.

p. 24 - John PECK, will; 17 May 1793, 2 Jun 1795
  whole est. real and personal, except the "life estate"
  hereafter carved out to my dear wife, to be kept
  together until my youngest son Emmanuel shall arrive
  at 21 years; other chil. John and Harriet; ex: Fleet
  COX and Willoughby NEWTON; wits: John J. MAUND, Wm.
  CARPENTER.

p. 25 - Christopher DEATLEY, Farn.Par., will; 27 Sep 1793, 1 Jun
  1795
  wife Eleanor; daus. Elizabeth FICKLIN (wife of Famous
  FICKLIN) and Sarah HOGAN (wife of Travers HOGAN); ex:
  wife, Famous FICKLIN, and Travers HOGAN; wits: William
  MISKELL, Richard BEALE, Ezekiel FOSTER.

  - Edward MOZINGO, will; 29 Mar 1794, 6 Oct 179[5]
  son Edward all land in Rich. Co. except what I hold
  a lease for from the late Landon CARTER Esq. of this
  county; dau. Winnie MOZINGO the use of the land and
  plant. whereon I now dwell during the term of the
  lease; son Pearce; grchil. Edward MOZINGO and Rebecca
  MOZINGO (chil. of Pearce MOZINGO); daus. Hannah
  CROOKHORN, Sarah TOMS, Mary BARRETT, and Rebecca AIRS;
  ex: Col. Vincent REDMAN, Thomas CROOKHORN, and son
  Edward; wits: William YATEMAN, Thomas YATEMAN, Reuben
  Bailey MOZINGO.

p. 26 - Samuel PEACHEY, NFP, will; 2 Apr 1795, 1 Jun 1795
  bro. William; cousin Mrs. Winifred ARMISTEAD for the
  particular care and attention to me during my illness;
  sisters Jane and Catharine and bro. William to be ex;
  no wits;
  Note, 27 Apr 1795; I do hereby certify that the late
  Samuel PEACHEY Jr., who departed this life at my house
  on the 25th of this present month, did in his last
  illness signify to me his intention of making a will,
  that the instrument of writing hereunto annexed was
  found in this pocket after his decease and delivered
  to my care, his bro. being absent, which sd. instrument
  I believe and am satisfied is wholly in his, the
  testator's, handwriting.
  /s/ William PEACHEY

p. 27 - Charles JONES, NFP, will; 28 Jan 1795, 1 Jun 1795
       est. to be eq. div. between three chil: William, John,
       and Eleanor; at the time my son William shall arrive
       to the age of 21 years...he shall have the two boy
       twins James and Samuel; ex: friends Vincent BRAMHAM
       and John PORTER; wits: Benjamin BRAMHAM, David DUNGAN.

    - William LUTTRELL, inv; 1 Jun 1795.

p. 28 - Richard SHACKLEFORD Jr., inv; 7 Sep 1795.

    - Hannah BROWN, Farn.Par., will; 10 Jul 1795, 7 Sep 1795
       all my part of my father's est., when div., to be
       given to my sis. Martha BROWN; cousins Peggy JACKSON
       and Elizabeth BRYANT; ex: Thaddeus JACKSON, wits:
       William FORRESTER, Peter SHIRLEY.

p. 29 - George NORTHEN, inv; 7 Sep 1795.

p. 30 - Joseph SCATES, will; 22 Jun 1795, 7 Sep 1795
       son Elijah my horse, saddle, and bridle upon these
       conditions, that his mother shall have the use of
       the sd. horse to plow on the land wherever she may
       live and to do her other plantation business, but for
       no other purpose; wife Sarah; all chil. [unnamed]; ex:
       wife; wits: Robert MITCHELL, George NEWMAN.

    - George SAUNDERS, inv; 5 Oct 1795.

p. 31 - George YERBY, inv; taken 10 Jul 1793, rec. 7 Dec 1795.

p. 32 - Robert STOTT, St. Stephen's Par., North. Co., will; 9 Aug
    1788, 7 Dec 1795
       all est. to wife Elizabeth, then to be sold and div.
       between all chil; dau. Milly WINSTEAD; ex: b-i-l.
       James MELEY and George ASHBURNE; wits: James C. KNOTT,
       Will. LEWIS, William WROE, George WROE.

p. 33 - Richard SYDNOR, will; 28 Aug 1794, 7 Dec 1795
       entire est. to father John, and after his death, to
       be eq. div. among his chil; ex: father, Ezekiel LEVY,
       and John SYDNOR Jr; wits: James SYDNOR, Eppa SYDNOR.

    - William PRATT, will; 28 Oct 1795, 7 Dec 1795
       entire est. to son William; no ex; wits: John CLARK,
       William HART.

p. 34 - Andrew MORGAN, inv; 7 Dec 1795.

p. 35 - Nathaniel GARNER, inv; 4 Jan 1796.

p. 36 - William SADLER, inv; 4 Apr 1796.

p. 37 - Thomas CLARK, NFP, will; 4 Mar 1796, 4 Apr 1796
       chil: Thomas, William, Catharine, Judith, Frances
       FRANCE; grson. Reuben (son of Rodham CLARK); ex: sons
       Thomas and William; wits: Benjamin MORGAN, William
       GARLAND, Garland MOORE.

p. 38 - Edward EIDSON, inv; 4 Apr 1796.

p. 39 - Ailcy DOBYNS, will; 29 Aug 1795, 4 Apr 1796
       bro. Daniel; sisters Nancy, Betsy, and Winnie DOBYNS
       and Frances DAVENPORT; ex: bro. Daniel and Cousin
       Leroy DOBYNS; wits: L.R. DOBYNS, William HAMMOND,
       Richard WOOLLARD.

p. 40 - Williamson BALL, inv; taken 24 Jun 1794, rec. 4 Jul 1796.

p. 44 - George FOWLES, inv; 4 Jul 1796.

p. 45 - Samuel TUNE, NFP, will; 22 Jun 1792, 4 Jul 1796
wife Sarah; son James land and plant., if he die without heirs, the land to be sold and the money eq. div.
amongst two sons and four daus: Joannah, Henry, Lewis,
Sally, Molly, and Caty; my desire is, that if my dau.
Joannah should not marry, she should live with my son
James until my youngest dau. Caty arrives to the age
of 16; sons Henry and Lewis to have sufficient schooling and then bound out to som good trade; ex: wife and
son James; wits: George T. GARLAND, Henry TUNE.

- Vincent JACKSON, inv; ord. 6 Feb 1792, rec. 4 Jul 1796.

p. 47 - Edward MOZINGO, inv. by Edward MOZINGO Jr.; 5 Sep 1796.

p. 48 - Milly BUNYAN, NFP, will; 3 May 1795, 5 Sep 1796
dau. Caty; sons Samuel DEW, Richard WEBB, and William
BUNYAN; Susannah RIVEER; ex: son Richard WEBB and
Richard BENNEHAN; wits: Sarah HANKS, Mary KEYSER.

p. 49 - John GLASCOCK, will; 24 Aug 1790, 5 Sep 1796
wife Susannah; son Washington; other chil. [unnamed];
ex: friends Robert and Richard MITCHELL; wits: Benj.
SMITH, Thomas YERBY, Charles BARNES. [John GLASCOCK
mar. Susannah MITCHELL, bond 28 Jun 1770. MRC, p.78;
The births of their fol. chil. are rec. in the NFPR:
Nancy (1771), Washington (1775), and John (1777),
NFPR, p. 71.]

- Robert TOMLIN, inv; 5 Dec 1796.

p. 51 - Robert TOMLIN Jr., inv; ord. 29 Dec 1794, rec. 5 Dec 1796.

p. 52 - Betty REYNOLDS, Lun.Par., will; 7 Oct 1796, 5 Dec 1796
daus. Fanny the house and land whereon I now live,
Elizabeth DAVIS, and Sally ROBINSON; sons Vincent,
John, William, James, Joseph, and Reuben; Jane (the
dau. of George REYNOLDS); ex: sons Joseph and Vincent;
wits: Patty [DUFF], Winifred BRICKEY, William BRICKEY.

p. 53 - Mary ALDERSON, will; 5 Jan 1796, 5 Dec 1796
dau. Rachel CHAMBERLAIN; son Jerry; adm: son Jerry;
wits: Griffin G. BERRICK, Joseph REDMAN, Thomas T.
REYNOLDS.

p. 54 - William BRUCE, inv; 5 Dec 1796.

- William SAUNDERS Sr., Lun.Par., will; 5 Sep 1793, 5 Dec 1796
wife Mary Lewis SAUNDERS; chil: William, John, Almond,
Alexander, and Thomas; ex: fr. Daniel WILSON and son
William; wits: Elisha NEWCOMB, Daniel JENKINS.

p. 55 - John JONES, will; 3 Mar 1796, 5 Dec 1796
dau. Molly RAINS; sons James and John; fr. Eliza
[OWINGS]; ex: son James and Rawleigh RAINS; wits:
Richard SMITHER, Thomas WHITE, Rawleigh BRYANT.

p. 56 - Anthony TUNE, NFP, will; 18 Apr 1795, 5 Dec 1796
wife Nancy; bro. Jesse; ex: fr. Capt. Richard SMITHER
and Col. George GLASCOCK; wits: John GORDON, Peter
BARNES, Launcelot SMITHER, James BOOTH. [Anthony TUNE,

the probable son of Anthony and Dorcas (MORRIS) TUNE,
mar. (1) Nancy SANDERS, 1787, and (2) Nancy TUNE,
1793. MRC, p.219.]

p. 57 - Thomas CLARK, inv; 5 Dec 1796.

p. 58 - John WILSON, inv; 5 Dec 1796.

p. 59 - Peggy JENKINS, will; 12 Sep 1796, 5 Dec 1796
all est. to mother Hannah Anne BROWN; no ex; wits:
James DIGMAN, Jeremiah JENKINS, Billy SANDERS.

- Rodham CLARK, inv; 2 Jan 1797.

p. 61 - William GARLAND, inv; 2 Jan 1797.

p. 62 - Francis Lightfoot LEE, will; 30 Dec 1795, 6 Feb 1797
wife Rebecca; nephew Thomas Ludwell LEE of Loudon all
my lots in the town of Matildaville; nephew George
LEE tract of land near Colchester in Fairfax; gold
enameled snuff-box and the picture set with diamonds
belonging to it, which was given to me by my ever-
lamented bro. Arthur LEE to go to my nephew Francis
Lightfoot LEE; much-estimed fr. Dr. William SHIPPEN
Jr. of Philadelphia; nephew Thomas Lee SHIPPEN of
Pennsylvania; ex: wife, nephew Ludwell LEE, Thomas
Ludwell LEE of Loudon, and George LEE; no wits.
[Francis L. LEE mar. Rebecca P. TAYLOE, 25 May 1769.
MRC, p.116.]

p. 63 - Samuel TUNE, inv; 3 Apr 1797.

p. 65 - Anne MITCHELL, inv; 3 Apr 1797.

p. 69 - Mary CLATOR, inv; 3 Apr 1797.

- William PRATT, inv; 3 Apr 1797.

p. 70 - John JONES, inv; 3 Apr 1797.

p. 71 - John SMITH, inv; 3 Apr 1797.

p. 72 - Ailcy DOBYNS, inv; 3 Apr 1797.

- John SMITH, will; 23 Mar 17[8]7, 5 Jun 1797
wife Lucy; son John tract of land purchased of James
SAMFORD; other chil: Meredith, Eliza BURWELL, Mary,
Lucy, Anne, Sarah, and Frances; ex: wife and son John;
no wits.

p. 73 - Barbary SANFORD, Lun.Par., will; 26 Apr 1797, [5 Jun 1797]
Thomas James BULGER, Richard BULGER; grson. John BULGER
Jr; William Henry SANFORD; no ex; wits: Abraham WHITE,
Nancy FOULS.

- Robert Wormeley CARTER of Sabine Hall, will; 16 Dec 1794,
5 Jun 1797
wife Winifred Travers lands and plantations whereon I
now live consisting of several tracts, also land known
as the Fork Plant. in Rich. Co. together with 30 working slaves (half male and half female), after her death,
to go to son Landon; son George to have all lands in
York and James City counties commonly known by the
name of Rippon Hall and my lots in Williamsburg, tract
of land in Stafford Co. known as the Park or Acquia

supposed to contain 3000 ac. more or less; waiting
man Simon and his wife Polly and their chil., except
Caty (dau. of sd. Polly by a former husband); daus.
Anne Beale CARTER and Elizabeth CARTER; and, whereas
I have heretofore given to my dau. Elizabeth during
her first marriage 1000 pounds which, although it was
nearly of eq. value to her husband with specie and
was applied by him to the discharge of his specie
debts, yet at is was paid in paper money when it was
in a depreciated state, I do now, in order to make up
the depreciation, give to her the further sum of 500
pounds specie; dau. Fanny LEE; godson Robert HAMILTON
(son of Mr. Gilbert HAMILTON late of Rich. Co.) lot
#45 of land occupied by Benjamin RUTHERFORD part of
lands on Apeceon supposed to be in Frederick Co; fr.
Richard PARKER and his wife Elizabeth; ex: sons-in-law
Landon CARTER of Cleve, Thomas L. LEE of Loudon, and
sons Landon and George; wits: William HARFORD, Hen.
HARFORD, Solomon ABRAHAM.

p. 77 - Samuel DONOWAY, inv; 5 Jun 1797.

p. 80 - James DIGMAN, inv; 3 Jul 1797.

p. 81 - Anthony TUNE, inv; 3 Jul 1797.

p. 82 - Francis L. LEE Esq., inv. taken at Manokin and pres. by
the ex. Mr. Ludwell LEE; 3 Jul 1797.

p. 84 - Anne ASBURY, inv; 4 Sep 1797.

     - William FAUNTLEROY, will; 9 Oct 1796, [4 Sep 1797]
wife Elizabeth all est. during her natural life, pro-
vided I have no chil. by her; chil. of sis. Catharine
HOOE; ex: friends Mr. William HOOE and Robert [Howsen]
HOOE of Stafford Co; wits: Richard BRUER, N. MOTHERS-
HEAD, James CURTIE.

p. 85 - Mary ALDERSON, inv; 4 Sep 1797.

p. 86 - Thomas JESPER, Farn. Par; will; 20 Sep 1786, 4 Sep 1797
wife Anne; chil. Elizabeth, Rubart (sic), Anne,
William, Sary, John, Rany, Mary Anne, and Elander;
no ex; wits: Jonathan WILLIAMS, Henry SPENCE,
Benedick SHORT.

p. 87 - Thomas JESPER, inv; 2 Oct 1797.

p. 88 - Betty REYNOLDS, inv; 2 Oct 1797.

p. 89 - John FAUNTLEROY, Farn. Par., will; 25 Dec 1794, 5 Feb 1798
wife Judith; son William Henry all lands in Naylor's
Hole Neck which I purchased of Dr. William FLOOD, my
bro. Joseph, and John ROBINS containing 582 ac; daus.
Louisa and Lettice Lee the land and plant. commonly
called the Old House Tract on the Rappahannock River
above Naylor's Hole containing 1000 ac. which land I
purchased of my late father Col. William FAUNTLEROY,
he reserving the use thereof to my bro. Dr. Moore
FAUNTLEROY during his life, after his death, it is
my desire that the sd. land be eq. div. between my
sd. daus; ex: wife, bro. Robert, and fr. Col. James
BALL; wits: James BALL, Robert FAUNTLEROY, Joseph
CHINN, Thomas DAVIS. [John FAUNTLEROY mar. Judith

(BALL) GRIFFIN, bond 8 Feb 1781; she was the wid. of
Maj. Leroy GRIFFIN. MRC, p. 68.]

p. 90 - Milly BUNYAN, inv; 5 Feb 1798.

p. 91 - Barbara SANFORD, inv; 5 Feb 1798.

- George Lee TURBERVILLE of Epping, will; 8 Oct 179[5], 2
Apr 1798
    my body to be deposited at the head of my dear departed
    mother's grave and that my coffin might touch that of
    my ever dear and lately departed wife in the old family
    burying ground at Hickory Hill in West. Co; son John
    (under 16) all my law books in the possession of Mr.
    Walter JONES, Mr. John WARDEN, Mr. John MONROE, and
    Mr. Baldwin LEE as well as all those that are in my
    own possession or elsewhere, also such of my other
    books as have his name written thereon, also a tract
    of land in West. Co. called Awbrey's; mentions mother
    of son John whose grfather was the late Richard CORBIN;
    I give to my son John, negro Tom and negro Charity and
    her increase whom I require him to treat as humble
    friends rather than slaves on account of their faith-
    ful services to me during his minority, I require and
    desire that they may be permitted to chose their
    masters or mistresses and that, in case of accident,
    infirmity, or old age that they be comfortably provided
    for; ex: daus. Eliza TAYLOE, Martha Felicia, bro.
    Richard Henry CORBIN, Mr. Walter JONES the younger
    (attorney at law), and Mr. John FAWCETT; bro. Richard
    H. CORBIN, Maj.Gen. Henry LEE, and Mr. John TAYLOE of
    Mt. Airy to be guardians to my daus; Walter JONES the
    younger and John FAWCETT to be guardians to my son;
    Cod., 13 Mar 1798, I revoke every bequest made in my
    will to my servant Tom; he has behaved so basely since
    that I cannot get over it, if I die before he is sold,
    I direct Mr. FAWCETT, my ex, to send him and old Lewis
    over the Allegheny and sell them to pay my debts;
    Charity's goodness for seven months, night and day,
    prompts me to leave her 50 ac. of my land that I die
    possessed of during her life; no wits.

p. 95 - William FAUNTLEROY, inv. in West. Co; 2 Jul 1798.

p. 96 - Elizabeth TEBBS, inv; 3 Sep 1798.

p. 99 - George GARLAND, Lun.Par., will; 24 Mar 1797, 3 Dec 1798
    son William land I now live on which was purchased of
    Capt. Williamson BALL, which land was principally his
    mother's maiden land; son George Taylor to have the
    land purchased of Capt. Moore FAUNTLEROY together with
    the land I purchased of Capt. Samuel KELSICK thereto
    adjoining and also my surveyor's instruments; mentions
    his bridges over Totuskey and Farnham Creeks; daus.
    Elizabeth, Melia, Sarah, and Henrietta land in Glou-
    cester Co; wife Mary; ex: fr. Walker TOMLIN and son
    George T.; no wits.

p.100 - Samuel BARKER, NFP, will; 10 Nov 1798, 3 Dec 1798
    sisters Lucy GARNER, Caty JONES, Nancy BARKER, Milly
    BARKER; sis-in-law Winifred HAFFORD; bro. John BARKER;
    Frederick Barker and Thomas (sons of Caty JONES); ex:
    bro. John and fr. Daniel DOBYNS Jr; wits: Edward I.
    NORTHEN, William SMITH Jr. [Samuel BARKER was the son
    of William and Anne BARKER; he was b. 28 Jan 1758.
    NFPR, p.8.]

p.101 - George HOW, inv; 4 Feb 1799.

p.102 - Richard SYDNOR, inv; 4 Feb 1799.

p.103 - James MORTON, inv. pres. by William REYNOLDS the adm;
       4 Feb 1799.

p.105 - Jeremiah ALDERSON, inv; 1 Apr 1799.

p.106 - Thomas WROE, inv; 3 Jun 1799.

     - Thomas WEYMOUTH, inv; 3 Jun 1799.

p.107 - Margaret NORTHEN, NFP, will; 10 Apr 1799, 3 Jun 1799
       mother; chil. Edward I., Winifred DOBYNS, Edmund,
       Barbara B., Samuel, and Polly; ex: sons Edward and
       Edmund; wits: John SMITH, Elizabeth ENGLISH, Elizabeth
       STUCKY. [Margaret JONES, dau. of Edward JONES, was
       the wid. of George NORTHEN whom she mar. between 1767
       and 1774. MRC, p.148; NFPR, p.139.]

p.108 - Job Sims STUCKY, NFP, will; 13 Dec 1798, 3 Jun 1799
       wife Mary[or Molly]; dau. Bennerama; ex: wife and
       neighbor William FORRESTER; wits: Mary HAMMOND, George
       SHEARLY, Thomas BRYANT. [Two daus., Griffin Warmouth
       [sic] (b.1782) and Hannah (b.1781) are described as
       chil. of Job STUCKY in the NFPR, p.177.]

p.109 - Samuel HIPKINS, will; 14 Jan 1799, 3 Jun 1799
       nephew Robert S. HIPKINS all lands in Rich. Co; bros.
       William Aug. HIPKINS and John HIPKINS; sisters Mary
       Anne ROANE and Patty [STHRESHLY]; Samuel W. HIPKINS;
       nephew William A. HIPKINS; ex: Robert S. and William
       A. HIPKINS; wits: Washington SAMFORD, Henry M. DOBYNS,
       William ADAMS.

p.110 - Pitman NASH, inv; 1 Jul 1799.

p.111 - William FAUNTLEROY, inv; 1 Jul 1799.

p.115 - John MORRIS Sr., inv; 1 Jul 1799.

p.117 - Morton WILSON, will; 29 Jun 1797, 1 Jul 1799
       wife Elizabeth whole est; the land I now live on,
       after wife's death, should go to the use of two daus.
       Eleanor and Martha; sons Thomas Ford, James, Richard,
       and Henry; ex: wife and fr. James KELLY; wits: Thomas
       ASBURY, Spicer KELLY. [Morton WILSON mar. Elizabeth
       FORD, bond 9 Jul 1753. MRC, p.233.]

p.118 - Elizabeth APPLEBY, NFP, will; 1 Apr 1799, 1 Jul 1799
       fr. Lucy WARNER; no ex; wit: James ALDERSON.

     - Charles T. McCARTY, NFP, will; 17 Apr 1798, 2 Sep 1799
       entire est. to wife Apphia Fauntleroy; ex: wife, fr.
       James WILLIAMS, and Samuel HIPKINS; wits: "Many of
       my friends can prove this to be all in my handwriting."
       [Charles Travers McCARTY, son of Maj. Charles McCARTY,
       mar. Apphia Fauntleroy TOMLIN, bond 12 Jan 1796. MRC,
       123.]

p.119 - George Lee TURBERVILLE, inv; 7 Oct 1799.

p.122 - John DODSON, NFP, will; 1 Jan 1795, 7 Oct 1799
       wife all of est; after her death, to be eq. div.

between two sons James and Thomas; ex: bro. Alexander
and William CORNISH; wits: William FORRESTER, William
STONUM.

p.123 - Thomas BEALE, Lun.Par., will; 7 Jun 1799, 3 Dec 1799
wife Sinah land I now live on called Chestnut Hill
as far as the main road leading from Dickerson's Mill
after her death, to go to son Thomas Smith; sons
James and Reuben the Burnt House tract of land where
Col. John GORDON formerly lived, to be eq. div. between
them; son Jesse Ball the tract called Old Field tract;
dau. Fanny FOUSHEE; son William Currie; other chil:
Anne H., Mildred, Eliza, Maria, Winifred Travis,
Charles, George, and Robert Taverner; ex: bros. William
and Reuben and wife; wits: John BROCKENBROUGH, John
YEATMAN, John H. FOUSHEE.

p.124 - Eleanor ROCHESTER, Lun.Par., will; 10 Oct 1791, 6 Jan 1800
land and plant. on which I now live to my two daus.
Anne JONES and Elizabeth JONES; son Jeremiah ROCHESTER;
ex: sons Jeremiah ROCHESTER and Charles JONES; wits:
Benjamin BRAMHAM, Molly NORTHEN, James WOOSONCRAFT,
Fanny REYNOLDS.

p.125 - Job STUCKY, inv; 6 Jan 1800.

p.127 - George WROE, NFP, will; 1 Jan 1799, 6 Jan 1800
wife Jane; bro. William WROE; sis. Jane STREET; nephew
George VANLANDINGHAM; ex: Samuel CRALLE, Richard STREET,
George MISKELL, and James BOOTH; wit: Samuel CRALLE.

- David AUSTIN, NFP, will; 31 Dec 1798, 7 Apr 1800
sons Chatman, Orville, Thomas, David, and Warner; ex:
friends Thomas PLUMMER and John DUDLEY; wits: John
SMITH, Thomas P. SMITH, Henry W. HEADLEY.

p.128 - John PECK, inv; 7 Apr 1800.

p.130 - Miss Eleanor TOMLIN, inv; 7 Apr 1800.

- Thomas BROWN, Lun.Par., will; 4 Dec 1799, 7 Apr 1800
wife Nancy; chil. [unnamed]; ex: kinsman William
MORRIS; wits: William BRAGG, James KELLY Jr., John
MORRIS, William MORRIS Jr. [Thomas BROWN mar. Nancy
MORRIS, bond 6 Jan 1789. MRC, p.26.]

p.131 - Samuel BAKER, inv; 2 Jun 1800.

p.132 - William MORRISON, inv; 2 Jun 1800.

- Peter BARNES, will; 24 Apr 1797, 2 Jun 1800
dau. Sally Tune (under 18) and her five aunts: Joanna
TUNE, Nancy TUNE, Sally TUNE, Molly TUNE, and Caty
TUNE; ex: fr. Joseph TAPSCOTT and Joanna TUNE; wits:
Thomas WILLIAMS, George LEWIS, William ALDERSON, L.R.
DOBYNS. [Peter BARNES mar. Winifred TUNE, bond 29 Dec
1787. MRC, p.10.]

p.133 - George THRIFT, Lun.Par., will; 6 May 1800, 2 Jun 1800
all est. to be div. among four chil: Mary, George,
William, and Betsy; ex: fr. Peter NORTHEN [Sr.], if
he should die before my oldest child comes of age,
Mr. William GARLAND, son of William GARLAND dec'd, in
the Fork of Totuskey should be my ex. in place of Mr.
NORTHEN; wits: James NORTHEN, William NORTHEN,
William LANDMAN.

- David AUSTIN, inv; 2 Jun 1800.

p.134 - Mrs. Anne QUINLAN, inv; 7 Jul 1800.

p.136 - George SCURLOCK, inv; 7 Jul 1800.

p.137 - John SHORTT, inv; 6 Oct 1800.

- Mary HARDWICK, NFP, will; 19 Sep 1796, 6 Oct 1800
  dau. Barbary HARDWICK; son John; ex: dau. Barbary,
  George SISSON, and Elizabeth SISSON; wits: William
  JESPER, Aaron HARDWICK.

p.138 - John PURCELL, will; 19 Mar 1797, 1 Dec 1800
  son George land and plant. on which I now live; daus.
  Margaret THRIFT and Sarah GOLDSBY; other sons Edward
  M., William, Reuben, and Benjamin; no ex; wits:
  Benjamin BRAMHAM, John HOW, Elizabeth HOW.

p.139 - James CRASK, inv; 1 Dec 1800.

189

INDEX OF PLACE NAMES

INDEX OF PERSONAL NAMES

205

218

WALLACE (cont.)
  Geo. 128, 171
  Margaret 128
  Walter 128
WALTER, Thomas 20
  [Mil.] 18
WALTON, John 10
  Samuel 10
  Sem 10
  Thomas 10
WANLESS, Benj. 114
  Sarah 114
WARD, Jeremiah 125
  Thomas 15, 18
WARDEN, John 185
WAREING, Alex. 67
WARNER, Betty Anne 130
  John 75
  Lucy 168, 186
  Mary 75
  Rob. 171
  Sarah 130
  Wm. 130, 156
WARREN, Abraham 15
WARRENER (see WARNER)
WARRICK, Obediah
WASCOLE, Mary 4
WATERS, Roger 2
  Thomas 24
WATERSON, Catharine 39
  Peter 20
WATSON, Thomas 114
  Wm. 7
WATTERS, Catharine 39
  Bersheba 39
  Margaret 39
  Petter 39
WATTS, Mary 143, 149, 175
  Rich. 12
WATTSON, Wm. 14
WAUGH, Joseph 43
WAUGHAN, Rich. 19
WEATHERS, John 173
  Rebecca B. 173
  Samuel 46, 65
WEBB, [?] 99
  Anne 50, 83, 101
  Barbary 55
  Betty 68, 101, 124, 126
  Charles 121, 141, 144,
    145, 156, 161
  Cuthburt 68, 121, 140,
    141, 144, 145, 153,
    155, 156, 159
  Drucilla 144
  Eliz. 70, 121, 126
  Frances 121, 144, 156,
    159, 163
  Giles 1, 2, 12, 40, 44,
    46, 54, 68, 121, 126
  Isaac 1, 2, 68, 76, 85,
    87, 89, 121, 122,
    126, 144, 156
  James 2, 60, 101, 121,
    138, 140, 144, 147,
    153
  John 1, 2, 55, 68, 101,
    121, 126, 144
  John S. 132
  John Spann 54, 68, 76,
    89, 98, 115
  Joseph 101
  Judy 101
  Lucy 126
  Margaret 1
  Mary 68, 101
  Nancy 121
  Priscilla 121, 156

WEBB (cont.)
  Rich. 182
  Sarah 101, 132
  Susannah 121, 124, 126
  Terence 5
  Wilalmira 132
  Wm. 115, 121, 132, 134,
    156
  Winifred 68, 76, 83,
    132, 142
  Winnie 121, 126, 144,
    156
WEBSTER, Eliz. 56, 62
  Geo. 62
  Henry 49, 62, 72
  Joyce 62, 96
  Judith 62
  Mary Anne 72
  Wm. 31, 132, 133, 146,
    149
  Winifred 71
WEEKS, Eliz. 114
WELCH, Edw. 11
  Eliz. 51
  James 18, 19
  Margaret 51
  Mary 53
  Reuben 50
  Rich. 53
  Thomas 51
  Wm. 51
WELDON, Anne 77
  Milly 159
WELLS, Absolom 54
  Barnaby 52, 66
  Eliz. 52, 54
  Geo. 52, 66, 131
  John 39, 51, 52, 78
  John Sr. 66, 67
  Milou 66
  Stephen 15, 17, 44, 52,
    54, 80
  Thomas 66
  Thomas Williams 54
WELSH, Eliz. 72
  Robert 61
WEMS, Alice 172
WEST, Rich. 7
  Wm. 20
[WESTT], Thomas 40
WEYMOUTH, John 174
  Thomas 172, 186
WHALEY, Eliz. 101
  James 95, 101, 103
  Thomas 101
  Wm. 101
WHARTON, Geo. 25
  John 47
  Rich. 4
  Samuel 35, 36
WHEELER, Wm. 3, 4
WHING, Aguthey 45
  Joseph 45
WHITE, Abraham 183
  Anne 92, 98
  Catharine 122
  Daniel 21, 45
  Eliz. 46, 69
  Frances 30
  Franky 165
  Geo. 21, 33, 44, 46
  Jane 21
  Jesse 165
  John 7, 16, 29, 69, 83
  Katharine 10
  Margaret 80
  Mary 165
  Mary Anne 164

WHITE (cont.)
  Presley 165
  Reuben 114
  Richard 2, 10, 16
  Sally 165
  Samuel 164
  Sarah 16
  Seleashea 165
  Sileicia 136
  Thomas 2, 7, 11, 16, 20,
    21, 30, 33, 61, 69,
    70, 164, 182
  W. 118
  Wm. 16, 39, 80, 98, 164,
    165
  Winifred 110, 129
  Zachariah 136, 162, 164,
    165
WHITEHILL, John 95, 96,
    108, 109
WHITING, Ralph 3
  Thomasin 3
WHITTLE, Anne 69
  Eliz. 46
  Thomas 46
WIGMORE, Rich. 77
WILCOCKS, John 16
  Godfrey 81, 103, 132
WILCOX (see WILCOCKS)
WILDMAN, Jane 23
  John 23
WILDY, Sarah 141
WILKERSON (see also
  WILKINSON)
  Jane 83
WILKEY, Eliz. 160
WILKIE, Wm. 160
WILKINS, Rich. 47
WILKINSON, Charles 60
  Jane 55
WILL 172
WILLESS, Robert 158
WILLETT, Walter 14
WILLIAM, David 41
WILLIAMS, [?] 120
  Abraham 89, 120, 142,
    164
  Anne 26, 59, 133, 149,
    164, 165
  Barbara 165
  Betsy A. 167
  Betty 140
  Betty A. 167
  Betty Anne 147, 179
  Butler 165
  Catharine 13, 40
  Cyrus 147
  Daniel 120
  David 59, 147, 167
  Edw. 55
  Eliz. 10, 11, 18, 87,
    101, 105, 119, 125,
    142, 157
  Evan 2
  Francis 55, 57, 76
  Geo. 85, 122, 125, 133
  Griffith 100
  Hannah 63
  Harris 165
  Henry 11, 15, 56, 60,
    89, 96, 104, 105, 120,
    159
  Hugh 71, 104
  Hukey 133
  Isaac 159
  James 63, 65, 186
  Jane 11, 105, 125, 132
  Joan 59